Pro iPhone Development with Swift 5

Design and Manage Top Quality Apps

Second Edition

Wallace Wang

Pro iPhone Development with Swift 5: Design and Manage Top Quality Apps

Wallace Wang
San Diego, CA, USA

ISBN-13 (pbk): 978-1-4842-4943-7   ISBN-13 (electronic): 978-1-4842-4944-4
https://doi.org/10.1007/978-1-4842-4944-4

Managing Director, Apress Media LLC: Welmoed Spahr
Acquisitions Editor: Aaron Black
Development Editor: James Markham
Coordinating Editor: Jessica Vakili

Cover image designed by Freepik (www.freepik.com)

Distributed to the book trade worldwide by Springer Science+Business Media New York, 233 Spring Street, 6th Floor, New York, NY 10013. Phone 1-800-SPRINGER, fax (201) 348-4505, e-mail orders-ny@springer-sbm.com, or visit www.springeronline.com. Apress Media, LLC is a California LLC and the sole member (owner) is Springer Science + Business Media Finance Inc (SSBM Finance Inc). SSBM Finance Inc is a **Delaware** corporation.

For information on translations, please e-mail rights@apress.com, or visit http://www.apress.com/rights-permissions.

Apress titles may be purchased in bulk for academic, corporate, or promotional use. eBook versions and licenses are also available for most titles. For more information, reference our Print and eBook Bulk Sales web page at http://www.apress.com/bulk-sales.

Any source code or other supplementary material referenced by the author in this book is available to readers on GitHub via the book's product page, located at www.apress.com/978-1-4842-4943-7. For more detailed information, please visit http://www.apress.com/source-code.

Printed on acid-free paper

The secret to success is persistence. Never give up, never doubt yourself. The path to any goal will never be easy, but that's exactly what makes striving for goals so rewarding. Talent, intelligence, and skill are never as important as persistence. Remember, never be afraid of failure. Be afraid of giving up too soon and never realizing your true potential in whatever dream you want to achieve. You may not always reach your dreams, but pursuing big dreams will always give you a far richer life than if you never bothered trying at all.

Table of Contents

About the Author

Wallace Wang has written dozens of computer books over the years beginning with ancient MS-DOS programs like WordPerfect and Turbo Pascal, migrating to writing books on Windows programs like Visual Basic and Microsoft Office, and finally switching to Swift programming for Apple products like the Macintosh and the iPhone. He currently teaches iOS programming through UCSD Extension in San Diego.

When he's not helping people discover the fascinating world of programming, he performs stand-up comedy and appears on two radio shows on KNSJ in San Diego (`http://knsj.org`) called *Notes from the Underground* (with Dane Henderson, Jody Taylor, and Kristen Yoder) and *Laugh In Your Face Radio* (with Chris Clobber and Sarah Burford).

He also writes a screenwriting/storytelling blog called *The 15 Minute Movie Method* (`http://15minutemoviemethod.com`) designed for screenwriters and novelists. For fun, he also writes a blog about the latest cat news on the Internet called *Cat Daily News* (`http://catdailynews.com`).

About the Technical Reviewer

Massimo has more than 22 years of experience in Security, Web and Mobile Development, Cloud, and IT Architecture. His true IT passions are Security and Android.

He has been programming and teaching how to program with Android, Perl, PHP, Java, VB, Python, C/C++, and MySQL for more than 20 years.

He holds a Master of Science in Computing Science from the University of Salerno, Italy.

He has worked as a Project Manager, Software Engineer, Research Engineer, Chief Security Architect, Information Security Manager, PCI/SCADA Auditor, and Senior Lead IT Security/Cloud/SCADA Architect for many years.

His technical skills include Security, Android, Cloud, Java, MySQL, Drupal, Cobol, Perl, Web and Mobile Development, MongoDB, D3, Joomla, Couchbase, C/C++, WebGL, Python, Pro Rails, Django CMS, Jekyll, Scratch, etc.

He currently works as Chief Information Security Officer (CISO) for Cargotec Oyj.

CHAPTER 1

Organizing Code

Programs are rewritten and modified far more often than they are ever created. That means most of the time developers will be changing and altering existing code either written by someone else or written by you sometime in the past. Since you may be writing code that you or someone else will eventually modify in the future, you need to make sure you organize your code to make it easy to understand.

While every developer has their own programming style and no two programmers will write the exact same code, programming involves writing code that works and writing code that's easy to understand.

Writing code that works is hard. Unfortunately once developers get their code to work, they rarely clean it up and optimize it. The end result is a confusing mix of code that works but isn't easy to understand. To modify that code, someone has to decipher how it works and then rewrite that code to make it cleaner to read while still working as well as the original code. Since this takes time and doesn't add any new features, it's often ignored.

Since few developers want to take time to clean up their code after they get it to work, it's best to get in the habit of writing clear, understandable code right from the start. That involves several tasks:

- Writing code in a consistent and understandable style

- Making the logic of your code clear so anyone reading it later can easily understand how it works

- Organizing code to make it easy to modify later

Writing code in a consistent and understandable style means predictability. For example, some programmers give all IBOutlet variables a prefix of "IB" to stand for IBOutlet such as

```
@IBOutlet var IBnameLabel: UILabel!
```

1

This type of programming style makes it easy to tell the difference between using an IBOutlet variable and an ordinary variable. Other programmers add a prefix or suffix to variable names to identify the type of data they contain such as

```
var nameStr : String
var ageInt : Int
var salaryDbl : Double
```

The ultimate goal is to write self-documenting code that makes it easy for anyone to understand at first glance. One huge trap that programmers often make is assuming they'll be able to understand their own code months or even years later. Yet even after a few weeks, your own code can seem confusing because you're no longer familiar with your assumptions and logic that you had when you wrote the code originally.

If you can't even understand your own code months or even weeks later, imagine how difficult other programmers will find your code when they have to modify it in your absence. Good code doesn't just work, but it's easy for other programmers to understand how it works and what it does as well.

When developing your own programming style, strive for consistency and organization. Consistency means you use the same convention for writing code whether it's naming variables with prefixes or suffixes that identify the data type or indenting code the same way to highlight specific steps.

Organization means using spacing and storing related code together such as putting IBOutlets and variables near the top and placing IBAction methods at the bottom with ordinary functions in the middle. This can group chunks of code in specific places to make looking for specific code easier as shown in Figure 1-1.

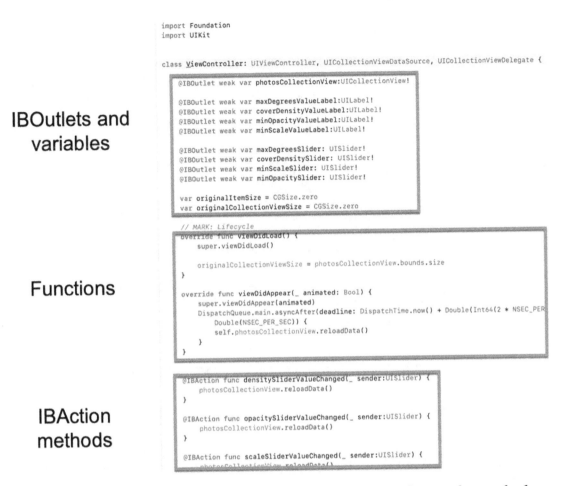

IBOutlets and variables

Functions

IBAction methods

Figure 1-1. *Grouping related code together makes it easy to know where to look for certain information*

The exact grouping of different parts of code is arbitrary, but what's important is that you organize code so it's easy to find what you want.

Using the // MARK: Comment

Besides physically grouping related items together such as IBOutlets and variables, you can also make searching for groups of related code easier by using the // MARK: comment. By placing a //MARK: comment, followed by descriptive text, you can make it easy to jump from one section of code to another through Xcode's pull-down menu as shown in Figure 1-2.

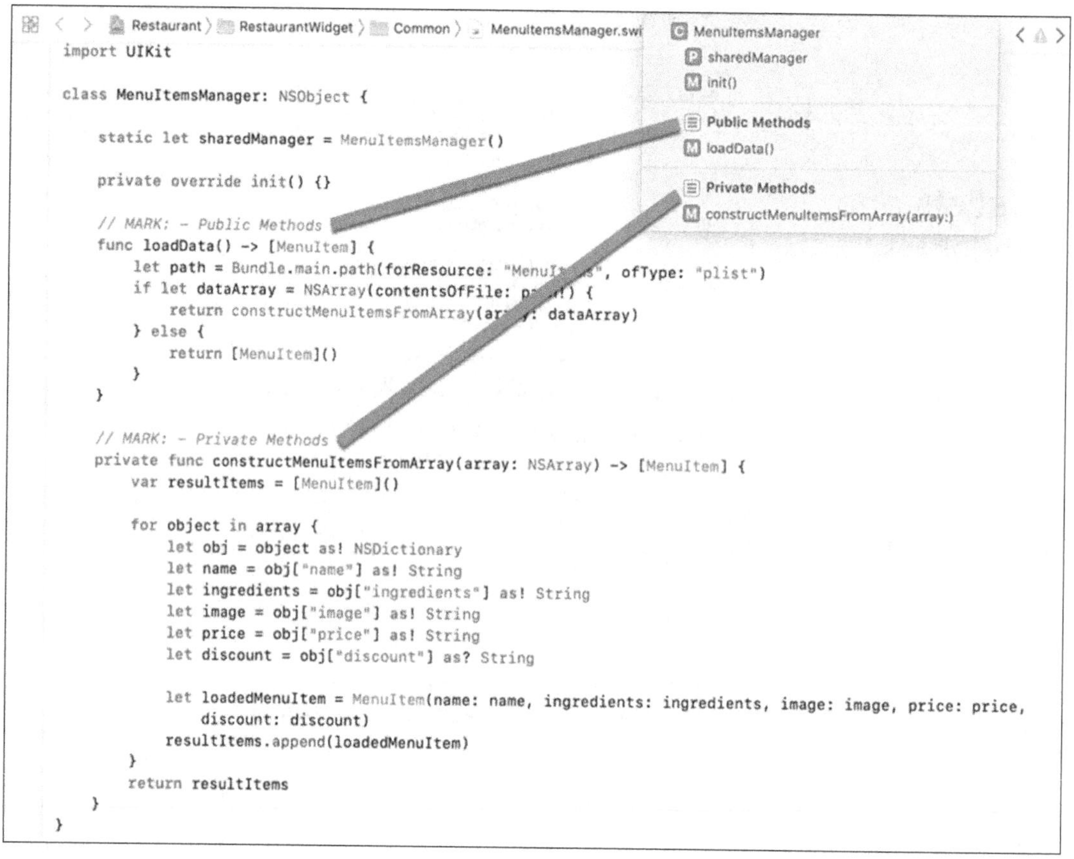

Figure 1-2. *The // MARK: comment creates categories in Xcode's pull-down menus*

The structure of the // MARK: comment looks like this:

```
// MARK: Descriptive text
```

The two // symbols define a comment. The MARK: text tells Xcode to create a pull-down menu category. The descriptive text can be any arbitrary text you want to identify the code that appears underneath.

Once you've defined one or more // MARK: comments, you can quickly jump to any of them by clicking the last item displayed above Xcode's middle pane to open a pull-down menu as shown in Figure 1-3.

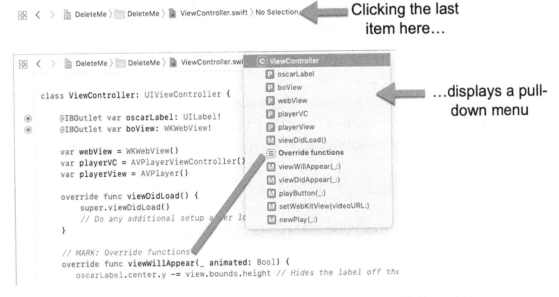

Figure 1-3. *Displaying Xcode's pull-down menu that lists all // MARK: comments*

Use the // MARK: comment generously throughout each .swift file. This will make it easy to jump to different parts of your code to modify it or simply study it later.

Using Extensions

When creating different classes, it's likely you'll need to extend them. For example, a class file that uses table views often needs to extend its class with UITableViewDataSource and UITableViewDelegate such as

```
class ViewController: UIViewController, UITableViewDelegate,
UITableViewDataSource {
```

Once you extend a class, you need to implement its required functions. For example, extending a class with UITableViewDataSource requires that you include the following two functions:

```
func tableView(_ tableView: UITableView, numberOfRowsInSection section:
Int) -> Int {
    // Code here
}
```

```swift
func tableView(_ tableView: UITableView, cellForRowAt indexPath:
IndexPath) -> UITableViewCell {
    // Code here
}
```

You can place these two functions anywhere in your .swift file, but it's generally a good idea to keep these two functions together. If you extend a ViewController class with UITableViewDelegate and UITableViewDataSource, the entire ViewController.swift file might look like this:

```swift
import UIKit

class ViewController: UIViewController, UITableViewDelegate,
UITableViewDataSource {

    @IBOutlet var petTable: UITableView!

    let petArray = ["cat", "dog", "parakeet", "parrot", "canary", "finch",
    "tropical fish", "goldfish", "sea horses", "hamster", "gerbil",
    "rabbit", "turtle", "snake", "lizard", "hermit crab"]

    let cellID = "cellID"

    override func viewDidLoad() {
        super.viewDidLoad()
        petTable.dataSource = self
        petTable.delegate = self
        // Do any additional setup after loading the view, typically from a nib.
    }

    func tableView(_ tableView: UITableView, numberOfRowsInSection section:
    Int) -> Int {
        return petArray.count
    }

    func tableView(_ tableView: UITableView, cellForRowAt indexPath:
    IndexPath) -> UITableViewCell {
        var cell = tableView.dequeueReusableCell(withIdentifier: cellID)
        if (cell == nil) {
            cell = UITableViewCell(
```

```swift
            style: UITableViewCell.CellStyle.default,
            reuseIdentifier: cellID)
    }
    cell?.textLabel?.text = petArray[indexPath.row]
    return cell!
}

func tableView(_ tableView: UITableView, didSelectRowAt indexPath:
IndexPath) {
    let selectedItem = petArray[indexPath.row]
    let alert = UIAlertController(title: "Your Choice", message: "\
    (selectedItem)", preferredStyle: .alert)

    let okAction = UIAlertAction(title: "OK", style: .default, handler:
    { action -> Void in
        //Just dismiss the action sheet
    })
    alert.addAction(okAction)

    self.present(alert, animated: true, completion: nil)
}

}
```

While it's easy to identify the three tableView functions (numberOfRowsInSection, cellForRowAt, and didSelectRowAt), it's not easy to see which functions belong to the UITableViewDelegate and which belong to UITableViewDataSource. Even more troublesome is that it's possible to insert multiple functions in between all three tableView functions.

To make it much easier to see which required functions are required by which class, you can extend a class a second way by adding specific extension code at the end of a class file as follows:

```swift
import UIKit

class ViewController: UIViewController {

    @IBOutlet var petTable: UITableView!
```

```swift
    let petArray = ["cat", "dog", "parakeet", "parrot", "canary", "finch",
    "tropical fish", "goldfish", "sea horses", "hamster", "gerbil",
    "rabbit", "turtle", "snake", "lizard", "hermit crab"]

    let cellID = "cellID"

    override func viewDidLoad() {
        super.viewDidLoad()
        petTable.dataSource = self
        petTable.delegate = self
        // Do any additional setup after loading the view.
    }

}

extension ViewController: UITableViewDataSource {
    func tableView(_ tableView: UITableView, numberOfRowsInSection section:
    Int) -> Int {
        return petArray.count
    }

    func tableView(_ tableView: UITableView, cellForRowAt indexPath:
    IndexPath) -> UITableViewCell {
        var cell = tableView.dequeueReusableCell(withIdentifier: cellID)
        if (cell == nil) {
            cell = UITableViewCell(
                style: UITableViewCell.CellStyle.default,
                reuseIdentifier: cellID)
        }
        cell?.textLabel?.text = petArray[indexPath.row]
        return cell!
    }
}

extension ViewController: UITableViewDelegate {
    func tableView(_ tableView: UITableView, didSelectRowAt indexPath:
    IndexPath) {
        let selectedItem = petArray[indexPath.row]
```

```swift
    let alert = UIAlertController(title: "Your Choice", message:
    "\(selectedItem)", preferredStyle: .alert)

    let okAction = UIAlertAction(title: "OK", style: .default, handler:
    { action -> Void in
        //Just dismiss the action sheet
    })
    alert.addAction(okAction)

    self.present(alert, animated: true, completion: nil)
    }
}
```

Notice that this method separates the tableView functions from the rest of the ViewController.swift code and explicitly shows that the numberOfRowsInSection and cellForRowAt tableView functions belong to the UITableViewDataSource while the didSelectRowAt tableView function belongs to the UITableViewDelegate.

By using the extension keyword at the end of .swift class files, it's much easier to group and organize related code. With the extension keyword, Xcode automatically identifies extensions in its pull-down menus to make it easier to find as shown in Figure 1-4.

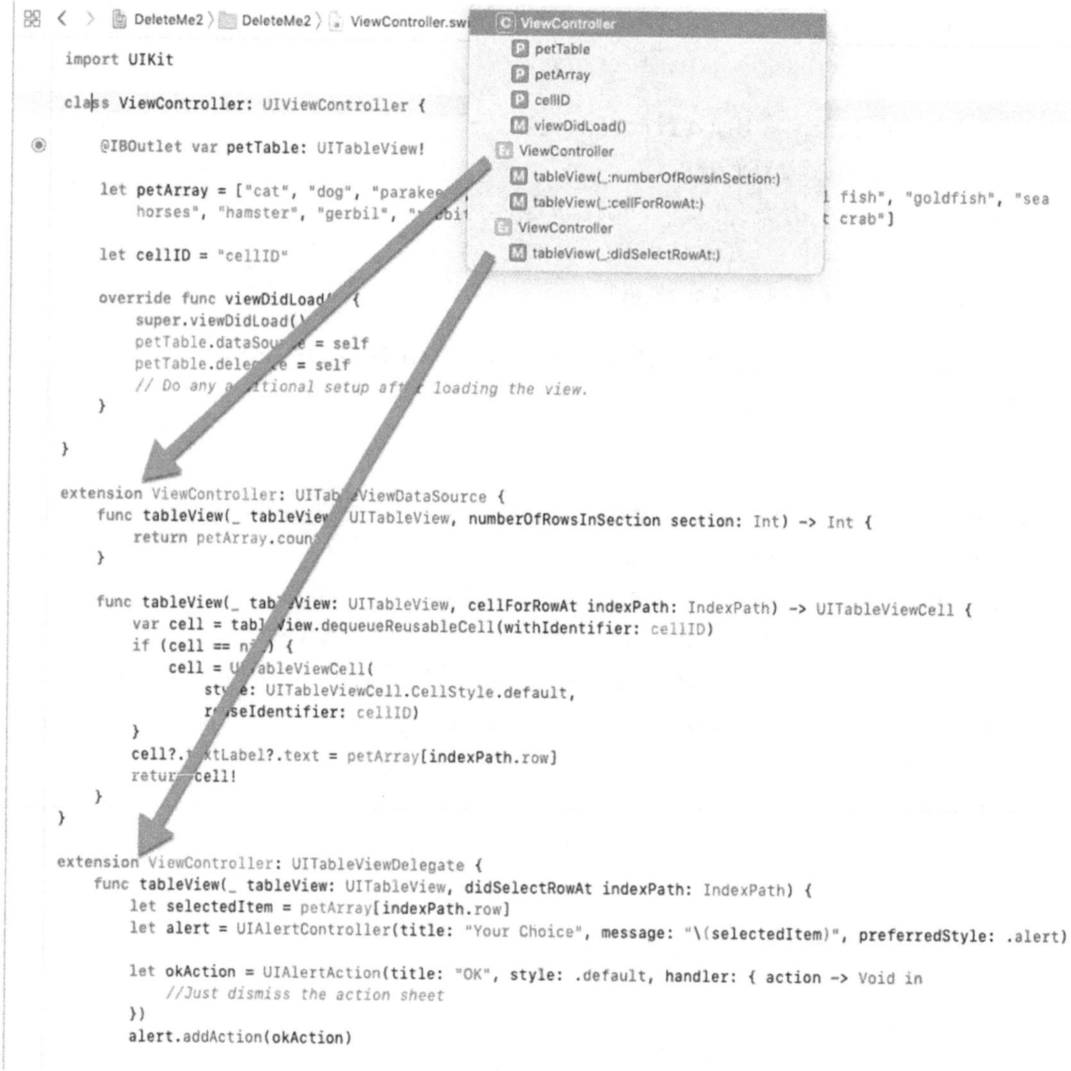

```
import UIKit

class ViewController: UIViewController {

    @IBOutlet var petTable: UITableView!

    let petArray = ["cat", "dog", "parakee...                     fish", "goldfish", "sea
        horses", "hamster", "gerbil", "rabbi...                   crab"]

    let cellID = "cellID"

    override func viewDidLoad() {
        super.viewDidLoad()
        petTable.dataSource = self
        petTable.delegate = self
        // Do any additional setup after loading the view.
    }

}

extension ViewController: UITableViewDataSource {
    func tableView(_ tableView: UITableView, numberOfRowsInSection section: Int) -> Int {
        return petArray.count
    }

    func tableView(_ tableView: UITableView, cellForRowAt indexPath: IndexPath) -> UITableViewCell {
        var cell = tableView.dequeueReusableCell(withIdentifier: cellID)
        if (cell == nil) {
            cell = UITableViewCell(
                style: UITableViewCell.CellStyle.default,
                reuseIdentifier: cellID)
        }
        cell?.textLabel?.text = petArray[indexPath.row]
        return cell!
    }
}

extension ViewController: UITableViewDelegate {
    func tableView(_ tableView: UITableView, didSelectRowAt indexPath: IndexPath) {
        let selectedItem = petArray[indexPath.row]
        let alert = UIAlertController(title: "Your Choice", message: "\(selectedItem)", preferredStyle: .alert)

        let okAction = UIAlertAction(title: "OK", style: .default, handler: { action -> Void in
            //Just dismiss the action sheet
        })
        alert.addAction(okAction)
```

Figure 1-4. *Displaying extensions in Xcode's pull-down menu*

The preceding two methods of extending a class are equivalent so it's just a matter of using which method you like best. Just be aware that using the extension keyword to separate code can help you organize code without any extra work on your part.

Using Files and Folders

Theoretically, you could create a single ViewController.swift file and cram it full of code. While this would work, it's likely to be troublesome to read and modify. A far better solution is to divide your project into multiple files and store those multiple files in separate folders in Xcode's Navigator pane.

Separate files and folders exist solely for your benefit to organize your project. Xcode ignores all folders and treats separate files as if they were all stored in a single file. When creating separate files, the two most common types of files to create are shown in Figure 1-5:

- Cocoa Touch Class

- Swift File

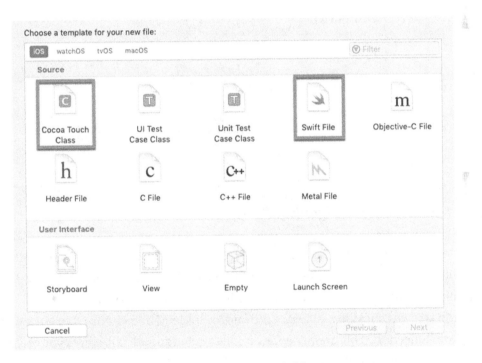

Figure 1-5. *The two most common types of .swift files in a project*

Cocoa Touch Class files are mostly used to connect to view controllers displayed in a storyboard. When you need a .swift file to control part of your app's user interface, use a Cocoa Touch Class file.

The Swift File option creates blank .swift files which are most often used to store and isolate code that you don't want to cram in an existing .swift file such as defining a list of variables, data structures, or classes.

The more .swift files you add to a project, the harder it can be to find any particular file. To help organize all the files that make up a project, Xcode lets you create folders. By using folders, you can selectively hide or display the contents of a folder as shown in Figure 1-6.

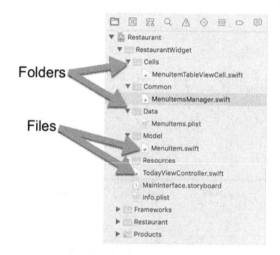

Figure 1-6. *Folders help organize all the files in a project*

To create an empty folder, choose File ➤ New ➤ Group. Once you've created an empty folder, you can drag and drop other folders or files into that empty folder.

Another option is to select one or more files and/or folders by holding down the Command key and clicking a different file and/or folder. Then choose File ➤ New ➤ Group from Selection. This creates a new folder and automatically stores your selected items into that new folder.

You can also right-click the Navigator pane to display a popup menu with the New Group or New Group from Selection commands as shown in Figure 1-7.

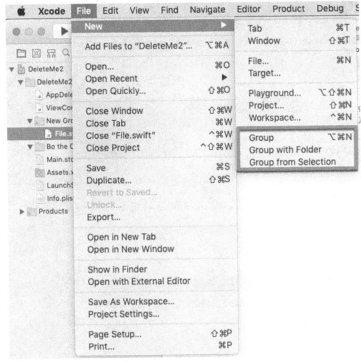

File pull-down menu

Right-click pop-up menu

Figure 1-7. *Menu commands to create a new folder*

Note   If the Group or Group from Selection commands are grayed out, click a .swift file to select it before choosing the File ➤ New ➤ Group or File ➤ New ➤ Group from Selection command.

Once you've created a folder, you can always delete that folder afterward. To delete a folder, follow these steps:

1. Click the folder you want to delete in the Navigator pane.

2. Choose Edit ➤ Delete, or right-click the folder, and when a popup menu appears, choose Delete. If the folder is not empty, Xcode displays a dialog to ask if you want to remove references to any stored files in that folder or just delete them all as shown in Figure 1-8.

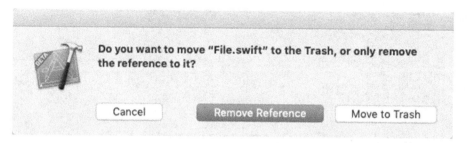

Figure 1-8. *Xcode alerts you if you're deleting a folder that contains files*

Note   Deleting a folder also deletes its contents, which can include other folders and files.

---

3. Click the Move to Trash button to delete the files completely (or click Remove Reference to keep the file and disconnect the file from your project but without deleting it).

Use Code Snippets

Remembering the exact syntax to create switch statements or for loops in Swift can be troublesome. As a shortcut, Xcode offers code snippets, which let you insert generic code in your .swift files that you can customize afterward. This lets you focus on the purpose of your code without worrying about the specifics of how Swift implements a particular way of writing branching or looping statements. In addition, code snippets help you write consistent code that's formatted the same way.

To use code snippets, follow these steps:

1. Click the .swift file where you want to type code.

2. Click the Library icon. The Snippets window appears as shown in Figure 1-9.

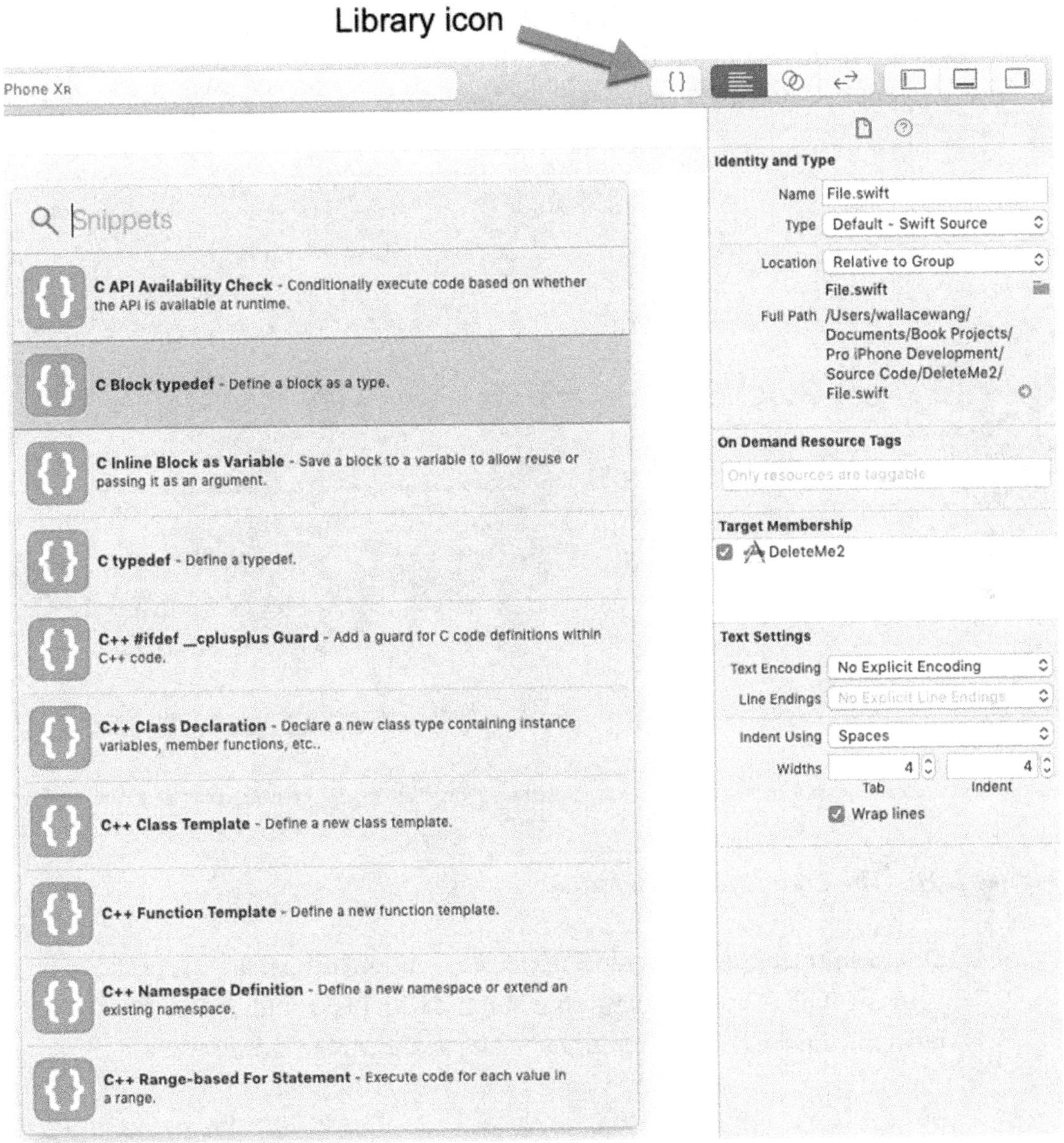

Library icon

Figure 1-9. *The Code Snippets window*

3. Scroll through the Code Snippets window and click a snippet
    you want to use. Xcode displays a brief description of that code
    snippet as shown in Figure 1-10.

Figure 1-10. *The Code Snippets window*

4. Drag a snippet from the Code Snippet window and drop it in
    your .swift file. Xcode displays your snippet with placeholders for
    customizing the code with your own data as shown in Figure 1-11.

```
if (condition) {
    statements
} else {
    statements
}
```

Figure 1-11. *A code snippet ready for customization*

Creating Custom Code Snippets

The Code Snippet window can make it easy to use common types of Swift statements without typing them yourself. However, you might create your own code that you might want to save and reuse between multiple projects. Rather than copy and paste from one project to another, you can store your own code in the Code Snippet window.

To store your own code as a snippet, follow these steps:

1. Select the code you want to store.

2. Choose Editor ➤ Create Code Snippet, or right-click your selected code, and when a popup menu appears, choose Create Code Snippet as shown in Figure 1-12. Xcode adds your selected code to the Code Snippet window as shown in Figure 1-13.

Editor pull-down menu

Right-click popup menu

Figure 1-12. *The Create Code Snippet command for adding your own code to the Code Snippet library*

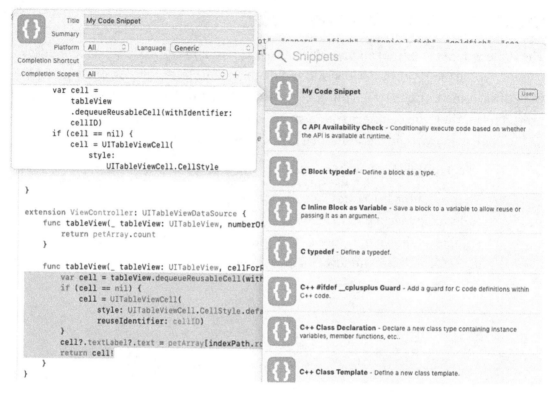

Figure 1-13. *Adding custom code to the Code Snippet window*

3. Click in the Title text field and type a descriptive name for your
    code snippet. You may also want to edit your code or modify other
    options. From now on, you'll be able to use your custom code
    snippet in any Xcode project.

Deleting Custom Code Snippets

After adding one or more code snippets, you may want to delete them. You can only
delete any code snippets you added to Xcode; you can never delete any of Xcode's
default code snippets. To delete a user-defined code snippet from the Code Snippet
window, follow these steps:

1. Click a .swift file in the Navigator pane.

2. Click the Library icon to open the Code Snippet library.

3. Click the code snippet you want to delete.

4. Press Shift+Delete. Xcode asks if you really want to delete the code snippet as shown in Figure 1-14.

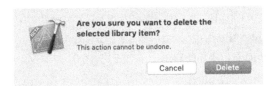

Figure 1-14. *Verifying the deletion of a code snippet*

5. Click Delete. Xcode removes your code snippet from the Code Snippet window.

Using @IBDesignable and @IBInspectable

When you design a user interface, you place various objects on a view such as buttons, sliders, labels, and text fields. To customize these objects, you have two choices:

- Write Swift code to modify objects programmatically.

- Change an object's properties in the Attributes Inspector.

As a general rule, it's always best to try to write as little code as possible because the less code you have, the easier it will be to examine and debug that code. Unfortunately, the Attributes Inspector doesn't list all possible ways to customize an object. That means you have to resort to writing Swift code to customize an object.

Suppose you wanted to create a button, define a border width and border color, and also a corner radius so the corners of the button appear rounded. You could create an IBOutlet variable and then modify that IBOutlet variable like this:

```
@IBOutlet var oldButton: UIButton!

override func viewDidLoad() {
    super.viewDidLoad()
    // Do any additional setup after loading the view.
    oldButton.layer.cornerRadius = 20
    oldButton.layer.borderWidth = 3
    oldButton.layer.borderColor = UIColor.red.cgColor
}
```

The preceding code programmatically changes the appearance of a button at runtime. However, if you don't like the appearance of the border width, color, or corner radius, you have to go back and modify the code all over again.

A far better solution would be to modify these properties in the Attributes Inspector and see your changes affect the appearance of a button at the same time. To do this, we need to use @IBInspectable and @IBDesignable.

@IBInspectable defines properties we want to appear in the Attributes Inspector. @IBDesignable tells Xcode to make any changes visible in Xcode. We need to create a Cocoa Touch Class file based on the object we want to customize. Then we need to make that class file @IBDesignable and create variables that are @IBInspectable.

To see how @IBDesignable and @IBInspectable work, follow these steps:

1. Create an iOS Single View App project and name it InspectableApp.

2. Click the Main.storyboard in the Navigator pane.

3. Click the Library icon and drag and drop two buttons onto the view where one button appears above the other.

4. Resize both buttons so they're larger and wider.

5. Choose Editor ➤ Resolve Auto Layout Issues ➤ Reset to Suggested Constraints. Xcode adds constraints to both buttons.

6. Double-click the top button, type **Custom Button**, and press Enter.

7. Double-click the bottom button, type **Old Button**, and press Enter.

8. Choose View ➤ Inspectors ➤ Assistant Editor ➤ Show Assistant Editor, or click the Assistant Editor icon in the upper right corner of the Xcode window. The Main.storyboard file and ViewController.swift file appear side by side.

9. Move the mouse pointer over the Old Button, hold down the Control key, and Ctrl-drag under the class ViewController line in the ViewController.swift file.

10. Release the Control key and the left mouse button. A popup window appears.

11. Click in the Name text field, type **oldButton**, and click the Connect button. Xcode creates an IBOutlet as follows:

```
@IBOutlet var oldButton: UIButton!
```

12. Edit the viewDidLoad method as follows:

```
override func viewDidLoad() {
    super.viewDidLoad()
    // Do any additional setup after loading the view.
    oldButton.layer.cornerRadius = 20
    oldButton.layer.borderWidth = 3
    oldButton.layer.borderColor = UIColor.red.cgColor
}
```

13. Click the Main.storyboard file in the Navigator pane.

14. Choose File ➤ New ➤ File. A template dialog appears.

15. Click Cocoa Touch Class under the iOS category and click the Next button. Another dialog appears, asking for a class name and subclass.

16. Click in the Class text field and type RoundedButton.

17. Click the Subclass of popup menu and choose UIButton as shown in Figure 1-15. (Note that if you wanted to customize a different user interface object such as a label, you would choose UILabel in the Subclass of popup menu.)

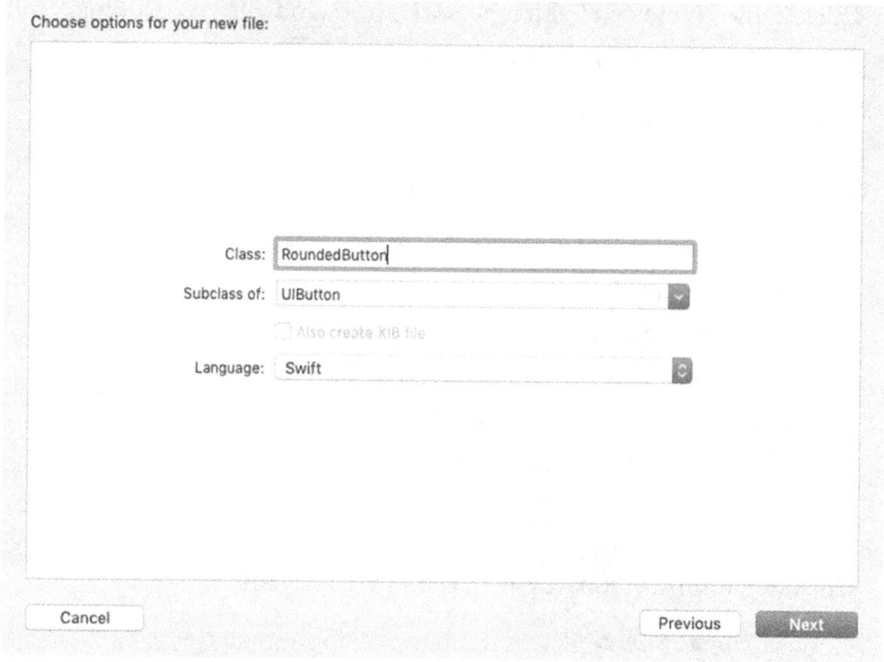

Figure 1-15. *Creating a new Cocoa Touch Class file for a UIButton*

18.   Click the Next button and then click the Create button. Xcode
      displays the RoundedButton.swift file in the Navigator pane.

19.   Click the Custom Button on the Main.storyboard to select it; then
      choose View ➤ Inspectors ➤ Show Identity Inspector, or click
      the Identity Inspector icon in the upper right corner of the Xcode
      window.

20.   Click the Class popup menu and choose RoundedButton. This
      links the RoundedButton.swift file to the button labelled Custom
      Button.

21.   Click the RoundedButton.swift file in the Navigator pane.

22.   Add the following code so the entire RoundedButton.swift looks
      like this:

```
import UIKit

@IBDesignable class RoundedButton: UIButton {

    @IBInspectable var cornerRadius : CGFloat = 0 {
```

```
        didSet {
            layer.cornerRadius = cornerRadius
        }
    }

    @IBInspectable var borderWidth : CGFloat = 1.0 {
        didSet {
            layer.borderWidth = borderWidth
        }
    }

    @IBInspectable var borderColor : UIColor = .white {
        didSet {
            layer.borderColor = borderColor.cgColor
        }
    }

}
```

The @IBDesignable keyword makes any object linked to this class file display its changes in Xcode when the user modifies the class file's defined properties.

The @Inspectable keyword makes all properties appear in the Attributes Inspector pane. Notice that each property uses the didSet keyword to immediately make any changes to these properties appear in the object displayed in Xcode.

23.   Click the Main.storyboard file in the Navigator pane.

24.   Click the Old Button and choose View ➤ Inspectors ➤ Show Attributes Inspector, or click the Attributes Inspector icon in the upper right corner of the Xcode window. Notice that the first options at the top of the Attributes Inspector display a Type, State Config, and Title popup menu as shown in Figure 1-16.

Figure 1-16. *An ordinary Attributes Inspector for a button*

25. Click the Custom Button. Notice that since this top button is
     connected to the RoundedButton.swift file that has defined three
     @Inspectable properties, those three properties now appear at the
     top of the Attributes Inspector as shown in Figure 1-17.

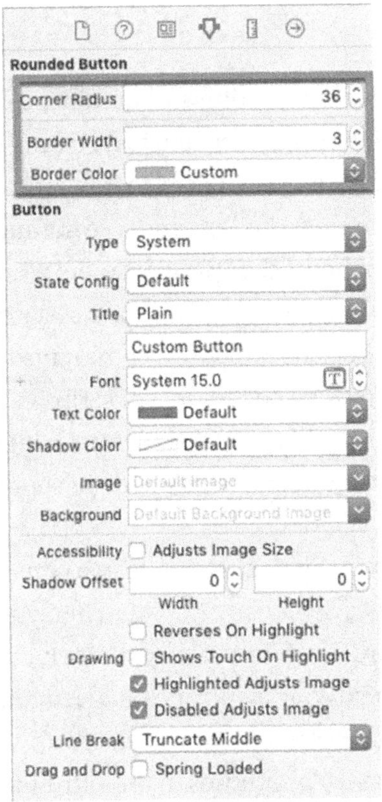

Figure 1-17. *A custom Attributes Inspector for a button*

26. Click in the Corner Radius text field and type a value such as 36. Notice that the higher the value, the more rounded the corners of the button.

27. Click in the Border Width text field and type a value such as 3. The higher the value, the thicker the border.

28. Click the Border Color popup menu and choose a color such as orange or red. Xcode displays the border in your chosen color.

By using the @IBInspectable, @IBDesignable, and didSet keywords, you can customize different user interface objects, make those custom properties appear in the Attributes Inspector, and see the changes in Xcode.

Summary

Writing iOS apps involves writing new code and modifying existing code. To do both tasks, you need to understand how any existing code works so you don't accidentally duplicate or break it. In many cases, you'll have to edit other people's code, which may or may not have been written in a clear, understandable manner.

Although you can't control how other programmers write code, you can control how you write code. The general principle is to write code that's easy to understand. This can involve adding comments (especially // MARK: comments to make it easy to jump to specific parts of your code). You should also use descriptive variable names and organize the related code in logical groups. You can do that by storing different parts of your code together. You can also organize code by storing code in separate files that you can group in folders.

To ensure you write common Swift statements in a consistent manner, you can use code snippets to insert the basic Swift code for you. Then you just have to customize it with your own data. For more flexibility, store your own code in the Code Snippet window. That way you can reuse your own code between multiple projects in Xcode.

If you want to customize a user interface object, create a separate Cocoa Touch Class file, use @IBInspectable to display properties in the Attributes Inspector pane, use didSet to make Xcode apply changes immediately, and use @IBDesignable to visually display those changes.

Organizing code is never necessary, but since most programs are modified multiple times, proper organization ahead of time can make modifying code much easier. Always assume that someone else will modify your code and make it easy on that person for the future, especially because that person could be you.

CHAPTER 2

Debugging Code

In the professional world of software, you'll actually spend more time modifying existing programs than you ever will creating new ones. When writing new programs or editing existing ones, it doesn't matter how much experience or education you might have because even the best programmers can make mistakes. In fact, you can expect that you will make mistakes no matter how careful you may be. Once you accept this inevitable fact of programming, you need to learn how to find and fix your mistakes.

In the world of computers, mistakes are commonly called "bugs," which gets its name from an early computer that used physical switches to work. One day the computer failed, and when technicians opened the computer, they found that a moth had been crushed within a switch, preventing the switch from closing. From that point on, programming errors have been called bugs and fixing computer problems has been known as debugging.

Three common types of computer bugs are

- Syntax errors – Occurs when you misspell something such as a keyword, variable name, function name, or class name or use a symbol incorrectly

- Logic errors – Occurs when you use commands correctly, but the logic of your code doesn't do what you intended

- Runtime errors – Occurs when a program encounters unexpected situations such as the user entering invalid data or when another program somehow interferes with your program unexpectantly

Syntax errors are the easiest to find and fix because they're merely misspellings of variable names that you created or misspelling of Swift commands that Xcode can help you identify. If you type a Swift keyword such as "var" or "let", Xcode displays that keyword in pink (or whatever color you specify for displaying keywords in the Xcode editor).

27

© Wallace Wang 2019
W. Wang, *Pro iPhone Development with Swift 5*, https://doi.org/10.1007/978-1-4842-4944-4_2

Now if you type a Swift keyword and it doesn't appear in its usual identifying color, then you know you probably typed it wrong somehow. By coloring your code, Xcode's editor helps you visually identify common misspellings or typos.

Besides using color, the Xcode editor provides a second way to help you avoid mistakes when you need to type the name of a method or class. As soon as Xcode recognizes that you might be typing a known item, it displays a popup menu of possible options. Now instead of typing the entire command yourself, you can simply select a choice in the popup menu and press the Tab or Enter key to let Xcode type your chosen command correctly as shown in Figure 2-1.

Figure 2-1. *Xcode displays a menu of possible commands you might want to use*

Syntax errors often keep your program from running at all. When a syntax error keeps your program from running, Xcode can usually identify the line (or the nearby area) of your program where the misspelled command appears so you can fix it as shown in Figure 2-2.

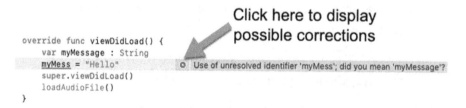

Figure 2-2. *Syntax errors often keep a program from running, which allows Xcode to identify the syntax error*

If you click the red dot that appears on the left of the error message, Xcode can often display possible suggestions for fixing your error. Then you can let Xcode fix the error for you by clicking the Fix button that appears to the right of the solution you want to use as shown in Figure 2-3.

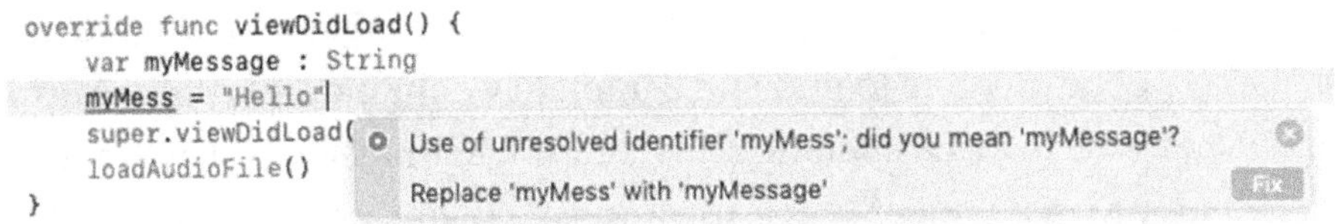

```
override func viewDidLoad() {
    var myMessage : String
    myMess = "Hello"|
    super.viewDidLoad(  ⊙  Use of unresolved identifier 'myMess'; did you mean 'myMessage'?          ⊗
    loadAudioFile()
}                          Replace 'myMess' with 'myMessage'                                    Fix
```

Figure 2-3. *Xcode can often suggest ways to fix errors*

Logic errors are much harder to find and detect than syntax errors. Logic errors occur when you use Swift code correctly, but it doesn't do what you want it to do. Since your code is actually valid, Xcode has no way of knowing that it's not working the way you intended. As a result, logic errors can be difficult to debug because you think you wrote your code correctly but you (obviously) did not.

How do you find a mistake in code that you thought you wrote correctly? Finding your mistake can often involve starting from the beginning of your program and exhaustively searching each line all the way until the end. (Of course there are faster ways than searching your entire program, line by line, which you'll learn about later in this chapter.)

Finally, the hardest errors to find and debug are runtime errors. Syntax errors usually keep your program from running, so if your program actually runs, you can assume that you have eliminated most, if not all, syntax errors in your code.

Logic errors can be tougher to find, but they're predictable. For example, if your program asks the user for a password but fails to give the user access even though the user types a correct password, you know you have a logic error. Each time you run your program, you can reliably predict when the logic error will occur.

Runtime errors are more insidious because they don't always occur predictably. For example, your app may run perfectly well on an iPhone, but the moment you run the same app on an iPad (or vice versa), the app fails. That's because conditions between two different iOS devices will never be exactly the same.

The problem is that unexpected, outside circumstances can affect an app's behavior such as another app taking up too much memory or one device might be running a different version of iOS than another device. Because runtime errors can't always be duplicated, they can be frustrating to find and even harder to fix since you can't always examine every possible condition your app might face when running on different iOS devices. Some apps can work perfectly – except if the user accidentally presses two keys at the same time. Other apps work just fine – until the user happens to save a file at the exact moment that another app tries to receive data over a WiFi connection.

Usually you can eliminate most syntax errors and find and fix most logic errors. However, it may not be possible to find and completely eliminate all runtime errors in a program. The best way to avoid spending time hunting for bugs is to strive to write code and test it carefully to make sure it's as error-free as possible.

Simple Debugging Techniques

When your app isn't working, you often have no idea what could be wrong. While you could tediously examine your code from beginning to end, it's often faster to simply guess where the mistake might be.

Once you have a rough idea what part of your app might be causing the problem, you have two choices. First, you can delete the suspicious code and run your app again. If the problem magically goes away, then you'll know that the code you deleted was likely the culprit.

However if your app still doesn't work, you have to retype your deleted code back into your program. A simpler solution might be to cut and paste code out of Xcode and store it in a text editor such as the TextEdit program that comes with every Macintosh, but this can be tedious.

That's why a second solution is to just temporarily hide code that you suspect might be causing a problem. Then if the problem persists, you can simply unhide that code and make it visible again. To do this in Xcode, you just need to turn your code into comments.

Remember, comments are text that Xcode completely ignores. You can create comments in three ways:

- Add the // symbols at the beginning of each line that you want to convert into a comment. This method lets you convert a single line into a comment.

- Add the /* symbols at the beginning of code and add the */ at the end of code you want to convert into a comment. This method lets you convert one or more lines into a comment.

- Select the lines of code you want to turn into a comment and choose Editor ➤ Structure ➤ Toggle Comments (or press Command+/). This method lets you convert one or more lines into a comment by placing the // symbols at the beginning of each line of code you selected.

> **Note**   Xcode color codes comments in green (or whatever color you may have defined to identify comments). After creating a comment, make sure Xcode color codes it properly to ensure you have created a comment. If Xcode fails to recognize your comments, it will treat your text as a valid Swift command, which will likely keep your code from running properly.

By turning code into comments, you essentially hide that code from Xcode. Now if you want to turn that comment back into code again, you just remove the // or /* and */ symbols that define your commented out code.

If you commented out code by choosing Editor ➤ Structure ➤ Toggle Comments (or pressing Command+/), just repeat the command again to convert that commented code back to working code once more.

Besides turning your code into comments to temporarily hide it, a second simple debugging technique is to use the print command. The idea is to put the print command in your code to print out the values of a variable wherever you think your code may be making a mistake.

By doing this, you can see what values one or more variables may contain. Putting multiple print commands throughout your program gives you a chance to make sure your program is running correctly.

To see how using the print command along with commenting out code can work to help you debug a program, follow these steps:

1. Choose File ➤ New ➤ Project to create a Single View App iOS project and name it **DebugApp**.

2. Click the ViewController.swift file in the Navigator pane and edit the ViewController.swift file as follows:

```swift
import UIKit

class ViewController: UIViewController {

    override func viewDidLoad() {
        super.viewDidLoad()
        var myMessage = "Temperature in Celsius:"
        let temp = 100.0
        print (myMessage + "\(temp)")
```

31

```swift
        myMessage = "Temperature in Fahrenheit:"
        print (myMessage + "\(C2F(tempC: temp))")
    }

    func C2F (tempC : Double) -> Double {
        var tempF : Double
        tempF = tempC + 32 * 9/5
        return tempF
    }

}
```

3. Click the Run button or choose Product ➤ Run. The Simulator window appears showing a blank screen.

4. Choose Simulator ➤ Quit Simulator. Notice that the debug area at the bottom of the middle Xcode pane displays the following text from the two print statements in our code:

Temperature in Celsius:100.0
Temperature in Fahrenheit:157.6

If you know anything about temperatures in Fahrenheit and Celsius, you know that the boiling point in Celsius is 100 degrees and the boiling point in Fahrenheit is 212 degrees. Yet our temperature conversion program calculates that 100 degrees Celsius is equal to 157.6 degrees in Fahrenheit, which means the Fahrenheit temperature should be 212 rather than 157.6. Obviously something is wrong, so let's use the print command and comments to help debug the problem.

1. Make sure the DebugApp project is loaded in Xcode.

2. Click the ViewController.swift file in the Navigator pane and edit the C2F function as follows:

```swift
func C2F (tempC : Double) -> Double {
    var tempF : Double
    tempF = tempC + 32 //* 9/5
    return tempF
}
```

This comment will let us check if the tempC parameter is properly coming into the C2F function and getting stored in the tempF variable.

3. Add a "print (tempC)" command above the return statement as follows:

```
func C2F (tempC : Double) -> Double {
    var tempF : Double
    tempF = tempC + 32 //* 9/5
    print (tempF)
    return tempF
}
```

4. Click the Run button or choose Product ➤ Run. The Simulator window appears showing a blank screen.

5. Choose Simulator ➤ Quit Simulator. Notice that the debug area at the bottom of the middle Xcode pane displays the following text from the two print statements in our code:

Temperature in Celsius:100.0
132.0
Temperature in Fahrenheit:132.0

By commenting out the calculation part of the code and using the "print (tempF)" command, we can see that the C2F function is storing 100.0 correctly in the tempC variable and adding 32 to this value before storing it in the tempF variable. Because we commented out the calculation part of the code, we can assume that the error must be in our commented out code.

Although the formula might look correct, the error occurs because of the way Swift (and most programming languages) calculate formulas. First, they start from left to right. Second, they calculate certain operations such as multiplication before addition.

The error occurs because our conversion formula first multiples 32 by 9 (288) and then divides the result (288) by 5 to get 57.6. Finally, it adds 57.6 to 100.0 to get the incorrect result of 157.6. What it should really be doing is multiplying 9/5 by the temperature in Celsius and then adding 32 to the result.

6. Modify the C2F function as follows:

```
func C2F (tempC : Double) -> Double {
    var tempF : Double
    tempF = tempC * (9/5) + 32
    print (tempF)
    return tempF
}
```

7. Click the Run button or choose Product ➤ Run. The Simulator window appears showing a blank screen.

8. Choose Simulator ➤ Quit Simulator. Look in the debug area and you'll see that the program now correctly converts 100 degrees Celsius to 212 degrees Fahrenheit.

For simple debugging, turning code temporarily into comments and using the print command can work, but it's fairly clumsy to keep adding and removing comment symbols and print commands. A much better solution is to use breakpoints and variable watching, which essentially duplicates using comments and print commands.

Using the Xcode Debugger

While comments and the print command can help you isolate problems in your code, they can be clumsy to use. The print command can be especially tedious since you have to type it into your code and then remember to remove it later when you're ready to ship your app.

Although leaving one or more print commands buried in your program won't likely hurt your program's performance, it's poor programming practice to leave code in your program that no longer serves any purpose.

As an alternative to typing the print command throughout your program, Xcode offers a more convenient alternative using the Xcode debugger. The debugger gives you two ways to hunt out and identify bugs in your program:

- Breakpoints
- Variable watching

Using Breakpoints

Breakpoints let you identify a specific line in your code where you want your program to stop. Once your program stops, you can step through your code, line by line. As you do so, you can also peek at the contents of one or more variables to check if the variables are holding the right values.

For example, if your program converts Celsius to Fahrenheit, but somehow converts 100 degrees Celsius into –41259 degrees Fahrenheit, you know your code isn't working right. By inserting breakpoints in your code and examining the values of your variables at each breakpoint, you can identify where your code calculates its values. The moment you spot the line where it miscalculates a value, you know the exact area of your program that you need to fix.

You can set a breakpoint by doing one of the following:

- Clicking to the left of the code where you want to set the breakpoint
- Moving the cursor to a line where you want to set the breakpoint and pressing Command+\
- Choosing Debug ➤ Breakpoints ➤ Add Breakpoint at Current Line

Xcode displays breakpoints as blue arrows in the left margin as shown in Figure 2-4.

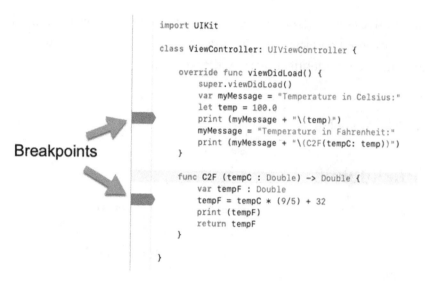

```
import UIKit

class ViewController: UIViewController {

    override func viewDidLoad() {
        super.viewDidLoad()
        var myMessage = "Temperature in Celsius:"
        let temp = 100.0
        print (myMessage + "\(temp)")
        myMessage = "Temperature in Fahrenheit:"
        print (myMessage + "\(C2F(tempC: temp))")
    }

    func C2F (tempC : Double) -> Double {
        var tempF : Double
        tempF = tempC * (9/5) + 32
        print (tempF)
        return tempF
    }

}
```

Breakpoints

Figure 2-4. Breakpoints appear in the left margin

Stepping Through Code

Once a breakpoint has stopped your program from running, you can step through your code line by line using the Step command. Xcode offers a variety of different Step commands, but the three most common are

- Step Over

- Step Into

- Step Out

The Step Over command examines the next line of code, treating function or method calls as a single line of code.

The Step Into command works exactly like the Step Over command until it highlights a function or method call. Then it jumps to the first line of code in that function or method.

The Step Out command is used to prematurely exit out of a function or method that you entered using the Step Into command. The Step Out command returns to the line of code where a function or method was called.

All three Step commands are used after a program temporarily stops at a breakpoint. By using a Step command, you can examine your code, line by line, and see how values stored in different variables may change.

Such variable watching lets you examine the contents of one or more variables to verify if it's holding the correct data. The moment you spot a variable holding incorrect data, you can zero in on the line of code that's creating that error.

The best part about breakpoints is that you can easily add and remove them since they don't modify your code at all, unlike comments and multiple print commands. Xcode can remove all breakpoints for you automatically so you don't have to hunt through your code to remove them one by one.

To see how to use breakpoints, step commands, and variable watching, follow these steps:

1. Make sure the DebugApp project is loaded in Xcode.

2. Click the ViewController.swift file in the Navigator pane and modify the C2F function as follows:

    ```swift
    func C2F (tempC : Double) -> Double {
        var tempF : Double
        tempF = tempC + 32 * 9/5
        return tempF
    }
    ```

3. Move the cursor on the following line in the viewDidLoad method:

    ```swift
    var myMessage = "Temperature in Celsius:"
    ```

4. Choose Debug ➤ Breakpoints ➤ Add Breakpoint at Current Line. Xcode displays a breakpoint as a blue arrow.

5. Click the Run button or choose Product ➤Run. The Simulator window appears showing a blank screen. Notice that Xcode highlights the line where the breakpoint appears and that the myMessage variable does not yet contain a value as shown in the debug area in Figure 2-5.

```
import UIKit

class ViewController: UIViewController {

    override func viewDidLoad() {
        super.viewDidLoad()
        var myMessage = "Temperature in Celsius:"
        let temp = 100.0
        print (myMessage + "\(temp)")
        myMessage = "Temperature in Fahrenheit:"
        print (myMessage + "\(C2F(tempC: temp))")
    }

    func C2F (tempC : Double) -> Double {
        var tempF : Double
        tempF = tempC + 32 * 9/5
        return tempF
    }

}
```

Figure 2-5. *A breakpoint temporarily stops a program from running*

6.   Choose Debug ➤ Step Over (or press F6). Xcode highlights the next line under your breakpoint. The information in the left-hand side of the debug area displays the current values that your program is using as shown in Figure 2-6. Notice that after the breakpoint code runs, the value of the myMessage variable is now defined as the string "Temperature in Celsius:".

```
import UIKit

class ViewController: UIViewController {

    override func viewDidLoad() {
        super.viewDidLoad()
        var myMessage = "Temperature in Celsius:"
        let temp = 100.0
        print (myMessage + "\(temp)")
        myMessage = "Temperature in Fahrenheit:"
        print (myMessage + "\(C2F(tempC: temp))")
    }

    func C2F (tempC : Double) -> Double {
        var tempF : Double
        tempF = tempC + 32 * 9/5
        return tempF
    }

}
```

Thread 1: step over

Debug App Thread 1 0 ViewController.viewDidLoad()

```
▶ self = (DebugApp.ViewController) 0x00007fbb14c12450      (lldb)
▶ myMessage = (String) "Temperature in Celsius:"
▶ $interpolation (DefaultStringInterpolation)
  temp = (Double) 100
```

Auto   Filter   All Output   Filter

Figure 2-6. *By watching how variables change, you can see how each line of code affects each variable*

7. Choose Debug ➤ Step Over (or press F6) several more times until Xcode highlights the following line:

```
print (myMessage + "\(C2F(tempC: temp))")
```

8. Choose Debug ➤ Step Into (or press F7). Xcode now highlights the first line of code in the C2F function as shown in Figure 2-7.

```
import UIKit

class ViewController: UIViewController {

    override func viewDidLoad() {
        super.viewDidLoad()
        var myMessage = "Temperature in Celsius:"
        let temp = 100.0
        print (myMessage + "\(temp)")
        myMessage = "Temperature in Fahrenheit:"
        print (myMessage + "\(C2F(tempC: temp))")
    }

    func C2F (tempC : Double) -> Double {
        var tempF : Double
        tempF = tempC + 32 * 9/5
        return tempF
    }

}
```

Thread 1: step in

DebugApp Thread 1 0 ViewController.C2F(tempC:)

tempC = (Double) 100
self = (DebugApp.ViewController) 0x00007fbb14c12450
tempF = (Double) 0

Temperature in Celsius:100.0
(lldb)

Auto ◇ | ◎ ①   ⊕ Filter   All Output ◇   ⊕ Filter   🗑 |⬜️⬜️

Figure 2-7. *The Step Into command lets you step through the code stored in a function or method*

9. Choose Debug ➤ Step Out (or press F8). Xcode now highlights the line that called the C2F function.

10. Choose Debug ➤ Continue to continue running the program until the next breakpoint. In this program there's only one breakpoint so the program displays its empty user interface.

11. Choose Simulator ➤ Quit Simulator to return back to Xcode.

12. Choose Debug ➤ Deactivate Breakpoints. Xcode dims the breakpoint. Xcode will ignore deactivated breakpoints.

13. Click the Run button or choose Product ➤ Run. The Simulator window appears showing a blank screen. Notice that since you deactivated breakpoints, Xcode runs the entire program without stopping at any of the breakpoints.

14. Choose Simulator ➤ Quit Simulator to return back to Xcode.

15. Choose Debug ➤ Activate Breakpoints. Notice that Xcode no longer dims the breakpoint arrow in the left margin any more.

16. Move the mouse pointer over the breakpoint and drag to the left or right.

17. Release the left mouse button. Xcode deletes the breakpoint.

Managing Breakpoints

There's no limit to the number of breakpoints you can put in a program so feel free to place as many as you need to help you track down an error. Of course if you place breakpoints in a program, you may lose track of how many breakpoints you've set and where they might be set. To help you manage your breakpoints, Xcode offers a Breakpoint Navigator.

You can open the Breakpoint Navigator in one of three ways:

- Choose View ➤ Navigators ➤ Show Breakpoint Navigator.

- Press Command+8.

- Click the Show Breakpoint Navigator icon in the Navigator pane.

The Breakpoint Navigator lists all the breakpoints set in your program and identifies the files the breakpoints are in and the line number of each breakpoint as shown in Figure 2-8.

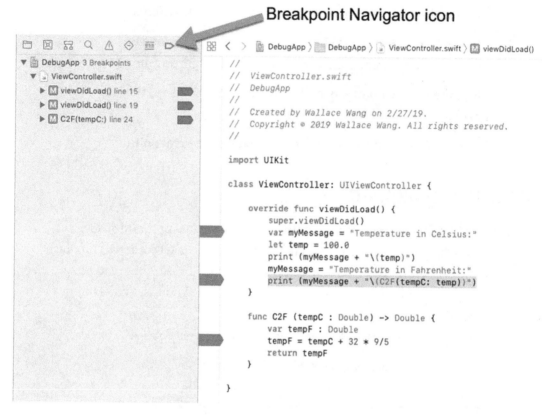

Figure 2-8. *The Breakpoint Navigator identifies all your breakpoints*

Since the Breakpoint Navigator identifies breakpoints by line number, you might want to display line numbers in the Xcode editor (see Figure 2-8). To turn on line numbers, follow these steps:

1. Choose Xcode ➤ Preferences. The Xcode Preferences window appears.

2. Click the Text Editing icon. The Text Editing options appear.

3. Select the "Line numbers" check box as shown in Figure 2-9.

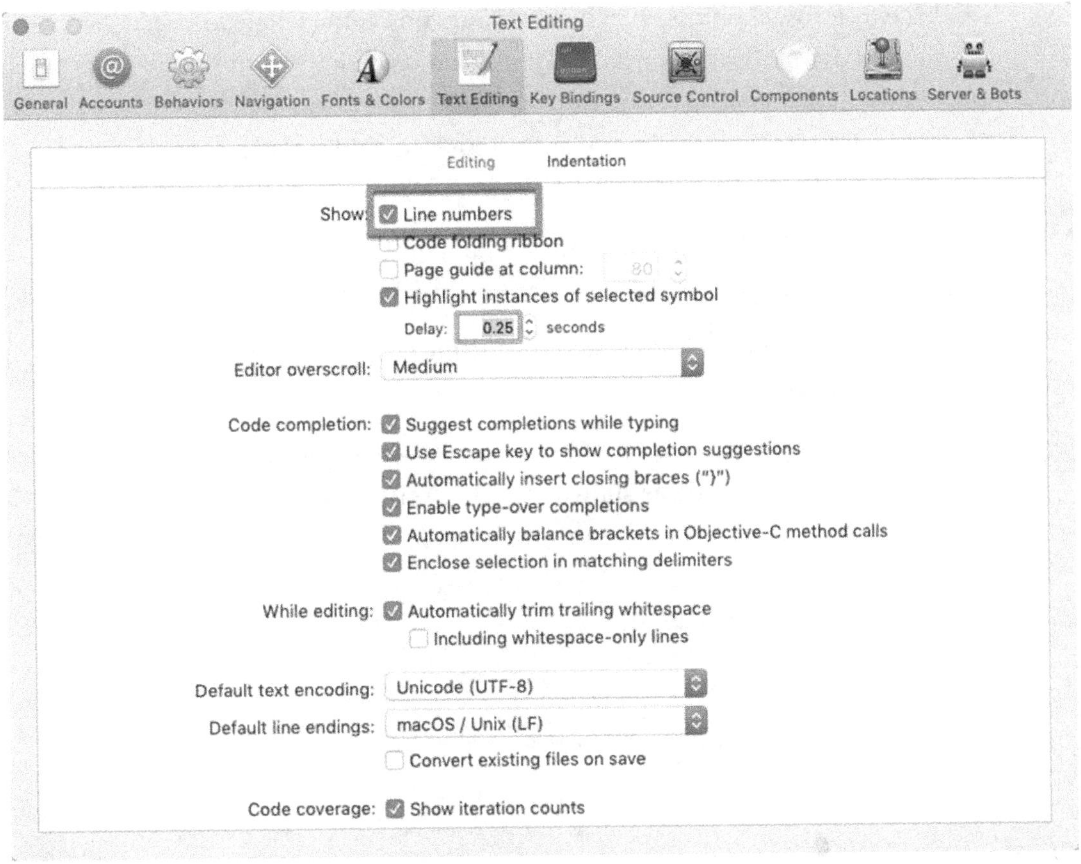

Figure 2-9. *The Line numbers check box lets you show or hide line numbers in the Xcode editor*

4. Click the close button (the red button) in the upper left corner of the Xcode Preferences window. Xcode now displays line numbers in the left margin of the editor.

To see how to use the Breakpoint Navigator, follow these steps:

1. Make sure the DebugApp project is loaded in Xcode.

2. Turn on line numbers in Xcode.

3. Click the ViewController.swift file in the Navigator pane.

4. Place three breakpoints anywhere in your code using whatever method you like best such as clicking in the left margin of the Xcode editor, pressing Command+\, or choosing Debug ➤ Breakpoints ➤ Add Breakpoint at Current Line). (The exact location doesn't matter.)

5. Choose View ➤ Navigators ➤ Show Breakpoint Navigator. The Breakpoint Navigator displays your three breakpoints.

6. Click any breakpoint. Xcode displays the file containing your chosen breakpoint.

7. Right-click any breakpoint in the Breakpoint Navigator pane. A popup menu appears as shown in Figure 2-10.

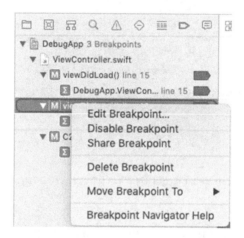

Figure 2-10. *The Breakpoint Navigator lets you see where you have placed breakpoints throughout a project*

8. Choose Disable Breakpoint. Notice this lets you deactivate or disable breakpoints individually instead of deactivating all of them at once through the Debug ➤ Deactivate Breakpoints command.

9. Right-click any breakpoint in the Breakpoint Navigator pane and choose Delete Breakpoint. (Another way to delete a breakpoint is to drag the breakpoint away from your code and release the left mouse button.)

10. Delete all your breakpoints until no more breakpoints are left.

Using Symbolic Breakpoints

When you create a breakpoint, you must place it on the line where you want your program's execution to temporarily stop. However, this often means guessing where the problem might be and then using the various step commands to examine your code line by line.

To avoid this problem, Xcode offers a Symbolic breakpoint. A Symbolic breakpoint stops program execution only when a specific function or method runs. In case you don't want your program's execution to stop every time a particular function or method runs, you can tell Xcode to ignore it a certain number of times such as 10. That means the function or method will run up to 10 times, and then on the 11th time it's called, the Symbolic breakpoint will temporarily halt execution so you can step through your code line by line.

To create a Symbolic breakpoint, you can define the following:

- Symbol – The name of the function or method to halt program execution

- Module – The file name containing the function or method defined by the Symbol text field

- Ignore – The number of times from 0 or more that you want the function or method to run before temporarily halting program execution

To see how a Symbolic breakpoint works, follow these steps:

1. Make sure the DebugApp project is loaded in Xcode.

2. Choose Debug ➤ Breakpoints ➤ Create Symbolic Breakpoint. A Symbolic Breakpoint popup window appears as shown in Figure 2-11.

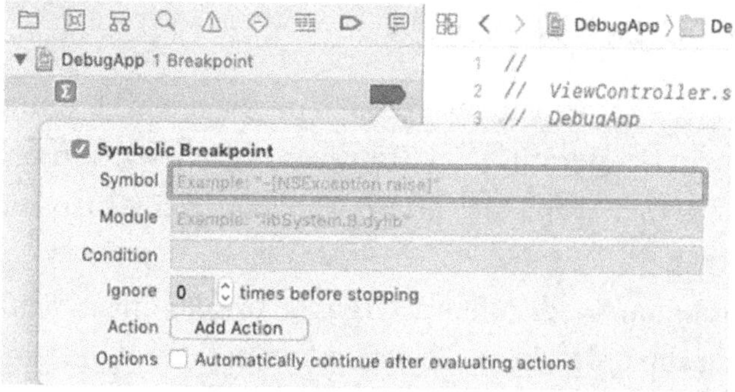

Figure 2-11. *The Symbolic Breakpoint popup window lets you define a breakpoint*

3. Click in the Symbol text field and type C2F, which is the name of the function or method you want to examine.

4. (Optional) If the function or method name you specified in the Symbol text field is used in other files, click in the Module text field and type a file name. This file name will limit the Symbolic breakpoint only to that function or method in that particular file. Since the C2F function is only used once, you can leave the Module text field empty.

5. (Optional) Click in the Ignore text field and type a number to specify how many times to ignore a function or method being called before halting program execution. In this case, leave 0 in the Ignore text field.

6. Click anywhere away from the Symbolic Breakpoint popup window to make it disappear.

7. Click the Run button or choose Product ➤ Run. The Simulator window appears showing a blank screen. The C2F Symbolic breakpoint causes the program to temporarily halt execution on the first line of code in the C2F function that calculates a result as shown in Figure 2-12.

Figure 2-12.   *The Symbolic breakpoint halts program execution in the C2F function defined by the Symbol text field*

8.   Choose Product ➤ Stop, or click the Stop button, to make your program stop running.

9.   Choose View ➤ Navigators ➤ Show Breakpoint Navigator. The Breakpoint Navigator pane appears.

10. Right-click the C2F breakpoint in the Breakpoint Navigator pane, and when a popup menu appears, choose Delete Breakpoint. There should be no breakpoints displayed in the Breakpoint Navigator pane.

Note   Another way to set a breakpoint without specifying a specific line of code is to create an Exception breakpoint. Normally if your program crashes, Xcode displays a bunch of cryptic error messages and you have no idea what caused the error. If you set an Exception breakpoint, Xcode can identify the line of code that created the crash so you can fix it.

Using Conditional Breakpoints

Breakpoints normally stop program execution at a specific line every time. However, you may want to stop program execution on a particular line only if a certain condition holds true, such as if a variable exceeds a certain value, which can signal when something has gone wrong.

To see how a Conditional breakpoint works, follow these steps:

1. Make sure the DebugApp project is loaded in Xcode.

2. Click the ViewController.swift file in the Navigator pane.

3. Place a breakpoint on the following line by clicking in the left margin or moving the cursor in the line and pressing Command+\ or choosing Debug ➤ Breakpoints ➤ Add Breakpoint at Current Line:

   ```
   print (myMessage + "\(C2F(tempC: temp))")
   ```

4. Choose View ➤ Navigators ➤ Show Breakpoint Navigator, or click the Breakpoint Navigator icon. The Breakpoint Navigator pane appears, showing the breakpoint you just created.

5. Right-click the breakpoint in the Breakpoint Navigator pane and choose Edit Breakpoint. A popup window appears.

6. Click in the Condition text field, and type C2F(tempC: temp) > 20 as shown in Figure 2-13.

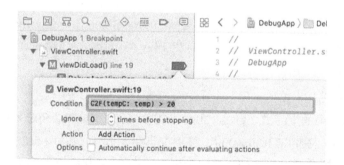

Figure 2-13. *The Symbolic breakpoint halts program execution in the C2F function defined by the Symbol text field*

7. Click the Run button or choose Product ➤ Run. Xcode highlights your breakpoint to temporarily stop program execution, which means that the condition (C2F(temp) > 20) must be true.

8. Choose Product ➤ Stop, or click the Stop button, to make your program stop running and return back to Xcode.

9. Choose View ➤ Navigators ➤ Show Breakpoint Navigator, right-click the breakpoint you created, and choose Edit Breakpoint. The popup window appears.

10. Click in the Condition text field and edit the text so it reads C2F(temp > 500). Press Enter.

11. Click the Run button or choose Product ➤ Run. Notice that this time your breakpoint does not stop program execution because its condition (C2F(temp) > 500) is not true. Because the breakpoint didn't stop your app, your app's blank user interface appears.

12. Choose Simulator ➤ Quit Simulator to return back to Xcode.

13. Drag the breakpoint away from the left margin and release the left mouse button to delete the breakpoint. (You can also right-click the breakpoint in the Breakpoint Navigator pane and choose Delete Breakpoint.)

Summary

Errors or bugs are unavoidable in any app. While syntax errors are easy to find and fix, logic errors can be tougher to find because you thought your code would create one type of result but it winds up creating a different result. Now you're left trying to figure out what you did wrong when you thought you were doing everything right. Even harder errors to track down are runtime errors that occur seemingly at random because of unknown conditions that affect an app.

To help you track down and eliminate most bugs, you can use the print command along with comments, but for most robust debugging, you should use Xcode's built-in debugger. With the debugger you can set breakpoints in your code and watch how values get stored in one or more variables.

A conditional breakpoint only stops program execution when a certain condition occurs. A Symbolic breakpoint only stops program execution when a specific function or method gets called. Once a breakpoint stops a program, you can continue examining your code line by line using various step commands. The Step Into command lets you view code stored inside a function or method, while the Step Out command lets you prematurely exit out of a function or method and jump back to the function or method call.

By using breakpoints and step commands, you can exhaustively examine how your program works, line by line, to eliminate as many errors as possible. The fewer errors your app contains, the happier your users will be.

CHAPTER 3

Understanding Closures

Reading a single sentence isn't difficult for most people, but when you combine
thousands of sentences together, reading a long mass of text can be cumbersome. That's
why people divide large amounts of text into parts such as paragraphs and chapters.
Programming is no different.

Rather than write code as one large mass of text, programmers typically divide a
large program into smaller functions where each function performs a single task. Not
only do functions help make a large program easier to understand, but functions also act
like building blocks that you can reuse in other programs.

You should already be familiar with the standard way to create a function by using
the func keyword followed by a descriptive name, parameter list, and a block of code
such as

```
func descriptiveName() {
    // Code here
}
```

To run a function, you have to call it by name such as

```
descriptiveName()
```

If a function returns a value, you can assign a function to represent a value such as

```
var x = descriptiveName()
```

To use functions, you need to follow a two-step process:

1. Create a function.

2. Call that function.

© Wallace Wang 2019
W. Wang, *Pro iPhone Development with Swift 5*, https://doi.org/10.1007/978-1-4842-4944-4_3

Another way to write a function is as a closure. Closures simply let you create and call a function in a single step. By using closures as a different way to write functions, you can write more concise code (with the drawback of being harder to read and understand). Closures are most often used in completion handlers that run as soon as another command finishes running as shown in Figure 3-1.

Completion handler
code goes here

Figure 3-1. *Closures are often used in completion handlers*

You could simply write one command followed by a function call immediately after it, but a completion handler makes it obvious that the command and its completion handler work together.

Closures can be written in several different ways. When you create a function, you need to use the func keyword followed by a descriptive name, a parameter list, and code that calculates a result such as

```
func multiplyBy2 (x: Int) -> Int {
    return x * 2
}
```

One way to rewrite this function as a closure involves dropping the func keyword and the function name, then enclose the rest of the code in curly brackets like this:

```
let y = {(x: Int) -> Int in return x * 2}
```

A second way to write a closure is to eliminate the parameter list altogether like this:

```
let z = {x in return x * 2}
```

Still another shortcut is to eliminate the return keyword altogether like this:

```
let w = {x in x * 2}
```

An even more condensed version of a closure simply displays the return calculation by eliminating any variables and replacing them with placeholders that identify different parameters such as

```
let v = {$0 * 2}
```

To see how to use closures, follow these steps:

1. Choose File ➤ New ➤ Playground and create an iOS Blank playground.

2. Name it **ClosurePlayground**.

3. Type the following:

```
print ("func multiplyBy2 (x: Int) -> Int {")
func multiplyBy2 (x: Int) -> Int {
    return x * 2
}

print(multiplyBy2(x: 4))
print(multiplyBy2(x: 17))

print("{(x: Int) -> Int in return x * 2}")
let y = {(x: Int) -> Int in return x * 2}
print (y(4))
print (y(17))

print("{x in return x * 2}")
let z = {x in return x * 2}
print (z(4))
print (z(17))

print("{x in x * 2}")
let w = {x in x * 2}
print (w(4))
print (w(17))

print("{$0 * 2}")
let v = {$0 * 2}
print(v(4))
print(v(17))
```

4. Click the Run button. The debug area prints the following:

```
func multiplyBy2 (x: Int) -> Int {
8
34
{(x: Int) -> Int in return x * 2}
8
34
{x in return x * 2}
8
34
{x in x * 2}
8
34
{$0 * 2}
8
34
```

Notice how all versions of the closure work exactly the same as the function declaration. The only difference is how concise each written closure appears. By understanding the different ways closures can be written, you can recognize them in code written by other people.

When it's time to write completion handlers, you can use a closure and write it out in whatever style you wish that makes most sense to you. For simplicity, many programmers use the concise version that uses $0 as a placeholder for the first passed parameter, $1 for the second passed parameter, $2 for the third passed parameter, and so on.

Closures with Multiple Parameters

When declaring a function, you need to explicitly define the data type of each parameter such as

```
func addNumbers (x: Int, y: Int) -> Int {
    return x + y
}
```

When using closures, you need to enclose all parameters inside parentheses. In many cases, you do not need to define the data type of each parameter since Swift can infer that value based on the data type of the return value. For example, if the return value data type is an integer, Swift infers that the passed parameters must be integers as well such as

```
{(x, y) -> Int in return x + y}
```

However, if there is any ambiguity, you must explicitly define the data types of your parameters such as

```
{(x: Int, y: Int) in return x + y}
{(x: Int, y: Int) in x + y}
{$0 as Int + $1 as Int}
```

Notice that the top two examples define the integer data type with a colon and the Int keyword, while the last example defines the integer data type with the "as" and Int keywords.

Modify your ClosurePlayground file as follows and click the Run button:

```
print ("func addNumbers (x: Int, y: Int) -> Int ")
func addNumbers (x: Int, y: Int) -> Int {
    return x + y
}

print(addNumbers(x: 4, y: 5))
print(addNumbers(x: 17, y: 9))

print("{(x, y) -> Int in return x + y}")
let y = {(x, y) -> Int in return x + y}
print (y(4, 5))
print (y(17, 9))

print("{(x: Int, y: Int) in return x + y}")
let z = {(x: Int, y: Int) in return x + y}
print (z(4, 5))
print (z(17, 9))
```

```
print("{(x: Int, y: Int) in x + y}")
let w = {(x: Int, y: Int) in x + y}
print (w(4, 5))
print (w(17, 9))

print("{$0 as Int + $1 as Int}")
let v = {$0 as Int + $1 as Int}
print(v(4, 5))
print(v(17, 9))
```

Understanding Value Capturing

When you declare variables and constants within a function, they can only be accessed inside that function. However, when you declare a variable or constant outside of a function, that function can access that value as shown in Figure 3-2.

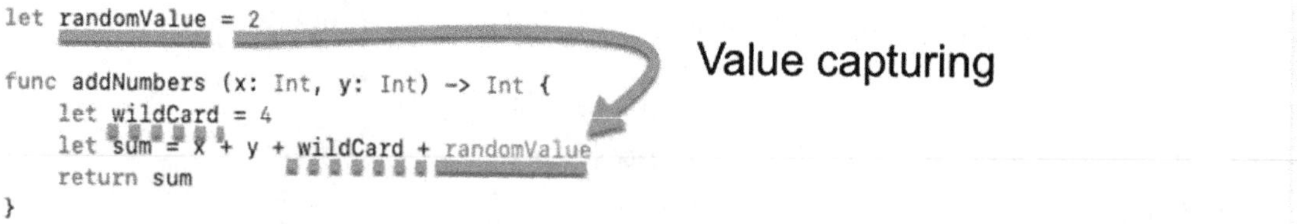

Figure 3-2. A function can access variables inside and above a function

In Figure 3-2, the "randomValue" constant is declared outside of the function but the function can still access its value. However, the "wildcard" constant is declared inside the function so it can only be accessed inside that function and nowhere else.

Since "wildcard" is declared inside the function, we cannot access that value outside that function as shown in Figure 3-3.

```
func addNumbers (x: Int, y: Int) -> Int {
    let wildCard = 4
    let sum = x + y + wildCard + randomValue
    return sum
}

print(wildCard)                    Use of unresolved identifier 'wildCard'
```

Figure 3-3. Values declared inside a function cannot be accessed outside that function

Because closures are just another way of writing a function, closures can also capture and modify values declared outside of their scope.

Using Closures Like Data

Perhaps the most versatile use of closures is to treat them like chunks of data that you can use like any fixed value. That means you can pass a closure as a parameter in a function (or another closure), store closures in data structures like arrays, or assign a closure to a variable.

When you declare a function, you must give that function a unique name such as

```
func addNumbers (x: Int, y: Int) -> Int {
    return x + y
}
```

To call this function, you would use the function name and pass it parameters such as

```
addNumbers(x: 17, y: 9)
```

Likewise, you can assign a closure to a variable name like this:

```
let addNumbers1 = {(x, y) -> Int in return x + y}
let addNumbers2 = {(x: Int, y: Int) in return x + y}
let addNumbers3 = {(x: Int, y: Int) in x + y}
let addNumbers4 = {$0 as Int + $1 as Int}
```

Then you can run this closure by using its name and pass it parameters such as

```
addNumbers1(17, 9)
addNumbers2(17, 9)
addNumbers3(17, 9)
addNumbers4(17, 9)
```

You can pass a closure as data to another closure like this:

```
addNumbers2(17, addNumbers1(17,9))
```

Since the value of addNumbers1(17,9) is 26, the preceding code is equivalent to

```
addNumbers2(17, 26)
```

This calculates the value 43 (17 + 26).

Another interesting use for closures is to store them in data structures. Unlike fixed values, the same closure can represent different values depending on its parameters. Modify the ClosurePlayground as follows and click the Run button:

```
let addNumbers1 = {(x, y) -> Int in return x + y}
let addNumbers2 = {(x: Int, y: Int) in return x + y}
let addNumbers3 = {(x: Int, y: Int) in x + y}
let addNumbers4 = {$0 as Int + $1 as Int}

let closureArray = [addNumbers1(9,1), addNumbers2(2,3), addNumbers3(7,6),
addNumbers4(10,2)]
print (closureArray.count)
for i in closureArray {
    print(i)
}
```

The first four lines define four different closures that work exactly alike, which is to accept two integers as parameters, add them together, and return the sum. The fifth line creates an array that holds each closure where each closure gets different parameters.

The sixth line prints the total number of items in the closureArray (4) and then the for-in loop prints each item in the closureArray so the output looks like this:

```
10
5
13
12
```

Remember, closures are functions. There are different ways to write a closure where each succeeding version gets sparser and more cryptic. Suppose you had a function like this:

```
func multiplyBy2 (x: Int) -> Int {
    return x * 2
}
```

You could rewrite this function as a closure in four different ways:

```
{(x: Int) -> Int in return x * 2}
{x in return x * 2}
{x in x * 2}
{$0 * 2}
```

When passing parameters into a closure, enclose them in parentheses. In case the data type of a closure's parameters might not be clear, explicitly define the data type like this:

```
{(x: Int, y: Int) in return x + y}
{(x: Int, y: Int) in x + y}
{$0 as Int + $1 as Int}
```

Summary

Closures are nothing more than another way to write a function. Instead of creating a function and then calling that function in a two-step process, you can create and use a closure in one step.

Be aware that closures can access and modify variables declared outside of the closure. You can assign closures to a name or simply use closures in place of data. Any place where you can use data, you can use a closure. Just be careful since closures aren't always obvious how they work. Closures offer efficiency in exchange for possible confusion so use closures sparingly or add comments to explain how a closure works.

CHAPTER 4

Multithreaded Programming Using Grand Central Dispatch

The next time you pay for groceries in a supermarket, look at the lines at the checkout stands. If there's only one open checkout stand, there's likely a long line of customers waiting to pay. That means everyone has to wait their turn before they can leave. However if there are multiple checkout stands open, more customers can pay at the same time and the wait time for everyone is much less. That's the basic idea behind multithreaded programming.

In the old days of computers, tasks were fairly simple so processors were fast enough to handle them one at a time no matter how many there might be. Gradually as software got more sophisticated and tasks got more complex, processors couldn't handle so many complicated tasks simultaneously. Speeding up the processor by itself could only solve the problem to a limited extent, so processors started offering multiple cores, which were essentially separate processors that could work on different tasks simultaneously.

While multicore processors offered a solution, the bigger problem was none of these multicore processors could work to their full potential unless the software took advantage of these multiple cores. This forced programmers to write code that could run at the same time known as concurrent programming. Writing code was hard enough, and writing additional code to make different parts of a program run at the same time was often confusing and difficult. As a result, most programmers didn't bother, which meant their software wouldn't take full advantage of multicore processors.

61

© Wallace Wang 2019
W. Wang, *Pro iPhone Development with Swift 5*, https://doi.org/10.1007/978-1-4842-4944-4_4

To solve the problem of managing code to run in parallel, Apple created a solution called **Grand Central Dispatch** (GCD), which provides support for concurrent code execution on multicore hardware in iOS and macOS. Instead of forcing developers to worry about the details of managing code to run in parallel, known as threads, Grand Central Dispatch lets developers simply identify which chunks of code to run at the same time, and Grand Central Dispatch takes care of the actual details to do so.

In the old days, software was mostly self-contained in that it didn't need to rely on anything else. Today, software often depends on external factors that are largely unpredictable such as waiting for a file to load or a network connection to complete. While waiting, the entire program is effectively paused. If this pause is too long, it makes the program look like it's frozen and unresponsive.

That's why you want to use Grand Central Dispatch to allow multiple threads of execution within a program. That way even if a single thread is stuck waiting for a specific event, the other threads can keep going. By using Grand Central Dispatch, your apps should never feel slow and unresponsive to the user.

Note   Grand Central Dispatch works identically in both iOS and macOS.

Understanding Threads

To fully understand the advantage of Grand Central Dispatch, it's important to see how delays can ruin the responsiveness of an app in the eyes of a user. To do this, we'll see what happens when a process runs for too long, essentially forcing the entire app to wait until the process finishes. During this time, the app appears frozen and unresponsive.

We'll deliberately create an app that will lock up the user interface. To see how to create an app that appears unresponsive, follow these steps:

1. Create a new iOS Single View App and name it ThreadApp.

2. Click the Main.storyboard file in the Navigator pane.

3. Click the Library icon to open the Object Library window.

4. Drag and drop a button, a text view, and a slider anywhere on the view as shown in Figure 4-1.

Button

Lorem ipsum dolor sit er elit lamet,
consectetaur cillium adipisicing
pecu, sed do eiusmod tempor
incididunt ut labore et dolore
magna aliqua. Ut enim ad minim
veniam, quis nostrud exercitation
ullamco laboris nisi ut aliquip ex ea

Figure 4-1. *Adding a button, a text view, and a slider to create the user interface*

5. Choose Editor ➤ Resolve Auto Layout Issues ➤ Reset to
    Suggested Constraints at the bottom half of the menu. Xcode adds
    constraints to the button, text view, and slider.

6. Choose View ➤ Assistant Editor ➤ Show Assistant Editor, or click
    the Assistant Editor icon in the upper right corner of the Xcode
    window. Xcode shows the Main.storyboard and ViewController.
    swift file side by side.

7. Move the mouse pointer over the text view, hold down the
    Control key, and Ctrl-drag from the text view to under the "class
    ViewController" line in the ViewController.swift file.

8. Release the Control key and the left mouse button. A popup
    window appears.

9. Click in the Name text field and type **resultsTextView**. Then click
    the Connect button. Xcode creates an IBOutlet as follows:

    ```
    @IBOutlet var resultsTextView: UITextView!
    ```

10. Move the mouse pointer over the button, hold down the Control
    key, and Ctrl-drag from the button to above the last curly bracket
    at the bottom of the ViewController.swift file.

11. Release the Control key and the left mouse button. A popup
    window appears.

12. Click in the Name text field, type **doButton**, click the Type popup menu and choose UIButton, then click the Connect button. Xcode creates a blank IBAction method as follows:

```
@IBAction func doButton(_ sender: UIButton) {
}
```

13. Choose View ➤ Standard Editor ➤ Show Standard Editor, or click the Standard Editor icon in the upper right corner of the Xcode window.

14. Click the ViewController.swift file in the Navigator pane.

15. Add the following code underneath the viewDidLoad method:

```
func fetchSomethingFromServer() -> String {
    Thread.sleep(forTimeInterval: 1)
    return "Hi there"
}

func processData(_ data: String) -> String {
    Thread.sleep(forTimeInterval: 2)
    return data.uppercased()
}

func calculateFirstResult(_ data: String) -> String {
    Thread.sleep(forTimeInterval: 3)
    let message = "Number of chars: \(String(data).count)"
    return message
}

func calculateSecondResult(_ data: String) -> String {
    Thread.sleep(forTimeInterval: 4)
    return data.replacingOccurrences(of: "E", with: "e")
}
```

16. Edit the doButton IBAction method as follows:

```swift
@IBAction func doButton(_ sender: UIButton) {
    let startTime = NSDate()
    self.resultsTextView.text = ""
    let fetchedData = self.fetchSomethingFromServer()
    let processedData = self.processData(fetchedData)
    let firstResult = self.calculateFirstResult(processedData)
    let secondResult = self.calculateSecondResult(processedData)
    let resultsSummary =
    "First: [\(firstResult)]\nSecond: [\(secondResult)]"
    self.resultsTextView.text = resultsSummary
    let endTime = NSDate()
    print("Completed in \(endTime.timeIntervalSince(startTime as
    Date)) seconds")
    }
```

The entire ViewController.swift file should look like this:

```swift
import UIKit

class ViewController: UIViewController {

    @IBOutlet var resultsTextView: UITextView!

    override func viewDidLoad() {
        super.viewDidLoad()
        // Do any additional setup after loading the view.
    }
    func fetchSomethingFromServer() -> String {
        Thread.sleep(forTimeInterval: 1)
        return "Hi there"
    }

    func processData(_ data: String) -> String {
        Thread.sleep(forTimeInterval: 2)
        return data.uppercased()
    }
```

```swift
func calculateFirstResult(_ data: String) -> String {
    Thread.sleep(forTimeInterval: 3)
    let message = "Number of chars: \(String(data).count)"
    return message
}

func calculateSecondResult(_ data: String) -> String {
    Thread.sleep(forTimeInterval: 4)
    return data.replacingOccurrences(of: "E", with: "e")
}

@IBAction func doButton(_ sender: UIButton) {
    let startTime = NSDate()
    self.resultsTextView.text = ""
    let fetchedData = self.fetchSomethingFromServer()
    let processedData = self.processData(fetchedData)
    let firstResult = self.calculateFirstResult(processedData)
    let secondResult = self.calculateSecondResult(processedData)
    let resultsSummary =
    "First: [\(firstResult)]\nSecond: [\(secondResult)]"
    self.resultsTextView.text = resultsSummary
    let endTime = NSDate()
    print("Completed in \(endTime.timeIntervalSince(startTime
    as Date)) seconds")
}

}
```

17. Click the Run button or choose Product ➤ Run. The Simulator
    screen appears as shown in Figure 4-2.

Button

Lorem ipsum dolor sit er elit lamet,
consectetaur cillium adipisicing
pecu, sed do eiusmod tempor
incididunt ut labore et dolore
magna aliqua. Ut enim ad minim
veniam, quis nostrud exercitation
ullamco laboris nisi ut aliquip ex ea

Figure 4-2. *The initial appearance of the user interface*

18. Drag the slider left and right. Notice that you can easily drag the
    slider back and forth.

19. Click the button. Notice that the button dims. Try dragging the
    slider back and forth. Because the app is running a process, the
    user interface now appears frozen and unresponsive for about 10
    seconds. After the process completes, it displays the results on the
    screen as shown in Figure 4-3.

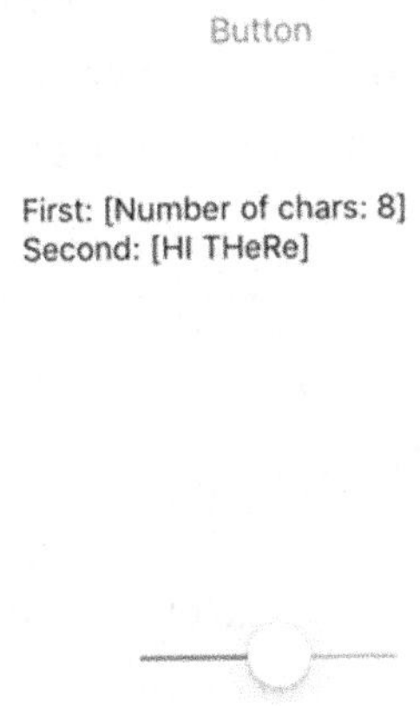

Button

First: [Number of chars: 8]
Second: [HI THeRe]

Figure 4-3. *The altered appearance of the user interface*

20. Drag the slider left and right. Notice that the slider now easily moves once again.

21. Choose Simulator ➤ Quit Simulator to return back to Xcode.

This example lets you see how a process can freeze an app and make it appear unresponsive even though the app is still running. If you submit an app that freezes its user interface periodically, Apple will reject it from the App Store.

Most modern operating systems (including iOS) support multiple threads of execution. If there's just one processor core, the operating system will switch between all executing threads, much like it switches between all executing processes. If more than one core is available, the threads will be distributed among them, just as processes are.

All threads in a process share the same executable program code and the same global data. Each thread can also have some data that is exclusive to the thread through a special structure called a **mutex** (short for **mutual exclusion**) or a lock. Such a lock ensures that a particular chunk of code can't be run by multiple threads at once, which can keep multiple threads from accessing the same data simultaneously.

When writing code, you need to make sure your code is **thread-safe**. As a general rule, any code that controls the user interface is not thread-safe. Because threads increase the chance of multiple processes interfering with each other, most programmers don't use threads directly. That's why Apple created Grand Central Dispatch (GCD) to help make concurrent programming easier and safer.

Note   To learn more about thread safety, read Apple's documentation:
`https://developer.apple.com/library/ios/documentation/`
`Cocoa/Conceptual/Multithreading/ThreadSafetySummary/`
`ThreadSafetySummary.html`

Using Grand Central Dispatch

A key concept of GCD is the **queue**. GCD splits tasks into units of work and puts those units into queues for execution. The system manages the queues for us, executing units of work on multiple threads. We don't need to start or manage the background threads directly, and we are freed from much of the bookkeeping that's usually involved in implementing multithreaded applications.

GCD provides a number of predefined queues, including a queue that's guaranteed to always do its work on the main thread which is perfect for code that manages the user interface (the non-thread-safe UIKit software framework). GCD lets you create as many queues as you need. Units of work added to a GCD queue will always be started in the order they were placed in the queue. That said, they may not always finish in the same order, since a GCD queue will automatically distribute its work among multiple threads, if possible.

To use GCD, we first need to create a queue using the DispatchQueue keyword such as

```
let queue1 = DispatchQueue(label: "queue1")
```

Once we've created a queue, we need to define the code to run in that queue. This code runs in a closure and can run synchronously or asynchronously. An asynchronous queue runs whenever the processor has time to complete it. A synchronous queue runs and must complete before any other code can run. In general, asynchronous queues are most useful when you want to run multiple tasks at the same time, but the order and time that they complete isn't important.

To make a queue run, we have to define whether it's asynchronous or synchronous and specify the code to run in a closure like this:

```
queue1.sync { () -> Void in
    // Code here
}

queue2.async { () -> Void in
    // Code here
}
```

To see how asynchronous queues can work, but may complete at different, unpredictable times, follow these steps:

1. Choose File ➤ New ➤ Playground and create a Blank iOS playground. Name this new playground **QueuePlayground**.

2. Edit the playground code so it looks like this:

    ```
    import UIKit

    let queue1 = DispatchQueue(label: "queue1")
    let queue2 = DispatchQueue(label: "queue2")
    let queue3 = DispatchQueue(label: "queue3")
    ```

```
queue1.async { () -> Void in
    print(queue1.label)
}

queue2.async { () -> Void in
    print(queue2.label)
}

queue3.async { () -> Void in
    print(queue3.label)
}

print("Program stopped")
```

This code creates three queues and then runs tasks in each queue that simply prints the name of the queue. Finally, the code ends by printing "Program stopped".

3. Click the Run button. Notice that the debug area displays the output of the code such as

    queue1
    Program stopped
    queue2
    queue3

4. Click the Run button to run the program again. Notice that the output may change such as

    Program stopped
    queue1
    queue3
    queue2

Even though the code is identical, asynchronous queues may complete at different times. Each time you click the Run button, you'll likely see a different result. While you can have multiple tasks running on different asynchronous queues, you cannot predict when any given queue will complete its task.

To see how synchronous queues work in the exact same order every time, modify the playground code to change all async calls to sync as follows:

```
import UIKit

let queue1 = DispatchQueue(label: "queue1")
let queue2 = DispatchQueue(label: "queue2")
let queue3 = DispatchQueue(label: "queue3")

queue1.sync { () -> Void in
    print(queue1.label)
}

queue2.sync { () -> Void in
    print(queue2.label)
}

queue3.sync { () -> Void in
    print(queue3.label)
}

print("Program stopped")
```

No matter how many times you run this code, the output will always be predictable and in order like this:

queue1
queue2
queue3
Program stopped

The only way you can change the order of the output is to change the position of the queues such as putting queue3 ahead of queue1. Since synchronous queues are little different than not using concurrency at all, asynchronous queues are used most often as long as the order of task completion isn't important.

Now that we know how GCD can run multiple tasks at the same time, we need to use GCD to fix the unresponsive user interface of our ThreadApp. First, we need to identify which code is causing the delay. In our example, it's this code inside the doButton IBAction method:

```
let fetchedData = self.fetchSomethingFromServer()
  let processedData = self.processData(fetchedData)
  let firstResult = self.calculateFirstResult(processedData)
  let secondResult = self.calculateSecondResult(processedData)
  let resultsSummary =
  "First: [\(firstResult)]\nSecond: [\(secondResult)]"
  self.resultsTextView.text = resultsSummary
  let endTime = NSDate()
  print("Completed in \(endTime.timeIntervalSince(startTime as Date))
  seconds")
```

Logically, it would seem like we could simply wrap this code inside a closure and run it in a queue. However, look out for this line:

```
self.resultsTextView.text = resultsSummary
```

This line updates the resultsTextView on the user interface. As a general rule, updating the user interface in a queue is not thread-safe, which means trying to update the user interface in a queue will cause an error. To see what happens when you try to update the user interface within a queue, follow these steps:

1. Make sure the ThreadApp project is loaded in Xcode.

2. Click the ViewController.swift file.

3. Edit the doButton IBAction method as follows:

```
@IBAction func doButton(_ sender: UIButton) {
    let startTime = NSDate()
    self.resultsTextView.text = ""
    let queue = DispatchQueue.global(qos: .default)
    queue.async {
```

```swift
        let fetchedData = self.fetchSomethingFromServer()
        let processedData = self.processData(fetchedData)
        let firstResult = self.calculateFirstResult(processedData)
        let secondResult = self.calculateSecondResult(processedDa
        ta)
        let resultsSummary =
        "First: [\(firstResult)]\nSecond: [\(secondResult)]"
        self.resultsTextView.text = resultsSummary
        let endTime = NSDate()
        print("Completed in \(endTime.timeIntervalSince(startTime
        as Date)) seconds")
    }
}
```

First, we grab a preexisting global queue that's always available, using the DispatchQueue.global() function. That function takes one argument to define a priority. If you specify a different priority in the argument, you will actually get a different global queue, which the system will prioritize differently. For now, we'll stick with the default global queue.

The queue is then passed to the queue.async() function, along with the closure. GCD takes the closure and puts it on the queue, from where it will be scheduled to run on a background thread and executed one step at a time, just as when it was running in the main thread.

Note that we defined a variable called startTime just before the closure is created, and then use its value at the end of the closure. Intuitively, this may not make sense because by the time the closure is executed, the doButton IBAction method has returned. However, the closure can "capture" the value of variables declared ahead of it, allowing access.

4. Click the Run button or choose Produce ➤ Run. Notice that Xcode displays an error message in the debug area with a message such as the following:

Main Thread Checker: UI API called on a background thread:
-[UITextView setText:]
PID: 94760, TID: 14970143, Thread name: (none), Queue name: com.
apple.root.default-qos, QoS: 0
Backtrace:

5. Choose Simulator ➤ Quit Simulator to return to Xcode where you can see another error message highlighting the line that caused the error as shown in Figure 4-4.

```
"First: [\(firstResult)]\nSecond: [\(secondResult)]"
self.resultsTextView.text = resultsSummary        🔲 UITextView.text must be used from main thread only  ?
let endTime = NSDate()
print("Completed in \(endTime.timeIntervalSince(startTime as Date)) seconds")
```

Figure 4-4. *Xcode highlights the line causing the error*

To fix this problem, we need to update the user interface on the main thread like this:

```
DispatchQueue.main.async {
        self.resultsTextView.text = resultsSummary
}
```

Note As a general rule, use the main thread any time you want to update the user interface.

---

6. Edit the doButton IBAction method like this:

```
@IBAction func doButton(_ sender: UIButton) {
    let startTime = NSDate()
    self.resultsTextView.text = ""
    let queue = DispatchQueue.global(qos: .default)
```

```swift
queue.async {
    let fetchedData = self.fetchSomethingFromServer()
    let processedData = self.processData(fetchedData)
    let firstResult = self.calculateFirstResult(processedData)
    let secondResult = self.calculateSecondResult(processedData)
    let resultsSummary =
    "First: [\(firstResult)]\nSecond: [\(secondResult)]"

    DispatchQueue.main.async {
        self.resultsTextView.text = resultsSummary
    }

    let endTime = NSDate()
    print("Completed in \(endTime.timeIntervalSince
    (startTime as Date)) seconds")
}
}
```

The entire ViewController.swift file should look like this:

```swift
import UIKit

class ViewController: UIViewController {

    @IBOutlet var resultsTextView: UITextView!

    override func viewDidLoad() {
        super.viewDidLoad()
        // Do any additional setup after loading the view.
    }

    func fetchSomethingFromServer() -> String {
        Thread.sleep(forTimeInterval: 1)
        return "Hi there"
    }

    func processData(_ data: String) -> String {
        Thread.sleep(forTimeInterval: 2)
        return data.uppercased()
    }
```

```swift
func calculateFirstResult(_ data: String) -> String {
    Thread.sleep(forTimeInterval: 3)
    let message = "Number of chars: \(String(data).count)"
    return message
}

func calculateSecondResult(_ data: String) -> String {
    Thread.sleep(forTimeInterval: 4)
    return data.replacingOccurrences(of: "E", with: "e")
}

@IBAction func doButton(_ sender: UIButton) {
    let startTime = NSDate()
    self.resultsTextView.text = ""
    let queue = DispatchQueue.global(qos: .default)
    queue.async {
        let fetchedData = self.fetchSomethingFromServer()
        let processedData = self.processData(fetchedData)
        let firstResult = self.calculateFirstResult(processedData)
        let secondResult = self.calculateSecondResult(processedData)
        let resultsSummary =
        "First: [\(firstResult)]\nSecond: [\(secondResult)]"

        DispatchQueue.main.async {
            self.resultsTextView.text = resultsSummary
        }

        let endTime = NSDate()
        print("Completed in \(endTime.timeIntervalSince
        (startTime as Date)) seconds")
    }
}
```

7. Click the Run button or choose Produce ➤ Run. The Simulator screen appears.

8. Click the button.

9. Drag the slider left and right. Notice that even though the app is processing, the user interface is still responsive. Eventually, the app finishes its processing and displays its results in the text view, but during that entire time, the user could still interact with the interface.

10. Choose Simulator ➤ Quit Simulator.

Displaying Feedback

Fixing the unresponsive user interface is a huge step, but there's still a perception problem. After the user taps the button, the app runs a process, but from the user's point of view, nothing seems to be happening. Whenever an app is busy processing, it's best to give the user some kind of visual feedback that the app is still running. To do that, we'll add an Activity Indicator View that displays a constantly spinning icon on the screen to show that the app is doing something. When the app is finished processing, the spinning icon will go away.

To add a spinning icon (Activity Indicator View), follow these steps:

1. Make sure the ThreadApp project is loaded in Xcode.

2. Click the Main.storyboard file in the Navigator pane.

3. Click the Library icon to open the Object Library window.

4. Drag and drop an Activity Indicator View in the middle of the view as shown in Figure 4-5.

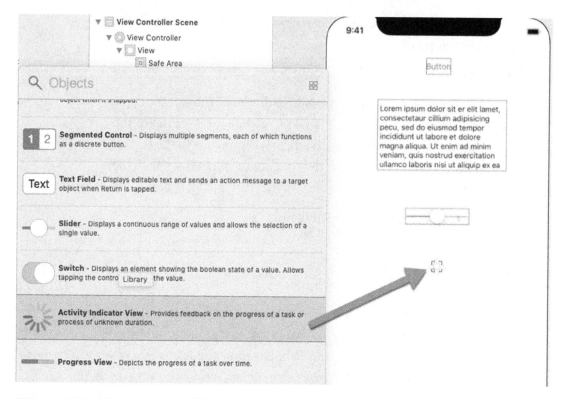

Figure 4-5. *The Activity Indicator View*

5. Click the Activity Indicator View to select it and then choose
    Editor ➤ Resolve Auto Layout Issues ➤ Reset to Suggested
    Constraints in the top half of the menu to set constraints on the
    Activity Indicator View.

6. Choose View ➤ Assistant Editor ➤ Show Assistant Editor, or click
    the Assistant Editor icon in the upper right corner of the Xcode
    window. Xcode shows the Main.storyboard and ViewController.
    swift file side by side.

7. Move the mouse pointer over the Activity Indicator View,
    hold down the Control key, and Ctrl-drag from the Activity
    Indicator View to under the "class ViewController" line in the
    ViewController.swift file.

8. Release the Control key and the left mouse button. A popup
    window appears.

9. Click in the Name text field and type **spinnerView**. Then click the Connect button. Xcode creates an IBOutlet as follows:

```
@IBOutlet var spinnerView: UIActivityIndicatorView!
```

10. Choose View ➤ Standard Editor ➤Show Standard Editor, or click the Standard Editor icon in the upper right corner of the Xcode window.

11. Click the ViewController.swift file in the Navigator pane.

12. Modify the viewDidLoad method as follows:

```
override func viewDidLoad() {
    super.viewDidLoad()
    spinnerView.hidesWhenStopped = true
}
```

This spinnerView.hidesWhenStopped line hides the Activity Indicator View until it starts animating. The moment it stops animating, it disappears from view again.

13. Edit the doButton IBAction method by adding a startAnimating line ahead of the queue and a stopAnimating line inside the main thread as follows:

```
@IBAction func doButton(_ sender: UIButton) {
    let startTime = NSDate()
    self.resultsTextView.text = ""
    spinnerView.startAnimating()
    let queue = DispatchQueue.global(qos: .default)
    queue.async {
        let fetchedData = self.fetchSomethingFromServer()
        let processedData = self.processData(fetchedData)
        let firstResult = self.calculateFirstResult(processedData)
        let secondResult = self.calculateSecondResult(processedData)
        let resultsSummary =
        "First: [\(firstResult)]\nSecond: [\(secondResult)]"
```

```
            DispatchQueue.main.async {
                self.resultsTextView.text = resultsSummary
                self.spinnerView.stopAnimating()
            }

            let endTime = NSDate()
            print("Completed in \(endTime.timeIntervalSince
            (startTime as Date)) seconds")
        }
    }
```

14. Click the Run button or choose Product ➤ Run. The Simulator
     screen appears.

15. Click the button. Notice that the Activity Indicator View appears
     and spins around. As soon as the app finishes processing, the
     Activity Indicator View disappears again.

16. Choose Simulator ➤ Quit Simulator to return back to Xcode.

Using Dispatch Groups

In the previous example, we created a background thread and then jumped back to
the main thread to update the user interface. While this is acceptable, we can optimize
the code a bit further using dispatch groups. Right now our calculateFirstResult() and
calculateSecondResult() methods are called in sequence, yet there's no reason to do this
since they're completely independent of each other.

A better solution is to call these two methods in a dispatch group. This lets each
function run independent of the other, which can improve performance since the
methods are now operating concurrently rather than sequentially. Finally, we can also
use dispatch_group_notify() to specify an additional closure that will run only when all
the other closures in the group have completed running.

To create a dispatch group, we just need to create a DispatchGroup object like this:

```
let group = DispatchGroup()
Then we run each queue inside this dispatch group like this:
    queue.async(group: group) {
```

```
        firstResult = self.calculateFirstResult(processedData)
}
```

To run a final closure after all other closures have finished, we create a group.notify queue like this:

```
group.notify(queue: queue) {
    let resultsSummary = "First: [\(firstResult!)]\nSecond: [\
    (secondResult!)]"
    DispatchQueue.main.async {
        self.resultsTextView.text = resultsSummary
        self.spinnerView.stopAnimating()
    }
    let endTime = Date()
    print("Completed in \(endTime.timeIntervalSince(startTime))
    seconds")
}
```

One final difference is that the group.notify and the queue.async queues need to access the firstResult and secondResult variables, so we need to declare them outside of both queues like this:

```
var firstResult: String!
var secondResult: String!
```

To see how to use dispatch groups, follow these steps:

1. Make sure the ThreadApp project is loaded in Xcode.

2. Click the Main.storyboard file in the Navigator pane.

3. Click the Library icon to open the Object Library window.

4. Drag and drop a second button anywhere near the first button.

5. Double-click this second button, type **Group,** and press Enter. The second button should now display "Group" as its title as shown in Figure 4-6.

Figure 4-6. *Adding a second button to the user interface*

6. Choose Editor ➤ Resolve Auto Layout Issues ➤ Reset to Suggested
    Constraints at the top half of the menu. Xcode adds constraints to
    the second button.

7. Choose View ➤ Assistant Editor ➤ Show Assistant Editor, or click
    the Assistant Editor icon in the upper right corner of the Xcode
    window. Xcode shows the Main.storyboard and ViewController.
    swift file side by side.

8. Move the mouse pointer over the second button, hold down the
    Control key, and Ctrl-drag from the button to above the last curly
    bracket in the ViewController.swift file.

9. Release the Control key and the left mouse button. A popup
    window appears.

10. Click in the Name text field and type **doGroupButton**. Click the
    Type popup menu and choose UIButton, then click the Connect
    button. Xcode creates an IBAction method.

11. Choose View ➤ Standard Editor ➤ Show Standard Editor, or click
    the Standard Editor icon in the upper right corner of the Xcode
    window.

12. Click the ViewController.swift file in the Navigator pane.

13. Edit the doGroupButton IBAction method as follows:

```swift
@IBAction func doGroupButton(_ sender: UIButton) {
    let startTime = Date()
    self.resultsTextView.text = ""
    spinnerView.startAnimating()
    let queue = DispatchQueue.global(qos: .default)
    queue.async {
        let fetchedData = self.fetchSomethingFromServer()
        let processedData = self.processData(fetchedData)
        var firstResult: String!
        var secondResult: String!
        let group = DispatchGroup()

        queue.async(group: group) {
            firstResult = self.calculateFirstResult(processedData)
        }
        queue.async(group: group) {
            secondResult = self.calculateSecondResult(processed
            Data)
        }

        group.notify(queue: queue) {
            let resultsSummary = "First: [\(firstResult!)]\
            nSecond: [\(secondResult!)]"
            DispatchQueue.main.async {
                self.resultsTextView.text = resultsSummary
                self.spinnerView.stopAnimating()
            }
            let endTime = Date()
            print("Completed in \(endTime.
            timeIntervalSince(startTime)) seconds")
        }
    }
}
```

The entire ViewController.swift file should look like this:

```swift
import UIKit

class ViewController: UIViewController {

    @IBOutlet var resultsTextView: UITextView!
    @IBOutlet var spinnerView: UIActivityIndicatorView!

    override func viewDidLoad() {
        super.viewDidLoad()
        spinnerView.hidesWhenStopped = true
    }

    func fetchSomethingFromServer() -> String {
        Thread.sleep(forTimeInterval: 1)
        return "Hi there"
    }

    func processData(_ data: String) -> String {
        Thread.sleep(forTimeInterval: 2)
        return data.uppercased()
    }

    func calculateFirstResult(_ data: String) -> String {
        Thread.sleep(forTimeInterval: 3)
        let message = "Number of chars: \(String(data).count)"
        return message
    }

    func calculateSecondResult(_ data: String) -> String {
        Thread.sleep(forTimeInterval: 4)
        return data.replacingOccurrences(of: "E", with: "e")
    }

    @IBAction func doButton(_ sender: UIButton) {
        let startTime = NSDate()
        self.resultsTextView.text = ""
        spinnerView.startAnimating()
        let queue = DispatchQueue.global(qos: .default)
```

```swift
queue.async {
    let fetchedData = self.fetchSomethingFromServer()
    let processedData = self.processData(fetchedData)
    let firstResult = self.calculateFirstResult(processed
    Data)
    let secondResult = self.calculateSecondResult(processe
    dData)
    let resultsSummary =
    "First: [\(firstResult)]\nSecond: [\(secondResult)]"

    DispatchQueue.main.async {
        self.resultsTextView.text = resultsSummary
        self.spinnerView.stopAnimating()
    }

    let endTime = NSDate()
    print("Completed in \(endTime.timeIntervalSince
    (startTime as Date)) seconds")
    }
}

@IBAction func doGroupButton(_ sender: UIButton) {
    let startTime = Date()
    self.resultsTextView.text = ""
    spinnerView.startAnimating()
    let queue = DispatchQueue.global(qos: .default)
    queue.async {
        let fetchedData = self.fetchSomethingFromServer()
        let processedData = self.processData(fetchedData)
        var firstResult: String!
        var secondResult: String!
        let group = DispatchGroup()

        queue.async(group: group) {
            firstResult = self.calculateFirstResult(processed
            Data)
        }
```

```
        queue.async(group: group) {
            secondResult = self.calculateSecondResult(processed
            Data)
        }

        group.notify(queue: queue) {
            let resultsSummary = "First: [\(firstResult!)]\
            nSecond: [\(secondResult!)]"
            DispatchQueue.main.async {
                self.resultsTextView.text = resultsSummary
                self.spinnerView.stopAnimating()
            }
            let endTime = Date()
            print("Completed in \(endTime.timeIntervalSince
            (startTime)) seconds")
        }
    }
}
```

14.   Click the Run button or choose Product ➤ Run. The Simulator
      screen appears.

15.   Click the first button. Notice that when the process completes,
      Xcode's debug area displays a message such as

Completed in 10.00560998916626 seconds

16.   Click the second button labelled "Group". Notice that when this
      process completes, Xcode's debug area displays a message such as

Completed in 7.014010071754456 seconds

17.   Choose Simulator ➤ Quit Simulator to return back to Xcode.

What was once a 10-second operation now takes just 7 seconds, thanks to the fact
that we're running both of the calculations simultaneously. Obviously, our contrived
example gets the maximum effect because these two "calculations" don't actually do
anything but cause the thread they're running on to sleep. In a real app, the speedup
would depend on what sort of work is being done and what CPU is available.

Summary

Grand Central Dispatch (GCD) is a way to run multiple parts of your code separately. You can do this using threads, but manipulating individual threads can be troublesome and error-prone. Instead of working with threads, you can use GCD, which takes care of the details needed to start, run, and stop different threads safely.

As you can see, GCD can help speed up bottlenecks in your code where a single process might take a long time to complete, which can make your app seem to freeze and be unresponsive. By using GCD at points in your app where speed is essential or where your app lags in responses to the user, you can easily provide a better user experience, even in situations where you can't improve the actual performance.

CHAPTER 5

Understanding the Application Life Cycle

Every time you create an iOS project, it will likely include at least two .swift files: ViewController.swift and AppDelegate.swift. A ViewController.swift file connects to a scene in a storyboard and lets you write code that manages the user interface. Each time you add another view controller scene to the storyboard, you'll likely need another ViewController.swift file (under a different name) to manage any user interface objects such as buttons, text fields, or switches.

Where a project can have multiple ViewController.swift files connected to different scenes in a storyboard, a project will have one AppDelegate.swift file that contains code to manage the different states of an app. Initially, an app is not running. When the user launches the app, the app becomes active and appears in the foreground. As long as the user continues interacting with the app, it remains active in the foreground. However, if the user switches to another app, this pushes the other app into the background. Finally, the user may simply shut down an app altogether.

The AppDelegate.swift file monitors these different states so the app can respond accordingly. When an app first launches, it might need to retrieve data such as the last document the user had been working on before exiting the app. The app might also need to load any custom settings the user might have defined earlier such as color settings.

If the user switches to another app and pushes the previously active app into the background, that app might need to save data in case the user later exits out of the app altogether without making it active again. Finally, if the user terminates the app completely, the app might need one last chance to save data before exiting.

© Wallace Wang 2019
W. Wang, *Pro iPhone Development with Swift 5*, https://doi.org/10.1007/978-1-4842-4944-4_5

The various states an app might be in during its life cycle include

- Not Running – This is the state that all apps are in on a freshly rebooted device.

- Active – This is the normal running state of an application when it's displayed on the screen to receive user input and update the display.

- Background – In this state, an app is given some time to execute some code, but it can't directly access the screen or get any user input. All apps enter this state briefly when the user presses the home button; most of them quickly move onto the Suspended state. Apps that want to do any sort of background processing stay in this state until they're made Active again.

- Suspended – A Suspended app is frozen. This is what happens to normal apps after their brief stint in the Background state. All the memory the app was using while it was active is held just as it was. If the user brings the app back to the Active state, it will pick up right where it left off. On the other hand, if the system needs more memory for whichever app is currently Active, any Suspended apps may be terminated (and placed back into the Not Running state) and their memory freed for other use.

- Inactive – An app enters the Inactive state only as a temporary rest stop between two other states. The only way an app can stay Inactive for any length of time is if the user is dealing with a system prompt (such as those shown for an incoming call or SMS message) or if the user has locked the screen. This state is basically a sort of limbo.

Getting State-Change Notifications

To manage changes between these states, the AppDelegate.swift file contains methods that its delegate can implement as follows:

- `application(_:didFinishLaunchingWithOptions:)` – Detects when an app starts running

- `applicationWillResignActive()` – Detects when the user returns to the Home screen, which will push the app into the background

- `applicationDidBecomeActive()` – Detects when an app, formerly in the background, reappears in the foreground once more

- `applicationDidEnterBackground()` – Detects when an app gets sent into the background

- `applicationWillEnterForeground()` – Detects when an app is about to be sent into the background

- `applicationWillTerminate()` – Detects when an app is about to stop running

The applicationWillResignActive() and applicationDidBecomeActive() methods can be useful when detecting interruptions such as someone using your app when a phone call comes in and interrupts your app. This pair of methods brackets the movement of an app from the Active state to the Inactive state, which makes them good places to enable and disable any animations, in-app audio, or other items that deal with the app's presentation to the user. Because of the multiple situations where applicationDidBecomeActive() is used, you may want to put some of your app initialization code there instead of in application(_:didFinishLaunchingWithOptions:). Note that you should not assume in applicationWillResignActive() that the application is about to be sent to the background; it may just be a temporary change that ends up with a move back to the Active state.

The two applicationDidEnterBackground() and applicationWillEnterForeground() methods deal with an app that is definitely being sent to the background. The applicationDidEnterBackground() method is where an app should free all resources such as saving all user data, closing network connections, and so forth. This is also the spot where you can request more time to run in the background if you need it, as we'll see shortly. If you spend too much time doing things in applicationDidEnterBackground() – more than about 5 seconds – the system will decide that your app is misbehaving and terminate it.

You should implement applicationWillEnterForeground() to re-create whatever was torn down in applicationDidEnterBackground(), such as reloading user data, reestablishing network connections, and so on. Note that when applicationDidEnterBackground() is called, you can safely assume that applicationWillResignActive() has also been recently called. Likewise, when applicationWillEnterForeground() gets called, you can assume that applicationDidBecomeActive() will soon be called as well.

Finally, applicationWillTerminate(), which you'll probably rarely use, if ever, is called only if your application is already in the background and the system decides to skip suspension for some reason and simply terminate the app.

Now that you have a basic theoretical understanding of the states an application transitions between, let's see how this works with a simple app that does nothing more than write a message to Xcode's console log each time one of these methods is called. We'll then manipulate the running app in a variety of ways, just as a user might, and see which transitions occur. To get the most out of this example, you'll need an iOS device. If you don't have one, you can use the Simulator and skip over the parts that require a device.

To see how the different AppDelegate.swift methods work, follow these steps:

1. Create a new iOS Single View App and name it StateApp.

2. Click the AppDelegate.swift file in the Navigator pane.

3. Edit the AppDelegate.swift file and add a print(#function) line in each method so the entire file looks like this:

```
import UIKit

@UIApplicationMain
class AppDelegate: UIResponder, UIApplicationDelegate {

    var window: UIWindow?

    func application(_ application: UIApplication,
    didFinishLaunchingWithOptions launchOptions: [UIApplication.
    LaunchOptionsKey: Any]?) -> Bool {
        print(#function)
        return true
    }
```

```swift
func applicationWillResignActive(_ application: UIApplication)
{
    // Sent when the application is about to move from active
    // to inactive state. This can occur for certain types of
    // temporary interruptions (such as an incoming phone call or
    // SMS message) or when the user quits the application and it
    // begins the transition to the background state.
    // Use this method to pause ongoing tasks, disable timers,
    // and invalidate graphics rendering callbacks. Games should
    // use this method to pause the game.
    print(#function)
}

func applicationDidEnterBackground(_ application:
UIApplication) {
    // Use this method to release shared resources, save user
    // data, invalidate timers, and store enough application
    // state information to restore your application to its
    // current state in case it is terminated later.
    // If your application supports background execution, this
    // method is called instead of applicationWillTerminate: when
    // the user quits.
    print(#function)
}

func applicationWillEnterForeground(_ application:
UIApplication) {
    // Called as part of the transition from the background to
    // the active state; here you can undo many of the changes
    // made on entering the background.
    print(#function)
}
```

```
func applicationDidBecomeActive(_ application: UIApplication) {
    // Restart any tasks that were paused (or not yet started)
    while the application was inactive. If the application was
    previously in the background, optionally refresh the user
    interface.
    print(#function)
}

func applicationWillTerminate(_ application: UIApplication) {
    // Called when the application is about to terminate. Save
    data if appropriate. See also applicationDidEnterBackground:.
    print(#function)
}
```

}

The literal expression #function evaluates to the name of the method in which it appears, and the print statement simply prints this information in Xcode's debug area. This allows us to track which method has been called at any given time.

4. Click the Run button or choose Product ➤ Run. The Simulator screen appears and displays a blank screen since we didn't design any type of user interface. Notice that the Xcode debug area displays the following:

```
application(_:didFinishLaunchingWithOptions:)
applicationDidBecomeActive(_:)
```

This shows that the :didFinishLaunchingWithOptions method runs first as soon as the app launches, followed by the applicationDidBecomeActive method.

5. Choose Hardware ➤ Home to emulate the user returning to the Home screen. Notice the following message appears in Xcode's debug area:

`applicationWillResignActive(_:)`
`applicationDidEnterBackground(_:)`

This shows that when the app is no longer active, the applicationWillResignActive method runs first, followed by the applicationDidEnterBackground method. These two lines show the app actually transitioning between two states: it first becomes Inactive and then goes to Background. What you can't see here is that the app also switches to a third state: Suspended. Remember that you do not get any notification that this has happened; it's completely outside your control.

6. Click the StateApp icon on the Home screen to relaunch it. Notice that the Xcode debug area now displays the following:

`applicationWillEnterForeground(_:)`
`applicationDidBecomeActive(_:)`

This shows that the app was previously Suspended, is woken up to Inactive, and then ends up Active again.

7. Press Command+Shift and press H twice in rapid succession. The sideways-scrolling screen of apps appears as shown in Figure 5-1.

Figure 5-1. *The sideways-scrolling view of currently running apps*

8. Move the mouse pointer over the StateApp screen and drag up until the StateApp screen disappears off the top of the Simulator screen. Notice that the Xcode debug area displays the following:

applicationDidEnterBackground(_:)

applicationWillTerminate(_:)

Note   Do not rely on the `applicationWillTerminate()` method being called to save the state of your application – do this in the `applicationDidEnterBack ground()` method instead.

By experimenting with the Simulator, you can see how the AppDelegate.swift file's various methods run at different times. If you have an iPhone, you can see what happens when an app runs and gets interrupted by a phone call.

To see how an app handles an interruption like a phone call, follow these steps:

1. Connect an iPhone to your Macintosh through its USB cable.

2. Make sure the StateApp project is loaded in Xcode.

3. Click the Active Scheme menu to choose the iPhone as shown in Figure 5-2.

Active Scheme menu

Figure 5-2. *Clicking the Active Scheme menu lets you choose to run the StateApp project on an iPhone instead of in the Simulator*

4. Click the Run button or choose Product ➤ Run. The StateApp appears on your iPhone. If you look in Xcode's debug area, you'll see these two lines showing that the app launched:

```
application(_:didFinishLaunchingWithOptions:)
applicationDidBecomeActive(_:)
```

5. From another phone, call the iPhone currently running the StateApp while connected to your Macintosh. Notice that the following line appears in Xcode's debug area:

```
applicationWillResignActive(_:)
```

This shows that the StateApp is no longer active since the iPhone screen displays the phone call information.

6. Stop the phone call from the other phone. Notice that the StateApp screen appears again (a blank screen) and that the Xcode debug area displays the following:

    `applicationDidBecomeActive(_:)`

7. Click the Stop button or choose Product ➤ Stop in Xcode to stop the StateApp on your iPhone.

Using Execution State Changes

Based on what was just demonstrated, each state change serves different purposes:

Active ➤ Inactive

Use applicationWillResignActive() to "pause" your app's display. If your app is a game, you probably already have the ability to pause the gameplay in some way. For other kinds of apps, make sure no time-critical demands for user input are running because your app won't be getting any user input for a while.

Inactive ➤ Background

Use applicationDidEnterBackground() to release any resources that don't need to be kept around when the app is tucked in the background (such as cached images or other easily reloadable data) or that might not survive backgrounding anyway (such as active network connections). Getting rid of excess memory usage here will make your app's eventual Suspended snapshot smaller, thereby decreasing the risk that your app will be purged from RAM entirely. You should also use this opportunity to save any application data that will help your users pick up where they left off the next time your app is relaunched. If your app comes back to the Active state, normally this won't matter; however, in case it's purged and must be relaunched, your users will appreciate starting off in the same place.

When this transition is underway, the system won't give your app an unlimited amount of time to save any changes; it just gives you a few seconds. If your app takes longer than that, then your app will be purged from memory and pushed into the Not Running state.

Background ➤ Inactive

Use applicationWillEnterForeground() to undo anything you did when switching from Inactive to Background. For example, here you can reestablish persistent network connections.

Inactive ➤ Active

Use applicationDidBecomeActive() to undo anything you did when switching from Active to Inactive. Note that, if your app is a game, this probably does not mean dropping out of pause straight to the game; you should let your users do that on their own. Also keep in mind that this method and notification are used when an app is freshly launched, so anything you do here must work in that context as well.

There is one special consideration for the Inactive ➤ Background transition. Not only does it have the longest description in the previous list, but it's also probably the most code- and time-intensive transition in applications because of the amount of bookkeeping you may want your app to do.

Displaying the Launch Screen

Every iOS project has a launch screen, which is actually the first screen that appears when the app first starts. After a few seconds, the launch screen disappears and the initial view controller appears. The launch screen, sometimes called a splash screen, appears first, which can give your initial view controller time to load. In addition, a launch screen typically displays a flashy graphic image of some kind that represents your app. By default, the launch screen is named LaunchScreen.storyboard, but you can choose a different .storyboard file to represent the launch screen.

To define the .storyboard file you want to use as the launch screen, follow these steps:

1. Click the project name at the top of the Navigator pane.

2. Click the Launch Screen File popup menu and choose the .storyboard file you want to use for your launch screen as shown in Figure 5-3.

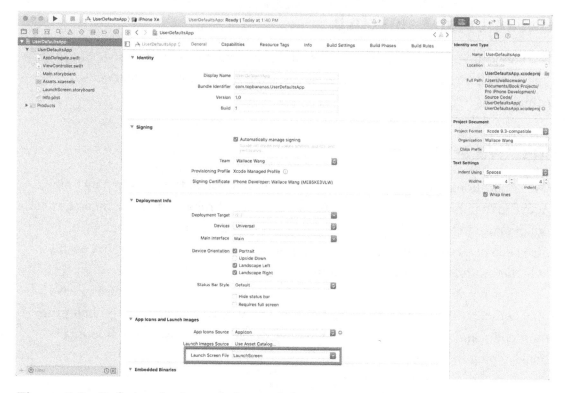

Figure 5-3. *Defining the Launch Screen File*

To see how launch screens work, follow these steps:

1. Create a new iOS Single View App and name it LaunchScreenApp.

2. Click the LaunchScreen.storyboard file in the Navigator pane. A blank view controller appears.

3. Click View Controller Scene ➤ View Controller ➤ View in the Document Outline.

4. Choose View ➤ Inspectors ➤ Show Attributes Inspector, or click the Attributes Inspector icon in the upper right corner of the Xcode window.

5. Click the Background popup menu and choose a color such as green or blue. This will make it easy to recognize when the launch screen appears and then disappears.

6. Click the Library icon to open the Object Library window.

7. Drag and drop a label anywhere on the view.

8. Double-click the label, type **Launch Screen**, then press Enter.

9. Click the Run button or choose Product ➤ Run. The Simulator screen appears. Notice that it displays the colored launch screen for a few seconds before displaying the blank screen of the initial view controller defined in the Main.storyboard file.

10. Choose Hardware ➤ Home to return to the Home screen.

11. Double-click the LaunchScreenApp icon. Notice that the launch screen does not appear.

12. Choose Simulator ➤ Quit Simulator to return back to Xcode.

The first time an app launches, it displays its launch screen for a few seconds before displaying the initial view controller in the Main.storyboard file. From now on, the launch screen will be hidden until the app completely terminates and restarts.

Using the Notification Center

The AppDelegate.swift file contains methods that can track different states of an app such as when an app starts, goes into the background, and becomes active again. However, you may want to track other states of your app such as when a user makes a certain choice by clicking different user interface objects. In that case, you can use the notification center.

To use the notification center, you need to follow several steps:

- Define a unique name for each action you want to detect.

- Define one or more notification center observers to receive notifications when certain actions occur.

- Write functions to run when a notification center observer receives a notification.

- Write code to send a notification when a certain action occurs.

Think of the notification center as a broadcasting station that allows certain parts of an app to listen and take action when certain actions occur.

To see how to use the notification center, follow these steps:

1. Create a new iOS Single View App and name it
    NotificationCenterApp.

2. Click the Main.storyboard file in the Navigator pane.

3. Click the Library icon to open the Object Library window.

4. Drag and drop a label onto the view and resize its width to make it
    stretch from the left edge to the right edge.

5. Drag and drop a button onto the view.

6. Choose Editor ➤ Resolve Auto Layout Issues ➤ Reset to Suggested
    Constraints. Xcode adds constraints to the label and the button.

7. Choose View ➤ Assistant Editor ➤ Show Assistant Editor, or click
    the Assistant Editor icon in the upper right corner of the Xcode
    window. Xcode displays the Main.storyboard file side by side with
    the ViewController.swift file.

8. Move the mouse pointer over the label, hold down the Control
    key, and Ctrl-drag under the "class ViewController" line in the
    ViewController.swift file.

9. Release the Control key and the left mouse button. A popup
    window appears.

10. Click in the Name text field, type **myLabel**, and click the Connect
    button. Xcode creates an IBOutlet as follows:

    ```
    @IBOutlet var myLabel: UILabel!
    ```

11. Choose View ➤ Standard Editor ➤ Show Standard Editor, or click
    the Standard Editor icon in the upper right corner of the Xcode
    window.

12. Click the ViewController.swift file in the Navigator pane.

13. Add the following underneath the "import UIKit" line:

```
import UIKit

extension Notification.Name {
    static let firstSegment = Notification.Name("first")
    static let secondSegment = Notification.Name("second")
    static let buttonPressed = Notification.Name("button")
}
```

This extension simply defines arbitrary names that will be used to identify our different notification center observers that we'll define next.

14. Add the following underneath the IBOutlet line:

```
@objc func firstSegmentTapped(notification: Notification) {
    myLabel.text = "First segment of segmented control tapped"
}

@objc func secondSegmentTapped(notification: Notification) {
    myLabel.text = "Second segment of segmented control tapped"
}

@objc func buttonTapped(notification: Notification) {
    myLabel.text = "Button tapped"
}
```

15. Edit the viewDidLoad method as follows:

```
override func viewDidLoad() {
    super.viewDidLoad()

    NotificationCenter.default.addObserver(self, selector:
    #selector(firstSegmentTapped(notification:)), name:
    .firstSegment, object: nil)
```

```swift
NotificationCenter.default.addObserver(self, selector:
#selector(secondSegmentTapped(notification:)), name:
.secondSegment, object: nil)

NotificationCenter.default.addObserver(self, selector:
#selector(buttonTapped(notification:)), name: .buttonPressed,
object: nil)

}
```

The entire ViewController.swift file should look like this:

```swift
import UIKit

extension Notification.Name {
    static let firstSegment = Notification.Name("first")
    static let secondSegment = Notification.Name("second")
    static let buttonPressed = Notification.Name("button")
}

class ViewController: UIViewController {

    @IBOutlet var myLabel: UILabel!

    @objc func firstSegmentTapped(notification: Notification) {
        myLabel.text = "First segment of segmented control tapped"
    }

    @objc func secondSegmentTapped(notification: Notification) {
        myLabel.text = "Second segment of segmented control tapped"
    }

    @objc func buttonTapped(notification: Notification) {
        myLabel.text = "Button tapped"
    }

    override func viewDidLoad() {
        super.viewDidLoad()

        NotificationCenter.default.addObserver(self, selector:
        #selector(firstSegmentTapped(notification:)), name:
        .firstSegment, object: nil)
```

```
        NotificationCenter.default.addObserver(self, selector:
        #selector(secondSegmentTapped(notification:)), name:
        .secondSegment, object: nil)

        NotificationCenter.default.addObserver(self, selector:
        #selector(buttonTapped(notification:)), name:
        .buttonPressed, object: nil)
    }

}
```

16. Click the Main.storyboard file in the Navigator pane.

17. Click the Library icon to open the Object Library window.

18. Drag and drop a View Controller into the storyboard as shown in
    Figure 5-4.

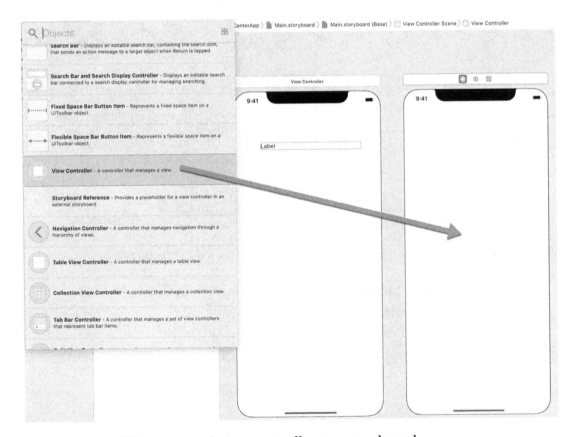

Figure 5-4. *Adding a second view controller to a storyboard*

19. Move the mouse pointer over the button on the first view
     controller, hold down the Control key, and Ctrl-drag onto the
     second view controller as shown in Figure 5-5.

Figure 5-5. *Ctrl-dragging from the button to the second view controller*

20. Release the Control key and the left mouse button. A popup menu
     appears as shown in Figure 5-6.

Figure 5-6. *Choosing a segue from the button to the second view controller*

21. Choose Show. This creates a segue that lets the button display the second view controller. Xcode displays a segue arrow connecting the two view controllers.

22. Click the Library icon to open the Object Library window.

23. Drag and drop a segmented control and a button anywhere on the second view controller.

24. Choose Editor ➤ Resolve Auto Layout Issues ➤ Reset to Suggested Constraints in the bottom half of the submenu. Xcode adds constraints to the segmented control and the button.

25. Choose File ➤ New ➤ File. A template dialog appears.

26. Click Cocoa Touch Class in the iOS category and click the Next button. Another dialog appears.

27. Click in the Name text field and type **SecondViewController**.

28. Make sure the Subclass of popup menu displays UIViewController.

29. Click the Next button and then click the Create button. Xcode displays SecondViewController.swift in the Navigator pane.

30. Click the Main.storyboard file in the Navigator pane.

31. Click the View Controller icon that appears on the second view controller (the one with the button and segmented control).

32. Choose View ➤ Inspectors ➤ Show Identity Inspector, or click the Identity Inspector icon in the upper right corner of the Xcode window.

33. Click the Class popup menu and choose SecondViewController as shown in Figure 5-7. Notice that Second View Controller now appears at the top of the second view controller.

Figure 5-7. *Connecting the SecondViewController.swift file to the second view controller*

34. Choose View ➤ Assistant Editor ➤ Show Assistant Editor, or click the Assistant Editor icon in the upper right corner of the Xcode window. Xcode displays the Main.storyboard file side by side with the SecondViewController.swift file.

35. Move the mouse pointer over the button, hold down the Control key, and Ctrl-drag above the last curly bracket at the bottom of the SecondViewController.swift file.

36. Release the Control key and the left mouse button. A popup window appears.

37. Make sure the Connection popup menu displays Action, then click in the Name text field and type **tapButton**.

38. Click the Type popup menu and choose UIButton, then click the Connect button. Xcode creates a tapButton IBAction method.

39. Move the mouse pointer over the segmented control, hold down the Control key, and Ctrl-drag above the last curly bracket at the bottom of the SecondViewController.swift file.

40. Release the Control key and the left mouse button. A popup window appears.

41. Make sure the Connection popup menu displays Action, then click in the Name text field and type **tapSegmentedControl**.

42. Click the Type popup menu and choose UISegmentedControl, then click the Connect button. Xcode creates a tapSegmentedControl IBAction method.

43. Click the segmented control to select it. Notice that the first segment appears highlighted.

44. Choose View ➤ Inspectors ➤ Show Attributes Inspector, or click the Attributes Inspector icon in the upper right corner of the Xcode window.

45. Clear the "Selected" check box as shown in Figure 5-8.

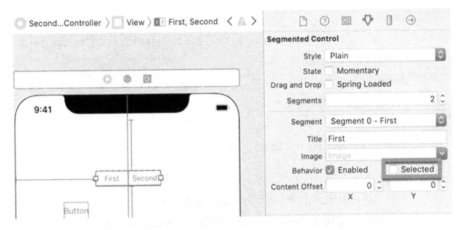

Figure 5-8. *Clearing the Selected check box*

46. Choose View ➤ Standard Editor ➤ Show Standard Editor, or click the Standard Editor icon in the upper right corner of the Xcode window.

47. Click the SecondViewController.swift file in the Navigator pane.

48.   Edit the tapButton IBAction method as follows:

```
@IBAction func tapButton(_ sender: UIButton) {
    NotificationCenter.default.post(name: .buttonPressed,
    object: nil)
    dismiss(animated: true, completion: nil)
}
```

This sends a notification that the user tapped the button on the second view controller.

49.   Edit the tapSegmentedControl IBAction method as follows:

```
@IBAction func tapSegmentedControl(_ sender: UISegmentedControl) {
    switch sender.selectedSegmentIndex {
    case 0:
        NotificationCenter.default.post(name: .firstSegment,
        object: nil)
    case 1:
        NotificationCenter.default.post(name: .secondSegment,
        object: nil)
    default:
        print ("Default")
    }
    dismiss(animated: true, completion: nil)
}
```

This sends a notification that the user tapped the segmented control and identifies which segment the user tapped, the first one or the second one.

50.   Click the Run button or choose Product ➤ Run. The Simulator screen appears, displaying the button and label.

51.   Click the button. The second view controller appears.

52. Click the button or the segmented control. The first view controller appears and displays a message, identifying whether you tapped the button or segmented control.

53. Choose Simulator ➤ Quit Simulator to return back to Xcode.

Summary

As you can see, an app often goes through multiple states just to load and stop. If the user returns to the Home screen or gets interrupted by another process such as a phone call, that can affect an app's state too. To help you track and respond to different states, you can use various methods stored in the AppDelegate.swift file, which monitors and responds to different states of an app.

When an app first launches, it may need to retrieve various setting information or data that the user was working on the last time your app ran. When the user returns to the Home screen or gets interrupted, an app may need to temporarily store data that it will need again once the user returns back to the app. When an app finally terminates, then the app may need to store data one last time to prepare for the next time the user launches the app.

The first time an app starts, it displays a launch screen, which is any .storyboard file you wish to use. After an app is running, it won't display its launch screen again until the user terminates the app and starts it up again. By using launch screens, you can display a distinctive visual image on the screen while loading the rest of your app.

If you want to track the specific actions on the user interface, you can use the notification center. This allows different parts of your project to receive notifications and respond to those notifications. Now you can track not only the different stages an app goes into but also what happens on the user interface.

CHAPTER 6

Understanding Data Persistence

All but the simplest apps need to store data. The Stocks app lets users track their favorite stocks, so it needs to store the list of stocks to follow that the user chose. Each time the user launches the Stocks app again, it displays the list of stocks the user inputted previously. If the user adds or deletes stocks from this list, the Stocks app needs to store this updated list and retrieve it again the next time the user loads the Stocks app.

Other types of apps may have various settings that allow users to customize an app such as defining its background color or sounds to play when certain events occur such as one sound to represent a text message received and another sound to represent a voicemail someone left you.

Storing and retrieving data is known as data persistence. The three common ways to store and retrieve data in an iOS app include

- UserDefaults

- Reading and writing files

- Core Data

Each method offers different advantages and disadvantages, so it depends on what type of data you want to store and its purpose that can define which storage method your app should use.

UserDefaults is generally used to store small amounts of data such as user preferences for a particular app. This method uses a dictionary data structure and saves data in a .plist file, similar to the Info.plist file that every Xcode project includes. It's the simplest method to save common types of data such as strings, numbers, dates, and data structures such as dictionaries or arrays and is best suited for small amounts of data.

113

© Wallace Wang 2019
W. Wang, *Pro iPhone Development with Swift 5*, https://doi.org/10.1007/978-1-4842-4944-4_6

Reading and writing data to a file can be useful to store longer amounts of data such as several lines of text. However, reading and writing to a file can be slow if you have lots of data, which requires code to search through the entire file to find specific data.

Core Data lets you store different types of data in groups called entities, which are similar to tables or records in a database. If you need to store large amounts of diverse data, use Core Data over the other two options for storing data.

Storing Preferences in UserDefaults

UserDefaults is meant to store small amounts of data such as a number, Boolean value, or a string. This makes UserDefaults best for storing an app's settings such as its default background color. Using UserDefaults involves a two-step process:

- Store data in UserDefaults.

- Retrieve data from UserDefaults.

To store data using UserDefaults, you need to define a key and the data you want to store in this format where "dataToSave" represents an actual value and "keyString" represents a unique string:

```
UserDefaults.standard.set(dataToSave, forKey: "keyString")
```

The set command saves the key and its associated data. To retrieve previously saved data, you need to know the key value and the type of data stored such as an integer, Boolean, or double data type. Knowing the data type you want to retrieve, you can use one of the following:

- integer(forKey: "keyString") – Returns an integer if the key exists, or 0 if not

- bool(forKey: "keyString") – Returns a Boolean if the key exists, or false if not

- float(forKey: "keyString") – Returns a float value if the key exists, or 0.0 if not

- string(forKey: "keyString") – Returns a string value if the key exists, or nil if not

- double(forKey: "keyString") – Returns a double value if the key exists, or 0.0 if not

- object(forKey: "keyString") – Returns AnyObject? so you'll need to conditionally typecast it to a specific data type, or nil if not

- url(forKey: "keyString") – Returns a URL if the key exists, or nil if not

To see how to save data as UserDefaults, follow these steps:

1. Create a new iOS Single View App and name it UserDefaultsApp.

2. Click the Main.storyboard file in the Navigator pane.

3. Click the Library icon to open the Object Library window.

4. Drag and drop a switch, a text field, and a slider. Then drag and drop three buttons on the view as well.

5. Double-click the left button, type **Save**, and press Enter.

6. Double-click the middle button, type **Clear**, and press Enter.

7. Double-click the right button, type **Load**, and press Enter. The user interface looks something like Figure 6-1.

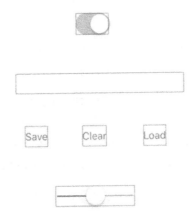

Figure 6-1. *Designing a user interface with a switch, text field, a slider, and three buttons*

8. Choose View ➤ Assistant Editor ➤ Show Assistant Editor, or click the Assistant Editor icon in the upper right corner of the Xcode window. Xcode displays the Main.storyboard file side by side with the ViewController.swift file.

9. Move the mouse pointer over the switch, hold down the Control key, and Ctrl-drag under the "class ViewController" line.

10. Release the Control button and the left mouse button. A popup window appears.

11. Click in the Name text field, type **mySwitch**, and click the Connect button. Xcode creates the following IBOutlet:

    @IBOutlet var mySwitch: UISwitch!

12. Move the mouse pointer over the slider, hold down the Control key, and Ctrl-drag under the "class ViewController" line.

13. Release the Control button and the left mouse button. A popup window appears.

14. Click in the Name text field, type **mySlider**, and click the Connect button. Xcode creates the following IBOutlet:

    @IBOutlet var mySlider: UISlider!

15. Move the mouse pointer over the text field, hold down the Control key, and Ctrl-drag under the "class ViewController" line.

16. Release the Control button and the left mouse button. A popup window appears.

17. Click in the Name text field, type **myTextField**, and click the Connect button. Xcode creates the following IBOutlet:

    @IBOutlet var myTextField: UITextField!

18. Move the mouse pointer over the Save button, hold down the Control key, and Ctrl-drag above the last curly bracket at the bottom of the ViewController.swift file.

19. Release the Control button and the left mouse button. A popup window appears.

20. Click in the Name text field, type **saveData**, click the Type popup menu and choose UIButton, and click the Connect button. Xcode creates a saveData IBAction method.

21. Move the mouse pointer over the Clear button, hold down the Control key, and Ctrl-drag above the last curly bracket at the bottom of the ViewController.swift file.

22. Release the Control button and the left mouse button. A popup window appears.

23. Click in the Name text field, type **clearData**, click the Type popup menu and choose UIButton, and click the Connect button. Xcode creates a clearData IBAction method.

24. Move the mouse pointer over the Load button, hold down the Control key, and Ctrl-drag above the last curly bracket at the bottom of the ViewController.swift file.

25. Release the Control button and the left mouse button. A popup window appears.

26. Click in the Name text field, type **loadData**, click the Type popup menu and choose UIButton, and click the Connect button. Xcode creates a loadData IBAction method.

27. Edit the saveData IBAction method as follows:

```
@IBAction func saveData(_ sender: UIButton) {
    UserDefaults.standard.set(myTextField.text, forKey: "Text")
    UserDefaults.standard.set(mySwitch.isOn, forKey: "Switch")
    UserDefaults.standard.set(mySlider.value, forKey: "Slider")
}
```

28.   Edit the clearData IBAction method as follows:

```
@IBAction func clearData(_ sender: UIButton) {
    mySwitch.isOn = true
    mySlider.value = 0.5
    myTextField.text = ""
}
```

29.   Edit the loadData IBAction method as follows:

```
@IBAction func loadData(_ sender: UIButton) {
    mySwitch.isOn = UserDefaults.standard.bool(forKey: "Switch")
    mySlider.value = UserDefaults.standard.float(forKey: "Slider")
    myTextField.text = UserDefaults.standard.string(forKey:
    "Text")
    }
```

Note that mySwitch.isOn retrieves Boolean data from
UserDefaults, mySlider.value retrieves a floating point value
(decimal number), and myTextField.text retrieves a string.

The entire ViewController.swift file should look like this:

```
import UIKit

class ViewController: UIViewController {

    @IBOutlet var mySwitch: UISwitch!
    @IBOutlet var mySlider: UISlider!
    @IBOutlet var myTextField: UITextField!

    override func viewDidLoad() {
        super.viewDidLoad()
        // Do any additional setup after loading the view.
    }
```

```
@IBAction func saveData(_ sender: UIButton) {
    UserDefaults.standard.set(myTextField.text, forKey:
    "Text")
    UserDefaults.standard.set(mySwitch.isOn, forKey: "Switch")
    UserDefaults.standard.set(mySlider.value, forKey:
    "Slider")
}

@IBAction func clearData(_ sender: UIButton) {
    mySwitch.isOn = true
    mySlider.value = 0.5
    myTextField.text = ""
}

@IBAction func loadData(_ sender: UIButton) {
    mySwitch.isOn = UserDefaults.standard.bool(forKey:
    "Switch")
    mySlider.value = UserDefaults.standard.float(forKey:
    "Slider")
    myTextField.text = UserDefaults.standard.string
    (forKey: "Text")
}
}
```

30.   Click the Run button or choose Product ➤ Run. The Simulator screen appears and displays the user interface.

31.   Click the switch to turn it off (the switch appears on the left).

32.   Click in the text field and type any text you wish such as **Hello, there!**

33.   Drag the slider to the far left.

34.   Click the Save button. This saves the settings in UserDefaults.

35.   Click the Clear button. Notice that the switch moves back to its default position (the switch on the right), the text field appears empty, and the slider moves back to its default position (the slider in the middle).

36. Click the Load button. Notice that this loads the data previously saved in UserDefaults, so the switch appears to the left, the text field displays the text you typed, and the slider moves back to the far left.

37. Choose Simulator ➤ Quit Simulator.

Storing Preferences in UserDefaults in the AppDelegate File

An app can always save data in UserDefaults anywhere and load them back again in a viewDidLoad method. In the previous example, we could simply load data from UserDefaults automatically like this:

```
override func viewDidLoad() {
    super.viewDidLoad()
    mySwitch.isOn = UserDefaults.standard.bool(forKey: "Switch")
    mySlider.value = UserDefaults.standard.float(forKey: "Slider")
    myTextField.text = UserDefaults.standard.string(forKey: "Text")
}
```

Rather than save and store data in separate .swift files, it's generally better to do all the saving and retrieving of UserDefaults data in the AppDelegate.swift file, which can save data before an app terminates and load data back again when the app starts up again.

The AppDelegate.swift file needs to store and retrieve UserDefaults data. That means the AppDelegate.swift file needs to retrieve data from other .swift files (so it can save it) and pass that data back to another .swift file (so that view controller can use the saved data).

That means we need a way for the AppDelegate.swift file to share data with the ViewController.swift file. One way to do this is through the Notification Center (see Chapter 5). Another way is through defining properties in both the AppDelegate.swift file and the ViewController.swift file and sending or retrieving data to and from those properties.

To see how to save and load UserDefaults data in the AppDelegate.swift file, follow these steps:

1. Create a new iOS Single View App and name it AppDelegateApp.

2. Click the Main.storyboard file in the Navigator pane.

3. Click the Library icon and then drag and drop a slider, text field, switch, and a button onto the view.

4. Double-click the button, type **Clear**, and press Enter. The user interface should look similar to Figure 6-2.

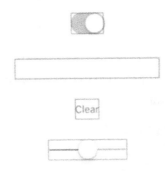

Figure 6-2. *Creating a user interface with a text field, switch, slider, and button*

5. Move the mouse pointer over the switch, hold down the Control key, and Ctrl-drag under the "class ViewController" line.

6. Release the Control button and the left mouse button. A popup window appears.

7. Click in the Name text field, type **mySwitch**, and click the Connect button. Xcode creates the following IBOutlet:

    `@IBOutlet var mySwitch: UISwitch!`

8. Move the mouse pointer over the slider, hold down the Control key, and Ctrl-drag under the "class ViewController" line.

9. Release the Control button and the left mouse button. A popup window appears.

10. Click in the Name text field, type **mySlider**, and click the Connect button. Xcode creates the following IBOutlet:

@IBOutlet var mySlider: UISlider!

11. Move the mouse pointer over the text field, hold down the Control key, and Ctrl-drag under the "class ViewController" line.

12. Release the Control button and the left mouse button. A popup window appears.

13. Click in the Name text field, type **myTextField**, and click the Connect button. Xcode creates the following IBOutlet:

@IBOutlet var myTextField: UITextField!

14. Move the mouse pointer over the Clear button, hold down the Control key, and Ctrl-drag above the last curly bracket at the bottom of the ViewController.swift file.

15. Release the Control button and the left mouse button. A popup window appears.

16. Click in the Name text field, type **clearData**, click the Type popup menu and choose UIButton, and click the Connect button. Xcode creates a clearData IBAction method.

17. Move the mouse pointer over the switch, hold down the Control key, and Ctrl-drag above the last curly bracket at the bottom of the ViewController.swift file.

18. Release the Control button and the left mouse button. A popup window appears.

19. Click in the Name text field, type **changeSwitch**, click the Type popup menu and choose UISwitch, and click the Connect button. Xcode creates a changeSwitch IBAction method.

20. Move the mouse pointer over the slider, hold down the Control key, and Ctrl-drag above the last curly bracket at the bottom of the ViewController.swift file.

21. Release the Control button and the left mouse button. A popup window appears.

22. Click in the Name text field, type **changeSlider**, click the Type popup menu and choose UISlider, and click the Connect button. Xcode creates a changeSlider IBAction method.

23. Move the mouse pointer over the text field, hold down the Control key, and Ctrl-drag above the last curly bracket at the bottom of the ViewController.swift file.

24. Release the Control button and the left mouse button. A popup window appears.

25. Click in the Name text field, type **changeTextField**, and click the Type popup menu and choose UITextField.

26. Click the Event popup menu and choose Editing Changed and then click the Connect button. Xcode creates a changeTextField IBAction method.

27. Choose View ➤ Standard Editor ➤ Show Standard Editor, or click the Standard Editor icon in the upper right corner of the Xcode window.

28. Click the AppDelegate.swift file in the Navigator pane.

29. Add the following under the var : UIWindow? Line:

```
var sliderData : Float = 0.5
var textFieldData = ""
var switchData = true

static func shared() -> AppDelegate {
    return UIApplication.shared.delegate as! AppDelegate
}
```

The first three lines create three properties that will later be accessed by ViewController.swift file to store data in. The shared() function allows another .swift file to access the AppDelegate.swift file's properties.

30. Modify the didFinishLaunchingWithOptions method as follows:

```
func application(_ application: UIApplication,
didFinishLaunchingWithOptions launchOptions: [UIApplication.
LaunchOptionsKey: Any]?) -> Bool {
    // Override point for customization after application launch.
    switchData = UserDefaults.standard.bool(forKey: "Switch")
    sliderData = UserDefaults.standard.float(forKey: "Slider")
    textFieldData = UserDefaults.standard.string(forKey: "Text")!
    return true
}
```

This method runs when the app starts up and retrieves any UserDefaults data. Then it stores this data in the AppDelegate. swift file's properties.

31. Modify the applicationDidEnterBackground method as follows:

```
func applicationDidEnterBackground(_ application: UIApplication) {
    // Use this method to release shared resources, save user
    data, invalidate timers, and store enough application state
    information to restore your application to its current state
    in case it is terminated later.
    // If your application supports background execution, this
    method is called instead of applicationWillTerminate: when the
    user quits.
    UserDefaults.standard.set(textFieldData, forKey: "Text")
    UserDefaults.standard.set(switchData, forKey: "Switch")
    UserDefaults.standard.set(sliderData, forKey: "Slider")
}
```

This method runs right before the app leaves the active state and goes into the background, which occurs when the user switches to another app. This saves all data in UserDefaults. The entire AppDelegate.swift file should look like this:

```swift
import UIKit

@UIApplicationMain
class AppDelegate: UIResponder, UIApplicationDelegate {

    var window: UIWindow?

    var sliderData : Float = 0.5
    var textFieldData = ""
    var switchData = true

    static func shared() -> AppDelegate {
        return UIApplication.shared.delegate as! AppDelegate
    }

    func application(_ application: UIApplication,
    didFinishLaunchingWithOptions launchOptions: [UIApplication.
    LaunchOptionsKey: Any]?) -> Bool {
        // Override point for customization after application
        launch.
        switchData = UserDefaults.standard.bool(forKey: "Switch")
        sliderData = UserDefaults.standard.float(forKey: "Slider")
        textFieldData = UserDefaults.standard.string(forKey: "Text")!
        return true
    }

    func applicationWillResignActive(_ application: UIApplication)
    {
        // Sent when the application is about to move from active
        to inactive state. This can occur for certain types of
        temporary interruptions (such as an incoming phone call or
        SMS message) or when the user quits the application and it
        begins the transition to the background state.
        // Use this method to pause ongoing tasks, disable timers,
        and invalidate graphics rendering callbacks. Games should
        use this method to pause the game.
    }
```

```swift
func applicationDidEnterBackground(_ application:
UIApplication) {
    // Use this method to release shared resources, save user
    data, invalidate timers, and store enough application
    state information to restore your application to its
    current state in case it is terminated later.
    // If your application supports background execution, this
    method is called instead of applicationWillTerminate: when
    the user quits.
    UserDefaults.standard.set(textFieldData, forKey: "Text")
    UserDefaults.standard.set(switchData, forKey: "Switch")
    UserDefaults.standard.set(sliderData, forKey: "Slider")
}

func applicationWillEnterForeground(_ application:
UIApplication) {
    // Called as part of the transition from the background to
    the active state; here you can undo many of the changes
    made on entering the background.
}

func applicationDidBecomeActive(_ application: UIApplication) {
    // Restart any tasks that were paused (or not yet started)
    while the application was inactive. If the application was
    previously in the background, optionally refresh the user
    interface.
}

func applicationWillTerminate(_ application: UIApplication) {
    // Called when the application is about to terminate. Save
    data if appropriate. See also applicationDidEnterBackground:.
}

}
```

32. Click the ViewController.swift file in the Navigator pane.

33. Edit the viewDidLoad method as follows:

```swift
override func viewDidLoad() {
    super.viewDidLoad()
    // Do any additional setup after loading the view.
    mySlider.value = AppDelegate.shared().sliderData
    mySwitch.isOn = AppDelegate.shared().switchData
    myTextField.text = AppDelegate.shared().textFieldData
}
```

This retrieves the data stored in the AppDelegate.swift file's properties, which contain the UserDefaults data loaded in from the didFinishLaunchingWithOptions method.

34. Edit the changeTextField IBAction method as follows:

```swift
@IBAction func changeTextField(_ sender: UITextField) {
    AppDelegate.shared().textFieldData = sender.text ?? ""
}
```

As the user edits the contents of the text field, this IBAction method stores the text field contents in the AppDelegate.swift file's textFieldData property.

35. Edit the changeSlider IBAction method as follows:

```swift
@IBAction func changeSlider(_ sender: UISlider) {
    AppDelegate.shared().sliderData = sender.value
}
```

When the user changes the slider, the slider's value gets stored in the AppDelegate.swift file's sliderData property.

36. Edit the changeSwitch IBAction method as follows:

```swift
@IBAction func changeSwitch(_ sender: UISwitch) {
    AppDelegate.shared().switchData = sender.isOn
}
```

When the user changes the switch, the switch's isOn property (true or false) gets stored in the AppDelegate.swift file's switchData property.

37.   Edit the clearData IBAction method as follows:

```swift
@IBAction func clearData(_ sender: UIButton) {
    mySwitch.isOn = true
    mySlider.value = 0.5
    myTextField.text = ""
}
```

This simply sets the switch back to true and the slider to 0.5 and clears the text field. The entire ViewController.swift file should look like this:

```swift
import UIKit

class ViewController: UIViewController {

    @IBOutlet var mySwitch: UISwitch!
    @IBOutlet var myTextField: UITextField!
    @IBOutlet var mySlider: UISlider!

    override func viewDidLoad() {
        super.viewDidLoad()
        // Do any additional setup after loading the view.
        mySlider.value = AppDelegate.shared().sliderData
        mySwitch.isOn = AppDelegate.shared().switchData
        myTextField.text = AppDelegate.shared().textFieldData
    }

    @IBAction func changeTextField(_ sender: UITextField) {
        AppDelegate.shared().textFieldData = sender.text ?? ""
    }

    @IBAction func changeSlider(_ sender: UISlider) {
        AppDelegate.shared().sliderData = sender.value
    }
```

```
@IBAction func changeSwitch(_ sender: UISwitch) {
    AppDelegate.shared().switchData = sender.isOn
}

@IBAction func clearData(_ sender: UIButton) {
    mySwitch.isOn = true
    mySlider.value = 0.5
    myTextField.text = ""
}

}
```

38. Click the Run button, or choose Product ➤ Run. The Simulator screen appears.

39. Click the switch so it appears to the left.

40. Click in the text field and type some text such as **Hello, there!**

41. Drag the slider all the way to the left.

42. Click the Clear button. Notice that the switch moves back to the right, the text field clears, and the slider moves back to the middle.

43. Press Command+Shift and press H twice in rapid succession to display the app screen shrunken as shown in Figure 6-3.

Figure 6-3. *Terminating the app in the Simulator*

44. Move the mouse pointer over the app screen and drag up to slide it out of sight. This terminates the app.

45. Double-click the AppDelegateApp icon on the Home screen to load the app again. This will load the UserDefaults data. When the app appears again, notice that the switch is on the left, the slider is to the left, and the text field displays the data you typed earlier.

46. Choose Simulator ➤ Quit Simulator to return back to Xcode.

Reading and Writing to Files

On ordinary computers like the Macintosh, it's common for a program to read data from a file and write data back to a file. On an iOS device, an iOS app can do that too. Writing data to a file offers another way an app can save data.

Although iOS shields users from the folder hierarchy of the operating system, it still exists. To write a file, we first need to use the FileManager object like this:

```
let fm = FileManager.default
```

Next, we need to define a location for the file, which is the document directory in the home folder:

```
let urls = fm.urls(for: .documentDirectory, in: .userDomainMask)
```

Finally, we need to create a file name (such as "file.txt") to store data like this:

```
let url = urls.last?.appendingPathComponent("file.txt")
```

Once we've stored text in a file, we can retrieve it by using the FileManager again and look for the file in the document directory in the home folder. To see how to write data to a file and then read it back again, follow these steps:

1. Create a new iOS Single View App and name it ReadWriteApp.

2. Click the Main.storyboard file in the Navigator pane.

3. Click the Library icon and then drag and drop two buttons and two text views onto the view. Place one text view at the top of the screen and the second text view near the middle of the screen. Put the two buttons in between the two text views.

4. Double-click one button, type **Write File**, and press Enter.

5. Double-click the second button, type **Read File**, and press Enter. The user interface should look similar to Figure 6-4.

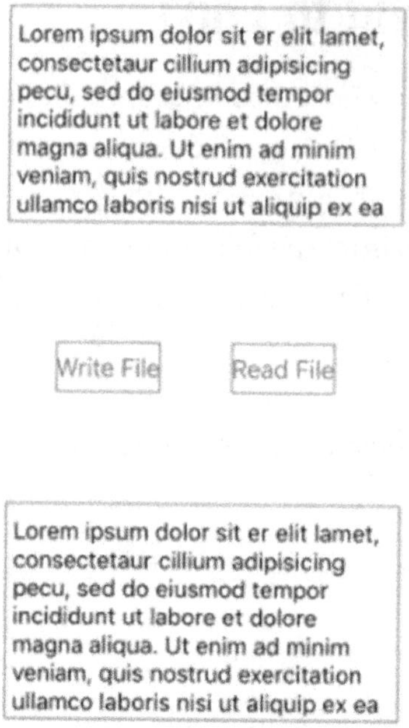

Lorem ipsum dolor sit er elit lamet,
consectetaur cillium adipisicing
pecu, sed do eiusmod tempor
incididunt ut labore et dolore
magna aliqua. Ut enim ad minim
veniam, quis nostrud exercitation
ullamco laboris nisi ut aliquip ex ea

Write File   Read File

Lorem ipsum dolor sit er elit lamet,
consectetaur cillium adipisicing
pecu, sed do eiusmod tempor
incididunt ut labore et dolore
magna aliqua. Ut enim ad minim
veniam, quis nostrud exercitation
ullamco laboris nisi ut aliquip ex ea

Figure 6-4. *Creating a user interface with two text views and two buttons*

6. Move the mouse pointer over the top text view, hold down the
    Control key, and Ctrl-drag below the class ViewController line in
    the ViewController.swift file.

7. Release the Control button and the left mouse button. A popup
    window appears.

8. Click in the Name text field, type **createText**, and click the
    Connect button. Xcode creates a createText IBOutlet as follows:

    @IBOutlet var createText: UITextView!

9. Move the mouse pointer over the bottom text view, hold down the
    Control key, and Ctrl-drag below the class ViewController line in
    the ViewController.swift file.

10. Release the Control button and the left mouse button. A popup
    window appears.

11. Click in the Name text field, type **displayText**, and click the
    Connect button. Xcode creates a createText IBOutlet as follows:

    ```
    @IBOutlet var displayText: UITextView!
    ```

12. Edit the viewDidLoad method as follows:

    ```
    override func viewDidLoad() {
        super.viewDidLoad()
        // Do any additional setup after loading the view.
        createText.text = "Type your text here"
        displayText.text = ""
    }
    ```

13. Move the mouse pointer over the Write File button, hold down
    the Control key, and Ctrl-drag above the last curly bracket in the
    bottom of the ViewController.swift file.

14. Release the Control button and the left mouse button. A popup
    window appears.

15. Click in the Name text field, type **writeFile**, click the Type popup
    menu and choose UIButton, and click the Connect button. Xcode
    creates a writeFile IBAction method.

16. Move the mouse pointer over the Read File button, hold down
    the Control key, and Ctrl-drag above the last curly bracket in the
    bottom of the ViewController.swift file.

17. Release the Control button and the left mouse button. A popup
    window appears.

18. Click in the Name text field, type **readFile**, click the Type popup
    menu and choose UIButton, and click the Connect button. Xcode
    creates a readFile IBAction method.

19. Edit the writeFile IBAction method as follows:

    ```
    @IBAction func writeFile(_ sender: UIButton) {
        let fm = FileManager.default
        let urls = fm.urls(for: .documentDirectory, in:
        .userDomainMask)
    ```

```
    let url = urls.last?.appendingPathComponent("file.txt")
    do {
        try createText.text.write(to: url!, atomically: true,
        encoding: String.Encoding.utf8)
    } catch {
        print("File writing error")
    }
}
```

20.   Edit the readFile IBAction method as follows:

```
@IBAction func readFile(_ sender: UIButton) {
    let fm = FileManager.default
    let urls = fm.urls(for: .documentDirectory, in:
    .userDomainMask)
    let url = urls.last?.appendingPathComponent("file.txt")
    do {
        let fileContent = try String(contentsOf: url!, encoding:
        String.Encoding.utf8)
        displayText.text = fileContent
    } catch {
        print("File reading error")
    }
}
```

The entire ViewController.swift file should look like this:

```
import UIKit

class ViewController: UIViewController {

    @IBOutlet var createText: UITextView!
    @IBOutlet var displayText: UITextView!

    override func viewDidLoad() {
        super.viewDidLoad()
        // Do any additional setup after loading the view.
        createText.text = "Type your text here"
        displayText.text = ""
```

```swift
    }

    @IBAction func writeFile(_ sender: UIButton) {
        let fm = FileManager.default
        let urls = fm.urls(for: .documentDirectory, in:
        .userDomainMask)
        let url = urls.last?.appendingPathComponent("file.txt")
        do {
            try createText.text.write(to: url!, atomically: true,
            encoding: String.Encoding.utf8)
        } catch {
            print("File writing error")
        }
    }

    @IBAction func readFile(_ sender: UIButton) {
        let fm = FileManager.default
        let urls = fm.urls(for: .documentDirectory, in:
        .userDomainMask)
        let url = urls.last?.appendingPathComponent("file.txt")
        do {
            let fileContent = try String(contentsOf: url!,
            encoding: String.Encoding.utf8)
            displayText.text = fileContent
        } catch {
            print("File reading error")
        }
    }
}
```

21. Click the Run button or choose Product ➤ Run. The Simulator screen appears, displaying your two buttons and the top text view that displays the text "Type your text here".

22. Edit the text in the top text view to contain any text you wish to write.

23. Click the Write File button. This saves the text in a file.

24.   Click the Read File button. Whatever text you saved in the file now appears in the bottom text view.

25.   Choose Simulator ➤ Quit Simulator to return back to Xcode.

Using Core Data

If you only need to store small amounts of data, you can store data in UserDefaults. If you need to store larger amounts of data that are unstructured, you can store them in a file. However, if you want to store large amounts of structured data, then it's better to use Core Data.

Core Data is a framework to help you manage data in an app. Core Data lets you define the type of data you want to save and the relationships between these different chunks of data. Then Core Data helps you manipulate this data and their relationships without worrying about the actual details of storing and retrieving the data or learning cryptic SQL database commands.

Core Data stores data using entities and attributes. An attribute defines a single chunk of data to store such as a name, address, age, gender, e-mail address, and phone number. An entity represents all of these attributes used to define a single chunk of related data such as a person as shown in Figure 6-5. Think of a Core Data entity like a database record or table and a Core Data attribute like a database field.

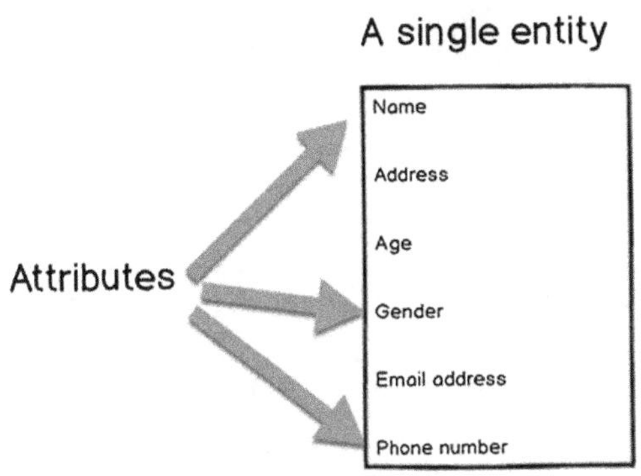

A single entity

Figure 6-5. *Core Data stores data in attributes, grouped together to represent a single entity*

The basic steps to using Core Data involve

- Creating entities and defining attributes in the Xcode data model editor

- Writing Swift code to manipulate data

Creating a Data Model File

A data model is a Core Data file that lets you define entities and attributes where an entity represents a single object such as a person and attributes represent details such as a name, phone number, and e-mail address. You can manually add a data model file to any project or let Xcode add a data model file when you create a new project.

To add a Core Data file manually to a project, follow these steps:

1. Choose File ➤ New ➤ File. A template dialog appears.

2. Click the iOS category.

3. Scroll down and click the Data Model under the Core Data category as shown in Figure 6-6.

4. Click the Next button. A dialog appears, letting you choose a name that ends with the .xcdatamodeld file extension.

Figure 6-6. *Creating a Core Data data model file*

5.   Choose a name for your Core Data file and click the Create button. Xcode displays your .xcdatamodeld Core Data file in the Navigator pane.

If you know ahead of time that you want to use Core Data, it's easier to create a Core Data file when you create a new project. This lets Xcode add the necessary Swift code to access Core Data.

To create a new project that includes a Core Data file, follow these steps:

1.   Choose File ➤ New ➤ Project. A template dialog appears.

2.   Click the iOS category and click the Single View App. Then click the Next button. Another dialog appears.

3.   Click in the Product Name text field and type **CoreDataApp**. (When creating your own projects, choose any name you wish.)

4.   Make sure the Use Core Data check box is selected as shown in Figure 6-7.

5.   Click the Next button and then click the Create button.

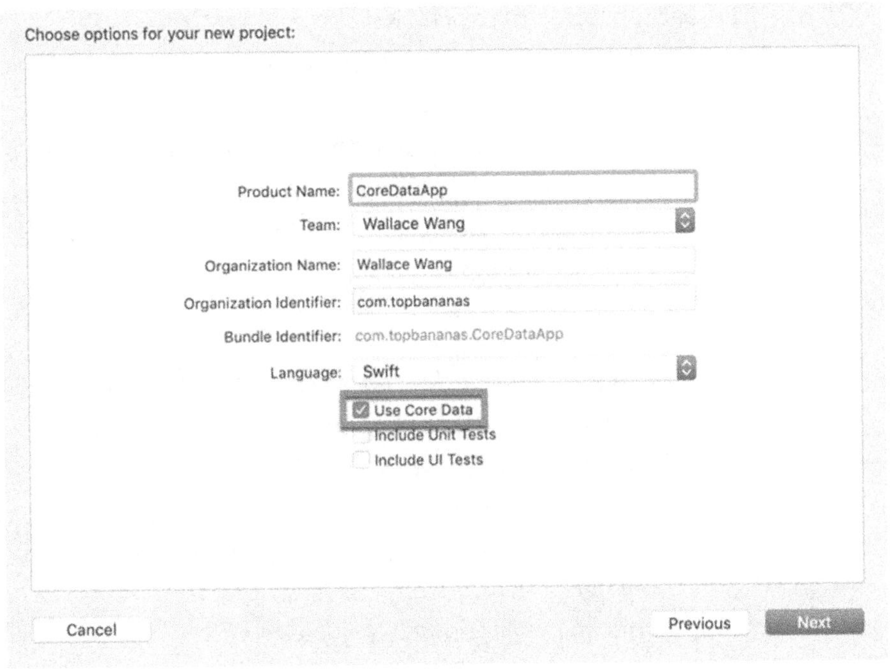

Figure 6-7. *Selecting the Use Core Data check box when creating a new project*

6. Click the AppDelegate.swift file in the Navigator pane. When you create a new project using Core Data, Xcode adds the following code at the end of the AppDelegate.swift file:

```
lazy var persistentContainer: NSPersistentContainer = {
    /*
    The persistent container for the application. This
    implementation creates and returns a container, having
    loaded the store for the application to it. This property is
    optional since there are legitimate error conditions that
    could cause the creation of the store to fail.
    */
    let container = NSPersistentContainer(name: "CoreDataApp")
    container.loadPersistentStores(completionHandler: {
    (storeDescription, error) in
```

```swift
            if let error = error as NSError? {
                // Replace this implementation with code to handle the
                error appropriately.
                // fatalError() causes the application to generate
                a crash log and terminate. You should not use this
                function in a shipping application, although it may be
                useful during development.

                /*
                 Typical reasons for an error here include:
                 * The parent directory does not exist, cannot be
                 created, or disallows writing.
                 * The persistent store is not accessible, due to
                 permissions or data protection when the device is
                 locked.
                 * The device is out of space.
                 * The store could not be migrated to the current
                 model version.
                 Check the error message to determine what the actual
                 problem was.
                 */
                fatalError("Unresolved error \(error), \(error.
                userInfo)")
            }
        })
        return container
    }()

    // MARK: - Core Data Saving support

    func saveContext () {
        let context = persistentContainer.viewContext
        if context.hasChanges {
            do {
                try context.save()
            } catch {
```

```
        // Replace this implementation with code to handle the
        error appropriately.
        // fatalError() causes the application to generate
        a crash log and terminate. You should not use this
        function in a shipping application, although it may be
        useful during development.
        let nserror = error as NSError
        fatalError("Unresolved error \(nserror),
        \(nserror.userInfo)")
      }
    }
  }
```

Note   If you add a Core Data file to an existing project, you'll need to add the preceding code to the AppDelegate.swift file.

Customizing a Data Model File

Creating a Core Data file creates a file with the .xcdatamodeld file extension. First, you'll need to create at least one entity and one or more attributes in each entity (see Figure 6-5) where an entity represents a group of related data such as a person that contains data such as a name, age, address, or phone number.

To create an entity in a Core Data file, follow these steps:

1. Click the .xcdatamodeld file in the Navigator pane. Xcode displays a data editor as shown in Figure 6-8.

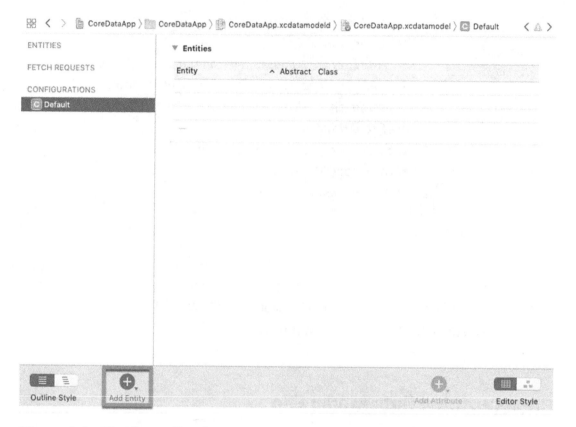

Figure 6-8. *The data editor lets you view and edit entities and attributes*

2. Click the Add Entity icon, or choose Editor ➤ Add Entity. Xcode displays an Entity under the ENTITIES category.

3. Click this Entity to select it and press Enter to highlight the entire name.

4. Type **Item** and press Enter. Entity names must always begin with an uppercase letter such as Item, Person, or Vehicle.

After you've created at least one entity, you'll need to add one or more attributes to hold data. An attribute consists of descriptive name (typed in lowercase) and the type of data the attribute will hold such as a string, integer, or date.

To define an attribute in an entity, follow these steps:

1. Click the .xcdatamodeld file in the Navigator pane. Xcode displays the data model editor (see Figure 6-8).

2. Click the Entity that you want to modify. Xcode displays an Attributes category as shown in Figure 6-9.

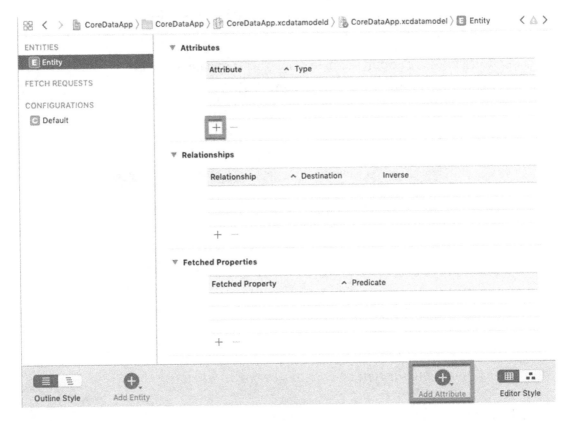

Figure 6-9. *The Add Attribute button appears in two places*

3. Click the Add Attribute button in the bottom of the Xcode window or underneath the Attribute column, or choose Editor ➤ Add Attribute. Xcode displays an attribute and a type as shown in Figure 6-10.

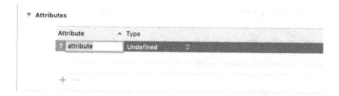

Figure 6-10. *Creating a new attribute*

4. Type **name** and press Enter. All attribute names must use lowercase letters.

5. Click the Type popup menu to display a list of data types the attribute can store as shown in Figure 6-11.

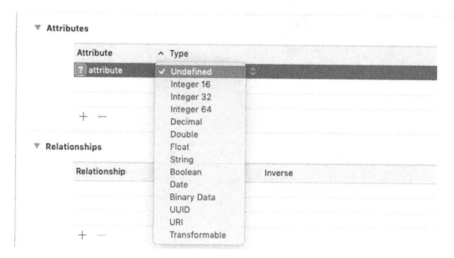

Figure 6-11. *Defining the type of data to store in an attribute*

6. Choose String.

7. Click the Add Attribute button in the bottom of the Xcode window or underneath the Attribute column, or choose Editor ➤ Add Attribute. Xcode displays an attribute and a type (see Figure 6-10).

8. Type **price** and press Enter.

9. Click the Type popup menu and choose String. The two attributes and one entity should look like Figure 6-12.

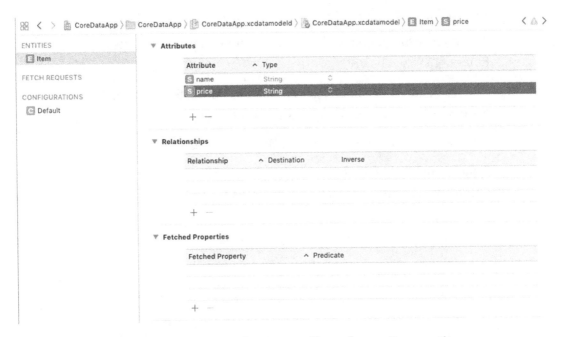

Figure 6-12. *Defining a name and price attribute for an Item entity*

Designing the User Interface

For our CoreDataApp project, we'll design a simple user interface that will consist of two text fields, two buttons, and a label. The two text fields will allow us to input data, the label will display all stored data, and the two buttons will let us add or delete data.

To design the user interface for the CoreDataApp project, follow these steps:

1. Make sure the CoreDataApp project is loaded into Xcode.

2. Click the Main.storyboard file in the Navigator pane.

3. Click the Library icon and drag and drop two text fields (one above the other), two buttons, and a label onto the view.

4. Resize the label and text fields to make them both wider.

5. Click the label and choose View ➤ Inspectors ➤ Show Attributes Inspector, or click the Attributes Inspector icon in the upper right corner of Xcode window.

6. Click in the Lines text field and change the value to 0. This will allow the label to display multiple lines of text.

7. Click the top text field, click in the Placeholder text field on the Attributes Inspector pane, type **Enter product name**, and press Enter.

8. Click the bottom text field, click in the Placeholder text field on the Attributes Inspector pane, type **Enter price**, and press Enter.

9. Double-click one button, type **Add Data**, and press Enter.

10. Double-click the second button, type **Delete Data**, and press Enter. The user interface should look similar to Figure 6-13.

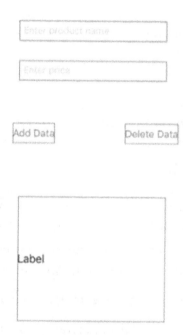

Figure 6-13. *The user interface of a text field, label, and two buttons*

11. Choose Editor ➤ Resolve Auto Layout Issues ➤ Reset to Suggested Constraints at the bottom half of the submenu. Xcode adds constraints to all the objects on the user interface.

12. Choose View ➤ Assistant Editor ➤ Show Assistant Editor, or click the Assistant Editor icon in the upper right corner of the Xcode window. Xcode displays the Main.storyboard file side by side with the ViewController.swift file.

13. Under the import UIKit line, add the following:

```
import Foundation
import CoreData
```

14. Move the mouse pointer over the top text field, hold down the Control key, and Ctrl-drag under the class ViewController line.

15. Release the Control key and the left mouse button. A popup window appears.

16. Click in the Name text field, type **myProductTextField**, and click the Connect button. Xcode creates an IBOutlet as follows:

```
@IBOutlet var myProductTextField: UITextField!
```

17. Move the mouse pointer over the bottom text field, hold down the Control key, and Ctrl-drag under the class ViewController line.

18. Release the Control key and the left mouse button. A popup window appears.

19. Click in the Name text field, type **myPriceTextField**, and click the Connect button. Xcode creates an IBOutlet as follows:

```
@IBOutlet var myPriceTextField: UITextField!
```

20. Move the mouse pointer over the label, hold down the Control key, and Ctrl-drag under the class ViewController line.

21. Release the Control key and the left mouse button. A popup window appears.

22. Click in the Name text field, type **myLabel**, and click the Connect button. Xcode creates an IBOutlet as follows:

```
@IBOutlet var myLabel: UILabel!
```

23. Under the IBOutlets, add the following two lines:

```
var dataManager : NSManagedObjectContext!
var listArray = [NSManagedObject]()
```

147

24. Move the mouse pointer over the Add Data button, hold down the Control key, and Ctrl-drag above the last curly bracket at the bottom of the ViewController.swift file.

25. Release the Control key and the left mouse button. A popup window appears.

26. Click in the Name text field, type **addDataButton**, click the Type popup menu and choose UIButton, and click the Connect button. Xcode creates an addDataButton IBAction method.

27. Move the mouse pointer over the Delete Data button, hold down the Control key, and Ctrl-drag above the last curly bracket at the bottom of the ViewController.swift file.

28. Release the Control key and the left mouse button. A popup window appears.

29. Click in the Name text field, type **deleteDataButton**, click the Type popup menu and choose UIButton, and click the Connect button. Xcode creates a deleteDataButton IBAction method.

30. Choose View ➤ Standard Editor ➤ Show Standard Editor, or click the Standard Editor icon in the upper right corner of the Xcode window.

Writing Swift Code

Once we've defined the user interface, it's time to write Swift code to save, search, and delete data. We need to write Swift code to add data from the two text fields when the user clicks the Add Data button. Then we need more Swift code to delete data when the user clicks the Delete Data button.

To write code to save, search, and delete data, follow these steps:

1. Make sure the CoreDataApp project is loaded into Xcode.

2. Click the ViewController.swift file in the Navigator pane.

3. Edit the viewDidLoad method as follows:

```
override func viewDidLoad() {
    super.viewDidLoad()
    // Do any additional setup after loading the view.
    let appDelegate = UIApplication.shared.delegate as! AppDelegate
    dataManager = appDelegate.persistentContainer.viewContext
    myLabel.text?.removeAll()
    fetchData()
}
```

The first two lines under the comment access the AppDelegate.
swift file, which contains persistentContainer (Core Data). The
next two lines simply clears the myLabel object on the user
interface and calls a function called fetchData().

4. Under the viewDidLoad method, add the fetchData() function as
follows:

```
func fetchData() {
    let fetchRequest : NSFetchRequest<NSFetchRequestResult> =
    NSFetchRequest(entityName: "Item")

    do {
        let result = try dataManager.fetch(fetchRequest)
        listArray = result as! [NSManagedObject]
        for item in listArray {
            let product = item.value(forKey: "name") as! String
            let cost = item.value(forKey: "price") as! String
            myLabel.text! += product + " " + cost + ", "
        }
    } catch {
        print ("Error retrieving data")
    }
}
```

This fetchData() function tries to retrieve data stored in the "Item" entity. Then it stores the item in listArray. A for-in loop retrieves the name and price for each item and adds it to the myLabel object.

5. Edit the addDataButton IBAction method as follows:

```
@IBAction func addDataButton(_ sender: UIButton) {
    let newEntity = NSEntityDescription.
    insertNewObject(forEntityName: "Item", into: dataManager)

    newEntity.setValue(myProductTextField.text!, forKey: "name")
    newEntity.setValue(myPriceTextField.text!, forKey: "price")

    do {
        try self.dataManager.save()
        listArray.append(newEntity)
    } catch {
        print ("Error saving data")
    }
    myLabel.text?.removeAll()
    myProductTextField.text?.removeAll()
    myPriceTextField.text?.removeAll()
    fetchData()
}
```

This creates new data for the "Item" entity and retrieves the data from myProductTextField and myPriceTextField into the name and price attributes. Then it saves the data and appends the new data to listArray, which stores all the data currently saved.

Finally it clears myLabel, myProductTextField, and myPriceTextField before calling fetchData(), which will display the updated data into the myLabel object.

6. Edit the deleteDataButton IBAction method as follows:

```
@IBAction func deleteDataButton(_ sender: UIButton) {
    let deleteItem = myProductTextField.text!
    for item in listArray {
        if item.value(forKey: "name") as! String == deleteItem {
        dataManager.delete(item)
        }
    }
    do {
        try self.dataManager.save()
    } catch {
        print ("Error deleting data")
    }
    myLabel.text?.removeAll()
    myProductTextField.text?.removeAll()
    fetchData()
}
```

This method retrieves whatever appears in the
myProductTextField object and then uses a for-in loop to see if
that item exists in the stored data. If so, then it deletes that item.

Then it saves the data and clears the myLabel object and the
myProductTextField object before calling fetchData(), which
displays the updated data in the myLabel object again.

7. Click the Run button or choose Product ➤ Run. The Simulator
    screen appears.

8. Click in the top text field and type **car**.

9. Click in the bottom text field and type any number such as **6000**.

10. Click the Add Data button. The myLabel object displays "car 6000,"
    on the screen.

11. Click in the top text field and type **oven**.

12. Click in the bottom text field and type any number such as **850**.

13. Click the Add Data button. The myLabel object displays "car 6000, oven 650" on the screen.

14. Choose Hardware ➤ Home. The Simulator displays the Home screen.

15. Double-click the CoreDataApp icon to make its user interface reappear. Notice that the data "car 6000, oven 650" still appears, which shows that Core Data saved the information. (You can even quit out of the Simulator here and run your app again to see that Core Data will save the data even if the app stops running.)

16. Click in the top text field and type **car**.

17. Click the Delete Data button. Notice that the myLabel object now only displays "oven 650," on the screen.

18. Click in the top text field and type **oven**.

19. Click the Delete Data button. Notice that the myLabel object now appears blank, showing that no data exists any more.

20. Choose Simulator ➤ Quit Simulator to return back to Xcode.

Summary

Many simple apps, such as the Calculator app, can run perfectly fine without the need to store data at all. However, most apps need to store data of some kind that the app can retrieve each time it loads. For example, the Stocks app lets users customize the list of stocks they want to follow. Once they enter this list, they want that list to appear every time they launch the Stocks app again.

To store app settings, store data in UserDefaults, which lets you store data in a dictionary so you'll need to define a unique key for each chunk of data you want to store. Once you've stored data in UserDefaults, you can always retrieve that data again by using the key associated with each chunk of data.

You can store and retrieve UserDefault data anywhere in an app, but it's often stored and retrieved in the AppDelegate.swift file that monitors when an app enters the background or returns to the foreground.

In addition to storing data in UserDefaults, you can also read or write data to a file. This can be handy for storing larger amounts of data in a sequential list.

If you need to store larger amounts of related data, use Core Data to save this information. Whether you store data in UserDefaults, files, or Core Data, you can always retrieve that data again so an app can display that data automatically without requiring the user to manually load data each time.

Beyond the technical aspects of storing data, data persistence also involves privacy and security issues. For example, users generally don't want to share their data with others without their permission, especially health data or other personal information. When storing data, be sure to keep security and privacy in mind so any data your app saves can't be accessed by another app.

CHAPTER 7

Passing Data Between Files

Every storyboard consists of one or more view controllers that displays a view or window of your program's user interface. To control the user interface objects on a scene, such as buttons or text fields, each view controller is connected to its own .swift class file where you can write Swift code to create IBOutlets and IBAction methods.

In most iOS projects, there is a single AppDelegate.swift file and one or more view controller files that manage the views and the user interface objects displayed on that view such as buttons, text fields, and labels. So you need to know how to share data between a view controller and the AppDelegate.swift file along with sharing data between two different view controllers.

Sharing Data with the AppDelegate.swift File

The AppDelegate.swift file tracks an app's various states such as when it first launches, when it goes into the background, and when it returns to the foreground. That means the AppDelegate.swift often needs to retrieve data from other view controllers to save the data before an app terminates or goes into the background.

Likewise, when the AppDelegate.swift file detects an app launching or returning to the foreground, it may need to retrieve stored data and pass that data to a view controller to display on the user interface.

155

© Wallace Wang 2019
W. Wang, *Pro iPhone Development with Swift 5*, https://doi.org/10.1007/978-1-4842-4944-4_7

To pass data to the AppDelegate.swift file, we need to make the AppDelegate.swift file accessible to any view controller. To do this, we just need the following function inside the AppDelegate.swift file:

```
static func shared() -> AppDelegate {
return UIApplication.shared.delegate as! AppDelegate
}
```

In addition, we also need to declare properties inside the AppDelegate.swift file to hold any passed data. When a view controller wants to pass data to the AppDelegate. swift file, it simply needs to use code like this:

```
AppDelegate.shared().propertyHere = dataToPass
```

In the preceding code, propertyHere is the name of a property defined inside the AppDelegate.swift file and dataToPass is the data being sent from a view controller to the AppDelegate.swift file.

To send data from the AppDelegate.swift file to a view controller, the Swift code in the view controller just needs to assign an AppDelegate property to a variable or property like this:

```
variable = AppDelegate.shared().propertyHere
```

To see how to pass data to and from a view controller to the AppDelegate.swift file, follow these steps:

1. Create a Single View App from the iOS category and name it AppDelegateDataApp.

2. Click the Main.storyboard file in the Navigator pane.

3. Click the Library icon and drag and drop a text field, a button, and a label onto the view. You may want to expand the width of both the text field and label as shown in Figure 7-1.

Figure 7-1. *Creating a user interface for passing data to and from the AppDelegate.swift file*

4. Choose Editor ➤ Resolve Auto Layout Issues ➤ Reset to Suggested Constraints at the bottom half of the submenu. Xcode adds constraints to all the user interface objects.

5. Choose View ➤ Assistant Editor ➤ Show Assistant Editor, or click the Assistant Editor icon in the upper right corner of the Xcode window. Xcode displays the Main.storyboard and ViewController. swift file side by side.

6. Move the mouse pointer over the text field, hold down the Control key, and Ctrl-drag underneath the class ViewController line in the ViewController.swift file.

7. Release the Control key and the left mouse button. A popup window appears.

8. Click in the Name text field, type **myTextField**, and click the Connect button. Xcode creates the following IBOutlet:

    @IBOutlet var myTextField: UITextField!

9. Move the mouse pointer over the label, hold down the Control key, and Ctrl-drag underneath the class ViewController line in the ViewController.swift file.

10. Release the Control key and the left mouse button. A popup window appears.

11.   Click in the Name text field, type **myLabel**, and click the Connect button. Xcode creates the following IBOutlet:

```
@IBOutlet var myLabel: UILabel!
```

12.   Move the mouse pointer over the button, hold down the Control key, and Ctrl-drag above the last curly bracket at the bottom of the ViewController.swift file.

13.   Release the Control key and the left mouse button. A popup window appears.

14.   Click in the Name text field, type **sendDataButton**, click the Type popup menu and choose UIButton, and click the Connect button. Xcode creates a sendDataButton IBAction method.

15.   Choose View ➤ Standard Editor ➤ Show Standard Editor, or click the Standard Editor icon in the upper right corner of the Xcode window.

16.   Click the AppDelegate.swift file in the Navigator pane.

17.   Under the var window: UIWindow? Line, add the following:

```
var receivedData : String = ""
var sentData : String = "Data from AppDelegate"

static func shared() -> AppDelegate {
    return UIApplication.shared.delegate as! AppDelegate
}
```

The receivedData property will hold the data passed to the AppDelegate.swift file from a view controller. The sentData property contains a string "Data from AppDelegate", which will be sent to a view controller. The shared() function will allow any view controller to access the AppDelegate.swift file to send or receive data.

18.   Edit the applicationDidEnterBackground method as follows:

```
func applicationDidEnterBackground(_ application: UIApplication) {
    print("The AppDelegate file received this data = " +
    receivedData)
}
```

This applicationDidEnterBackground method will run when the user returns to the Home screen. Then a message will appear in Xcode's debug area, showing that the AppDelegate.swift file received data from a view controller.

The entire AppDelegate.swift file should look like this:

```
import UIKit

@UIApplicationMain
class AppDelegate: UIResponder, UIApplicationDelegate {

    var window: UIWindow?

    var receivedData : String = ""
    var sentData : String = "Data from AppDelegate"

    static func shared() -> AppDelegate {
        return UIApplication.shared.delegate as! AppDelegate
    }

    func application(_ application: UIApplication,
    didFinishLaunchingWithOptions launchOptions: [UIApplication.
    LaunchOptionsKey: Any]?) -> Bool {
        // Override point for customization after application
        launch.
        return true
    }

    func applicationWillResignActive(_ application: UIApplication) {

    }
```

```
func applicationDidEnterBackground(_ application:
UIApplication) {
    print("The AppDelegate file received this data = " +
    receivedData)
}

func applicationWillEnterForeground(_ application: UIApplication) {

}

func applicationDidBecomeActive(_ application: UIApplication) {

}

func applicationWillTerminate(_ application: UIApplication) {

}
}
```

19. Click the ViewController.swift file in the Navigator pane.

20. Edit the sendDataButton IBAction method as follows:

```
@IBAction func sendDataButton(_ sender: UIButton) {
    AppDelegate.shared().receivedData = myTextField.text ??
    "default value"
    myLabel.text = AppDelegate.shared().sentData
}
```

The first line retrieves the text in the myTextField object and stores it in the AppDelegate.swift file's receivedData property. Then the second line retrieves the sentData property from the AppDelegate. swift file and stores it in the myLabel object on the user interface.

The entire ViewController.swift file should look like this:

```
import UIKit

class ViewController: UIViewController {

    @IBOutlet var myTextField: UITextField!
    @IBOutlet var myLabel: UILabel!
```

```
override func viewDidLoad() {
    super.viewDidLoad()
    // Do any additional setup after loading the view.
}

@IBAction func sendDataButton(_ sender: UIButton) {
    AppDelegate.shared().receivedData = myTextField.text ??
    "default value"
    myLabel.text = AppDelegate.shared().sentData
}

}
```

21. Click the Run button, or choose Product ➤ Run. The Simulator screen appears.

22. Click in the text field and type a message such as **Data from view controller**.

23. Click the button. Notice that the label now displays Data from AppDelegate, which is the data sent from the AppDelegate to the ViewController.swift file.

24. Choose Hardware ➤ Home. The Home screen appears on the Simulator. Notice that the debug area in Xcode now displays "The AppDelegate file received this data = Data from view controller" (or whatever data you typed into the text field). This shows that the AppDelegate.swift file received data sent from the ViewController. swift file.

25. Choose Simulator ➤ Quit Simulator to return back to Xcode.

Sharing Data Between View Controllers

Many times view controllers need to pass data to each other. Normally when a view controller receives data from its user interface, that data remains trapped in the .swift file connected to that view controller in the Identity Inspector pane. Fortunately, view controllers can pass data to other view controllers.

For example, suppose you have two view controllers labelled SceneA and SceneB where a segue links SceneA to SceneB. That means the user first sees SceneA then taps a button to view SceneB. Tapping another button can make SceneA appear again.

If the user enters data in SceneA, you want to pass that data forward to SceneB. If a segue points from SceneA to SceneB, you can use a special segue function that runs when SceneA uses a segue to display SceneB. Within this segue function, you can create an object from SceneB's .swift class file and pass data to this object.

However, what if you want to pass data back from SceneB to SceneA? SceneB can't create an object from SceneA's Swift class file because this risks creating a circular reference where SceneA creates an object from SceneB and SceneB turns around and creates an object from SceneA. Instead, you must pass data back to a view controller using a delegate. SceneB passes data to a delegate and then this delegate then passes data back to SceneA.

Essentially when you're passing data forward from one view controller to another through a segue, you can pass data using objects, but when you're passing data backward from one view controller to another without a segue, you must pass data using a delegate as shown in Figure 7-2.

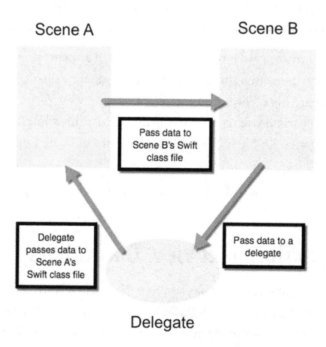

Figure 7-2. *Passing data forward and backward between scenes in a storyboard*

Passing Data Forward

Before you can pass data between two view controllers, you need to connect them with a segue. Then you need to make sure that each view controller has its own .swift file that you can connect it to through the Identity Inspector. Finally, you need to write Swift code in the .swift files of both view controllers to send and receive data.

To see how to pass data forward between two view controllers, follow these steps:

1. Create a Single View App from the iOS category and name it PassForwardApp.

2. Click the Main.storyboard file in the Navigator pane.

3. Click the Library icon and drag and drop a button and a text field onto the view. You may want to expand the width of the text field.

4. Choose Editor ➤ Resolve Auto Layout Issues ➤ Reset to Suggested Constraints in the bottom half of the submenu. Xcode adds constraints to the button and text field.

5. Click the Library icon and drag and drop a View Controller into the storyboard.

6. Move the mouse pointer over the button on the first view controller, hold down the Control key, and Ctrl-drag from the button over the second view controller as shown in Figure 7-3.

Figure 7-3. *Ctrl-dragging from a button to another view controller creates a segue*

7. Release the Control key and the left mouse button. A popup menu appears as shown in Figure 7-4.

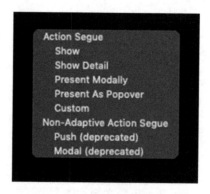

Figure 7-4. *Choosing the type of segue between view controllers*

8. Choose Show. Xcode creates a segue (arrow) connecting the two view controllers in the storyboard.

9. Click the Library icon and drag and drop a label and a button onto the second view controller. You may want to expand the width of the label.

10. Choose Editor ➤ Resolve Auto Layout Issues ➤ Reset to Suggested Constraints in the bottom half of the submenu. Xcode adds constraints to all the user interface objects. The entire storyboard should look similar to Figure 7-5.

Figure 7-5. *The complete user interface*

11.   Choose File ➤ New ➤ File. A template window appears.

12.   Click Cocoa Touch Class under the iOS category and click the Next button. Another window appears asking for a Class name and Subclass.

13.   Click in the Class text field and type **SecondViewController**.

14.   Click the Subclass popup menu and choose UIViewController. Then click the Next button and the Create button. Xcode adds the SecondViewController.swift file in the Navigator pane.

15.   Click the Main.storyboard file in the Navigator pane.

16.   Click the second View Controller Scene in the Document Outline to select the second view controller.

17.   Choose View ➤ Inspectors ➤ Show Identity Inspector, or click the Identity Inspector icon in the upper right corner of the Xcode window.

18.   Click the Class popup menu and choose SecondViewController as shown in Figure 7-6.

Figure 7-6. *Connecting the SecondViewController.swift file to the second view controller in the storyboard*

At this point, we've designed a simple user interface where the first view controller contains a text field and a button. We'll be able to type in the text field on the first view controller, click the button, and pass the data to the second view controller so the text appears in the label on that second view controller.

First, we need to define a property in the SecondViewController. swift to hold any passed data. Then we need to load that data into the label.

19. Click Second View Controller Scene in the Document Outline.

20. Choose View ➤ Assistant Editor ➤ Show Assistant Editor, or click the Assistant Editor icon in the upper right corner of the Xcode window. Xcode displays the Main.storyboard file and the SecondViewController.swift file side by side.

21. Move the mouse pointer over the label, hold down the Control key, and Ctrl-drag under the class ViewController line in the ViewController.swift file.

22. Release the Control key and the left mouse button. A popup window appears.

23. Click in the Name text field, type **myLabel**, and click the Connect button. Xcode creates the following IBOutlet:

```
@IBOutlet var myLabel: UILabel!
```

24. Underneath this IBOutlet, add the following property:

```
var receivedData : String = ""
```

25. Edit the viewDidLoad method as follows:

```
override func viewDidLoad() {
    super.viewDidLoad()
    myLabel.text = receivedData
    // Do any additional setup after loading the view.
}
```

26. Move the mouse pointer over the button, hold down the Control key, and Ctrl-drag above the last curly bracket at the bottom of the ViewController.swift file.

27. Release the Control key and the left mouse button. A popup window appears.

28. Click in the Name text field, type **closeButton**, click the Type popup menu and choose UIButton, and click the Connect button. Xcode creates a closeButton IBAction method.

29. Edit this closeButton IBAction method as follows:

```swift
@IBAction func closeButton(_ sender: UIButton) {
    dismiss(animated: true, completion: nil)
}
```

The entire SecondViewController.swift file should look like this:

```swift
import UIKit

class SecondViewController: UIViewController {

    @IBOutlet var myLabel: UILabel!
    var receivedData : String = ""

    override func viewDidLoad() {
        super.viewDidLoad()
        myLabel.text = receivedData
        // Do any additional setup after loading the view.
    }

    @IBAction func closeButton(_ sender: UIButton) {
        dismiss(animated: true, completion: nil)
    }

}
```

30. Click View Controller Scene in the Document Outline to select the first view controller. Xcode displays the Main.storyboard file and the ViewController.swift file side by side.

31. Move the mouse pointer over the text field, hold down the Control key, and Ctrl-drag under the class ViewController line in the ViewController.swift file.

32. Release the Control key and the left mouse button. A popup window appears.

33. Click in the Name text field, type **myTextField**, and click the Connect button. Xcode creates the following IBOutlet:

```
@IBOutlet var myTextField: UITextField!
```

34. Add the following function under the viewDidLoad method:

```
override func prepare(for segue: UIStoryboardSegue, sender: Any?) {
    if let secondVC = segue.destination as? SecondViewController {
        secondVC.receivedData = myTextField.text ?? "default value"
    }
}
```

The entire ViewController.swift file should look like this:

```
import UIKit

class ViewController: UIViewController {

    @IBOutlet var myTextField: UITextField!

    override func viewDidLoad() {
        super.viewDidLoad()
        // Do any additional setup after loading the view.
    }

    override func prepare(for segue: UIStoryboardSegue, sender:
    Any?) {
        if let secondVC = segue.destination as?
        SecondViewController {
```

```
                        secondVC.receivedData = myTextField.text ??
                        "default value"
                }
            }

        }
```

35. Click the Run button or choose Product ➤ Run. The Simulator
     screen appears, showing the user interface of the first view
     controller (a button and a text field).

36. Click in the text field and type any text such as **Hello, there!**

37. Click the button. The user interface of the second view controller
     appears (a button and a label) where the label displays the text
     you typed into the first view controller.

38. Click the button. The second view controller disappears and the
     first view controller appears again. Repeat steps 35–36 as often as
     you like, typing different text into the text field to see how the data
     gets passed forward from the first view controller to the second
     view controller.

39. Choose Simulator ➤ Quit Simulator to return back to Xcode.

In this app, we passed data using a segue such as

```swift
override func prepare(for segue: UIStoryboardSegue, sender: Any?) {
    if let secondVC = segue.destination as? SecondViewController {
        secondVC.receivedData = myTextField.text ?? "default value"
    }
}
```

This code creates a constant called secondVC (you can use any arbitrary name you
want) and checks to make sure the segue links to the second view controller, which
is linked to the SecondViewController.swift file. If so, then it takes the text that the
user typed in the text field and stores it in the receivedData property defined in the
SecondViewController.swift file. (If the user did not type any text in the text field, then
the receivedData property gets sent "default value" instead.)

There's another way to pass data through a segue that involves giving the segue a name. Then your code can run depending on the segue name. This method can be handy in case you have multiple segues linked to the same view controller.

To see how to pass data forward using segue names, follow these steps:

1. Create a Single View App from the iOS category and name it PassForwardNameApp.

2. Click the Main.storyboard file in the Navigator pane.

3. Click the Library icon and drag and drop two buttons, a text field, and a slider onto the view. You may want to expand the width of the text field.

4. Double-click one button, type **Pass Text**, and press Enter.

5. Double-click the second button, type **Pass Value**, and press Enter.

6. Choose Editor ➤ Resolve Auto Layout Issues ➤ Reset to Suggested Constraints in the bottom half of the submenu. Xcode adds constraints to all the user interface objects. The user interface should look similar to Figure 7-7.

Figure 7-7. *The user interface of the first view controller*

7. Click the Library icon and drag and drop a View Controller into the storyboard.

8. Move the mouse pointer over the Pass Text button on the first view controller, hold down the Control key, and Ctrl-drag from the button over the second view controller.

9. Release the Control key and the left mouse button. A popup menu appears (see Figure 7-4).

10. Choose Show. Xcode creates a segue (arrow) connecting the two view controllers in the storyboard.

11. Click the segue or click Show segue to "View Controller" in the Document Outline.

12. Choose View ➤ Inspectors ➤ Show Attributes Inspector, or click the Attributes Inspector icon in the upper right corner of the Xcode window.

13. Click in the Identifier text field, type **textSegue**, and press Enter as shown in Figure 7-8.

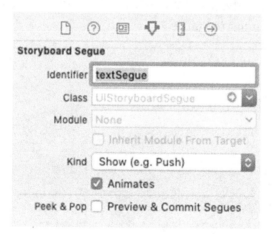

Figure 7-8. *Giving a segue an identifier*

14. Move the mouse pointer over the Pass Value button on the first view controller, hold down the Control key, and Ctrl-drag from the button over the second view controller.

15. Release the Control key and the left mouse button. A popup menu appears (see Figure 7-4).

16. Choose Show. Xcode creates a second segue (arrow) connecting the two view controllers in the storyboard.

17. Click the segue or click Show segue to "View Controller" in the Document Outline.

18. Choose View ➤ Inspectors ➤ Show Attributes Inspector, or click the Attributes Inspector icon in the upper right corner of the Xcode window.

19. Click in the Identifier text field, type **sliderSegue**, and press Enter. At this point, we have two segues that point to the same view controller.

20. Click the Library icon and drag and drop a label and a button onto the second view controller. You may want to expand the width of the label.

21. Choose Editor ➤ Resolve Auto Layout Issues ➤ Reset to Suggested Constraints in the bottom half of the submenu. Xcode adds constraints to all the user interface objects. The entire storyboard should look similar to Figure 7-9. Notice the two segues linking the view controllers.

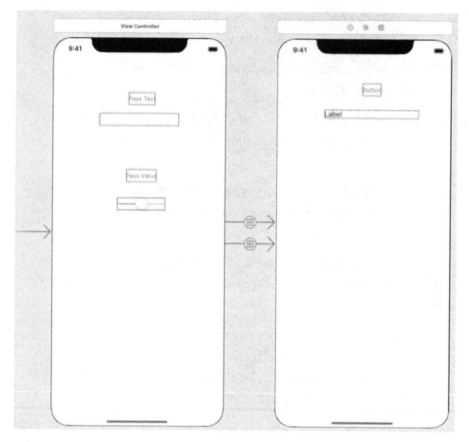

Figure 7-9. *The complete user interface*

22. Choose File ➤ New ➤ File. A template window appears.

23. Click Cocoa Touch Class under the iOS category and click the Next
     button. Another window appears asking for a Class name and
     Subclass.

24. Click in the Class text field and type **SecondViewController**.

25. Click the Subclass popup menu and choose UIViewController.
     Then click the Next button and the Create button. Xcode adds the
     SecondViewController.swift file in the Navigator pane.

26. Click the Main.storyboard file in the Navigator pane.

27. Click the second View Controller Scene in the Document Outline
     to select the second view controller.

28. Choose View ➤ Inspectors ➤ Show Identity Inspector, or click the Identity Inspector icon in the upper right corner of the Xcode window.

29. Click the Class popup menu and choose SecondViewController (see Figure 7-6).

   At this point, we've designed a simple user interface where the first view controller contains a text field, a slider, and two buttons. If we type in the text field and click the Pass Text button, we'll pass text to the second view controller. If we drag the slider left or right and click the Pass Value button, we'll pass a numeric value to the second view controller. Depending on which segue opens the second view controller, the label on the second view controller will display either the text (from the text field) or a value (from the slider).

   First, we need to define a property in the SecondViewController. swift to hold any passed data. Then we need to load that data into the label.

30. Click Second View Controller Scene in the Document Outline.

31. Choose View ➤ Assistant Editor ➤ Show Assistant Editor, or click the Assistant Editor icon in the upper right corner of the Xcode window. Xcode displays the Main.storyboard file and the SecondViewController.swift file side by side.

32. Move the mouse pointer over the label, hold down the Control key, and Ctrl-drag under the class ViewController line in the ViewController.swift file.

33. Release the Control key and the left mouse button. A popup window appears.

34. Click in the Name text field, type **myLabel**, and click the Connect button. Xcode creates the following IBOutlet:

   ```
   @IBOutlet var myLabel: UILabel!
   ```

35. Underneath this IBOutlet, add the following property:

   ```
   var receivedData : String = ""
   ```

36. Edit the viewDidLoad method as follows:

```
override func viewDidLoad() {
    super.viewDidLoad()
    myLabel.text = receivedData
    // Do any additional setup after loading the view.
}
```

37. Move the mouse pointer over the button, hold down the Control key, and Ctrl-drag above the last curly bracket at the bottom of the SecondViewController.swift file.

38. Release the Control key and the left mouse button. A popup window appears.

39. Click in the Name text field, type **closeButton**, click the Type popup menu and choose UIButton, and click the Connect button. Xcode creates a closeButton IBAction method.

40. Edit this closeButton IBAction method as follows:

```
@IBAction func closeButton(_ sender: UIButton) {
    dismiss(animated: true, completion: nil)
}
```

The entire SecondViewController.swift file should look like this:

```
import UIKit

class SecondViewController: UIViewController {

    @IBOutlet var myLabel: UILabel!
    var receivedData : String = ""

    override func viewDidLoad() {
        super.viewDidLoad()
        myLabel.text = receivedData
        // Do any additional setup after loading the view.
    }
```

```
@IBAction func closeButton(_ sender: UIButton) {
    dismiss(animated: true, completion: nil)
}
```

}

41. Click View Controller Scene in the Document Outline to select the first view controller. Xcode displays the Main.storyboard file and the ViewController.swift file side by side.

42. Move the mouse pointer over the text field, hold down the Control key, and Ctrl-drag under the class ViewController line in the ViewController.swift file.

43. Release the Control key and the left mouse button. A popup window appears.

44. Click in the Name text field, type **myTextField**, and click the Connect button. Xcode creates the following IBOutlet:

```
@IBOutlet var myTextField: UITextField!
```

45. Move the mouse pointer over the slider, hold down the Control key, and Ctrl-drag under the class ViewController line in the ViewController.swift file.

46. Release the Control key and the left mouse button. A popup window appears.

47. Click in the Name text field, type **mySlider**, and click the Connect button. Xcode creates the following IBOutlet:

```
@IBOutlet var mySlider: UISlider!
```

48. Add the following function under the viewDidLoad method:

```
override func prepare(for segue: UIStoryboardSegue, sender: Any?) {
    let secondVC = segue.destination as? SecondViewController
    if segue.identifier == "textSegue" {
        secondVC?.receivedData = myTextField.text ?? "default value"
    }
```

```
    if segue.identifier == "sliderSegue" {
        secondVC?.receivedData = "Slider value = \(mySlider.value)"
    }
}
```

The entire ViewController.swift file should look like this:

```
import UIKit

class ViewController: UIViewController {

    @IBOutlet var myTextField: UITextField!
    @IBOutlet var mySlider: UISlider!

    override func viewDidLoad() {
        super.viewDidLoad()
        // Do any additional setup after loading the view.
    }

    override func prepare(for segue: UIStoryboardSegue, sender: Any?) {
        let secondVC = segue.destination as? SecondViewController
        if segue.identifier == "textSegue" {
            secondVC?.receivedData = myTextField.text ?? "default
            value"
        }

        if segue.identifier == "sliderSegue" {
            secondVC?.receivedData = "Slider value = \(mySlider.
            value)"
        }
    }
}
```

49. Click the Run button or choose Product ➤ Run. The Simulator
     screen appears, showing the user interface of the first view
     controller (two buttons, a text field, and a slider).

50. Click in the text field and type any text such as **Hello, there!**

51. Click the Pass Text button. The user interface of the second view controller appears (a button and a label) where the label displays the text you typed into the first view controller.

52. Click the button. The second view controller disappears and the first view controller appears again.

53. Drag the slider to the far left and click the Pass Value button. The second view controller appears where the label displays the value from the slider on the first view controller.

54. Click the button to make the second view controller disappear and make the first view controller appear again. Repeat the preceding steps with different text and slider values to see how the first view controller passes data to the second view controller depending on which segue runs.

55. Choose Simulator ➤ Quit Simulator to return back to Xcode.

Passing Data Backward with a Protocol

The first step to passing data backward between view controllers in a storyboard is to define a protocol. You can give this protocol any arbitrary name you wish, but the key feature is that the protocol must define a function that accepts one or more parameters that represent the data you want to send back.

So the three parts of the protocol you must define are

- The protocol name (which can be anything you wish)

- A function name (which can also be anything you wish)

- One or more parameters that represent the data and data type (such as String or Int) that you want to pass back

A protocol declaration can look as simple as this:

```
protocol ProtocolName {
    func functionName(dataToSendBack : DataType)
}
```

In the preceding example, the function's parameter list contains one item, which means it can pass back one item, but if you want, you could add more items to the function's parameter list to send back two or more items.

You need to place the protocol declaration above the class line in the Swift class file such as

```
import UIKit

protocol MyProtocol {
    func sendBackData(thisData: String)
}

class SecondViewController: UIViewController {
```

After defining a protocol, you just create a delegate inside the class like this:

```
class SecondViewController: UIViewController {

    var delegate : MyProtocol?
```

You must use the exact word "delegate" but the protocol name can be anything you wish.

Once you've defined a delegate, you must then use that delegate, combined with the function defined by the protocol, to send back data such as

```
delegate?.functionName(valueSent: DatatoSend)
```

To see how to pass data forward between two view controllers, follow these steps:

1. Create a Single View App from the iOS category and name it PassBackwardApp.

2. Click the Main.storyboard file in the Navigator pane.

3. Click the Library icon and drag and drop two buttons and a label onto the view. You may want to expand the width of the label.

4. Double-click one button, type **Open**, and press Enter.

5. Double-click the other button, type **View Data**, and press Enter. The user interface should look similar to Figure 7-10.

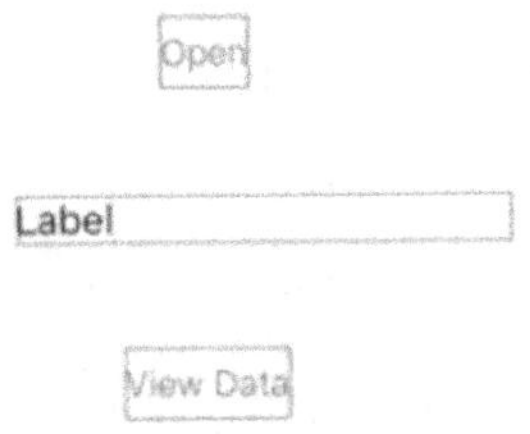

Open

Label

View Data

Figure 7-10. *Designing the user interface of the initial view controller*

6. Choose Editor ➤ Resolve Auto Layout Issues ➤ Reset to Suggested Constraints in the bottom half of the submenu. Xcode adds constraints to all the user interface objects.

7. Choose View ➤ Assistant Editor ➤ Show Assistant Editor, or click the Assistant Editor icon in the upper right corner of the Xcode window. Xcode displays the Main.storyboard file and the ViewController.swift file side by side.

8. Move the mouse pointer over the label, hold down the Control key, and Ctrl-drag under the class ViewController line in the ViewController.swift file.

9. Release the Control key and the left mouse button. A popup window appears.

10. Click in the Name text field, type **myLabel**, and click the Connect button. Xcode creates the following IBOutlet:

    @IBOutlet var myLabel: UILabel!

11. Under this IBOutlet, add the following property:

    var receivedData : String = ""

12. Move the mouse pointer over the View Data button, hold down the Control key, and Ctrl-drag above the last curly bracket at the bottom of the ViewController.swift file.

13. Release the Control key and the left mouse button. A popup window appears.

14. Click in the Name text field, type **viewDataButton**, click the Type popup menu and choose UIButton, and click the Connect button. Xcode creates a viewDataButton IBAction method.

15. Edit this viewDataButton IBAction method as follows:

```
@IBAction func viewDataButton(_ sender: UIButton) {
    myLabel.text = receivedData
    }
```

This completes the user interface of the first (initial) view controller. At this point, we need to add a second view controller to the storyboard, design its user interface, and write Swift code to define a protocol. After we're done writing Swift code in the second view controller, we'll need to go back to the first view controller .swift file and finish editing the code there.

Let's design the second view controller, attach a .swift file to this view controller, and write Swift code in its .swift file.

1. Choose View ➤ Standard Editor ➤ Show Standard Editor, or click the Standard Editor icon in the upper right corner of the Xcode window.

2. Click the Main.storyboard file in the Navigator pane.

3. Click the Library icon and drag and drop a View Controller in the storyboard.

4. Move the mouse pointer over the Open button on the first view controller, hold down the Control key, and Ctrl-drag over the second view controller.

5. Release the Control key and the left mouse button. A popup menu appears.

6. Choose Show. Xcode displays a segue between the two view controllers.

7. Choose File ➤ New ➤ File. A template window appears.

8. Click Cocoa Touch Class under the iOS category and click the Next button. Another window appears asking for a Class name and Subclass.

9. Click in the Class text field and type **SecondViewController**.

10. Click the Subclass popup menu and choose UIViewController. Then click the Next button and the Create button. Xcode adds the SecondViewController.swift file in the Navigator pane.

11. Click the Main.storyboard file in the Navigator pane.

12. Click the second View Controller Scene in the Document Outline to select the second view controller.

13. Choose View ➤ Inspectors ➤ Show Identity Inspector, or click the Identity Inspector icon in the upper right corner of the Xcode window.

14. Click the Class popup menu and choose SecondViewController (see Figure 7-6).

15. Click the Library icon and drag and drop a button and a text field onto the view. You may want to expand the width of the text field.

16. Choose View ➤ Assistant Editor ➤ Show Assistant Editor, or click the Assistant Editor icon in the upper right corner of the Xcode window. Xcode displays the Main.storyboard file and the SecondViewController.swift file side by side.

17. Move the mouse pointer over the text field, hold down the Control key, and Ctrl-drag under the class SecondViewController line in the SecondViewController.swift file.

18. Release the Control key and the left mouse button. A popup window appears.

19. Click in the Name text field, type **myTextField**, and click the Connect button. Xcode creates the following IBOutlet:

    ```
    @IBOutlet var myTextField: UITextField!
    ```

20. Add the following under the import UIKit line:

    ```
    protocol MyProtocol {
        func sendBackData(thisData: String)
    }
    ```

This defines our protocol, which we'll have to implement in the ViewController.swift file.

21. Add the following variable under the IBOutlet as follows:

var delegate : MyProtocol?

22. Move the mouse pointer over the button, hold down the Control key, and Ctrl-drag above the last curly bracket at the bottom of the SecondViewController.swift file.

23. Release the Control key and the left mouse button. A popup window appears.

24. Click in the Name text field, type **closeButton**, click the Type popup menu and choose UIButton, and click the Connect button. Xcode creates a closeButton IBAction method.

25. Edit this closeButton IBAction method as follows:

```
@IBAction func closeButton(_ sender: UIButton) {
    delegate?.sendBackData(thisData: myTextField.text ?? "default
    value")
    dismiss(animated: true, completion: nil)
    }
```

This code uses the protocol function to send data back from myTextField. Then it removes the second view controller from the screen. The entire SecondViewController.swift file should look like this:

```
import UIKit

protocol MyProtocol {
    func sendBackData(thisData: String)
}

class SecondViewController: UIViewController {

    @IBOutlet var myTextField: UITextField!
    var delegate : MyProtocol?
```

```swift
override func viewDidLoad() {
    super.viewDidLoad()

    // Do any additional setup after loading the view.
}

@IBAction func closeButton(_ sender: UIButton) {
    delegate?.sendBackData(thisData: myTextField.text ??
    "default value")
    dismiss(animated: true, completion: nil)
}

}
```

26. Click the ViewController.swift file in the Navigator pane. We now have to make sure the ViewController.swift file conforms to the protocol we just defined in the SecondViewController.swift file.

27. Add MyProtocol to the class ViewController line like this:

```swift
class ViewController: UIViewController, MyProtocol {
```

28. Add the following function underneath the viewDidLoad method:

```swift
func sendBackData(thisData: String) {
    self.receivedData = thisData
}
```

29. Add the following function above the viewDataButton IBAction method:

```swift
override func prepare(for segue: UIStoryboardSegue, sender: Any?) {
    let secondVC = segue.destination as! SecondViewController
    secondVC.delegate = self
}
```

The entire ViewController.swift file should look like this:

```
import UIKit

class ViewController: UIViewController, MyProtocol {

    @IBOutlet var myLabel: UILabel!
    var receivedData : String = ""

    override func viewDidLoad() {
        super.viewDidLoad()
        // Do any additional setup after loading the view.
    }

    func sendBackData(thisData: String) {
        self.receivedData = thisData
    }

    override func prepare(for segue: UIStoryboardSegue, sender: Any?) {
        let secondVC = segue.destination as! SecondViewController
        secondVC.delegate = self
    }

    @IBAction func viewDataButton(_ sender: UIButton) {
        myLabel.text = receivedData
    }

}
```

30. Click the Run button or choose Product ➤ Run. The Simulator screen appears.

31. Click the Open button. The second view controller appears on the screen.

32. Click in the text field and type any text such as **Hello, there!**

33. Click the button. The second view controller disappears and the first view controller appears.

34. Click the View Data button. Notice that the label now displays the text typed from the second view controller.

Passing Data Backward with a Delegate

Another way to pass data backward is to declare the first view controller as a delegate. Then define properties in both view controllers that hold the data you want to pass back from the second view controller.

To see how to use a delegate to pass data backward, follow these steps:

1. Create a Single View App from the iOS category and name it PassBackDelegateApp.

2. Click the Main.storyboard file in the Navigator pane.

3. Click the Library icon and drag and drop a button and a label onto the view. You may want to expand the width of the label.

4. Choose Editor ➤ Resolve Auto Layout Issues ➤ Reset to Suggested Constraints in the bottom half of the submenu. Xcode adds constraints to all the user interface objects.

5. Choose View ➤ Assistant Editor ➤ Show Assistant Editor, or click the Assistant Editor icon in the upper right corner of the Xcode window. Xcode displays the Main.storyboard file and the ViewController.swift file side by side.

6. Move the mouse pointer over the label, hold down the Control key, and Ctrl-drag under the class ViewController line in the ViewController.swift file.

7. Release the Control key and the left mouse button. A popup window appears.

8. Click in the Name text field, type **myLabel**, and click the Connect button. Xcode creates the following IBOutlet:

```
@IBOutlet var myLabel: UILabel!
```

9. Underneath this IBOutlet, add the following to define a property:

```
var receivedText : String = ""
```

10. Add the following method in the ViewController.swift file:

```
override func viewWillAppear(_ animated: Bool) {
    myLabel.text = receivedText
}
```

11. Choose View ➤ Standard Editor ➤ Show Standard Editor, or click the Standard Editor icon in the upper right corner of the Xcode window.

12. Click the Main.storyboard file in the Navigator pane.

13. Click the Library icon and drag and drop a View Controller in the storyboard.

14. Move the mouse pointer over the button on the first view controller, hold down the Control key, and Ctrl-drag anywhere over the second view controller.

15. Release the Control key and the left mouse button. A popup menu appears (see Figure 7-4).

16. Choose Show. Xcode adds a segue from the first view controller to the second view controller.

17. Click the Library icon and drag and drop a button and a text field onto the second view controller. You may want to resize the width of the text field.

18. Choose Editor ➤ Resolve Auto Layout Issues ➤ Reset to Suggested Constraints in the bottom half of the submenu. Xcode adds constraints to all the user interface objects.

19. Choose File ➤ New ➤ File. A template window appears.

20. Click Cocoa Touch Class under the iOS category and click the Next button. Another window appears asking for a Class name and Subclass.

21. Click in the Class text field and type **SecondViewController**.

22. Click the Subclass popup menu and choose UIViewController. Then click the Next button and the Create button. Xcode adds the SecondViewController.swift file in the Navigator pane.

23. Click the Main.storyboard file in the Navigator pane.

24. Click the second View Controller Scene in the Document Outline
     to select the second view controller.

25. Choose View ➤ Inspectors ➤ Show Identity Inspector, or click
     the Identity Inspector icon in the upper right corner of the Xcode
     window.

26. Click the Class popup menu and choose SecondViewController
     (see Figure 7-6).

27. Choose View ➤ Assistant Editor ➤ Show Assistant Editor, or
     click the Assistant Editor icon in the upper right corner of the
     Xcode window. Xcode displays the Main.storyboard file and the
     SecondViewController.swift file side by side.

28. Move the mouse pointer over the text field, hold down the Control
     key, and Ctrl-drag under the class SecondViewController line in
     the SecondViewController.swift file.

29. Release the Control key and the left mouse button. A popup
     window appears.

30. Click in the Name text field, type **myTextField**, and click the
     Connect button. Xcode creates the following IBOutlet:

     ```
     @IBOutlet var myTextField: UITextField!
     ```

31. Add the following under the IBOutlet to define a delegate and a
     property to hold a string:

     ```
     var sentText : String = ""
     var delegate : ViewController!
     ```

     Move the mouse pointer over the button, hold down the Control
     key, and Ctrl-drag above the last curly bracket at the bottom of the
     SecondViewController.swift file.

32. Release the Control key and the left mouse button. A popup
     window appears.

33. Click in the Name text field, type **closeButton**, click the Type popup menu and choose UIButton, and click the Connect button. Xcode creates a closeButton IBAction method.

34. Edit this closeButton IBAction method as follows:

```swift
@IBAction func closeButton(_ sender: UIButton) {
    sentText = myTextField.text ?? "default value"
    delegate.receivedText = sentText
    dismiss(animated: true, completion: nil)
}
```

This closeButton IBAction method takes the text from the text field and stores it in the receivedText property of the delegate, which is defined as the ViewController.swift file connected to the first view controller.

The entire SecondViewController.swift file should look like this:

```swift
import UIKit

class SecondViewController: UIViewController {

    @IBOutlet var myTextField: UITextField!

    var sentText : String = ""
    var delegate : ViewController!

    override func viewDidLoad() {
        super.viewDidLoad()

        // Do any additional setup after loading the view.
    }

    @IBAction func closeButton(_ sender: UIButton) {
        sentText = myTextField.text ?? "default value"
        delegate.receivedText = sentText
        dismiss(animated: true, completion: nil)
    }

}
```

35. Choose View ➤ Standard Editor ➤ Show Standard Editor, or click the Standard Editor icon in the upper right corner of the Xcode window.

36. Click the ViewController.swift file in the Navigator pane.

37. Add the following method:

```
override func prepare(for segue: UIStoryboardSegue, sender: Any?) {
    let vc = segue.destination as! SecondViewController
    vc.sentText = self.receivedText
    vc.delegate = self
}
```

This method defines a constant called vc that represents the segue destination, which is the second view controller that's connected to the SecondViewController.swift file. Then it sends the receivedText value (in the first view controller) to the sentText property (in the second view controller). Finally, it defines itself (the ViewController.swift file) as the delegate declared in the second view controller.

The entire ViewController.swift file should look like this:

```
import UIKit

class ViewController: UIViewController {

    @IBOutlet var myLabel: UILabel!

    var receivedText : String = ""

    override func viewDidLoad() {
        super.viewDidLoad()
        // Do any additional setup after loading the view.
    }

    override func viewWillAppear(_ animated: Bool) {
        myLabel.text = receivedText
    }
```

```
override func prepare(for segue: UIStoryboardSegue, sender: Any?) {
    let vc = segue.destination as! SecondViewController
    vc.sentText = self.receivedText
    vc.delegate = self
}

}
```

38. Click the Run button or choose Product ➤ Run. The Simulator screen appears, displaying a button.

39. Click the button. The second view controller appears with a button and a text field.

40. Click in the text field and type text such as **Hello, there!**

41. Click the button. The first view controller appears, displaying the text (from the second view controller) in its label.

42. Choose Simulator ➤ Quit Simulator to return back to Xcode.

Passing Data with the Notification Center

Yet another way to pass data between view controller files is through the notification center. Using the notification center to pass data can be especially useful when you need to share data between two or more view controllers at the same time, or if the view controllers are not connected by a segue. There's a three-step process to using notification center:

- Define a unique name for a notification center.

- Add an observer to that notification center.

- Send a notification to the observer and pass data.

To define a name for a notification center, you can choose any arbitrary name such as

```
static let notificationName = Notification.Name("myNotification")
```

To add a notification center observer involves defining a function to run when it receives a notification and defining the name of the notification center to observe. This can be done with a statement like this:

```
NotificationCenter.default.addObserver(self, selector: #selector(functionNa
me(notification:)), name: notificationName, object: nil)
```

Where "functionName" is the name of your function to run when the notification is received, and "notificationName" is the name of the notification center you defined.

Finally, you need to send a notification and pass data at the same time. This can be done using this statement:

```
NotificationCenter.default.post(name: NSNotification.Name(rawValue:
"Notification Name"), object: dataSent)
```

Where "Notification Name" is the name you chose for the notification center, and "dataSent" is any data you wish to pass to a notification observer.

To see how to pass data using notifications, follow these steps:

1. Create a new iOS Single View App and name it NotificationPassApp.

2. Click the Main.storyboard file in the Navigator pane.

3. Click the Library icon and drag and drop a button and a label onto the view. You may want to resize the label to make it wider.

4. Choose Editor ➤ Resolve Auto Layout Issues ➤ Reset to Suggested Constraints at the bottom half of the submenu. Xcode adds constraints to the button and label.

5. Choose View ➤ Assistant Editor ➤ Show Assistant Editor, or click the Assistant Editor icon in the upper right corner of the Xcode window. Xcode displays the Main.storyboard file side by side with the ViewController.swift file.

6. Move the mouse pointer over the label, hold down the Control key, and Ctrl-drag under the class ViewController line.

7. Release the Control key and the left mouse button. A popup window appears.

8. Click in the Name text field, type **myLabel**, and click the Connect button. Xcode creates an IBOutlet as follows:

```
@IBOutlet var myLabel: UILabel!
```

9. Choose View ➤ Standard Editor ➤ Show Standard Editor, or click the Standard Editor icon in the upper right corner of the Xcode window.

10. Click the Main.storyboard file in the Navigator pane.

11. Click the Library icon and drag and drop a View Controller in the storyboard.

12. Move the mouse pointer over the button on the initial (first) view controller, hold down the Control key, and Ctrl-drag anywhere over the second view controller.

13. Release the Control key and the left mouse button. A popup menu appears (see Figure 7-4).

14. Choose Show. Xcode adds a segue between the two view controllers.

15. Click the Library icon and drag and drop a button and a text field onto the second view controller.

16. Choose Editor ➤ Resolve Auto Layout Issues ➤ Reset to Suggested Constraints at the bottom half of the submenu. Xcode adds constraints to the button and text field.

17. Choose File ➤ New ➤ File. A template window appears.

18. Click Cocoa Touch Class under the iOS category and click the Next button. Another window appears asking for a Class name and Subclass.

19. Click in the Class text field and type **SecondViewController**.

20. Click the Subclass popup menu and choose UIViewController. Then click the Next button and the Create button. Xcode adds the SecondViewController.swift file in the Navigator pane.

21. Click the Main.storyboard file in the Navigator pane.

22. Click the second View Controller Scene in the Document Outline to select the second view controller.

23. Choose View ➤ Inspectors ➤ Show Identity Inspector, or click the Identity Inspector icon in the upper right corner of the Xcode window.

24. Click the Class popup menu and choose SecondViewController (see Figure 7-6).

25. Choose View ➤ Assistant Editor ➤ Show Assistant Editor, or click the Assistant Editor icon in the upper right corner of the Xcode window. Xcode displays the Main.storyboard file side by side with the SecondViewController.swift file.

26. Move the mouse pointer over the text field, hold down the Control key, and Ctrl-drag under the class SecondViewController line in the SecondViewController.swift file.

27. Release the Control key and the left mouse button. A popup window appears.

28. Click in the Name text field, type **myTextField**, and click the Connect button. Xcode creates an IBOutlet as follows:

```
@IBOutlet var myTextField: UITextField!
```

29. Move the mouse pointer over the button, hold down the Control key, and Ctrl-drag above the last curly bracket at the bottom of the SecondViewController.swift file.

30. Release the Control key and the left mouse button. A popup window appears.

31. Click in the Name text field, type **closeButton**, click the Type popup menu and choose UIButton, and click the Connect button. Xcode creates a closeButton IBAction method.

32. Choose View ➤ Standard Editor ➤ Show Standard Editor, or click the Standard Editor icon in the upper right corner of the Xcode window.

33. Click the ViewController.swift file in the Navigator pane.

34. Add the following under the IBOutlet to give the notification center a unique name:

```
static let notificationName = Notification.Name("myNotification")
```

35. Add the following function under the static let line you just write in the previous step:

```
@objc func onNotification(notification:Notification)
{
    let data = notification.object
    let temp = String(describing: data!)
    myLabel.text =  temp
}
```

This function is called "onNotification" although you can choose any arbitrary name for the function. First, it stores the notification. object in a constant called "data" (this can be any arbitrary name). The notification.object is the data sent.

Next, another constant called "temp" (which can be any arbitrary name) takes the string value of the passed data and unwraps it since it's an optional. Finally, it stores this string in the myLabel object. The entire ViewController.swift file should look like this:

```
import UIKit

class ViewController: UIViewController {

    @IBOutlet var myLabel: UILabel!

    static let notificationName = Notification.
    Name("myNotification")
```

```swift
@objc func onNotification(notification:Notification)
{
    let data = notification.object
    let temp = String(describing: data!)
    myLabel.text =  temp
}

override func viewDidLoad() {
    super.viewDidLoad()
    // Do any additional setup after loading the view.
    NotificationCenter.default.addObserver(self, selector:
    #selector(onNotification(notification:)), name:
    ViewController.notificationName, object: nil)
}
}
```

36. Click the SecondViewController.swift file in the Navigator pane.

37. Edit the closeButton IBAction method as follows:

```swift
@IBAction func closeButton(_ sender: UIButton) {
    let dataSent = myTextField.text
    NotificationCenter.default.post(name: NSNotification.
    Name(rawValue: "myNotification"), object: dataSent)
    dismiss(animated: true, completion: nil)
}
```

This IBAction method retrieves the text in the text field and stores it in a constant called "dataSent" (which can be any arbitrary name). Next, this IBAction method sends a notification with the post command. This post command identifies the notification center by name ("myNotification") and then passes data ("dataSent") to any observer. Finally, the dismiss command makes the second view controller disappear.

The entire SecondViewController.swift file should look like this:

```swift
import UIKit

class SecondViewController: UIViewController {

    @IBOutlet var myTextField: UITextField!

    override func viewDidLoad() {
        super.viewDidLoad()
        // Do any additional setup after loading the view.
    }

    @IBAction func closeButton(_ sender: UIButton) {
        let dataSent = myTextField.text
        NotificationCenter.default.post(name: NSNotification.
        Name(rawValue: "myNotification"), object: dataSent)
        dismiss(animated: true, completion: nil)
    }

}
```

38. Click the Run button or choose Product ➤ Run. The Simulator screen appears.

39. Click the button. The second view controller appears, displaying a button and a text field.

40. Click in the text field and type text such as **Hello, there!**

41. Click the button. This first view controller appears, displaying the text sent by the second view controller.

42. Choose Simulator ➤ Quit Simulator to return back to Xcode.

Summary

Most apps will likely contain multiple view controllers. Data entered into one view controller will likely need to be used by another view controller. By adding a shared() function in the AppDelegate.swift file, you can make the AppDelegate.swift file accessible to any other .swift file in a project. That way the AppDelegate.swift file can receive data from another file or send data to another file.

If the two view controllers are connected by a segue, you can pass data using the prepare for segue function. You can even name segues to make it easy to identify which segue is used to display the next view controller. Passing data from one view controller to another one, connected by a segue, passes data forward.

If you need to pass data backward from one view controller that does not have a segue leading to the previous view controller, you need to use a protocol as a middleman to temporarily hold data before passing it to the previous view controller.

Another way to pass data between view controllers is through the notification center. This can be especially handy to pass data to multiple view controllers at once or to view controllers that are not connected by a segue.

Passing data between different files helps avoid the use of global variables. By using different ways to pass data, your app can access data no matter which view controller it came from.

CHAPTER 8

Translating with Localization

Most people create apps in their native language, but if you translate your app into other languages, you could sell and distribute your app to other parts of the world. Translating text from one language to another requires an experienced translator, but from a technical point of view, how do you create a single app and let it display different languages?

The hard way is to create separate apps for each language. The easy way is to create a single app and use something called localization. The idea behind localization is that you create your app once, then instead of typing text to appear in the app, you use a special localized string that represents the text to display.

Now you store different text in separate files stored in a localization folder. Depending on the language the user's iOS device uses, your app then yanks out the correct file that matches the user's language. So if you wanted your app to display text in English, Arabic, and Russian, you would create one file containing English words to appear in your app, a second file containing Arabic words that represent equivalent English text, and a third file containing Russian words that represent equivalent text.

If the user switches the settings on their iOS device to display text in Russian, then your app will automatically replace all text with Russian text. If the user switches to Arabic, then your app will automatically replace all text with Arabic text. By creating text in different languages, you can create an app that adapts to different languages.

An app that supports localization will likely need to replace the following to adjust to different languages:

- Text in the user interface such as buttons and labels

- Images

- Text displayed by code

- The name of the app displayed on the Home screen

© Wallace Wang 2019
W. Wang, *Pro iPhone Development with Swift 5*, https://doi.org/10.1007/978-1-4842-4944-4_8

Besides changing text and images that appear on the user interface, localization also needs to adjust the app's user interface. For example, buttons that may look perfect when displayed in English may look too small when displaying equivalent text in German or may look too big when displaying equivalent text in Chinese. When designing a user interface, you need to consider the size of displayed text and make sure your user interface adapts to different size text.

Besides the size and text itself, you must also consider how different cultures and regions display dates and numbers. In some areas, people separate decimal numbers with a period such as 3.1415, while in others, people separate decimal numbers with a comma such as 3,1415.

Likewise, some areas display dates with the month first followed by the day and the year like June 4, 2019, while other places display dates differently such as 4 June 2019. So not only must your app display the proper text adjusted on the user interface to appear correctly, but your app must also recognize different number and date formats.

Designing the User Interface

When you place objects on the user interface that display text such as buttons or labels, you generally resize these objects so the text appears completely visible. However when replacing your native language with equivalent words in other languages, those words may be shorter or longer. That means your user interface objects need to adapt to text.

Xcode helps you design user interfaces in two ways. First, always define constraints on your user interface objects. This uses Auto Layout that allows the user interface to dynamically adapt to longer or shorter text of different languages. When setting constraints, avoid defining fixed values such as widths.

Second, Xcode offers a preview feature that lets you see how user interface objects will look with different pseudolanguages that mimic real languages by displaying extra-long text or text with accent characters above and below text. This lets you see if your user interface provides enough width and height to display different types of text.

To see how to design a user interface for different languages, follow these steps:

1. Create a Single View App from the iOS category and name it LocalApp.

2. Click the Main.storyboard file in the Navigator pane.

3. Click the Library icon and drag and drop three labels onto the view similar to Figure 8-1.

Figure 8-1. *Designing a user interface for multiple languages*

4. Choose View ➤ Assistant Editor ➤ Show Assistant Editor, or click the Assistant Editor icon in the upper right corner of the Xcode window. Xcode displays the Main.storyboard and ViewController. swift file side by side.

5. Click the double circle icon at the top in the assistant editor (the window on the right). A popup menu appears as shown in Figure 8-2.

Figure 8-2. *Choosing the preview of the user interface*

6. Choose Preview ➤ Main.storyboard (Preview). Xcode displays a preview of the Main.storyboard file in the assistant editor (the right pane). In the bottom right corner of the assistant editor, a Language button displays your native language such as English.

7. Click this Language button that displays your current language (such as English). A popup menu appears as shown in Figure 8-3.

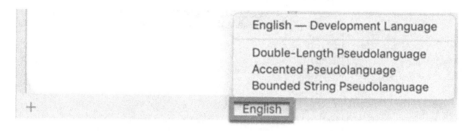

Figure 8-3. *Choosing a different pseudolanguage*

8. Choose Double-Length Pseudolanguage, which simply duplicates your current text to show you how longer text will look on your user interface. Notice that the labels cut off text, which tells you that the labels are not wide enough.

9. Click the Language button and choose Accented Pseudolanguage. Xcode displays text with accent characters above and below the text as shown in Figure 8-4.

$$L\overset{\circ}{a}\tilde{b}\ddot{e}\grave{l}$$

$$L\overset{\circ}{a}\tilde{b}\ddot{e}\grave{l}$$

$$L\overset{\circ}{a}\tilde{b}\ddot{e}\grave{l}$$

Figure 8-4. *Viewing accented pseudolanguage*

10. Click the Language button and choose Bounded String Pseudolanguage. Xcode displays the text cut off, which shows that the labels are not wide enough.

11. Click View Controller Scene in the Document Outline and then choose Editor ➤ Resolve Auto Layout Issues ➤ Reset to Suggested Constraints in the bottom half of the submenu. Xcode adds constraints to all the user interface objects.

12. Click the Language button in the assistant editor and choose Double-Length Pseudolanguage, Accented Pseudolanguage, and Bounded String Pseudolanguage. Notice that with constraints defined, Auto Layout automatically adjusts the width of the label to accommodate larger and shorter text.

13. Choose View ➤ Standard Editor ➤ Show Standard Editor, or click the Standard Editor icon in the upper right corner of the Xcode window.

By using Xcode's Auto Layout features (constraints) and the preview feature of the assistant editor, you can design a user interface that adapts to different languages.

Creating a Localization File

Localization works by creating multiple files to store the text you want to display in other languages. To create localization files, you need to define which languages you want your Xcode project to support. For each language you want your app to support, you'll need to define one localization setting.

To see how to add localization to a project, follow these steps:

1. Make sure the LocalApp project is loaded into Xcode.

2. Click the project name at the top of the Navigator pane as shown in Figure 8-5. Xcode displays information about the project in the middle pane.

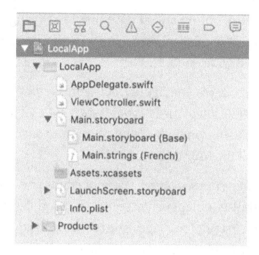

Figure 8-5. *Selecting the project name*

3. Click the Select popup menu in the upper left corner of the middle Xcode pane. A popup menu appears as shown in Figure 8-6.

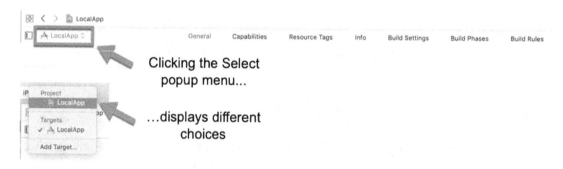

Figure 8-6. *Selecting the project name*

4. Click the project name (such as LocalApp) under the Project category at the top of the popup menu.

5. Click Info at the top of the middle Xcode pane. Xcode displays an Info pane as shown in Figure 8-7.

Figure 8-7. *The project Info pane*

6.   Click the + icon under the Localizations category. A popup menu appears of different languages as shown in Figure 8-8.

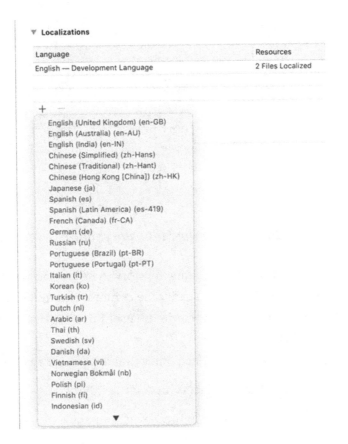

Figure 8-8. *The project Info pane*

7. Choose a language you want your app to support. For this example, choose French. A window appears, displaying all the files to localize.

8. Make sure all options are selected and click the Finish button. Notice that Xcode now displays a gray disclosure triangle to the left of the Main.storyboard file in the Navigator pane.

9. Click this gray disclosure triangle to the left of the Main.storyboard file. Notice that Xcode has now created two additional files: Main. storyboard (Base) that represents your native language and Main. strings (French) (or whatever language you chose) as shown in Figure 8-9.

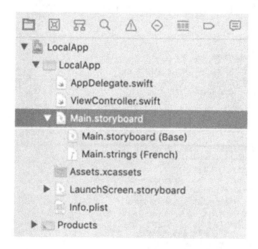

Figure 8-9. *Viewing multiple files in the Main.storyboard*

The Main.storyboard (Base) file contains the storyboard of your project where you can design the user interface. The Main.strings file contains text to display on the user interface. Xcode identifies the text to appear in the user interface by the Object ID, which appears on the Identity Inspector pane.

To view the Object ID of a user interface object, follow these steps:

1. Make sure the LocalApp project is loaded into Xcode.

2. Click the Main.storyboard file in the Navigator pane.

3. Click a user interface object and choose View ➤ Inspectors ➤ Show Identity Inspector, or click the Identity Inspector icon in the upper right corner of the Xcode window. The Object ID appears as shown in Figure 8-10.

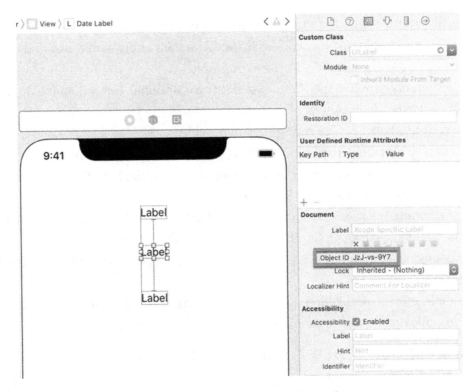

Figure 8-10. *Finding the Object ID of a user interface object*

Storing Text

The most common way to store text in an app is by simply typing it in code such as

var greeting = "Hello"

Unfortunately, such "hard coding" of text makes it difficult to change the text for other languages. Instead of typing the actual text to appear, we need to identify where we want text to appear and then let our app replace the text with the appropriate words depending on the user's language displayed on the iOS device.

If you're familiar with mail merge, the idea is to insert fields where you want specific names and addresses to appear. String localization works the same way. Instead of typing the actual text, we identify all text with NSLocalizedString like this:

```
var greeting = NSLocalizedString("Hello", comment: String)
```

You still type the actual text to appear but it appears as an NSLocalizedString. Then you'll need to create a list of NSLocalizedStrings with their equivalent translated text into another language such as French, Russian, or Arabic.

The comment portion of the NSLocalizedString is optional, but is meant to help a translator understand the context of the text. This can help a translator more accurately translate your text based on the comment you provide.

Once you've identified text in your code as NSLocalizedString, the next step is to edit the Main.strings file that shows the user interface (identified by Object ID) and its equivalent word or term in another language.

In our example, let's assume that we want to display a greeting in the top label, the date in the middle label, and a number in the bottom label. That means we'll need both our native language text and the foreign language text to appear in each label, identified by its Object ID.

When we define a localization file (such as French), Xcode automatically creates a Main.strings file that identifies user interface objects by their Object ID such as

```
/* Class = "UILabel"; text = "Label"; ObjectID = "FBY-Dx-bNj"; */
"FBY-Dx-bNj.text" = "Label";

/* Class = "UILabel"; text = "Label"; ObjectID = "JzJ-vs-9Y7"; */
"JzJ-vs-9Y7.text" = "Label";

/* Class = "UILabel"; text = "Label"; ObjectID = "aby-R3-3e4"; */
"aby-R3-3e4.text" = "Label";
```

What we need to do is customize this Main.strings file to display the foreign language equivalent. To do this with the LocalApp project, follow these steps:

1. Make sure the LocalApp project is loaded into Xcode and that you have defined a localization file for French.

2. Click the Main.storyboard file in the Navigator pane.

3. Choose View ➤ Assistant Editor ➤ Show Assistant Editor, or click the Assistant Editor icon in the upper right corner of the Xcode window. Xcode displays the Main.storyboard and ViewController. swift file side by side.

4. Move the mouse pointer over the top label, hold down the Control key, and Ctrl-drag underneath the class ViewController line in the ViewController.swift file.

5. Release the Control key and the left mouse button. A popup window appears.

6. Click in the Name text field, type **greetingLabel**, and click the Connect button.

7. Repeat steps 4–6 for the middle and bottom label, except name the middle label **dateLabel** and the bottom label **numberLabel**. You should have the following three IBOutlets:

```
@IBOutlet var greetingLabel: UILabel!
    @IBOutlet var dateLabel: UILabel!
    @IBOutlet var numberLabel: UILabel!
```

8. Edit the viewDidLoad method as follows:

```
override func viewDidLoad() {
        super.viewDidLoad()
        // Do any additional setup after loading the view.
        greetingLabel.text = NSLocalizedString("Hello",
        comment: "Formal greeting")
        dateLabel.text = NSLocalizedString("Date", comment:
        "Date format")
        numberLabel.text = NSLocalizedString("Number",
        comment: "Number format")
}
```

This code defines the text to appear in each label when the app runs. In this case, the top label will display "Hello", the middle label will display "Date", and the bottom label will display "Number".

9. Click the Main.strings (French) file in the Navigator pane under the Main.storyboard group. Notice that Xcode identifies each label by its Object ID, which is a mix of letters and numbers such as *JzJ-vs-9Y7*. (The exact Object ID of your labels will be different for every Xcode project.)

10. Edit the Main.strings file similar to the following:

```
/* Class = "UILabel"; text = "Label"; ObjectID = "FBY-Dx-bNj"; */
"FBY-Dx-bNj.text" = "Bonjour";

/* Class = "UILabel"; text = "Label"; ObjectID = "JzJ-vs-9Y7"; */
"JzJ-vs-9Y7.text" = "La date";

/* Class = "UILabel"; text = "Label"; ObjectID = "aby-R3-3e4"; */
"aby-R3-3e4.text" = "Nombre";
```

11. Click the Main.storyboard file in the Navigator pane.

12. Choose View ➤ Assistant Editor ➤ Show Assistant Editor, or click the Assistant Editor icon in the upper right corner of the Xcode window. Xcode displays the Main.storyboard and ViewController. swift file side by side.

13. Click the double circle icon at the top in the assistant editor (the window on the right). A popup menu appears (see Figure 8-2).

14. Choose Preview ➤ Main.storyboard (Preview). Xcode displays a preview of the Main.storyboard file in the assistant editor (the right pane). In the bottom right corner of the assistant editor, a Language button displays your native language such as English.

15. Click this Language button that displays your current language (such as English). A popup menu appears (see Figure 8-3).

16. Choose French. Notice that Xcode now displays the French translated text in the user interface as shown in Figure 8-11.

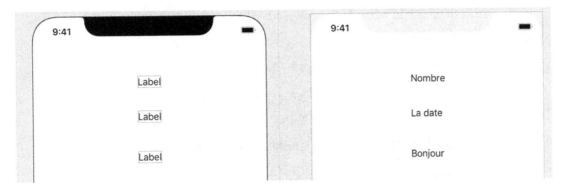

Figure 8-11. *The preview pane showing French text defined in the Main.strings (French) file*

17. Choose View ➤ Standard Editor ➤ Show Standard Editor, or click the Standard Editor icon in the upper right corner of the Xcode window.

Creating a Localized String File

At this point if you run our localApp, it will always display the text "Hello", "Date format", and "Number format" in the labels that appear on the user interface regardless of the iOS device's language preference. That's because even though we defined what French text to appear on the user interface through the Main.strings (French) file, we still need to define what strings to appear when the app actually runs. The Main.strings (French) file just lets us preview our user interface with different languages, but does not define which foreign language words to use while the app runs.

To do this, we need to define each text to replace everywhere we defined text as NSLocalizedString. That means we need to follow these steps:

- Replace text everywhere in our NSLocalizedString code to define placeholder text to appear.

- Create a localized string file that defines which native language terms to replace in the placeholder text.

- Create one or more additional localized string files to define which foreign language terms to replace in the placeholder text.

To see how to create localized string files for each foreign language you want to support, follow these steps:

1. Make sure the LocalApp project is loaded in Xcode.

2. Make sure you have created at least one localization file for an additional foreign language to support such as French.

3. Choose File ➤ New ➤ File. A template dialog appears.

4. Scroll down and click the Strings File icon under the Resource category under iOS as shown in Figure 8-12.

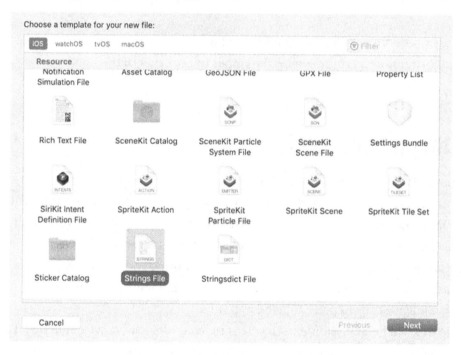

Figure 8-12. *Creating a Strings File*

5. Click the Next button. A dialog appears, asking where you want to save the file.

6. Change the file name to **Localizable.strings**.

7. Click the Create button. Xcode adds the Localizable.strings file
    to the Navigator pane and also displays a File Inspector pane as
    shown in Figure 8-13.

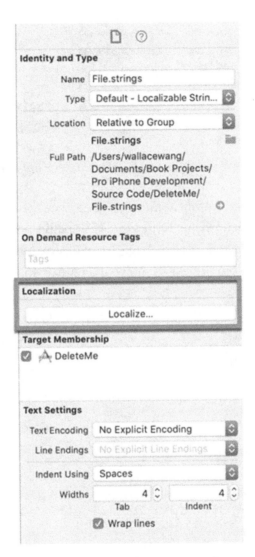

Figure 8-13. *The File Inspector pane for the Strings File*

8. Click the Localize button in the File Inspector pane. A dialog
    appears asking if you want to localize this file as shown in
    Figure 8-14.

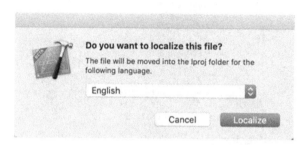

Figure 8-14. *Xcode asks if you want to localize the Strings File*

9. Click the Localize button. Xcode displays a Localization category
    in the File Inspector pane. Notice that your native language check
    box appears selected (such as English), while the other foreign
    language check box is clear as shown in Figure 8-15.

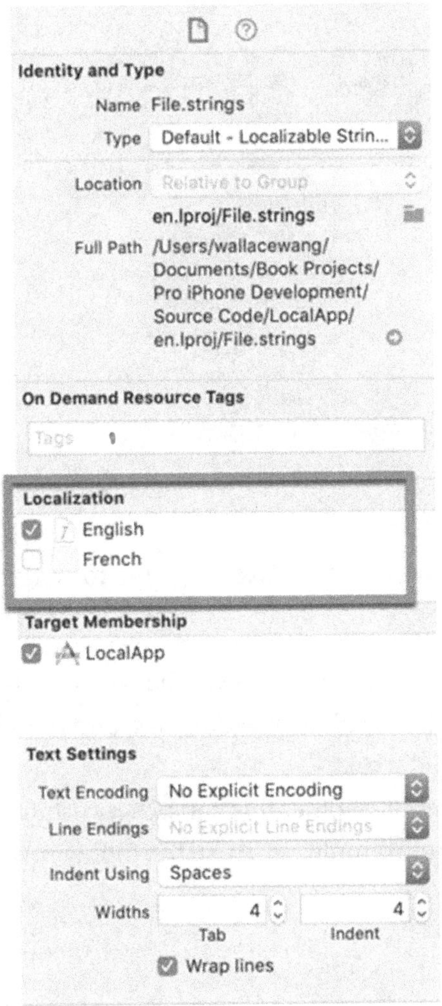

Identity and Type

Name File.strings

Type Default - Localizable Strin...

Location Relative to Group

en.lproj/File.strings

Full Path /Users/wallacewang/
Documents/Book Projects/
Pro iPhone Development/
Source Code/LocalApp/
en.lproj/File.strings

On Demand Resource Tags

Tags

Localization

☑ _I_ English

☐ French

Target Membership

☑ LocalApp

Text Settings

Text Encoding No Explicit Encoding

Line Endings No Explicit Line Endings

Indent Using Spaces

Widths 4   4
Tab   Indent

☑ Wrap lines

Figure 8-15. *The Localization category in the File Inspector pane*

10. Select the French check box. Xcode displays a gray disclosure triangle to the left of Localizable.strings in the Navigator pane.

11. Click the gray disclosure triangle that appears to the left of Localizable.strings. Notice that Xcode has now created two Localizable.strings, one for each language you want to support as shown in Figure 8-16.

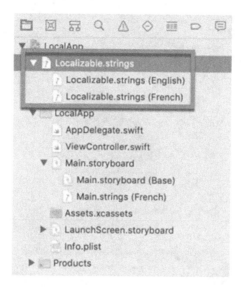

Figure 8-16. *Xcode creates a separate .strings file for each language you want to support in your app*

At this point, both .strings files are empty. What we need to do is go through our code, put placeholder text in all NSLocalizedStrings, and define what actual text we want to appear for each placeholder text.

The names we give our placeholder text can be any arbitrary text as long as it's distinct and unique. For our example, we'll use the following placeholder text:

```
[GREETING]
[DATE]
[NUMBER]
```

We could just as easily choose the following for our placeholder text, which shows that the placeholder text style isn't as important as its uniqueness:

```
Greeting.screen1
Date.screen1
Number.screen1
```

To see how to display text in foreign languages in our app, follow these steps:

1. Make sure the LocalApp project is loaded in Xcode.

2. Make sure you have created at least one localization file for an additional foreign language to support such as French.

3. Make sure you have created a separate .strings file for each
    language you want your app to support (such as two .strings files
    for English and French).

4. Click the ViewController.swift file in the Navigator pane.

5. Edit the viewDidLoad method as follows:

```swift
override func viewDidLoad() {
    super.viewDidLoad()
    // Do any additional setup after loading the view.
    greetingLabel.text = NSLocalizedString("[GREETING]", comment:
    "Formal greeting")
    dateLabel.text = NSLocalizedString("[DATE]", comment: "Date
    format")
    numberLabel.text = NSLocalizedString("[NUMBER]", comment:
    "Number format")
}
```

The entire ViewController.swift file should look like this:

```swift
import UIKit

class ViewController: UIViewController {

    @IBOutlet var greetingLabel: UILabel!
    @IBOutlet var dateLabel: UILabel!
    @IBOutlet var numberLabel: UILabel!

    override func viewDidLoad() {
        super.viewDidLoad()
        // Do any additional setup after loading the view.
        greetingLabel.text = NSLocalizedString("[GREETING]",
        comment: "Formal greeting")
        dateLabel.text = NSLocalizedString("[DATE]", comment:
        "Date format")
        numberLabel.text = NSLocalizedString("[NUMBER]",
        comment: "Number format")
    }

}
```

219

6. Click the Localizable.strings (English) file in the Navigator pane.

7. Add the following inside the Localizable.strings (English) file:

```
"[GREETING]" = "Hello";
"[DATE]" = "Date";
"[NUMBER]" = "Number";
```

Note   Make sure you put a semicolon at the end of each line or else Xcode won't know where the line ends and your project won't run.

---

8. Click the Localizable.strings (French) file in the Navigator pane.

9. Add the following inside the Localizable.strings (French) file:

```
"[GREETING]" = "Bonjour";
"[DATE]" = "La Date";
"[NUMBER]" = "Nombre";
```

Now that we've defined placeholder text along with English and French words to appear when the app runs, it's time to test the app as if the iOS Simulator were running in a different language. To change the language of the iOS Simulator, you need to define a different language in the project scheme.

To change the iOS Simulator language for your app to run in, follow these steps:

1. Click the Scheme button (it displays your project's name) that appears in the upper left corner of the Xcode window. A popup menu appears as shown in Figure 8-17.

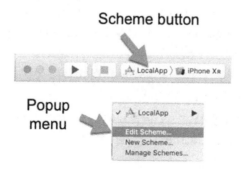

Figure 8-17. *The Scheme popup menu*

2. Choose Edit Scheme. A window appears.

3. Click Options.

4. Click Run in the left pane.

5. Click the Application Language popup menu and choose the
    language you want the Simulator to mimic such as French
    (see Figure 8-18).

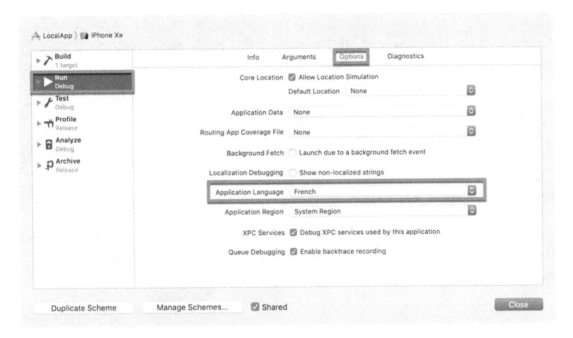

Figure 8-18. *The Application Language popup menu*

6. Click the Close button.

7. Click the Run button or choose Product ➤ Run. If you chose
    French as the Application Language in step 5, then the Simulator
    will load the French version of your app.

8. Choose Simulator ➤ Quit Simulator.

Localizing Images

To localize text, we needed to insert placeholder text in our code. Then we had to create two separate Localizable.strings files where each .strings file contained both the placeholder text we used and its actual text we want the app to use for different languages such as

```
"[GREETING]" = "Hello";
```

Localizing images is no different except you use placeholder text to specify a file name to display. Then you need a different image for each language such as an image for English and a different image for French such as

```
let imageFile = NSLocalizedString("[FLAG]", comment: "National flag")
 myImageView.image = UIImage(named: imageFile)
```

In each language's Localizable.strings file, you need to specify the exact file name such as

```
"[FLAG]" = "usaFlag";
```

Now you just need an image named usaFlag in your project. You can create your own images, have someone create one for you, or download images off the Internet. Some free sources of images include

- pixnio.com

- publicdomainvectors.org

- www.pdclipart.org

Visit one of these sites and download an American flag and a French flag image and make sure they have distinct names. For the purposes of this project, we'll assume the American flag image is called usaFlag.png and the French flag is called franceFlag.png.

Drag both flag images into your LocalApp project's Navigator pane. When a dialog appears, click Finish button. Xcode should now display the two flag images in the Navigator pane.

To see how to display these different images in an app, follow these steps:

1. Make sure the LocalApp project is loaded into Xcode.

2. Make sure you have added two flag images into the Navigator pane.

3. Click the Main.storyboard file in the Navigator pane.

4. Click the Library icon and drag and drop an Image View onto the view as shown in Figure 8-19.

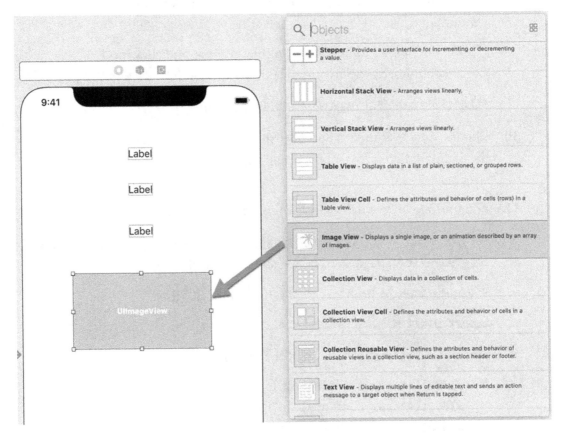

Figure 8-19. *Adding an Image View to the user interface*

5. Choose Editor ➤ Resolve Auto Layout Issues ➤ Reset to Suggested Constraints in the top half of the submenu. Xcode adds constraints to the image view.

6. Choose View ➤ Assistant Editor ➤ Show Assistant Editor, or click the Assistant Editor icon in the upper right corner of the Xcode window. Xcode displays the Main.storyboard file and the ViewController.swift file side by side.

7. Move the mouse pointer over the image view, hold down the Control key, and Ctrl-drag under the class ViewController line in the ViewController.swift file.

8. Release the Control key and the left mouse button. A popup window appears.

9. Click in the Name text field, type **flagImageView**, and click the Connect button. Xcode creates the following IBOutlet:

```
@IBOutlet var flagImageView: UIImageView!
```

10. Choose View ➤ Standard Editor ➤ Show Standard Editor, or click the Standard Editor icon in the upper right corner of the Xcode window.

11. Add the following two lines inside the viewDidLoad method:

```
let imageFile = NSLocalizedString("[FLAG]", comment: "National flag")
flagImageView.image = UIImage(named: imageFile)
```

The entire ViewController.swift file should look like this:

```
import UIKit

class ViewController: UIViewController {

    @IBOutlet var greetingLabel: UILabel!
    @IBOutlet var dateLabel: UILabel!
    @IBOutlet var numberLabel: UILabel!
    @IBOutlet var flagImageView: UIImageView!

    override func viewDidLoad() {
        super.viewDidLoad()
        // Do any additional setup after loading the view.
        greetingLabel.text = NSLocalizedString("[GREETING]",
        comment: "Formal greeting")
        dateLabel.text = NSLocalizedString("[DATE]", comment:
        "Date format")
        numberLabel.text = NSLocalizedString("[NUMBER]", comment:
        "Number format")
```

```
    let imageFile = NSLocalizedString("[FLAG]",
    comment: "National flag")
    flagImageView.image = UIImage(named: imageFile)
}

}
```

12. Click the Localizable.strings (English) file and add the following line:

    ```
    "[FLAG]" = "usaFlag";
    ```

13. Click the Localizable.strings (French) file and add the following line:

    ```
    "[FLAG]" = "franceFlag";
    ```

14. Click the Scheme button (it displays your project's name) that appears in the upper left corner of the Xcode window. A popup menu appears (see Figure 8-17).

15. Choose Edit Scheme. A window appears.

16. Click Options.

17. Click Run in the left pane.

18. Click the Application Language popup menu and choose the language you want the Simulator to mimic such as French (see Figure 8-18).

19. Click the Close button.

20. Click the Run button or choose Product ➤ Run. If you chose French as the Application Language in step 5, then the Simulator will load the French version of your app and display the French flag.

21. Repeat steps 14–20 except choose English in step 18. Notice that when you run the app under English, the American flag image appears on the Simulator screen.

22. Choose Simulator ➤ Quit Simulator.

Customizing the App Name

One final step to localization is customizing the app name. To do this, you need to create a separate InfoPlist.strings file for each language you want to support. Then in each InfoPlist.strings file, you define the CFBundleDisplayName value such as

```
"CFBundleDisplayName" = "App Name";
```

Whatever name you define here is what appears underneath the app's icon when it appears on the Home screen.

To see how to localize the name for your app, follow these steps:

1.   Make sure the LocalApp project is loaded into Xcode.

2.   Choose File ➤ New ➤ File. A template dialog appears.

3.   Scroll down and click the Strings File icon under the Resource category under iOS (see Figure 8-12).

4.   Click the Next button. A dialog appears, asking where you want to save the file.

5.   Change the file name to **InfoPlist.strings**.

6.   Click the Create button. Xcode adds the InfoPlist.strings file to the Navigator pane and also displays a File Inspector pane (see Figure 8-13).

7.   Click the Localize button in the File Inspector pane. A dialog appears asking if you want to localize this file (see Figure 8-14).

8.   Click the Localize button. Xcode displays a Localization category in the File Inspector pane. Notice that your native language check box appears selected (such as English), while the other foreign language check box is clear (see Figure 8-15).

9.   Select the French check box. Xcode displays a gray disclosure triangle to the left of InfoPlist.strings in the Navigator pane.

10.   Click the gray disclosure triangle that appears to the left of InfoPlist.strings. Notice that Xcode has now created two InfoPlist.strings, one for each language you want to support.

11. Click the InfoPlist.strings (English) file in the Navigator pane.

12. Add the following to the InfoPlist.strings (English) file:

    ```
    "CFBundleName" = "$(PRODUCT_NAME)";

    "CFBundleDisplayName" = "USA App";
    ```

13. Click the InfoPlist.strings (French) file in the Navigator pane.

14. Add the following to the InfoPlist.strings (French) file:

    ```
    "CFBundleDisplayName" = "French App";
    ```

15. Click the Run button or choose Product ➤ Run. The Simulator screen appears.

Note   Although you have defined the French version of the app to display "French App" as the app name on the Home screen, you must also change the language on the Simulator (or on a real iOS device) to make the app name change.

---

16. Choose Hardware ➤ Home to display the Home screen on the Simulator.

17. Click the Settings icon.

18. Click General.

19. Click Language & Region.

20. Click iPhone Language. A list of languages appears.

21. Choose French and then click Done. Notice that now your app displays "French App" on the Home screen. You may want to repeat steps 17–21 to change the Simulator's language back to your native language again.

22. Choose Simulator ➤ Quit Simulator to return back to Xcode.

Formatting Numbers and Dates

Every region tends to display numbers and dates in different ways. To make your app format data such as numbers and dates based on the user's language and region, use Apple's various Formatters such as NumberFormatter or DateFormatter.

Apple's various formatters can automatically adjust the appearance of data based on the iOS device's language and region. Your app just needs to calculate the data to appear on the user interface. To learn more about the different formatters available, read Apple's documentation (`https://developer.apple.com/documentation/foundation/formatter`).

The basic step to using a formatter involves choosing which formatter to use such as

```
let formatter = DateFormatter()
```

Then define one or more settings for how to format the information such as

```
formatter.dateStyle = .full
```

Finally, use the formatter to convert the data such as

```
let myDate = formatter.string(from: Date())
```

To see how to use formatters to display data in different languages and regions, follow these steps:

1. Make sure the LocalApp project is loaded into Xcode.

2. Click the ViewController.swift file in the navigator pane.

3. Edit the viewDidLoad method as follows:

```
override func viewDidLoad() {
    super.viewDidLoad()
    // Do any additional setup after loading the view.
    let formatter = DateFormatter()
    formatter.dateStyle = .full
    let myDate = formatter.string(from: Date())

    let formatter2 = NumberFormatter()
    formatter2.numberStyle = .currency
    let myMoney = formatter2.string(from: 123456)
```

```
greetingLabel.text = NSLocalizedString("[GREETING]",
comment: "Formal greeting")

dateLabel.text = NSLocalizedString("\(myDate)", comment:
"Date format")
numberLabel.text = NSLocalizedString("\(myMoney!)",
comment: "Number format")

let imageFile = NSLocalizedString("[FLAG]", comment:
"National flag")
flagImageView.image = UIImage(named: imageFile)
}
```

To see the differences in how the formatters work, we need to run our app as if we're in a different region of the world. So not only can we set the language for the Simulator to use, but we can also define the region for the Simulator to mimic.

The entire ViewController.swift file should look like this:

```
import UIKit

class ViewController: UIViewController {

    @IBOutlet var greetingLabel: UILabel!
    @IBOutlet var dateLabel: UILabel!
    @IBOutlet var numberLabel: UILabel!
    @IBOutlet var flagImageView: UIImageView!

    override func viewDidLoad() {
        super.viewDidLoad()
        // Do any additional setup after loading the view.
        let formatter = DateFormatter()
        formatter.dateStyle = .full
        let myDate = formatter.string(from: Date())

        let formatter2 = NumberFormatter()
        formatter2.numberStyle = .currency
        let myMoney = formatter2.string(from: 123456)
```

```
    greetingLabel.text = NSLocalizedString("[GREETING]",
    comment: "Formal greeting")

    dateLabel.text = NSLocalizedString("\(myDate)", comment:
    "Date format")
    numberLabel.text = NSLocalizedString("\(myMoney!)",
    comment: "Number format")

    let imageFile = NSLocalizedString("[FLAG]", comment:
    "National flag")
    flagImageView.image = UIImage(named: imageFile)
  }

}
```

4. Click the Scheme button (it displays your project's name) that
    appears in the upper left corner of the Xcode window. A popup
    menu appears (see Figure 8-17).

5. Choose Edit Scheme. A window appears.

6. Click Options.

7. Click Run in the left pane.

8. Click the Application Language popup menu and choose the
    language you want the Simulator to mimic such as French
    (see Figure 8-18).

9. Click the Application Region popup menu and choose a different
    region such as France as shown in Figure 8-20.

Figure 8-20. *Choosing a region for the Simulator to mimic*

10.   Click the Close button.

11.   Click the Run button or choose Product ➤ Run. If you chose French as the Application Language and France as the Application Region, then the Simulator will load the French version of your app and display the date and currency as shown in Figure 8-21.

Bonjour

mardi 12 mars 2019

123 456,00 €

Figure 8-21. *The French version of the app displays dates and currency in French format*

12. Choose Simulator ➤ Quit Simulator.

13. Repeat steps 5–10 except choose English as the language and the United States as the region. Notice that when you run the app under English, the date and currency appear in the format familiar to America as shown in Figure 8-22.

Hello

Tuesday, March 12, 2019

$123,456.00

Figure 8-22. *The English version of the app displays dates and currency in American format*

14. Choose Simulator ➤ Quit Simulator to return back to Xcode.

Summary

Creating an app in your native language may be fine, but if you want to reach other markets, you need to translate the text of your app into other languages. By using Xcode's preview feature, you can mimic other languages to make sure your user interface adapts to longer or shorter text. You can also display text in other languages to see how specific foreign words and phrases will look on your app's user interface.

Once you've defined the layout of your user interface and added constraints through Auto Layout, you can define all text in your app as NSLocalizedStrings. Then you can create a list of equivalent text to appear wherever your code finds an NSLocalizedString. You'll need to create a different file for each language you want your app to support.

Finally, don't forget that some languages and regions display data differently such as dates and numbers. Use a formatter to let your app adapt automatically to different regional differences. You can simulate different languages and regions by changing the scheme of your app before running it in the Simulator.

Creating an app can be hard work, so it only makes sense to distribute your app as broadly as possible so it can reach as many people as possible.

CHAPTER 9

Using 3D Touch

When Apple introduced the iPhone, smartphones often displayed rows of buttons or sported keyboards that folded or flipped out. Having to display so many buttons meant that the smartphone couldn't display much of the screen. Fortunately, the iPhone changed the smartphone world when they introduced the touch screen interface. Instead of crowding the smartphone with physical buttons, the touch screen interface displayed a single screen that could offer virtual buttons.

Such virtual buttons meant the screen could adapt to the user's needs. If you were typing an e-mail message, the virtual keyboard could display characters to type. If you were browsing the Internet, the virtual keyboard could display commonly used keys such as the @ symbol or the .com extension. Virtual keyboards made the iPhone far more versatile than older smartphones that relied on physical buttons.

The touch screen interface of the iPhone initially focused on taps and gestures. Tapping an icon on the screen would select it, while swiping on that same icon might make it move or slide away. While useful, such two-dimensional interaction can be limiting. That's why the latest iPhones offer a third way to interact with the touch screen called 3D Touch.

The idea behind 3D Touch is to add a third dimension to interaction with the touch screen: pressure. By pressing your finger on an icon for an extended period of time, 3D Touch can display shortcuts. By adding support for 3D Touch, your app can take advantage of the iPhone's latest touch gestures.

Note Only the iPhone 6s and later support 3D Touch with the exception of the iPhone Xr. The iPad does not support 3D Touch.

© Wallace Wang 2019
W. Wang, *Pro iPhone Development with Swift 5*, https://doi.org/10.1007/978-1-4842-4944-4_9

Understanding 3D Touch

3D Touch first appeared on the iPhone 6s and has been a standard feature of every iPhone (with the exception of the iPhone Xr) since then. The two most common ways to interact with 3D Touch are from the Home screen and from within your app itself. 3D Touch works by detecting the amount of pressure a user places on the touch screen.

When you use 3D Touch from the Home screen, a popup menu appears, listing several common actions you're most likely to want from that app. This popup menu can display shortcuts, called Quick Actions, that consist of up to two lines of text and an icon as shown in Figure 9-1.

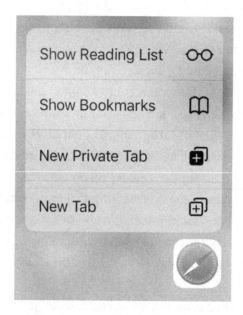

Figure 9-1.   *3D Touch can display Quick Actions*

By tapping on a Quick Action, users can immediately access common features of an app. The second common way to use 3D Touch is within an app itself, which can involve three steps:

- Peek availability

- Peek

- Peek quick actions

When you first press on an item within an app, peek availability blurs the surrounding screen to show you that it supports 3D Touch as shown in Figure 9-2.

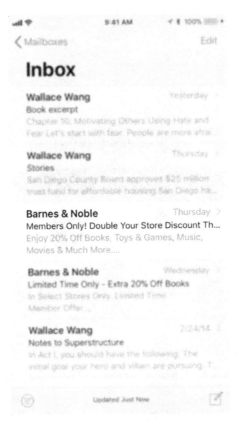

Figure 9-2. *Peek availability blurs the surrounding area to show that the app supports 3D Touch*

Once an app reveals that it supports 3D Touch through blurring the screen, the user can continue pressing to peek at more detailed information in a window that doesn't quite fill up the screen. This Peek action lets you view information without taking the time to open it as shown in Figure 9-3.

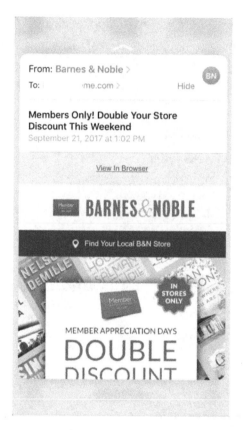

Figure 9-3. *Peek lets you view information without opening it fully in an app*

If you release your finger from the screen, this Peek information will disappear. However, if you swipe up, a menu of Peek Quick Actions appears at the bottom of the screen. This lets you perform common actions without opening the data within the app. At this point, the user can stop touching the screen to tap on one of the Peek Quick Actions as shown in Figure 9-4.

Figure 9-4. *A Peek Quick Action menu lets the user choose a common action for the displayed data*

To make this Peek Quick Action menu go away, the user can tap the top of the screen.

Detecting 3D Touch Availability

Since your app may be used on an iPad, iPhone Xr, or iPhone model earlier than the iPhone 6s, your app must first check if a device supports 3D Touch or not. To see how 3D Touch works, follow these steps:

1. Create a new iOS Single View App project and name it 3DTouchApp.

2. Click the ViewController.swift file in the Navigator pane.

3. Add the following underneath the viewDidLoad method:

```
override func touchesMoved(_ touches: Set<UITouch>, with event:
UIEvent?) {
        if touches.first != nil {
            if #available(iOS 9.0, *) {
                if traitCollection.forceTouchCapability ==
                UIForceTouchCapability.available {
                    print ("3D Touch available!")
                } else {
                    print ("3D Touch not available")
                }
            } else {
                print ("Need iOS 9 or higher")
            }
        }
}
```

This code first detects a touch and then checks if the device is
running iOS 9 or higher. That's because 3D Touch is only supported
by iOS 9 and higher. The next if statement checks if 3D Touch
capability is available. If 3D Touch is available and the device is
running iOS 9 or higher, then the preceding code prints "3D Touch
available!" It's best to ensure a device can support 3D Touch to avoid
possible crashes.

Note   To test 3D Touch in the Simulator, you need a Magic Trackpad that's either
built-in to a Macintosh laptop or a separate accessory that works with a desktop
Macintosh.

---

4. Click the Scheme button in the upper left corner of the Xcode
window and choose iPhone 8 as shown in Figure 9-5.

Figure 9-5. Choosing an iPhone 8 in the Scheme button

5. Click the Run button or choose Product ➤ Run. The Simulator screen appears.

6. Choose Hardware ➤ Touch Pressure and make sure a check mark appears in front of Use Trackpad Force as shown in Figure 9-6.

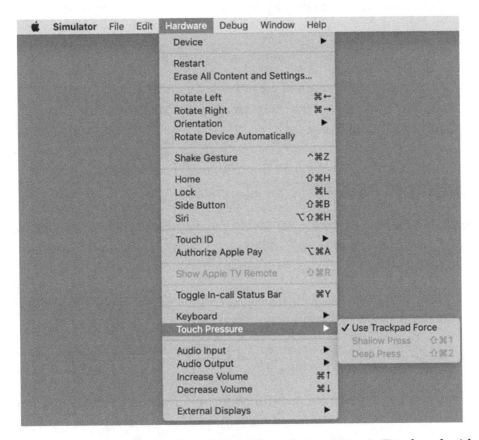

Figure 9-6. *Choosing Use Trackpad Force if you have a Magic Trackpad with your Macintosh*

7. Move the mouse pointer over the Simulator screen and press and hold down on the trackpad to simulate a 3D Touch. Notice that the debug area in Xcode displays the message "3D Touch is available!"

8. Choose Simulator ➤ Quit Simulator to return back to Xcode.

9. Click the Scheme button in the upper left corner of the Xcode window and choose iPhone Xr.

10. Click the Run button or choose Product ➤ Run. The Simulator screen appears.

11. Move the mouse pointer over the Simulator screen and press and hold down on the trackpad to simulate a 3D Touch. Notice that the debug area in Xcode now displays the message "3D Touch is not available!"

12. Choose Simulator ➤ Quit Simulator to return back to Xcode.

13. Click the Scheme button in the upper left corner of the Xcode window and choose iPhone 8 so you can continue testing 3D Touch in the Simulator.

Detecting Pressure

Once you know that a device offers 3D Touch, you may want to detect the pressure from the user pressing down on the screen. To simulate 3D Touch, you need to run your app on one of the following:

- In the Simulator running on a laptop Macintosh with a touch pad or a desktop Macintosh with a Magic Trackpad

- On an iPhone 6s or later (except for an iPhone Xr) connected to a Macintosh through its USB cable

The two properties for detecting the pressure of 3D Touch includes "force" and "maximumPossibleForce". The force property measures the current amount of pressure, while the maximumPossibleForce property defines the maximum pressure iOS can recognize.

To see how to detect pressure with 3D Touch, follow these steps:

1. Make sure the 3DTouchApp project is loaded into Xcode.

2. Click the Main.storyboard file in the Navigator pane.

3. Click the Library icon and drag and drop a label onto the view. You may want to expand the width of the label.

4. Choose Editor ➤ Resolve Auto Layout Issues ➤ Reset to Suggested Constraints. Xcode adds constraints to the label.

5. Choose View ➤ Assistant Editor ➤ Show Assistant Editor, or click the Assistant Editor icon in the upper right corner of the Xcode window. Xcode shows the Main.storyboard side by side with the ViewController.swift file.

6. Move the mouse pointer over the label, hold down the Control key, and Ctrl-drag under the class ViewController line in the ViewController.swift file.

7. Release the Control key and the left mouse button. A popup window appears.

8. Click in the Name text field, type **forceLabel**, and click the Connect button. Xcode creates the following IBOutlet:

    ```
    @IBOutlet var forceLabel: UILabel!
    ```

9. Choose View ➤ Standard Editor ➤ Show Standard Editor, or click the Standard Editor icon in the upper right corner of the Xcode window.

10. Click the ViewController.swift file in the Navigator pane.

11. Edit the touchesMoved function as follows:

    ```
    override func touchesMoved(_ touches: Set<UITouch>, with event:
    UIEvent?) {
    if touches.first != nil {
        if #available(iOS 9.0, *) {
            if traitCollection.forceTouchCapability ==
            UIForceTouchCapability.available {
                //print ("3D Touch available!")
                let touch = touches.first
                let force = Float(touch!.force)/Float(touch!.
                maximumPossibleForce)
                forceLabel.text = "\(force * 100)% force"
    ```

```
        } else {
            print ("3D Touch not available")
        }
    } else {
        print ("Need iOS 9 or higher")
    }
}
}
```

Once we know that 3D Touch is available (touches.first is not nil), then we can assign a constant "touch" to represent the value stored in touches.first. Then we divide the force of the touch by the maximumPossibleForce to get a numeric result (converted into Float data types). Finally, we display this force, multiplied by 100 to show a percentage, in the label on the user interface.

12. Click the Run button or choose Product ➤ Run. The Simulator screen appears.

13. Click the Simulator screen with a trackpad press down. The Simulator screen displays the amount of force as shown in Figure 9-7.

Figure 9-7. Detecting the amount of pressure from a 3D Touch

14.   Choose Simulator ➤ Quit Simulator to return back to Xcode.

Creating Home Screen Quick Actions

Quick Actions give the user the option of opening an app using different options. For example, when you use Quick Actions on the Safari icon on the Home screen, you'll have the option of opening a new tab, a privacy tab, a reading list, or a list of bookmarks (see Figure 9-1). Quick Actions provide shortcuts to commonly used features in an app.

There are two parts to creating Quick Actions. First, you need to create a menu of up to four Quick Actions by defining multiple strings in a dictionary stored in the info.plist file. Each Quick Action can display a title, a subtitle, and an icon. Second, you need to write Swift code in a method to handle every Quick Action.

To see how to create Home screen Quick Actions, follow these steps:

1. Make sure the 3DTouchApp project is loaded into Xcode.

2. Click the Info.plist file in the Navigator pane.

3. Click the mouse pointer over the up/down arrow icons that appear to the right of any key item in the property list. A + and a – icon appears to the right of the up/down arrow as shown in Figure 9-8.

Key	Type	Value
▼ Information Property List	Dictionary	(13 items)
Localization native development re... ↕	String	$(DEVELOPMENT_LANGUAGE)
Executable file ↕	String	$(EXECUTABLE_NAME)
Bundle identifier ↕	String	$(PRODUCT_BUNDLE_IDENTIFIER)
InfoDictionary version ↕	String	6.0
Bundle name ↕	String	$(PRODUCT_NAME)
Bundle OS Type code ↕	String	APPL
Bundle versions string, short ↕	String	1.0
Bundle version ↕	String	1
Application requires iPhone enviro... ↕	Boolean	YES
Launch screen interface file base... ↕	String	LaunchScreen
Main storyboard file base name ↕	String	Main
▶ Required device capabilities ↕	Array	(1 item)
▶ Supported interface orientati... ↕ ⊕⊖	Array	(3 items)

Figure 9-8. *Clicking on the up/down arrows displays a + and – icon*

4. Click the + icon to create a new property list item. Xcode creates a new property list item.

5. Click in the new property list item key column, type **UIApplicationShortcutItems**, and press Enter.

6. Click the popup menu in the Type column and choose Array as shown in Figure 9-9.

Key	Type	Value
▼ Information Property List	Dictionary	(14 items)
Localization native development re... ⌄	String	$(DEVELOPMENT_LANGUAGE)
Executable file ⌄	String	$(EXECUTABLE_NAME)
Bundle identifier ⌄	String	$(PRODUCT_BUNDLE_IDENTIFIER)
InfoDictionary version ⌄	String	6.0
Bundle name ⌄	String	$(PRODUCT_NAME)
Bundle OS Type code ⌄	String	APPL
Bundle versions string, short ⌄	String	1.0
Bundle version ⌄	String	1
Application requires iPhone enviro... ⌄	Boolean	YES
Launch screen interface file base... ⌄	String	LaunchScreen
Main storyboard file base name ⌄	String	Main
▶ Required device capabilities ⌄	Array	(1 item)
▶ Supported interface orientations ⌄	Array	(3 items)
▶ UIApplicationShortcutItems ⌄ ⊕ ⊝	Array	⌄ (0 items)

Figure 9-9. *Defining a new property list item as UIApplicationShortcutItems as an Array type*

7. Click the + icon to create a new property list item and name this Item 0 with a Type of Dictionary.

8. Click the + icon to create a new property list item and name this Item 1 with a Type of Dictionary.

9. Right-click Item 0. A popup menu appears as shown in Figure 9-10.

Figure 9-10. *Indenting a row in the Info.plist file*

10. Choose Shift Row Right. Xcode indents Item 0 under the UIApplicationShortcutItems key.

11.   Right-click Item 1. A popup menu appears (see Figure 9-10).

12.   Choose Shift Row Right. Xcode indents Item 1 under the UIApplicationShortcutItems key.

13.   Create three additional rows under Item 0 and Item 1 and shift them to the right so they appear indented under each item.

14.   Name these three rows under each item as follows:

   • UIApplicationShortcutItemTitle – Defines the Quick Action shortcut title (required)

   • UIApplicationShortcutItemSubtitle – Defines the Quick Action shortcut subtitle that appears in a smaller font size under the title text (optional)

   • UIApplicationShortcutItemType – Defines a required string to create a Quick Action shortcut menu (required)

For our 3D Touch app, we'll just create two Quick Action shortcuts to create nine new rows in the Information Property List that looks like the following table and Figure 9-11:

Key	Type	Value
UIApplicationShortcutItems	Array	(2 items)
Item 0	Dictionary	(3 items)
UIApplicationShortcutItemTitle	String	View
UIApplicationShortcutItemSubtitle	String	View favorite items
UIApplicationShortcutItemType	String	$(PRODUCT_BUNDLE_IDENTIFIER).First
Item 1	Dictionary	(3 items)
UIApplicationShortcutItemTitle	String	Share
UIApplicationShortcutItemSubtitle	String	Share items with friends
UIApplicationShortcutItemType	String	$(PRODUCT_BUNDLE_IDENTIFIER).Second

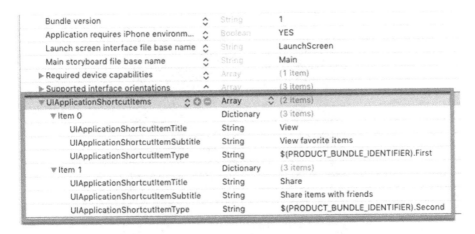

Bundle version	○	String	1
Application requires iPhone environm...	○	Boolean	YES
Launch screen interface file base name	○	String	LaunchScreen
Main storyboard file base name	○	String	Main
▶ Required device capabilities	○	Array	(1 item)
▶ Supported interface orientations	^	Array	(3 items)
▼ UIApplicationShortcutItems	○○⊖	Array	(2 items)
▼ Item 0		Dictionary	(3 items)
UIApplicationShortcutItemTitle		String	View
UIApplicationShortcutItemSubtitle		String	View favorite items
UIApplicationShortcutItemType		String	$(PRODUCT_BUNDLE_IDENTIFIER).First
▼ Item 1		Dictionary	(3 items)
UIApplicationShortcutItemTitle		String	Share
UIApplicationShortcutItemSubtitle		String	Share items with friends
UIApplicationShortcutItemType		String	$(PRODUCT_BUNDLE_IDENTIFIER).Second

Figure 9-11. *Defining Quick Action shortcuts in the Information Property List*

Note   Use a real iPhone that supports 3D Touch to test your app.

---

15. Connect an iPhone that supports 3D Touch to your Macintosh through a USB cable.

16. Click the Scheme button in the upper left corner of the Xcode window and choose the iPhone connected to your Macintosh as shown in Figure 9-12.

Figure 9-12. *You must choose an actual iOS device that supports 3D Touch to test your app*

17. Click the Run button or choose Product ➤ Run. The 3DTouchApp appears on your iPhone.

18. Press the Home button or swipe up from the bottom of the screen to return back to the Home screen.

19. Press firmly on the 3DTouchApp icon on the Home screen. The Quick Action shortcut menu appears as shown in Figure 9-13.

Figure 9-13. *Quick Action shortcuts appear next to the icon*

20. Click the Stop button in Xcode to stop running the app.

    If you notice the Quick Action menu, the title appears in large font and the subtitle appears in a smaller font. However, you may notice a black dot. This is where you can define an icon to appear. Apple provides icons to represent common tasks such as sharing, adding, or choosing a favorite item. To view a complete list of available icons, visit `https://developer.apple.com/documentation/uikit/uiapplicationshortcuticontype`.

21. Click the Info.plist file in the Navigator pane.

22. Create an additional row under Item 0 and Item 1 for each Quick Action shortcut that defines UIApplicationShortcutItemIconType. Then define this as an icon using UIApplicationShortcutIconTypeFavorite and UIApplicationShortcutIconTypeShare as shown in Figure 9-14.

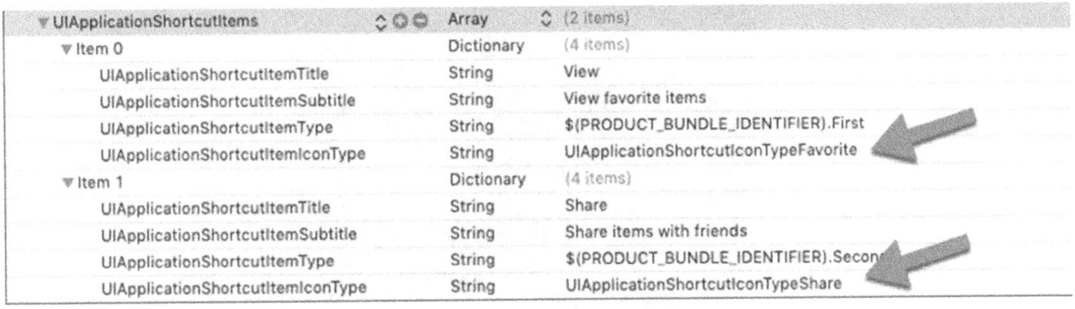

▼ UIApplicationShortcutItems	Array	(2 items)
▼ Item 0	Dictionary	(4 items)
UIApplicationShortcutItemTitle	String	View
UIApplicationShortcutItemSubtitle	String	View favorite items
UIApplicationShortcutItemType	String	$(PRODUCT_BUNDLE_IDENTIFIER).First
UIApplicationShortcutItemIconType	String	UIApplicationShortcutIconTypeFavorite
▼ Item 1	Dictionary	(4 items)
UIApplicationShortcutItemTitle	String	Share
UIApplicationShortcutItemSubtitle	String	Share items with friends
UIApplicationShortcutItemType	String	$(PRODUCT_BUNDLE_IDENTIFIER).Secon
UIApplicationShortcutItemIconType	String	UIApplicationShortcutIconTypeShare

Figure 9-14. *Adding icons to the Quick Action menu items*

Note   Make sure you spell everything (including uppercase and lowercase letters) exactly right. Be especially careful when defining an icon type. Under the Key column heading, you must use UIApplicationShortcutItemIconType (UI Application Shortcut Item Icon Type) but under the Value column heading, you need to use UIApplicationShortcutIconType (UI Application Shortcut Icon Type) followed by the icon name you want to use such as Share or Favorite.

23. Make sure your project will run on an iPhone connected to your Macintosh. Then click the Run button or choose Product ➤ Run. The 3DTouchApp's screen appears on the iPhone.

24. Press the Home button or swipe up from the bottom of the screen to return back to the Home screen.

25. Press firmly on the 3DTouchApp icon on the Home screen. The Quick Action shortcut menu appears with icons as shown in Figure 9-15.

Figure 9-15. *Displaying icons in the Quick Action menu items*

26.   Click the Stop button in Xcode to stop running the app.

Responding to Quick Action Items

Once you've created a list of Quick Action menu items, the last step is to write Swift code to respond to the Quick Action the user chose. To do that, you need to write Swift code in the AppDelegate.swift file of your project. The AppDelegate.swift file needs to contain an enumeration that identifies each Quick Action item with a descriptive name.

There are two parts to creating an enumeration. First, you must create an enumeration that has an equal number of Quick Actions you want to display. So if you want to respond to four Quick Actions, you must have four items defined in the enumeration.

In our project, we just have two Quick Action menu items, so our enumeration only needs to define two items like this:

```
enum MenuItems: String {
    case First
    case Second
}
```

The exact name of your enumeration is arbitrary (such as MenuItems). Also the name you give for each item in the enumeration is also arbitrary (First and Second). Next, we need to initialize the enumeration items using the following code as part of the enumeration:

```
enum MenuItems: String {
    case First
    case Second

    init?(fullType: String) {
        guard let last = fullType.components(separatedBy: ".").last
        else { return nil }

        self.init(rawValue: last)
    }

    var type: String {
        return Bundle.main.bundleIdentifier! + ".\(self.rawValue)"
    }
}
```

To respond to Quick Action items, we need a variable of the type UIApplicationShortcutItem in the AppDelegate.swift file like this:

```
var launchedShortcutItem: UIApplicationShortcutItem?
```

The AppDelegate.swift file needs two application functions. The first application function runs when the user selects a Quick Action item. This function stores the selected Quick Action selection in the launchedShortcutItem variable like this:

```
func application(_ application: UIApplication,
didFinishLaunchingWithOptions launchOptions: [UIApplication.
LaunchOptionsKey: Any]?) -> Bool {
```

```
    if let shortcutItem = launchOptions?[UIApplication.
    LaunchOptionsKey.shortcutItem] as? UIApplicationShortcutItem {

        launchedShortcutItem = shortcutItem
    }
    return true
}
```

The second application function does nothing more than call a function to handle the completion of the user choosing a Quick Action item:

```
func application(_ application: UIApplication, performActionFor
shortcutItem: UIApplicationShortcutItem, completionHandler: @escaping
(Bool) -> Void) {

    completionHandler(handleShortCutItem(shortcutItem))
}
```

The preceding function calls a function called handleShortCutItem (this name is arbitrary and can be anything you want to call it). This handleShortCutItem function does the actual work of deciding how to respond to which Quick Action item the user chose.

Now we need to write the handleShortCutItem function to respond to the Quick Action the user chose. There are two ways to identify the user's chosen Quick Action. One way is to identify the choice defined by the enumeration. The second way is to identify the localizedTitle property, which identifies the UIApplicationShortcutItemTitle for the Quick Action shortcut you defined in the Info.plist file.

However you want to identify the Quick Action the user chose, you'll likely need a switch statement to identify the chosen Quick Action and then respond to it. In our project, we'll just identify the Quick Action chosen. Add the handleShortCutItem function to the AppDelegate.swift file as follows:

```
func handleShortCutItem(_ shortcutItem: UIApplicationShortcutItem) ->
Bool {
    var handled = false

    guard MenuItems(fullType: shortcutItem.type) != nil else {
        return false
    }
```

```swift
guard let shortCutType = shortcutItem.type as String? else {
    return false
}

switch (shortCutType) {
case MenuItems.First.type:
    print ("View favorites")
    handled = true
case MenuItems.Second.type:
    print ("Share")
    handled = true
default:
    break
}

let alertController = UIAlertController(title: "Shortcut Chosen",
message: "\"\(shortcutItem.localizedTitle)\"", preferredStyle:
.alert)
let okAction = UIAlertAction(title: "OK", style: .default,
handler: nil)
alertController.addAction(okAction)
window!.rootViewController?.present(alertController, animated:
true, completion: nil)

    return handled
}
```

First, we need to declare a Boolean variable called handled and set it to false. Then we have two guard statements to ensure that a Quick Action was actually chosen. The switch statement identifies the chosen Quick Action by its enumeration value. Then an alert dialog appears to display the chosen Quick Action by its UIApplicationShortcutItemTitle value.

To see how to respond to Quick Action items, follow these steps:

1. Make sure the 3DTouchApp project is loaded into Xcode.

2. Click the AppDelegate.swift file in the Navigator pane.

3. Modify the AppDelegate.swift file so it appears like this:

```swift
import UIKit

@UIApplicationMain
class AppDelegate: UIResponder, UIApplicationDelegate {

    enum MenuItems: String {
        case First
        case Second

        init?(fullType: String) {
            guard let last = fullType.components(separatedBy:
            ".").last else { return nil }

            self.init(rawValue: last)
        }

        var type: String {
            return Bundle.main.bundleIdentifier! + ".\(self.rawValue)"
        }
    }

    var window: UIWindow?

    var launchedShortcutItem: UIApplicationShortcutItem?

    func application(_ application: UIApplication,
    didFinishLaunchingWithOptions launchOptions: [UIApplication.
    LaunchOptionsKey: Any]?) -> Bool {

        if let shortcutItem = launchOptions?[UIApplication.
        LaunchOptionsKey.shortcutItem] as?
        UIApplicationShortcutItem {

            launchedShortcutItem = shortcutItem
        }
        return true
    }

    func application(_ application: UIApplication,
    performActionFor shortcutItem: UIApplicationShortcutItem,
    completionHandler: @escaping (Bool) -> Void) {
```

```swift
        completionHandler(handleShortCutItem(shortcutItem))
}

func handleShortCutItem(_ shortcutItem:
UIApplicationShortcutItem) -> Bool {
    var handled = false

    guard MenuItems(fullType: shortcutItem.type) != nil else {
        return false
    }

    guard let shortCutType = shortcutItem.type as String? else {
        return false
    }

    switch (shortCutType) {
    case MenuItems.First.type:
        print ("View favorites")
        handled = true
    case MenuItems.Second.type:
        print ("Share")
        handled = true
    default:
        break
    }

    let alertController = UIAlertController(title: "Shortcut
    Chosen", message: "\"\(shortcutItem.localizedTitle)\"",
    preferredStyle: .alert)
    let okAction = UIAlertAction(title: "OK", style: .default,
    handler: nil)
    alertController.addAction(okAction)
    window!.rootViewController?.present(alertController,
    animated: true, completion: nil)

    return handled
}
```

```swift
func applicationWillResignActive(_ application: UIApplication) {

}

func applicationDidEnterBackground(_ application: UIApplication) {

}

func applicationWillEnterForeground(_ application: UIApplication) {

}

func applicationDidBecomeActive(_ application: UIApplication) {

}

func applicationWillTerminate(_ application: UIApplication) {

}

}
```

4. Make sure your project will run on an iPhone connected to your Macintosh. Then click the Run button or choose Product ➤ Run. The 3DTouchApp's screen appears on the iPhone.

5. Press the Home button or swipe up from the bottom of the screen to return back to the Home screen.

6. Press firmly on the 3DTouchApp icon on the Home screen. The Quick Action shortcut menu appears with icons (see Figure 9-15).

7. Tap on a Quick Action item. An alert dialog appears, displaying your chosen Quick Action by its UIApplicationShortcutItemTitle value as shown in Figure 9-16.

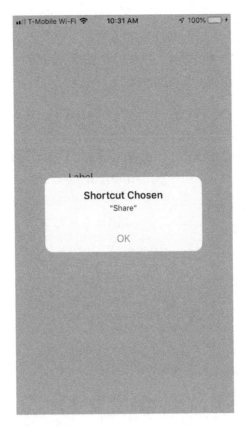

Figure 9-16. *An alert dialog shows the Quick Action shortcut the user chose*

8.   Tap OK to make the alert dialog go away.

9.   Click the Stop button in Xcode.

Adding Dynamic Home Screen Quick Actions

The two Quick Actions we defined so far are known as static actions because they appear all the time. A second type of Quick Action is known as Dynamic Quick Actions, which you can create in Swift code to appear after your app is already running. This allows the Quick Action menu to display different options depending on what the user might be doing at the moment.

Note   Remember, you can only have a maximum of four Quick Actions such as one static Quick Action and three Dynamic Quick Actions or four static Quick Actions and zero Dynamic Quick Actions.

To add Dynamic Quick Actions, you must modify the enumeration for each Dynamic Quick Action you want to add. In our project, we had two items in our enumeration so we need to add two more for the two Dynamic Quick Actions we want to add such as

```swift
enum MenuItems: String {
    case First
    case Second
    case Third
    case Fourth

    init?(fullType: String) {
        guard let last = fullType.components(separatedBy: ".").last
        else { return nil }

        self.init(rawValue: last)
    }

    var type: String {
        return Bundle.main.bundleIdentifier! + ".\(self.rawValue)"
    }
}
```

Note   The Quick Action defined by the top enumeration value will appear at the bottom of the Quick Action menu. So the Quick Action defined by Fourth will appear at the top, the one defined by Third will appear second, the one defined by Second will appear third, and the one defined by First will appear at the bottom as shown in Figure 9-17.

Figure 9-17. *Displaying the Quick Action menu with a maximum of four items*

Now we need to modify the existing application didFinishLaunchingWithOptions functions in two ways. First, we need to define each Dynamic Quick Action by identifying its place in the enumeration list (such as Third and Fourth) and giving it a localizedTitle and localizedSubtitle and a corresponding icon (UIApplicationShortcutIcon) such as

```
if let shortcutItems = application.shortcutItems, shortcutItems.
isEmpty {

    let shortcut3 = UIMutableApplicationShortcutIt
    em(type: MenuItems.Third.type, localizedTitle:
    "Play", localizedSubtitle: "Play audio", icon:
    UIApplicationShortcutIcon(type: .play)
    )
```

261

```
let shortcut4 = UIMutableApplicationShortcutIte
m(type: MenuItems.Fourth.type, localizedTitle:
"Add", localizedSubtitle: "Add an item", icon:
UIApplicationShortcutIcon(type: .add)
)

// Update the application providing the initial "dynamic"
shortcut items
application.shortcutItems = [shortcut3, shortcut4]

}
```

To see how to add Dynamic Quick Action items, follow these steps:

1. Make sure the 3DTouchApp project is loaded into Xcode.

2. Click the AppDelegate.swift file in the Navigator pane.

3. Modify the AppDelegate.swift file so it appears like this:

```
import UIKit

@UIApplicationMain
class AppDelegate: UIResponder, UIApplicationDelegate {

    enum MenuItems: String {
        case First
        case Second
        case Third
        case Fourth

        init?(fullType: String) {
            guard let last = fullType.components(separatedBy:
            ".").last else { return nil }

            self.init(rawValue: last)
        }

        var type: String {
            return Bundle.main.bundleIdentifier! + ".\(self.rawValue)"
        }
    }
```

```swift
var window: UIWindow?

var launchedShortcutItem: UIApplicationShortcutItem?

func application(_ application: UIApplication,
didFinishLaunchingWithOptions launchOptions: [UIApplication.
LaunchOptionsKey: Any]?) -> Bool {
    // If a shortcut was launched, display its information and
    take the appropriate action
    if let shortcutItem = launchOptions?[UIApplication.
    LaunchOptionsKey.shortcutItem] as?
    UIApplicationShortcutItem {

        launchedShortcutItem = shortcutItem
    }

    // Install our two extra dynamic Quick Action items
    if let shortcutItems = application.shortcutItems,
    shortcutItems.isEmpty {

        let shortcut3 = UIMutableApplicationShortcutIt
        em(type: MenuItems.Third.type, localizedTitle:
        "Play", localizedSubtitle: "Play audio", icon:
        UIApplicationShortcutIcon(type: .play)
        )

        let shortcut4 = UIMutableApplicationShortcutIte
        m(type: MenuItems.Fourth.type, localizedTitle:
        "Add", localizedSubtitle: "Add an item", icon:
        UIApplicationShortcutIcon(type: .add)
        )

        // Update the application providing the initial
        "dynamic" shortcut items
        application.shortcutItems = [shortcut3, shortcut4]

    }

    return true
}
```

```swift
func application(_ application: UIApplication,
performActionFor shortcutItem: UIApplicationShortcutItem,
completionHandler: @escaping (Bool) -> Void) {

    completionHandler(handleShortCutItem(shortcutItem))
}
func handleShortCutItem(_ shortcutItem:
UIApplicationShortcutItem) -> Bool {
    var handled = false

    guard MenuItems(fullType: shortcutItem.type) != nil else {
        return false
    }

    guard let shortCutType = shortcutItem.type as String? else {
        return false
    }

    switch (shortCutType) {
    case MenuItems.First.type:
        print ("View favorites")
        handled = true
    case MenuItems.Second.type:
        print ("Share")
        handled = true
    default:
        break
    }

    let alertController = UIAlertController(title: "Shortcut
    Chosen", message: "\"\(shortcutItem.localizedTitle)\"",
    preferredStyle: .alert)
    let okAction = UIAlertAction(title: "OK", style: .default,
    handler: nil)
    alertController.addAction(okAction)
    window!.rootViewController?.present(alertController,
    animated: true, completion: nil)
```

```
    return handled
}

func applicationWillResignActive(_ application: UIApplication) {

}

func applicationDidEnterBackground(_ application: UIApplication) {

}

func applicationWillEnterForeground(_ application: UIApplication) {

}

func applicationDidBecomeActive(_ application: UIApplication) {

}

func applicationWillTerminate(_ application: UIApplication) {

}

}
```

4. Make sure your project will run on an iPhone connected to your Macintosh. Then click the Run button or choose Product ➤ Run. The 3DTouchApp's screen appears on the iPhone.

5. Press the Home button or swipe up from the bottom of the screen to return back to the Home screen.

6. Press firmly on the 3DTouchApp icon on the Home screen. The Quick Action shortcut menu appears with icons (see Figure 9-15).

7. Tap on a Quick Action item. An alert dialog appears, displaying your chosen Quick Action by its UIApplicationShortcutItemTitle value (see Figure 9-16).

8. Tap OK to make the alert dialog go away.

9. Click the Stop button in Xcode.

Adding Peeking, Popping, and Previewing

The final use of 3D Touch is to add peeking to our project. Peeking lets the user press on an item to focus just on that item (see Figure 9-2). Holding a finger over that item pops up a new view of itself in a smaller form (see Figure 9-3). Previewing lets you view a menu of items to perform a task of some kind (see Figure 9-4).

Peeking and popping involve two different views. The first view displays an item, and when the user presses on an item, a second view pops up. Because you're working with two different views, you need to write code in the view controller files connected to each view (such as ViewController.swift).

To see how peeking, popping, and previewing work, follow these steps:

1. Create a new Single View App iOS project and name it
    3DPeekPopApp.

2. Click the Main.storyboard file in the Navigator pane.

3. Click the Library icon and drag and drop a button in the middle of
    the view.

4. Double-click the button, type **Touch Me to Peek**, and press Enter.

5. Choose View ➤ Inspectors ➤ Show Attributes inspector, or click
    the Attributes Inspector icon in the upper right corner of the
    Xcode window.

6. Click the Background popup menu and choose a distinctive color
    such as yellow or orange to make the button easier to see.

7. Choose Editor ➤ Resolve Auto Layout Issues ➤ Reset to Suggested
    Constraints. Xcode adds constraints to the button. The user
    interface should look similar to Figure 9-18.

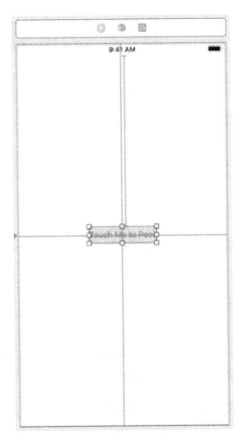

Figure 9-18. *The initial user interface of the 3DPeekPopApp project*

8. Choose View ➤ Assistant Editor ➤ Show Assistant Editor, or click the Assistant Editor icon in the upper right corner of the Xcode window. Xcode displays the Main.storyboard and ViewController. swift file side by side.

9. Move the mouse pointer over the button, hold down the Control key, and Ctrl-drag under the class ViewController line in the ViewController.swift file.

10. Release the Control key and the left mouse button. A popup window appears.

11. Click in the Name text field, type **peekButton**, and click the Connect button. Xcode creates an IBOutlet as follows:

```
@IBOutlet var peekButton: UIButton!
```

267

12. Choose View ➤ Standard Editor ➤ Show Standard Editor, or click the Standard Editor icon in the upper right corner of the Xcode window.

13. Click the ViewController.swift file in the Navigator pane.

14. Edit the viewDidLoad method as follows to make sure 3D Touch is available:

```
override func viewDidLoad() {
    super.viewDidLoad()

    if traitCollection.forceTouchCapability == .available {
        registerForPreviewing(with: self, sourceView: view)
    }
}
```

15. Edit the class ViewController line as follows:

```
class ViewController: UIViewController,
UIViewControllerPreviewingDelegate {
```

The UIViewControllerPreviewingDelegate requires two previewingContext functions to work. The first function runs when the user first presses down on an item. This function must identify a second view to appear and verify that the user pressed within on an item such as our UIButton. Then this function needs to define a smaller size for displaying the second view.

16. Add the following function to the ViewController.swift file:

```
func previewingContext(_ previewingContext:
UIViewControllerPreviewing, viewControllerForLocation location:
CGPoint) -> UIViewController? {
    guard let showMyView = storyboard?.instantiateViewController(withI
    dentifier: "PeekVC"), peekButton.frame.contains(location) else {
        return nil
    }
    showMyView.preferredContentSize = CGSize(width: 0.0, height: 300.0)
        return showMyView
    }
```

Note that the second view (which we haven't created yet) needs a Storyboard ID of "PeekVC".

17. Add the following function to the ViewController.swift file:

```swift
func previewingContext(_ previewingContext:
UIViewControllerPreviewing, commit viewControllerToCommit:
UIViewController) {
    show(viewControllerToCommit, sender: self)
}
```

The complete code for the ViewController.swift file should look like this:

```swift
import UIKit

class ViewController: UIViewController,
UIViewControllerPreviewingDelegate {

    @IBOutlet var peekButton: UIButton!

    override func viewDidLoad() {
        super.viewDidLoad()

        if traitCollection.forceTouchCapability == .available {
            registerForPreviewing(with: self, sourceView: view)
        }
    }

    func previewingContext(_ previewingContext:
    UIViewControllerPreviewing, viewControllerForLocation
    location: CGPoint) -> UIViewController? {
        guard let showMyView = storyboard?.instantiateViewCon
        troller(withIdentifier: "PeekVC"), peekButton.frame.
        contains(location) else {
            return nil
        }
        showMyView.preferredContentSize = CGSize(width: 0.0,
        height: 300.0)
        return showMyView
    }
```

```
func previewingContext(_ previewingContext:
UIViewControllerPreviewing, commit viewControllerToCommit:
UIViewController) {
    show(viewControllerToCommit, sender: self)
}

}
```

18. Click the Main.storyboard file in the Navigator pane.

19. Click the Library icon and drag and drop a View Controller next to the existing view.

20. Click the Library icon and drag and drop a label near the top of this new view controller.

21. Resize the label. Double-click the label, type **Touch Me to Peek**, and press Enter.

22. Choose View ➤ Inspectors ➤ Show Attributes inspector, or click the Attributes Inspector icon in the upper right corner of the Xcode window.

23. Click the Background popup menu and choose a distinctive color such as green or purple to make the label different from the button on the other view controller.

24. Click the Center icon in the Alignment group to center text. The Main.storyboard file should look similar to Figure 9-19.

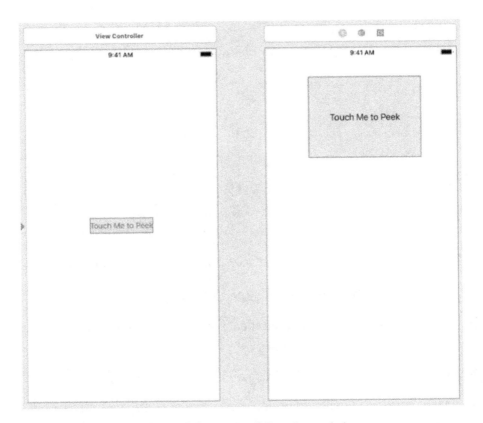

Figure 9-19. *The second view of the 3DPeekPopApp project*

25. Click the View Controller Scene in the Document Outline that represents this second view controller.

26. Choose View ➤ Inspectors ➤ Show Identity inspector, or click the Identity Inspector icon in the upper right corner of the Xcode window.

27. Click in the Storyboard ID text field and type **PeekVC**, then press Enter as shown in Figure 9-20.

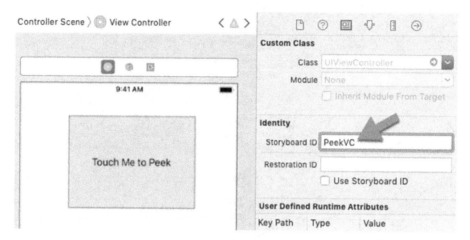

Figure 9-20. *Identifying the second view controller with a Storyboard ID of PeekVC*

28. Choose File ➤ New ➤ File. A template dialog appears.

29. Click Cocoa Touch Class under the iOS category and click the Next button. Another window appears.

30. Click in the Class text field and type **PeekViewController**.

31. Make sure the Subclass of popup menu displays UIViewController and then click the Next button and then click the Create button. Xcode displays a PeekViewController.swift file in the Navigator pane.

32. Click the Main.storyboard file and click View Controller Scene in the Document Outline that represents the second view controller that contains the large label.

33. Choose View ➤ Inspectors ➤ Show Identity inspector, or click the Identity Inspector icon in the upper right corner of the Xcode window.

34. Click in the Class popup menu and choose PeekViewController. This connects the PeekViewController.swift file with the second view controller on the storyboard.

35. Choose View ➤ Standard Editor ➤ Show Standard Editor, or click the Standard Editor icon in the upper right corner of the Xcode window.

36. Click the PeekViewController.swift file in the Navigator pane.

37. Add the following to the PeekViewController.swift file:

```swift
override var previewActionItems : [UIPreviewActionItem] {

    let defaultAction = UIPreviewAction(title: "Default style",
    style: .default) { (action, viewController) -> Void in
        print("Default")
    }

    let selectAction = UIPreviewAction(title: "Selected style",
    style: .selected) { (action, viewController) -> Void in
        print("Selected")
    }

    let destructiveAction = UIPreviewAction(title: "Destructive
    style", style: .destructive) { (action, viewController) ->
    Void in
        print("Destructive")
    }

    return [defaultAction, selectAction, destructiveAction]
}
```

The entire PeekViewController.swift file should look like this:

```swift
import UIKit

class PeekViewController: UIViewController {
    override func viewDidLoad() {
        super.viewDidLoad()

        // Do any additional setup after loading the view.
    }
```

```
override var previewActionItems : [UIPreviewActionItem] {

    let defaultAction = UIPreviewAction(title: "Default style",
    style: .default) { (action, viewController) -> Void in
        print("Default")
    }

    let selectAction = UIPreviewAction(title: "Selected style",
    style: .selected) { (action, viewController) -> Void in
        print("Selected")
    }

    let destructiveAction = UIPreviewAction(title:
    "Destructive style", style: .destructive) { (action,
    viewController) -> Void in
        print("Destructive")
    }

    return [defaultAction, selectAction, destructiveAction]
    }

}
```

Note   To test 3D Touch in the Simulator, your Macintosh needs a Magic Trackpad.

---

38. Click the Scheme button in the upper left corner of the Xcode window and choose iPhone 8 (or any iPhone model that supports 3D Touch).

39. Click the Run button, or choose Product ➤ Run. The Simulator screen appears, displaying your first Touch Me to Peek button.

40. Move the mouse pointer over this Touch Me to Peek button and press one finger down on the Magic Trackpad. The second view controller displaying the large label appears.

41. Swipe up. The Touch Me to Peek label slides up and displays a
    menu underneath displaying different styles (Default, Selected,
    and Destructive) as shown in Figure 9-21.

Figure 9-21. *Displaying three different types of preview menu items*

42. Click any of the menu options such as Default style or Destructive
    style. The initial view controller appears again displaying the
    Touch Me to Peek button.

43. Choose Simulator ➤ Quit Simulator to return to Xcode.

Summary

3D Touch provides another way for users to interact with your app. Although 3D Touch is currently only available on the iPhone (but not the iPad or certain iPhone models such as the iPhone Xr), adding 3D Touch to your app can provide users with the latest features they've come to expect from iPhone apps.

When testing 3D Touch, you need a Magic Trackpad to test in the Simulator, but it's more reliable to test on an actual iPhone connected to your Macintosh through a USB cable. Just make sure that iPhone supports 3D Touch.

3D Touch isn't crucial for any app, but it's just an added feature that can make your app feel modern and up to date with the latest version of iOS.

CHAPTER 10

Detecting Motion and Orientation

Mobile computer devices like the iPhone and iPad essentially put a PC in your pocket, letting you use a computer wherever you happen to be. However, unlike a desktop or even a laptop PC, mobile computers can track movement and orientation. This can come in handy for tracking the user's arm movements in a game or helping you measure angles.

To track motion and orientation, every iOS device comes with a built-in accelerometer that can detect movement. In addition to the accelerometer, the iOS devices also include a gyroscope to detect positions of the iOS device. By adding motion and orientation detection, you can create apps that respond to physical gestures as well as touch gestures.

Detecting Shake Gestures

The shake gesture is the easiest gesture to detect. Many apps use the shake gesture as a shortcut to undo actions. If you type text in the Notes app on an iPhone or iPad, you can shake your device to undo the last text you typed. Detecting a shake gesture involves using the motionEnded function:

```
override func motionEnded(_ motion: UIEvent.EventSubtype, with event:
UIEvent?) {
}
```

Inside this motionEnded function, you need to check if the motion that ended was the .motionShake event (a shake gesture) like this:

```
if motion == .motionShake {

}
```

© Wallace Wang 2019
W. Wang, *Pro iPhone Development with Swift 5*, https://doi.org/10.1007/978-1-4842-4944-4_10

Once you detect that the motion is a shake gesture, then your app can respond. To see how to detect a shake gesture, follow these steps:

1. Create a new iOS Single View App project and name it ShakeApp.

2. Click the Main.storyboard file in the Navigator pane.

3. Choose View ➤ Assistant Editor ➤ Show Assistant Editor, or click the Assistant Editor icon in the upper right corner of the Xcode window. Xcode shows the Main.storyboard side by side with the ViewController.swift file.

4. Move the mouse pointer over the middle of the view controller, hold down the Control key, and Ctrl-drag under the class ViewController line in the ViewController.swift file.

5. Release the Control key and the left mouse button. A popup window appears.

6. Click in the Name text field, type **myLabel**, and click the Connect button. Xcode creates the following IBOutlet:

    @IBOutlet var myView: UIView!

7. Choose View ➤ Standard Editor ➤ Show Standard Editor, or click the Standard Editor icon in the upper right corner of the Xcode window.

8. Click the ViewController.swift file in the Navigator pane.

9. Add the following underneath the viewDidLoad method:

```swift
override func motionEnded(_ motion: UIEvent.EventSubtype, with
event: UIEvent?) {
    if motion == .motionShake {
        if myView.backgroundColor == UIColor.red {
            myView.backgroundColor = UIColor.green
        } else {
            myView.backgroundColor = UIColor.red
        }
    }
}
```

This code simply detects a shaking gesture and alternates between changing the background color to red and green each time it detects another shake gesture. The entire ViewController.swift file should look like this:

```swift
import UIKit

class ViewController: UIViewController {

    @IBOutlet var myView: UIView!

    override func viewDidLoad() {
        super.viewDidLoad()
        // Do any additional setup after loading the view.
    }

    override func motionEnded(_ motion: UIEvent.EventSubtype, with
    event: UIEvent?) {
        if motion == .motionShake {
            if myView.backgroundColor == UIColor.red {
                myView.backgroundColor = UIColor.green
            } else {
                myView.backgroundColor = UIColor.red
            }
        }
    }

}
```

10. Click the Run button or choose Product ➤ Run. The Simulator screen appears.

11. Choose Hardware ➤ Shake Gesture as shown in Figure 10-1. Notice that the Simulator screen turns red.

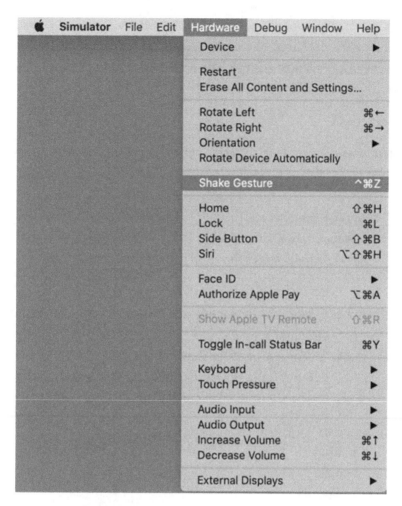

Figure 10-1. *Choosing the Shake Gesture in the Simulator*

12.   Choose Hardware ➤ Shake Gesture. Notice that this time the
      Simulator screen turns green. If you keep choosing the Shake
      Gesture command, the Simulator screen will alternate between
      red and green.

13.   Choose Simulator ➤ Quit Simulator to return back to Xcode.

Understanding Core Motion

To detect movement beyond simple shakes, Apple provides a software framework called Core Motion. Core Motion lets an app access the following types of motion data:

- Acceleration in three dimensions

- Rotation around the x, y, and z axes

- Magnetometer data that measures the device's orientation relative to the Earth's magnetic field

- Device motion data such as its orientation relative to gravity

---

Note   To test motion and orientation, you need a real iOS device connected to your Macintosh through a USB cable. The Simulator can only detect shaking motions but cannot detect changes in physical movements and different orientations.

To use Core Motion in an app, you need to import the CoreMotion framework and then create a CMMotionManager object like this:

```
import CoreMotion

let motionManager = CMMotionManager()
```

To detect motion, your app first needs to check if the iOS device contains the necessary equipment such as an accelerator or a gyroscope. This can be done by checking to make sure one of the following is true:

- .isAccelerometerAvailable

- .isGyroAvailable

- .isMagnetometerAvailable

- .isDeviceMotionAvailable

Next, we need to determine a time interval to detect data such as

- accelerometerUpdateInterval

- gyroUpdateInterval

- magnetometerUpdateInterval

- deviceMotionUpdateInterval

Finally, you need to check for data updates on a special queue called OperationQueue. Without this OperationQueue, motion-detecting data could arrive faster than the app could process it, making the app feel frozen or unresponsive.

Detecting Acceleration

The accelerometer can measure both acceleration and gravity in three dimensions. The accelerometer can determine not only how an iOS device is being held, but also whether it's lying face down or face up on a flat surface such as a table. Accelerometers measure g-forces (**g** for gravity), so a value of 1.0 returned by the accelerometer means that 1 g is sensed in a particular direction, as in these examples:

- If the device is being held perfectly upright, in portrait orientation, it will detect and report about 1 g of force exerted on its y axis.

- If the device is being held at an angle, that 1 g of force will be distributed along different axes depending on how it is being held. When held at a 45-degree angle, the 1 g of force will be split roughly equally between two of the axes.

Sudden movement can be detected by looking for accelerometer values considerably larger than 1 g. In normal usage, the accelerometer does not detect significantly more than 1 g on any axis. If you shake, drop, or throw your device, the accelerometer will detect a greater amount of force on one or more axes as shown in Figure 10-2.

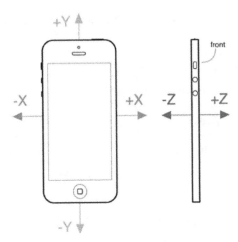

Figure 10-2. *The iPhone accelerometer's axes in three dimensions. The front view of an iPhone on the left shows the x and y axes. The side view on the right shows the z axis.*

To see how to use the accelerometer, follow these steps:

1. Create a new iOS Single View App project and name it AccelerateApp.

2. Click the Main.storyboard file in the Navigator pane.

3. Click the Library icon and drag and drop a label onto the view. Expand the width and height of the label.

4. Choose View ➤ Inspectors ➤ Show Attributes inspector, or click the Attributes Inspector in the upper right corner of the Xcode window.

5. Click in the Lines text field and change it to 0. A 0 value means that the label can hold an unlimited number of lines of text.

6. Choose Editor ➤ Resolve Auto Layout Issues ➤ Reset to Suggested Constraints. Xcode adds constraints to the label.

7. Choose View ➤ Assistant Editor ➤ Show Assistant Editor, or click the Assistant Editor icon in the upper right corner of the Xcode window. Xcode shows the Main.storyboard side by side with the ViewController.swift file.

8. Move the mouse pointer over the label, hold down the Control key, and Ctrl-drag under the class ViewController line in the ViewController.swift file.

9. Release the Control key and the left mouse button. A popup window appears.

10. Click in the Name text field, type **myLabel**, and click the Connect button. Xcode creates the following IBOutlet:

```
@IBOutlet var myLabel: UILabel!
```

11. Choose View ➤ Standard Editor ➤ Show Standard Editor, or click the Standard Editor icon in the upper right corner of the Xcode window.

12. Click the ViewController.swift file in the Navigator pane.

13. Add the following underneath the IBOutlet to access the Core Motion manager:

```
let motionManager = CMMotionManager()
```

14. Edit the viewDidLoad method as follows:

```
override func viewDidLoad() {
    super.viewDidLoad()
    // Do any additional setup after loading the view.
    if motionManager.isAccelerometerAvailable {
        motionManager.accelerometerUpdateInterval = 2.5
        motionManager.startAccelerometerUpdates(to:
        OperationQueue.main) { (motion, error) -> Void in
            if let trackMotion = motion {
                let userAcceleration = trackMotion.acceleration
                let displayText = "x: \(userAcceleration.x) \ny: \
                (userAcceleration.y) \nz: \(userAcceleration.z)"
                DispatchQueue.main.async {
                    self.myLabel.text = displayText
                }
            }
        }
    }
}
```

Once we know that the accelerometer is available, we can assign an arbitrary update interval as 2.5 seconds. This will update the values slowly so we can see the different values as we move the iOS device. Finally, we track the acceleration of the iOS device and store this data in a string (displayText), which uses the \n character to define a new line. Finally, we display this string in the label. Notice that updating this label occurs on the main thread because the label is part of the user interface and updating the user interface always needs to occur on the main thread.

15.   Connect an iOS device to your Macintosh through a USB cable.

16.   Click the Run button or choose Product ➤ Run.

17.   Lay the iOS device on a flat surface such as a table. The z value should appear close to –1.0.

18.   Hold the iOS device in portrait orientation so it's vertical. The y value should appear close to –1.0.

19.   Lay the iOS device on its side. The x value should appear close to –1.0.

20.   Click the Stop button in Xcode.

Detecting Rotation with the Gyroscope

A gyroscope measures orientation and rotation around the x, y, and z axes. Rotation around the x axis occurs when the iOS device tumbles backward or forward around its horizontal center. Rotation around the y axis occurs when the iOS device twists around its vertical center. Rotation around the z axis occurs when the iOS device rotates clockwise or counterclockwise as if pierced by a line through its front and back as shown in Figure 10-3.

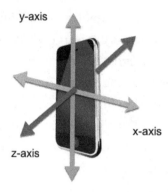

Figure 10-3. *Rotation around the x, y, and z axes*

To see how to use the gyroscope to detect and measure rotation, follow these steps:

1. Create a new iOS Single View App project and name it
    RotationApp.

2. Create the user interface exactly as you created the AccelerateApp
    in the previous example with an enlarged label connected to the
    IBOutlet in the ViewController.swift file.

3. Click the RotationApp project name at the top of the Navigator
    pane.

4. Click General and clear the Landscape Left and Landscape Right
    check boxes so only the Portrait check box remains selected
    as shown in Figure 10-4. This will keep the user interface from
    changing when you rotate the iOS device around.

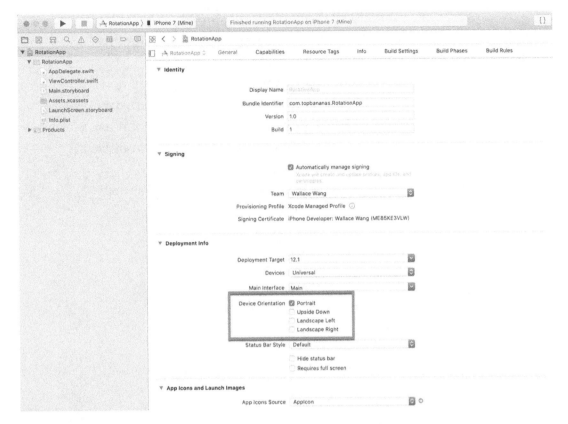

Figure 10-4. *Defining Portrait orientation only*

5. Click the ViewController.swift file in the Navigator pane.

6. Edit the ViewController.swift file so the entire file looks like the following:

```
import UIKit
import CoreMotion

class ViewController: UIViewController {

    @IBOutlet var myLabel: UILabel!

    let motionManager = CMMotionManager()

    override func viewDidLoad() {
        super.viewDidLoad()
        // Do any additional setup after loading the view.
        if motionManager.isGyroAvailable {
```

```
motionManager.gyroUpdateInterval = 2.5
motionManager.startGyroUpdates(to: OperationQueue.
main) { (motion, error) -> Void in
    if let trackMotion = motion {
        let userRotation = trackMotion.rotationRate
        let displayText = "x: \(userRotation.x) \ny: \
        (userRotation.y) \nz: \(userRotation.z)"
        DispatchQueue.main.async {
            self.myLabel.text = displayText
        }
    }
}
}
}
}
```

7. Connect an iOS device to your Macintosh through a USB cable.

8. Click the Run button or choose Product ➤ Run.

9. Rapidly dip your iOS device forward and backward across its horizontal center (x axis). Notice that the x value displayed on the screen changes drastically away from 0 such as reaching a value of –8 or 10.

10. Twist your iOS device around its vertical center (y axis). Notice that the y value displayed on the screen changes drastically away from 0 such as reaching a value of 7 or –6.

11. Rotate your iOS device clockwise and counterclockwise around its z axis that pierces the front and back of the device. Notice that the z value displayed on the screen changes drastically away from 0 such as reaching a value of –6 or 5.

12. Click the Stop button in Xcode to stop running the app.

Detecting Magnetic Fields

A magnetometer measures the Earth's magnetic field relative to the iOS device that contains the magnetometer. The values returned measure the Earth's magnetic field in microteslas where the x value measures horizontal displacement to the nearest magnetic field, the y value measures the vertical displacement, and the z value measures the altitude above/below the Earth's magnetic field.

To see how to get data from the magnetometer, follow these steps:

1. Create a new iOS Single View App project and name it MagnetApp.

2. Create the user interface exactly as you created the AccelerateApp in the previous example with an enlarged label connected to the IBOutlet in the ViewController.swift file.

3. Click the ViewController.swift file in the Navigator pane.

4. Edit the ViewController.swift file so the entire file looks like the following:

```swift
import UIKit
import CoreMotion

class ViewController: UIViewController {

    @IBOutlet var myLabel: UILabel!

    let motionManager = CMMotionManager()

    override func viewDidLoad() {
        super.viewDidLoad()
        // Do any additional setup after loading the view.
        if motionManager.isMagnetometerAvailable {
            motionManager.magnetometerUpdateInterval = 0.5
            motionManager.startMagnetometerUpdates(to:
            OperationQueue.main) { (motion, error) -> Void in
                if let trackMotion = motion {
                    let userField = trackMotion.magneticField
                    let displayText = "x: \(userField.x) \ny: \
                    (userField.y) \nz: \(userField.z)"
```

```
                    DispatchQueue.main.async {
                        self.myLabel.text = displayText
                    }
                }
            }
        }
    }
}
```

5. Connect an iOS device to your Macintosh through a USB cable.

6. Click the Run button or choose Product ➤ Run.

7. Move your iOS device around to see the x, y, and z values change.

8. Click the Stop button in Xcode to stop running the app.

Detecting Device Motion Data

Detecting device motion data lets you retrieve roll, pitch, and yaw data. Roll measures the rotation around the vertical axis, pitch measures the rotation around the horizontal axis, and yaw measures the rotation around an axis that pierces through the front and back of an iOS device as shown in Figure 10-5.

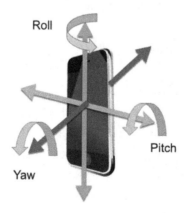

Figure 10-5. *Identifying roll, pitch, and yaw on an iOS device*

To see how to detect roll, pitch, and yaw, follow these steps:

1. Create a new iOS Single View App project and name it
   DeviceMotionApp.

2. Create the user interface exactly as you created the AccelerateApp
   in the previous example with an enlarged label connected to the
   IBOutlet in the ViewController.swift file.

3. Click the ViewController.swift file in the Navigator pane.

4. Edit the ViewController.swift file so the entire file looks like the following:

```swift
import UIKit
import CoreMotion

class ViewController: UIViewController {

    @IBOutlet var myLabel: UILabel!

    let motionManager = CMMotionManager()

    override func viewDidLoad() {
        super.viewDidLoad()
        // Do any additional setup after loading the view.
        if motionManager.isDeviceMotionAvailable {
            motionManager.deviceMotionUpdateInterval = 2.5
            motionManager.startDeviceMotionUpdates(to:
            OperationQueue.main) { (motion, error) -> Void in
                if let trackMotion = motion {
                    let userField = trackMotion.attitude
                    let displayText = "Roll: \(userField.roll) \nPitch:
                    \(userField.pitch) \nYaw: \(userField.yaw)"
                    DispatchQueue.main.async {
                        self.myLabel.text = displayText
                    }
                }
            }
        }
    }
}
```

5. Connect an iOS device to your Macintosh through a USB cable.

6. Click the Run button or choose Product ➤ Run.

7. Lay your iOS device flat on a table. The x, y, and z values should be near 0.

8. Twist your iOS device around its vertical axis. The Roll value should deviate from 0 such as –2 or 3.

9. Flip the front of your iOS device backward and forward. The Pitch value should deviate from 0 such as 1 or –2.

10. Rotate your iOS device on the flat surface clockwise and counterclockwise. The Yaw value should deviate from 0 such as –2 to 1.

11. Click the Stop button in Xcode to stop running the app.

Summary

Every iOS device comes with built-in sensors to measure movement. Shake gestures are the easiest to detect, which an app can use to represent the Undo command for reversing the last action a user took. To detect other types of movements of an iOS device, you need to use the CoreMotion framework.

Some of the different types of motion data an app can detect includes acceleration, rotation, and even nearby magnetic fields. Detecting the movement of an iOS device lets an app respond appropriately, giving movement another way to control an app.

CHAPTER 11

Using Location and Maps

One of the most useful features of mobile computers like smartphones and tablets is the ability to identify their location in the real world. Just this feature alone has made possible ride-sharing services that allow devices to track the position of both cars and waiting passengers in real time.

Tracking the location of an iOS device involves Global Positioning System (GPS), cell ID location, and WiFi positioning service (WPS). By using three different services, Apple's Core Location framework can pinpoint the location of an iOS device with varying degrees of accuracy.

Fortunately, Core Location hides the details of using these various technologies. Instead, Core Location lets you simply specify the degree of accuracy you wish, such as finding the location of an iOS device within 10 or 200 meters while also detecting any changes in the location of an iOS device. By tracking locations within a specified degree of accuracy and the distance an iOS device must travel before detecting movement, Core Location makes it easy for any app to identify the location of any iOS device.

Note   The more accurate and more often you need to track the movement of an iOS device's location, the more battery power the app will require, so you need to trade off between greater accuracy and constant updates against longer battery life.

Using Core Location

The first step to using Core Location is to import the Core Location framework into an app like this:

```
import CoreLocation
```

© Wallace Wang 2019
W. Wang, *Pro iPhone Development with Swift 5*, https://doi.org/10.1007/978-1-4842-4944-4_11

After importing the Core Location framework, the next step is to access the location manager with any arbitrary name such as locationManager like this:

```
let locationManager = CLLocationManager()
```

A class needs to conform to the CLLocationManagerDelegate protocol, which you can do in one of two ways. First, you can simply add this to the class line like this:

```
class ViewController: UIViewController, CLLocationManagerDelegate {
```

Then you can declare that this class is the CLLocationManagerDelegate inside the viewDidLoad method:

```
override func viewDidLoad() {
    super.viewDidLoad()
    locationManager.delegate = self
}
```

The other way to conform to the CLLocationManagerDelegate protocol is to use an extension at the end of the class ViewController file like this:

```
extension CLLocationManagerDelegate {

}
```

Then you can declare that this class is the CLLocationManagerDelegate inside the viewDidLoad method:

```
override func viewDidLoad() {
    super.viewDidLoad()
    locationManager.delegate = self as? CLLocationManagerDelegate
}
```

Defining Accuracy

When using Core Location, you need to define the amount of accuracy you want. Remember, the greater the accuracy, the more power the iOS device will require so it's best to choose the level of accuracy your app absolutely needs. If you just need to identify the user's geographical location such as a city, then you don't need specific accuracy. However, if your app needs to know the iOS device's precise location to locate the user such as for a ride-sharing service that needs to know where to pick up a passenger, then you'll need greater precision.

You can define a specific level of accuracy in meters such as 150 meters. However, Core Location provides several constants you can use that define varying degrees of accuracy:

- kCLLocationAccuracyBestForNavigation – The highest possible accuracy used for navigation apps

- kCLLocationAccuracyNearestTenMeters – Accurate to within 10 meters

- kCLLocationAccuracyHundredMeters – Accurate to within 100 meters

- kCLLocationAccuracyKilometer – Accurate to the nearest kilometer

- kCLLocationAccuracyThreeKilometers – Accurate to the nearest 3 kilometers

To define accuracy, you need to set the desiredAccuracy property to a value or to one of the preceding constants like this:

```
locationManager.desiredAccuracy = kCLLocationAccuracyNearestTenMeters.
```

Defining a Distance Filter

In addition to defining the accuracy you want, you can also define a distance filter that specifies how far the iOS device needs to move to detect movement. The default value is stored in a constant called kCLDistanceFilterNone, which tells an app to be notified of all movement.

However, if you define a specific value in meters, you can modify this distance filter such as only detecting movement when an iOS device travels 100 meters such as

```
locationManager.distanceFilter = 100
```

Requesting a Location

Core Location gives you two ways to request the location of an iOS device. The first method requests the location once. This can be useful for apps that don't need constant updating to track movement. To request location once, use the requestLocation method like this:

```
locationManager.requestLocation()
```

Because the requestLocation method only checks for a location once, it requires far less power than the second method, which requests locations continuously. To track locations continuously, you need to use the startUpdatingLocation and stopUpdatingLocation methods like this:

```
locationManager.startUpdatingLocation()
locationManager.stopUpdatingLocation()
```

Core Location also offers two Boolean values you can modify as follows:

- pausesLocationUpdatesAutomatically – Allows an app to temporarily pause updating a location

- allowsBackgroundLocationUpdates – Defines whether an app can continue receiving location updates even when the app is suspended

Retrieving Location Data

When Core Location retrieves the location of an iOS device, it provides several different types of values:

- coordinate.latitude and coordinate.longitude – Returns the latitude and longitude of a location

- horizontalAccuracy – Returns a distance of how accurate Core Location believes the defined location might be, measured in meters

- altitude – Returns the distance above or below sea level, measured in meters

- verticalAccuracy – Returns a distance of how accurate Core Location believes the altitude might be, measured in meters

- floor – Returns the floor of a building where the iOS device is located

- timestamp – Returns the time the location was retrieved

Requesting Authorization

Apps often need to request permission to access many hardware features of an iOS device. By forcing an app to request permission, Apple wants to make sure users authorize an app's access to features such as the camera, the microphone, and the device's location. Requesting authorization provides privacy for users and allows them to know exactly when an app might need to request access to specific hardware features.

Any app that uses Core Location must request authorization to track an iOS device's location. Core Location provides two ways to request authorization:

- requestWhenInUseAuthorization() – Uses location services only when your app is running

- requestAlwaysAuthorization() – Uses location services all the time

In most cases, you'll only want to use location services while your app is running. Besides using one of the preceding methods, an app also needs to modify its Info.plist file and add the Privacy – Location When In Use Usage Description key as shown in Figure 11-1. In addition, you'll need to add descriptive text explaining why your app needs to access location services.

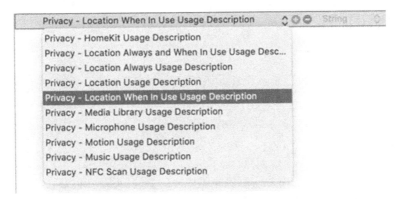

Figure 11-1. *Requesting to use location services in the Info.plist file*

Adding a Map

While you could display location data as text, you'll more likely want to display a location visually on a map. To do this, you need to use a Map Kit View, which displays a map on the screen. Then you'll need to import the MapKit framework such as

import MapKit

Finally, you'll need to make the Map Kit View display the current location. To do this, you just need to set the showsUserLocation property to true such as

```
@IBOutlet var mapView: MKMapView!
mapView.showsUserLocation = true
```

To see how to identify the location of an iOS device and display it on a map, follow these steps:

1. Create a new iOS Single View App project and name it LocationApp.

2. Click the Main.storyboard file in the Navigator pane.

3. Click the Library icon and drag and drop a Map Kit View at the top and a text view at the bottom of the view controller as shown in Figure 11-2.

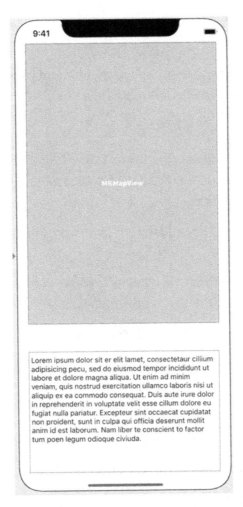

Figure 11-2. *Placing a Map Kit View and a text view on the user interface*

4.   Choose Editor ➤ Resolve Auto Layout Issues ➤ Reset to Suggested
      Constraints at the bottom half of the submenu. Xcode adds
      constraints to the Map Kit View and the text view.

5.   Choose View ➤ Assistant Editor ➤ Show Assistant Editor, or click
      the Assistant Editor icon in the upper right corner of the Xcode
      window. Xcode shows the Main.storyboard side by side with the
      ViewController.swift file.

6.   Move the mouse pointer over the Map Kit View, hold down the
      Control key, and Ctrl-drag under the class ViewController line in
      the ViewController.swift file.

7. Release the Control key and the left mouse button. A popup window appears.

8. Click in the Name text field, type **mapView**, and click the Connect button. Xcode creates the following IBOutlet:

```
@IBOutlet var mapView: MKMapView!
```

9. Move the mouse pointer over the text view, hold down the Control key, and Ctrl-drag under the class ViewController line in the ViewController.swift file.

10. Release the Control key and the left mouse button. A popup window appears.

11. Click in the Name text field, type **myTextView**, and click the Connect button. Xcode creates the following IBOutlet:

```
@IBOutlet var myTextView: UITextView!
```

12. Choose View ➤ Standard Editor ➤ Show Standard Editor, or click the Standard Editor icon in the upper right corner of the Xcode window.

13. Click the ViewController.swift file in the Navigator pane.

14. Add the following underneath the import UIKit line:

```
import CoreLocation
import MapKit
```

This code imports the Core Location framework to retrieve location data and imports the MapKit framework to allow the Map Kit View to display a scrollable map.

15. Add the following under the IBOutlets:

```
let locationManager = CLLocationManager()
```

16. Edit the class ViewController line as follows:

```
class ViewController: UIViewController, CLLocationManagerDelegate {
```

This makes the ViewController.swift file the CLLocationManagerDelegate. That means we need to define the ViewController.swift file as the delegate later.

17. Edit the viewDidLoad method as follows:

```
override func viewDidLoad() {
    super.viewDidLoad()
    // Do any additional setup after loading the view.
    locationManager.delegate = self
    locationManager.desiredAccuracy = kCLLocationAccuracyNearestTenMeters
    locationManager.requestWhenInUseAuthorization()
    locationManager.startUpdatingLocation()
    mapView.showsUserLocation = true
}
```

This code makes the ViewController.swift file the CLLocationManager delegate. Then it defines the accuracy to 10 meters. The next line requests authorization to use location services, which means we'll need to edit the Info.plist file later.

The startUpdatingLocation() method retrieves location data, while the showsUserLocation property is set to true to allow the Map Kit View to display the location. The entire ViewController.swift file should look like this:

```
import UIKit
import CoreLocation
import MapKit

class ViewController: UIViewController, CLLocationManagerDelegate {

    @IBOutlet var myTextView: UITextView!
    @IBOutlet var mapView: MKMapView!

    let locationManager = CLLocationManager()

    override func viewDidLoad() {
        super.viewDidLoad()
        // Do any additional setup after loading the view.
```

```
        locationManager.delegate = self
        locationManager.desiredAccuracy = kCLLocationAccuracy
        NearestTenMeters
        locationManager.requestWhenInUseAuthorization()
        locationManager.startUpdatingLocation()
        mapView.showsUserLocation = true
    }

    func locationManager(_ manager: CLLocationManager,
    didUpdateLocations locations: [CLLocation]) {
        if let newLocation = locations.last {

            let latitudeString = "\(newLocation.coordinate.latitude)"
            let longitudeString = "\(newLocation.coordinate.longitude)"

            myTextView.text = "Latitude: " + latitudeString + "\
            nLongitude: " + longitudeString

        }
    }

}
```

18. Click the Info.plist file in the Navigator pane.

19. Move the mouse pointer over the bottom row until a + and – icon appears. Click the + icon to add another row.

20. Click in the newly added row, and when a popup menu appears, choose Privacy – Location When In Use Usage Description (see Figure 11-1).

21. Click in the Value column of this row and type a message such as "Need to access location services".

22. Click the Run button or choose Product ➤ Run. The Simulator screen appears.

23. Choose Debug ➤ Location ➤ Apple to mimic the location of Apple's headquarters as shown in Figure 11-3. You can mimic a two-finger pinch gesture by holding down the Option key and dragging the mouse so you can zoom in and out of the displayed map.

Figure 11-3. *Displaying the location of Apple's headquarters on a map*

24.   Choose Simulator ➤ Quit Simulator to return back to Xcode.

Note   If you run this app on a real iOS device, you can see your actual location in the world.

Zooming in a Location

Although Core Location can find coordinates to our current location (or a simulated location such as Apple's headquarters), the app currently displays the location on a large map. While the user could pinch to zoom in, ideally the app should display a closer view of our location automatically.

To do this, not only do we need to know a location, but we also need to define a region to show around that location. Defining a region around a location involves defining the following:

- latitudeDelta – Measures north-to-south distance (measured in degrees) to display

- longitudeDelta – Measures east-to-west distance (measured in degrees) to display

To see how to zoom in on a location, follow these steps:

1. Make sure the LocationApp project is loaded into Xcode.

2. Click the ViewController.swift file in the Navigator pane.

3. Edit the class ViewController line as follows:

```
class ViewController: UIViewController, CLLocationManagerDelegate,
MKMapViewDelegate {
```

The MKMapViewDelegate gives us access to a mapView function that will let us zoom in to the defined location. After defining a MKMapViewDelegate, the next step is to make sure the map knows that the ViewController.swift file is the delegate.

4. Edit the viewDidLoad method by adding the mapView.delegate = self line at the end as follows:

```
override func viewDidLoad() {
    super.viewDidLoad()
    // Do any additional setup after loading the view.
    locationManager.delegate = self
    locationManager.desiredAccuracy = kCLLocationAccuracy
    NearestTenMeters
    locationManager.requestWhenInUseAuthorization()
    locationManager.startUpdatingLocation()
    mapView.showsUserLocation = true
    mapView.delegate = self
}
```

5. Add the following mapView function:

```
func mapView(_ mapView: MKMapView, didUpdate userLocation:
MKUserLocation) {
    let zoomArea = MKCoordinateRegion(center: self.mapView.
    userLocation.coordinate, span: MKCoordinateSpan
    (latitudeDelta: 0.05, longitudeDelta: 0.05))
    self.mapView.setRegion(zoomArea, animated: true)
}
```

The latitudeDelta and longitudeDelta values are 0.05, but
you can experiment with larger or smaller values. The entire
ViewController.swift file should look like this:

```
import UIKit
import CoreLocation
import MapKit

class ViewController: UIViewController, CLLocationManagerDelegate,
MKMapViewDelegate {

    @IBOutlet var myTextView: UITextView!
    @IBOutlet var mapView: MKMapView!

    let locationManager = CLLocationManager()

    override func viewDidLoad() {
        super.viewDidLoad()
        // Do any additional setup after loading the view.
        locationManager.delegate = self
        locationManager.desiredAccuracy = kCLLocationAccuracy
        NearestTenMeters
        locationManager.requestWhenInUseAuthorization()
        locationManager.startUpdatingLocation()
        mapView.showsUserLocation = true
        mapView.delegate = self
    }

    func locationManager(_ manager: CLLocationManager,
    didUpdateLocations locations: [CLLocation]) {
```

```
    if let newLocation = locations.last {

        let latitudeString = "\(newLocation.coordinate.latitude)"
        let longitudeString = "\(newLocation.coordinate.longitude)"

        myTextView.text = "Latitude: " + latitudeString + "\
        nLongitude: " + longitudeString
    }
}

func mapView(_ mapView: MKMapView, didUpdate userLocation:
MKUserLocation) {
    let zoomArea = MKCoordinateRegion(center:
    self.mapView.userLocation.coordinate, span:
    MKCoordinateSpan(latitudeDelta: 0.05, longitudeDelta:
    0.05))
    self.mapView.setRegion(zoomArea, animated: true)
}

}
```

6. Click the Run button or choose Product ➤ Run. The Simulator
    screen appears and zooms in on the location of Apple's
    headquarters as shown in Figure 11-4.

Figure 11-4. *Zooming in on a location on a map*

7.   Choose Simulator ➤ Quit Simulator to return back to Xcode.

Adding Annotations

An annotation allows the user to identify a location and place a cartoon pin on a map along with descriptive text. An annotation needs a location, which we can define by wherever the user presses on the map for an extended period of time, known as a long press.

Once we know where the user pressed on the map, we can display the annotation by adding it to the map along with any additional text. In addition, we'll store the annotations in an array and include a button to clear the annotations from the map.

To see how to add annotations, follow these steps:

1. Make sure the LocationApp project is loaded into Xcode.

2. Click the ViewController.swift file in the Navigator pane.

3. Add the following under the IBOutlets to define an array to hold all annotations added to the map:

```
var myAnnotations = [CLLocation]()
```

4. Edit the viewDidLoad method to recognize a long press gesture and add it to the map view as follows:

```
override func viewDidLoad() {
    super.viewDidLoad()
    // Do any additional setup after loading the view.
    locationManager.delegate = self
    locationManager.desiredAccuracy = kCLLocationAccuracy
    NearestTenMeters
    locationManager.requestWhenInUseAuthorization()
    locationManager.startUpdatingLocation()
    mapView.showsUserLocation = true
    mapView.delegate = self

    let longGesture = UILongPressGestureRecognizer(target: self,
    action: #selector(addPin(longGesture:)))
    mapView.addGestureRecognizer(longGesture)
}
```

This long press gesture defines a function called addPin to respond to a long press, which means we now need to create that addPin function.

5. Add the following function under the viewDidLoad method:

```
@objc func addPin(longGesture: UIGestureRecognizer) {
    let touchPoint = longGesture.location(in: mapView)
    let touchLocation = mapView.convert(touchPoint,
    toCoordinateFrom: mapView)
```

```
let location = CLLocation(latitude: touchLocation.latitude,
longitude: touchLocation.longitude)

let myAnnotation = MKPointAnnotation()
myAnnotation.coordinate = touchLocation
myAnnotation.title = "\(touchLocation.latitude) \
(touchLocation.longitude)"
myAnnotations.append(location)
self.mapView.addAnnotation(myAnnotation)
}
```

6. Click the Main.storyboard file in the Navigator pane.

7. Click the Library icon and drag and drop a button on the user interface such as between the map view and the text view.

8. Double-click the button, type **Clear Pins**, and press Enter.

9. Choose View ➤ Assistant Editor ➤ Show Assistant Editor, or click the Assistant Editor icon in the upper right corner of the Xcode window. Xcode shows the Main.storyboard side by side with the ViewController.swift file.

10. Move the mouse pointer over the button, hold down the Control key, and Ctrl-drag above the last curly bracket at the bottom of the ViewController.swift file.

11. Release the Control key and the left mouse button. A popup window appears.

12. Click in the Name text field, type **clearPins**, click the Type popup menu and choose UIButton, and click the Connect button. Xcode creates a clearPins IBAction method.

13. Edit this clearPins IBAction method as follows:

```
@IBAction func clearPins(_ sender: UIButton) {
    mapView.removeAnnotations(mapView.annotations)
    myAnnotations.removeAll()
}
```

14.   Click the Run button or choose Product ➤ Run. The LocationApp
appears on your iPhone.

15.   Move the mouse pointer to different parts of the map and hold
down the left mouse button until a pin appears. Repeat as often as
you like to see multiple pins placed wherever you hold down the
left mouse button as shown in Figure 11-5.

Figure 11-5. *Placing multiple annotations on a map*

16.   Click the Clear Pins button. Notice that all the annotations
disappear off the map.

17.   Choose Simulator ➤ Quit Simulator to return back to Xcode.

Summary

Mobile devices such as the iPhone and iPad can be especially useful when tracking the user's current location. When combined with a map display, an app can show the location of the user and the locations of other places or people as well.

When identifying a user's location, you can define the accuracy you want and the magnification of the map. To add annotations, you can detect a long press gesture and place a cartoon pin wherever the user presses on the map.

Remember that the greater the accuracy you need, the more power the app will require, which can drain the iOS device's battery, so only use greater accuracy when you need it. Also make sure that any app that uses location services requests permission to do so. An app won't be able to use location services until the user gives permission to do so.

CHAPTER 12

Playing Audio and Video

Not every app needs audio and video, but playing audio and video within an app can create an interesting way to deliver information to the user. For example, an app might want to play music or different sounds to alert the user or play a video to demonstrate steps for the user to follow. With both audio and video, an app can provide a more dynamic user experience.

When working with audio and video files, it's important to identify the file format. Some popular audio formats supported by iOS include

- .mp3 – Popular format that compresses audio files

- .aac – Advanced Audio Coding format that improves upon the mp3 format

- .aif – Audio Interchange File Format

- .wav – Waveform Audio file mostly found on Windows PCs

- .mp4 – MPEG-4 audio file

Some popular video formats supported by iOS include

- .mov – QuickTime media format

- .mp4 – MPEG-4 video file

- .m4v – An MPEG-4 video file, often called an iTunes video file because this is the format of videos downloaded from the iTunes Store

---

Note   If you have an audio or video file stored in a different format, you'll need to convert it to a format that iOS can recognize.

© Wallace Wang 2019
W. Wang, *Pro iPhone Development with Swift 5*, https://doi.org/10.1007/978-1-4842-4944-4_12

Playing an Audio File

To play audio, you need to import AVFoundation into your project like this:

`import AVFoundation`

After you've imported AVFoundation into your project, you can create a variable to represent the AVAudioPlayer such as

`var audioPlayer: AVAudioPlayer!`

To play an audio file, you need to drag and drop an audio file into the Navigator pane. Then you need to write code that loads the audio file into the AVAudioPlayer variable. Finally, you can use the play(), pause(), and stop() methods to control the playing of the audio file.

To complete this example, you'll need an audio file stored in a supported file format such as .mp3 or .mov. If you don't have any audio files stored on your Macintosh, you can download free audio files from the following sites:

- soundbible.com

- archive.org

- pond5.com

- gamesounds.xyz

You can also record audio files on a Macintosh by loading the QuickTime Player program and choosing File ➤ New Audio Recording. Once you have an audio file, either one you downloaded or created through QuickTime Player program, you can test how to play an audio file in an iOS app.

When working with files of any type, you need to specify the file name and the file path. The file name is the complete name of the file and its file extension such as HappyBirthday.mp3 or JingleBells.mov. The file path defines the location of the file within your app.

To retrieve the file path, you need to identify the file name and type you want to find such as

`let audioFilePath = Bundle.main.path(forResource: "Streetlife", ofType: "mp3")`

Once you know the path of the file you want to play, then you can load that file and path into the AVAudioPlayer to play it.

To see how to play an audio file, follow these steps:

1. Create a new iOS project using the Single View App template and name this new project PlayAudioApp. This creates a single view for the user interface.

2. Click the Main.storyboard file in the Navigator pane. Xcode displays the single view.

3. Click the Library icon to open the Object Library window.

4. Drag and drop a Toolbar onto the view as shown in Figure 12-1.

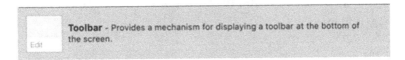

Figure 12-1. *The Toolbar in the Object Library window*

5. Click the Library icon to open the Object Library window. Then drag and drop three Bar Button Items on the Toolbar as shown in Figure 12-2.

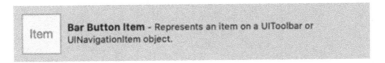

Figure 12-2. *The Bar Button Item in the Object Library window*

6. Click the Library icon to open the Object Library window. Then drag and drop two Flexible Space Bar Button Items on the Toolbar as shown in Figure 12-3. One Bar Button Item should appear on the left followed by a Flexible Space Bar Button. Then the second Bar Button Item appears in the middle followed by the second Flexible Space Bar Button. Finally, the last Bar Button Item appears on the far right.

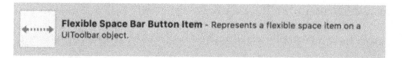

Figure 12-3. *The Flexible Space Bar Button Item in the Object Library window*

7. Click the Bar Button Item on the far left of the Toolbar to select it.

8. Choose View ➤ Inspectors ➤ Show Attributes Inspector, or click the Attributes Inspector icon in the upper right corner of the Xcode window.

9. Click the System Item popup menu. A popup menu appears as shown in Figure 12-4.

Figure 12-4. *Defining a Bar Button Item's System Item property*

10. Choose Pause.

11. Click the middle Bar Button Item.

12. Click the System Item popup menu in the Attributes Inspector pane and choose Play.

13. Click the far right Bar Button Item.

14. Click the System Item popup menu in the Attributes Inspector pane and choose Stop. Your Toolbar should display three Bar Button Items with icons as shown in Figure 12-5.

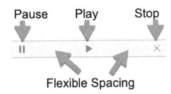

Figure 12-5. *The completed Toolbar with three Bar Button Items separated by two Flexible Space Bar Button Items*

The Toolbar with three Bar Button Items (separated by two Flexible Space Bar Button Items) represents the entire user interface. The next steps involve connecting the three Bar Button Items to IBAction methods to load, play, pause, and stop the audio file.

To write Swift code to play an audio file, follow these steps:

1. Make sure the PlayAudioApp project is loaded into Xcode.

2. Click the Main.storyboard file in the Navigator pane.

3. Choose View ➤ Assistant Editor ➤ Show Assistant Editor, or click the Assistant Editor icon in the upper right corner of the Xcode window. Xcode displays the Main.storyboard file side by side with the ViewController.swift file.

4. Move the mouse pointer over the Pause button (the button on the far left) in the Toolbar, hold down the Control key, and Ctrl-drag just above the last curly bracket at the bottom of the ViewController.swift file.

5. Release the Control key and the left mouse button. A popup window appears. Make sure the Connection popup menu displays Action.

6. Click in the Name text field, type **pauseAudio**, and press Enter.

7. Click in the Type popup menu and choose UIBarButtonItem. Then click the Connect button. Xcode creates an empty IBAction method as follows:

```
@IBAction func pauseAudio(_ sender: UIBarButtonItem) {

}
```

8. Move the mouse pointer over the Play button (the button in the middle) in the Toolbar, hold down the Control key, and Ctrl-drag just above the last curly bracket at the bottom of the ViewController.swift file.

9. Release the Control key and the left mouse button. A popup window appears. Make sure the Connection popup menu displays Action.

10. Click in the Name text field, type **playAudio**, and press Enter.

11. Click in the Type popup menu and choose UIBarButtonItem. Then click the Connect button. Xcode creates an empty IBAction method.

12. Move the mouse pointer over the Stop button (the button on the far right) in the Toolbar, hold down the Control key, and Ctrl-drag just above the last curly bracket at the bottom of the ViewController.swift file.

13. Release the Control key and the left mouse button. A popup window appears. Make sure the Connection popup menu displays Action.

14. Click in the Name text field, type **stopAudio**, and press Enter.

15. Click in the Type popup menu and choose UIBarButtonItem. Then click the Connect button. Xcode creates an empty IBAction method.

16. Choose View ➤ Standard Editor ➤ Show Standard Editor, or click the Standard Editor icon on the upper right corner of the Xcode window.

17. Click the ViewController.swift file in the Navigator pane.

18. Add the following underneath the import UIKit line:

import AVFoundation

19. Add the following underneath the classViewController line to create a variable that represents the AVAudioPlayer:

var audioPlayer: AVAudioPlayer!

20. Drag and drop an audio file from the Finder window into the Navigator pane as shown in Figure 12-6. Xcode displays a window for different options in adding a file to a project.

Figure 12-6. Adding an audio file to an Xcode project

21. Click the Finish button. Notice that your audio file now appears in the Navigator pane.

22. Type the following function underneath the audioPlayer variable as follows:

```
func loadAudioFile() {
    guard let audioFilePath = Bundle.main.path(forResource:
    "Streetlife", ofType: "mp3") else {
        print("Audio file not found")
        return
    }
```

```
let audioFileUrl = NSURL.fileURL(withPath: audioFilePath)

do {
    audioPlayer = try AVAudioPlayer(contentsOf: audioFileUrl,
    fileTypeHint: nil)
    audioPlayer.numberOfLoops = 0
} catch {
    print ("AVAudioPlayer error = \(error)")
}
}
```

The preceding code creates a constant to represent the audio file named "Streetlife" that's stored in the .mp3 file format (identified by its .mp3 file extension). Replace this file name and extension with the name and file type of your own audio file that you added to the Navigator pane in step 20.

The guard statement loads the audio file into a constant called audioFilePath to make sure that the audio file exists. If the audio file does exist, it creates a path to that audio file (audioFileUrl) and then loads that audio file into the audioPlayer variable. Otherwise it prints an error message.

Finally, notice the numberOfLoops property, which is set to 0. This property defines how many times the audio file plays after playing once, so a value of 0 means the audio file plays exactly once and then stops, a value of 1 means the audio file plays once and then plays one more time, a value of 2 means the audio file plays once and then plays two more times, and so on.

If the value of numberOfLoops is set to a negative number, the audio file will loop endlessly, which can be handy for background music while your app runs.

23. Modify the viewDidLoad method as follows:

```
override func viewDidLoad() {
    super.viewDidLoad()
    loadAudioFile()
}
```

The viewDidLoad file runs as soon as the view loads in memory. Then it calls the loadAudioFile to load the audio file into memory.

24. Edit the pauseAudio IBAction method as follows:

```swift
@IBAction func pauseAudio(_ sender: UIBarButtonItem) {
    audioPlayer.pause()
}
```

25. Edit the playAudio IBAction method as follows:

```swift
@IBAction func playAudio(_ sender: UIBarButtonItem) {
    audioPlayer.play()
}
```

26. Edit the stopAudio IBAction method as follows:

```swift
@IBAction func stopAudio(_ sender: UIBarButtonItem) {
    audioPlayer.stop()
    loadAudioFile()
}
```

This stopAudio IBAction method stops the audio and then reloads it to set it back to the beginning. The entire ViewController.swift file should look like this:

```swift
import UIKit
import AVFoundation

class ViewController: UIViewController {

    var audioPlayer: AVAudioPlayer!

    func loadAudioFile() {
        guard let audioFilePath = Bundle.main.path(forResource:
        "Streetlife", ofType: "mp3") else {
            print("Audio file not found")
            return
        }
```

```
        let audioFileUrl = NSURL.fileURL(withPath: audioFilePath)

        do {
            audioPlayer = try AVAudioPlayer(contentsOf:
            audioFileUrl, fileTypeHint: nil)
            audioPlayer.numberOfLoops = 0
        } catch {
            print ("AVAudioPlayer error = \(error)")
        }
    }

    override func viewDidLoad() {
        super.viewDidLoad()
        loadAudioFile()
    }

    @IBAction func pauseAudio(_ sender: UIBarButtonItem) {
        audioPlayer.pause()
    }

    @IBAction func playAudio(_ sender: UIBarButtonItem) {
        audioPlayer.play()
    }

    @IBAction func stopAudio(_ sender: UIBarButtonItem) {
        audioPlayer.stop()
        loadAudioFile()
    }

}
```

27. Click the Run button or choose Product ➤ Run. The Simulator appears, displaying the Toolbar and the pause, play, and stop buttons.

28. Click the play button. The Simulator starts playing your audio file.

29. Click the pause button. The Simulator halts playing of your audio file.

30. Click the play button. The Simulator plays the audio file starting from the point where it was paused.

31. Click the stop button. The Simulator stops playing the audio file.

32. Click the play button. Notice now the Simulator starts playing the audio file from the beginning again.

33. Click the stop button.

34. Choose Simulator ➤ Quit Simulator to return back to Xcode.

Experiment with different audio files and file formats such as a .wav or .mov audio file. Remember to modify your code to use the exact name and file format of each new audio file you test in this project. Also experiment with changing the numberOfLoops property defined in the loadAudioFile() function. By changing the value of numberOfLoops, you can make the audio file play multiple times.

Playing Video

Videos can display tutorials or tips on how to use an app. Just keep in mind that video files tend to be much larger than audio files, so you'll generally want to use short videos to avoid taking up too much space.

To play videos, your app needs the AVKit framework. Then you need to retrieve the path of the video file by defining the video file name and file extension such as "SaturnV" as the file name and "mov" as the file extension like this:

```
let videoFilePath = Bundle.main.path(forResource: "SaturnV", ofType: "mov")
```

After retrieving the path of a video file, you can then use the AVPlayer to play the video file. To display the video along with controls to let you fast-forward, pause, or rewind, you can use the AVPlayerViewController. To complete the following exercise, you'll need a video file. You can record your own videos using the QuickTime Player on a Macintosh or record a video on an iOS device such as an iPhone or iPad. You can also find free video files at the following sites:

- nasa.gov

- publicdomainfiles.com

- archive.org

To see how to play a video, follow these steps:

1. Create a new iOS project using the Single View App template and name this new project PlayVideoApp. This creates a single view for the user interface.

2. Click the Main.storyboard file in the Navigator pane. Xcode displays the single view.

3. Click the Library icon to open the Object Library window, and then drag and drop a button on the view.

4. Double-click the button, type **Play Video**, and press Enter.

5. Choose Editor ➤ Resolve Auto Layout Issues ➤ Reset to Suggested Constraints. Xcode adds constraints to the button.

6. Choose View ➤ Assistant Editor ➤ Show Assistant Editor, or click the Assistant Editor icon in the upper right corner of the Xcode window. Xcode displays the Main.storyboard file side by side with the ViewController.swift file.

7. Move the mouse pointer over the Play Video button, hold down the Control key, and Ctrl-drag just above the last curly bracket at the bottom of the ViewController.swift file.

8. Release the Control key and the left mouse button. A popup window appears.

9. Click in the Name text field, type **playVideo**, click the Type popup menu and choose UIButton, and click the Connect button. Xcode creates a playVideo IBAction method.

10. Choose View ➤ Standard Editor ➤ Show Standard Editor, or click the Standard Editor icon in the upper right corner of the Xcode window.

11. Click the ViewController.swift file in the Navigator pane.

12. Add the following underneath the import UIKit line:

```
import AVKit
```

13. Add the following underneath the class ViewController line:

```
var player:AVPlayer?
var vcPlayerController = AVPlayerViewController()
```

14. Drag and drop a video file into the Navigator pane. When a dialog appears displaying options for copying the file into your project, click the Finish button. Note the name of the video file (such as "SaturnV") and its file extension (such as ".mov").

15. Edit the viewDidLoad method as follows:

```
override func viewDidLoad() {
    super.viewDidLoad()

    guard let videoFilePath = Bundle.main.path(forResource:
    "SaturnV", ofType: "mov") else {
        print ("Video file not found")
        return
    }

    let videoURL = NSURL(fileURLWithPath: videoFilePath)
    player = AVPlayer(url: videoURL as URL)
    vcPlayerController.player = player
}
```

The guard statement makes sure that the video file exists. Make sure you substitute the name and file extension of your own video file here to replace the preceding example, which loads a video file called SaturnV.mov.

If the guard statement finds the video file defined by its name and file extension, the next step is to load that path as an NSURL into the videoURL constant. This videoURL constant is then passed to the AVPlayer so it knows which file to play. Finally, the AVPlayerViewController (defined by vcPlayerController) loads the AVPlayer and displays it on the screen.

16. Edit the playVideo IBAction method as follows:

```
@IBAction func playVideo(_ sender: UIButton) {
    present(self.vcPlayerController, animated: true, completion: {
        self.vcPlayerController.player?.play()
    })
}
```

This displays the vcPlayerController on the screen, and as soon as it fills the screen, it starts playing the video.

17. Click the Run button or choose Product ➤ Run. The Simulator screen appears.

18. Click the Play Video button. The video player appears and starts playing the video file you defined. Notice that the video player displays controls that let you pause, fast-forward, rewind, or stop the video as shown in Figure 12-7.

Figure 12-7. *Playing a video on an iOS device*

19.   Choose Simulator ➤ Quit Simulator.

Playing Videos on the Internet

One huge problem with videos is that each video file takes up a large amount of space. Just adding one or two videos to your app will greatly bloat its size. As an alternative, you can store videos on a video-sharing site like YouTube. Then you can simply provide a link to that video that your app can run.

The advantage of using a link is that it avoids bloating the size of your app with large video files. The disadvantage is that unlike a stored video file, an app may not be able to play a video if the iOS device does not have an Internet connection through WiFi or through a cellular telephone network.

The basic idea to playing Internet videos in an app involves using the AVKit framework to play videos and the WebKit framework to access web pages. Then you need to add a WebKit View to your user interface, which essentially adds a browser to your app. Now you just need to define the video URL to load.

To see how to play a video, follow these steps:

1. Create a new iOS project using the Single View App template and name this new project PlayInternetVideoApp. This creates a single view for the user interface.

2. Click the ViewController.swift file in the Navigator pane.

3. Add the following under the import UIKit line:

```
import WebKit
import AVKit
```

4. Click the Main.storyboard file in the Navigator pane.

5. Click the Library icon to open the Object Library window, and then drag and drop a WebKit View onto the user interface as shown in Figure 12-8.

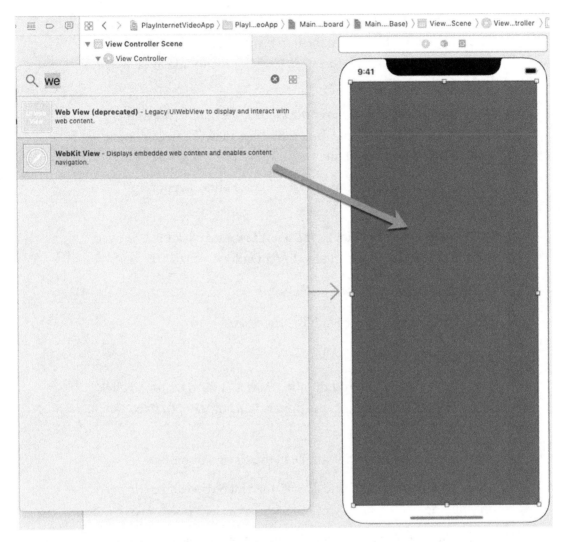

Figure 12-8. *Adding a WebKit View*

Note   Make sure you drag and drop a WebKit View and not a WebKit View, which has been deprecated and is far less versatile.

---

6. Resize the WebKit View to fill the screen.

7. Choose Editor ➤ Resolve Auto Layout Issues ➤ Reset to Suggested Constraints. Xcode adds constraints to the WebKit View.

8. Choose View ➤ Assistant Editor ➤ Show Assistant Editor, or click the Assistant Editor icon in the upper right corner of the Xcode window. Xcode displays the Main.storyboard file side by side with the ViewController.swift file.

9. Move the mouse pointer over the WebKit View, hold down the Control key, and Ctrl-drag under the class ViewController line in the ViewController.swift file.

10. Release the Control key and the left mouse button. A popup window appears.

11. Click in the Name text field, type **webView**, and click the Connect button. Xcode creates the following IBOutlet:

    @IBOutlet var webView: WKWebView!

12. Add the following underneath the IBOutlet:

    var myView = WKWebView()

13. Choose View ➤ Standard Editor ➤ Show Standard Editor, or click the Standard Editor icon in the upper right corner of the Xcode window.

14. Click the ViewController.swift file in the Navigator pane.

15. Open your browser and find a YouTube video you want to display in your app.

16. Right-click the YouTube video. A popup menu appears as shown in Figure 12-9.

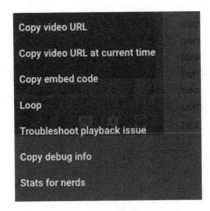

Figure 12-9. *Getting the video URL*

17. Choose Copy video URL.

18. Edit the viewDidLoad method as follows:

```
override func viewDidLoad() {
    super.viewDidLoad()

    if let url = URL(string: "Your video URL goes here") {
        let request = URLRequest(url: url)
        webView.load(request)
    } else {
        print ("Couldn't find file to load")
    }
}
```

Make sure you replace the text "Your video URL goes here"
with the video URL of the file you copied in step 17. The entire
ViewController.swift file should look like this with your video URL
replacing the string "Your video URL goes here":

```
import UIKit
import WebKit
import AVKit

class ViewController: UIViewController {

    @IBOutlet var webView: WKWebView!
    var myView = WKWebView()
```

```
override func viewDidLoad() {
    super.viewDidLoad()

    if let url = URL(string: "https://youtu.be/bivXtOhVufk") {
        let request = URLRequest(url: url)
        webView.load(request)
    } else {
        print ("Couldn't find file to load")
    }
}
```

19. Click the Run button or choose Product ➤ Run. The Simulator screen appears, displaying your chosen video.

20. Click the Play button on the video to watch it play. WebKit View essentially adds a browser to your app.

21. Chose Simulator ➤ Quit Simulator.

Summary

Any app can enhance the user's experience by playing audio or video. Audio files can play in the background, while an app runs or plays only when the user requests it. The audio file can play once, multiple times, or repeat continuously in a loop.

Video files let you display movies that users can watch. Because video files can take up large amounts of space, use video files sparingly or else the size of your app can dramatically increase in size each time you add another video file to an app.

To avoid gobbling up large amounts of storage space for video files, another alternative is to play videos off the Internet. This keeps an app's size down because it doesn't need to load one or more video files. However, the drawback is that the app can only play a video if it can connect to the Internet through WiFi or a fast cellular telephone network. Audio and video can enhance a user's experience with an app.

CHAPTER 13

Using the Camera

One of the most useful accessories on every smartphone has been the camera. While early smartphone cameras could only capture low-resolution images, today's cameras on the iPhone can capture amazingly high-quality images with resolutions that rival professional cameras of just a few generations ago. Not surprisingly, the camera is one of the most popular hardware accessories for an app to access and control.

To access the camera in an iOS device, you need to follow several steps:

- Set privacy settings in the Info.plist file to request access to both the camera and the photo library.

- Use the image picker controller to access the camera (and check to make sure the iOS device has a camera).

- Display the image on the screen so the user can capture an image.

- Optionally save the image in the photo library.

Note You can only test the camera on a real iOS device such as an iPhone or iPad because the Simulator cannot duplicate a camera.

Setting Privacy Settings

By default, no app can access the camera in an iOS device for privacy reasons. This prevents apps from recording images without the user's knowledge. So if an app wants to access the camera, it must request permission. There are two privacy settings you need to modify in the Info.plist file:

- Privacy – Camera Usage Description

- Privacy – Photo Library Additions Usage Description

© Wallace Wang 2019
W. Wang, *Pro iPhone Development with Swift 5*, https://doi.org/10.1007/978-1-4842-4944-4_13

The Privacy – Camera Usage Description key in the Info.plist file requests permission to access the camera. The Privacy – Photo Library Additions Usage Description key requests permission to store images in the Photos library. Only if the user grants permission to accessing the camera and the photo library can an app retrieve images through the camera and save them in the Photos library.

To see how to set privacy settings in an app, follow these steps:

1. Create a new iOS Single View App project and name it CameraApp.

2. Click the Info.plist file in the Navigator pane.

3. Move the mouse pointer over the last row displayed. A + and – button appears.

4. Click the + button to add a new row in the Info.plist file. Xcode displays a popup menu as shown in Figure 13-1.

Figure 13-1. *An app needs to request permission in the Info.plist file to access the camera and photo library*

5. Scroll down the list and choose Privacy – Camera Usage Description.

6. Click in the Value column and type any arbitrary text to display to the user such as "Need to access camera".

7. Move the mouse pointer over the last row until a + and – button appears.

8. Click the + button to add a new row. Xcode displays a popup menu (see Figure 13-1).

9. Scroll down the list and choose Privacy – Photo Library Additions Usage Description.

10. Click in the Value column and type any arbitrary text to display to the user such as "Need to access photo library". You should now have two privacy keys in the Info.plist as shown in Figure 13-2.

Key		Type	Value
▼ Information Property List		Dictionary	(16 items)
Localization native development region	⌄	String	$(DEVELOPMENT_LANGUAGE)
Executable file	⌄	String	$(EXECUTABLE_NAME)
Bundle identifier	⌄	String	$(PRODUCT_BUNDLE_IDENTIFIER)
InfoDictionary version	⌄	String	6.0
Bundle name	⌄	String	$(PRODUCT_NAME)
Bundle OS Type code	⌄	String	APPL
Bundle versions string, short	⌄	String	1.0
Bundle version	⌄	String	1
Application requires iPhone environment	⌄	Boolean	YES
Launch screen interface file base name	⌄	String	LaunchScreen
Main storyboard file base name	⌄	String	Main
▶ Required device capabilities	⌄	Array	(1 item)
▶ Supported interface orientations	⌄	Array	(3 items)
▶ Supported interface orientations (iPad)	⌄	Array	(4 items)
Privacy - Camera Usage Description	⌄	String	Need to access camera
Privacy - Photo Library Additions Usage Description	⌄	String	Need to access photo library

Figure 13-2. Accessing the camera and photo library requires setting two privacy keys in the Info.plist file

Once you've defined the two privacy settings to access the camera and photo library, you'll be ready to design the user interface and write Swift code.

Checking for a Camera

Most iOS devices come with a built-in camera. However, older iOS devices, such as the first iPod touch and early iPad models, did not come with a camera. In case your app may run on older iOS devices without a camera, you need to check to make sure a camera is available.

To access the camera in an iOS device, we need to use the UIImagePickerController. This allows us to not only detect if a camera exists but also to specify which camera to use, the front or rear camera. If you don't specify a camera to use, your app will default to using the rear camera.

To check if a camera exists, follow these steps:

1. Make sure the CameraApp is loaded into Xcode.

2. Click the ViewController.swift file in the Navigator pane.

3. Edit the class ViewController line as follows:

    ```
    class ViewController: UIViewController, UIImagePicker
    ControllerDelegate, UINavigationControllerDelegate {
    ```

    This allows the ViewController.swift file to access the camera through the image picker controller and view the image that the camera currently sees.

4. Edit the viewDidLoad method as follows:

    ```
    override func viewDidLoad() {
        super.viewDidLoad()
        if !UIImagePickerController.isSourceTypeAvailable(.camera){
            let alertController = UIAlertController.init(title: nil,
            message: "No camera available.", preferredStyle: .alert)

            let okAction = UIAlertAction.init(title: "OK", style:
            .default, handler: {(alert: UIAlertAction!) in
            })

            alertController.addAction(okAction)
            self.present(alertController, animated: true, completion: nil)
        }
    }
    ```

This code simply checks if a camera is available. If it is not true that a camera is available, then it displays "No camera available" in an alert that pops up on the screen. In a shipping app, you'd also want the app to shut down if it lacks a camera.

Designing a Simple User Interface

The user interface for our CameraApp project will consist of the following:

- Two buttons

- A single image view

One button will access the camera and let us take a picture. After we take a picture, we can show that picture in the image view. Now we'll be able to use the second button to save the picture into the Photos library.

To create the user interface for our CameraApp project, follow these steps:

1. Make sure the CameraApp project is loaded into Xcode.

2. Click the Main.storyboard file in the Navigator pane.

3. Click the Library icon and drag and drop two buttons and an image view onto the user interface.

4. Double-click one button, type **Take Picture**, and press Enter.

5. Double-click the second button, type **Save Picture**, and press Enter. The user interface should look similar to Figure 13-3.

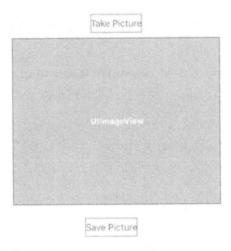

Figure 13-3. *The user interface of the CameraApp project*

6. Choose Editor ➤ Resolve Auto Layout Issues ➤ Reset to Suggested Constraints. Xcode adds constraints to the buttons and image view.

7. Choose View ➤ Assistant Editor ➤ Show Assistant Editor, or click the Assistant Editor icon in the upper right corner of the Xcode window. Xcode shows the Main.storyboard side by side with the ViewController.swift file.

8. Move the mouse pointer over the image view, hold down the Control key, and Ctrl-drag under the class ViewController line in the ViewController.swift file.

9. Release the Control key and the left mouse button. A popup window appears.

10. Click in the Name text field, type **imageView**, and click the Connect button. Xcode creates the following IBOutlet:

    @IBOutlet var imageView: UIImageView!

11. Move the mouse pointer over the Take Picture button, hold down the Control key, and Ctrl-drag above the last curly bracket at the bottom of the ViewController.swift file.

12. Release the Control key and the left mouse button. A popup window appears.

13. Click in the Name text field, type **takePicture**, and click the Connect button. Xcode creates a takePicture IBAction method.

14. Move the mouse pointer over the Save Picture button, hold down the Control key, and Ctrl-drag above the last curly bracket at the bottom of the ViewController.swift file.

15. Release the Control key and the left mouse button. A popup window appears.

16. Click in the Name text field, type **savePicture**, and click the Connect button. Xcode creates a savePicture IBAction method.

Taking a Picture

Before taking a picture, we first verify that the device has a camera. Then we use UIImagePickerController and define its source to be the camera in the iOS device. By default, the UIImagePickerController will use the rear camera, but if we want to specify the front camera, we'll need to use the following:

```
let picker = UIImagePickerController()
picker.cameraDevice = UIImagePickerController.CameraDevice.front
```

After we take a picture and capture an image, we need to store that image in the image view and dismiss the camera view.

To see how to take a picture and display it in the image view, follow these steps:

1. Make sure the CameraApp project is loaded into Xcode.

2. Click the ViewController.swift file in the Navigator pane.

3. Edit the takePicture IBAction method as follows:

```
@IBAction func takePicture(_ sender: UIButton) {
    if (UIImagePickerController.isSourceTypeAvailable(UIImagePicke
    rController.SourceType.camera)){
        let picker = UIImagePickerController()
        picker.delegate = self
        picker.sourceType = UIImagePickerController.SourceType.camera
        //picker.cameraDevice = UIImagePickerController.CameraDevice.
          front
        self.present(picker, animated: true, completion: nil)
    }
}
```

The if statement checks to make sure a camera exists in the iOS device. If so, then it creates a UIImagePickerController object, sets the delegate to the ViewController.swift file, and accesses the camera through the image picker controller. By default, the camera chosen will be the rear camera, but we can specify the front camera. Finally, the image displayed in the camera appears on the screen.

Now we need to write two additional functions. First, the camera view will display a Cancel button so we need to make this Cancel button hide the camera view. Second, if the user takes a picture, we need to hide the camera view and display this image in the image view.

4. Add the following two functions in the ViewController.swift file:

```swift
func imagePickerController(_ picker: UIImagePickerController,
didFinishPickingMediaWithInfo info: [UIImagePickerController.
InfoKey : Any]) {
    if let capturedImage = info[UIImagePickerController.InfoKey.
    originalImage] as? UIImage {
        picker.dismiss(animated: true, completion: nil)
        imageView.contentMode = .scaleToFill
        imageView.image = capturedImage
    }
}

func imagePickerControllerDidCancel(_ picker:
UIImagePickerController) {
    picker.dismiss(animated: true, completion: nil)
}
```

Saving a Picture

After the user takes a picture with the camera, our app displays that image in the image view. Now the user has the option of saving this image in the Photos library.

To save images in an image view and store them in the Photos library, follow these steps:

1. Make sure the CameraApp project is loaded into Xcode.

2. Click the ViewController.swift file in the Navigator pane.

3. Modify the savePicture IBAction method as follows:

```swift
@IBAction func savePicture(_ sender: UIButton) {
    let imageData = imageView.image!.pngData()
    let compressedImage = UIImage(data: imageData!)
```

```
UIImageWriteToSavedPhotosAlbum(compressedImage!, nil, nil, nil)

    let alert = UIAlertController(title: "Saved", message: "Your
    image has been saved", preferredStyle: .alert)
    let okAction = UIAlertAction(title: "OK", style: .default,
    handler: nil)
    alert.addAction(okAction)
    self.present(alert, animated: true, completion: nil)
}
```

The entire ViewController.swift file should look like this:

```
import UIKit

class ViewController: UIViewController,
UIImagePickerControllerDelegate, UINavigationControllerDelegate {

    @IBOutlet var imageView: UIImageView!

    override func viewDidLoad() {
        super.viewDidLoad()
        if !UIImagePickerController.isSourceTypeAvailable(.camera){
            let alertController = UIAlertController.init(title: nil,
            message: "No camera available.", preferredStyle: .alert)

            let okAction = UIAlertAction.init(title: "OK",
            style: .default, handler: {(alert: UIAlertAction!) in
            })

            alertController.addAction(okAction)
            self.present(alertController, animated: true,
            completion: nil)
        }
    }

    func imagePickerController(_ picker: UIImagePickerController,
    didFinishPickingMediaWithInfo info: [UIImagePickerController.
    InfoKey : Any]) {
        if let capturedImage = info[UIImagePickerController.
        InfoKey.originalImage] as? UIImage {
```

341

```
            picker.dismiss(animated: true, completion: nil)
            imageView.contentMode = .scaleToFill
            imageView.image = capturedImage
        }
    }

    func imagePickerControllerDidCancel(_ picker:
    UIImagePickerController) {
        picker.dismiss(animated: true, completion: nil)
    }

    @IBAction func takePicture(_ sender: UIButton) {
        if (UIImagePickerController.isSourceTypeAvailable(UIImage
        PickerController.SourceType.camera)){
            let picker = UIImagePickerController()
            picker.delegate = self
            picker.sourceType = UIImagePickerController.
            SourceType.camera
            //picker.cameraDevice = UIImagePickerController.
             CameraDevice.front
            self.present(picker, animated: true, completion: nil)
        }
    }

    @IBAction func savePicture(_ sender: UIButton) {
        let imageData = imageView.image!.pngData()
        let compressedImage = UIImage(data: imageData!)
        UIImageWriteToSavedPhotosAlbum(compressedImage!, nil, nil, nil)

        let alert = UIAlertController(title: "Saved", message:
        "Your image has been saved", preferredStyle: .alert)
        let okAction = UIAlertAction(title: "OK", style: .default,
        handler: nil)
        alert.addAction(okAction)
        self.present(alert, animated: true, completion: nil)
    }

}
```

4. Connect an iOS device to your Macintosh through a USB cable.

5. Click the Run button or choose Product ➤ Run. The CameraApp's screen appears.

6. Tap the Take Picture button. The camera view appears displaying a Cancel button, a round white button to take a picture, and a camera icon that lets you switch between the rear and front camera as shown in Figure 13-4.

Figure 13-4. *The camera view provides buttons for controlling the camera*

7. Tap the round white button to capture an image. Your chosen image now appears in the image view on the user interface.

8. Tap the Save Picture button. An alert appears, letting you know that the image has been saved in your Photos library.

9. Click the Stop button in Xcode.

10. Open the Photos app on your iOS device and you'll see that your image has been saved to the Photos library.

Summary

The camera has steadily improved over the years to the point where many professional photographers even use the iPhone's camera to take pictures instead of using a dedicated camera. Because of the popularity of photography on the iPhone, all current models of the iPad also include a camera. With cameras available in all the latest iOS devices, it's important to know how to access the camera in any iOS device.

Just keep in mind that if your app runs on older iOS devices such as early iPad models or the first-generation iPod touch, there won't be a camera available. Even though most iOS devices will come with a camera, make sure your app doesn't assume a camera exists so check for the existence of a camera before trying to capture a picture.

After taking a picture, save it in the Photos library. By adding the ability to access an iOS device's camera, your app can take full advantage of the user's iOS device.

CHAPTER 14

Using WebKit

If you ever used the Safari browser on a Macintosh, iPhone, or iPad, you've used an open source framework called WebKit (webkit.org). To give your apps the power of a complete browser, you can include the WebKit View. By using WebKit View, your apps can display web pages from anywhere on the Internet or simply display web pages stored within your app as HTML (HyperText Markup Language) files.

Note Xcode actually provides two objects that can display HTML web pages: Web View and WebKit View. Web View is an older and less versatile object that Apple no longer supports. As a result, always use WebKit View. If you ever modify older projects, replace Web View with WebKit View instead.

Displaying Web Pages from the Internet

Because WebKit View represents a complete browser, adding WebKit View to your app can give that app the ability to display any web pages available on the Internet.

To see how to display web pages from the Internet, follow these steps:

1. Create a new iOS Single View App project and name it WebKitApp.

2. Click the Main.storyboard file in the Navigator pane.

3. Click the Library icon and drag and drop a text field and two buttons and a WebKit View onto the user interface. Resize the text field and WebKit View so the text field appears at the top and extends across the width and the WebKit View fills the rest of the view as shown in Figure 14-1.

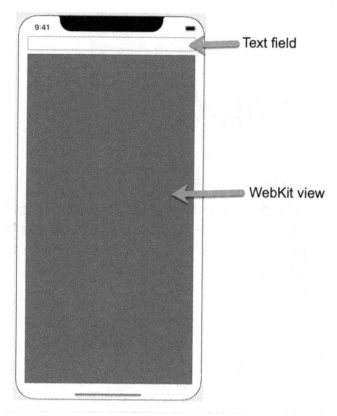

Figure 14-1. *The user interface of the WebKitApp project*

4. Choose Editor ➤ Resolve Auto Layout Issues ➤ Reset to Suggested
    Constraints. Xcode adds constraints to the text field and WebKit
    View.

5. Choose View ➤ Assistant Editor ➤ Show Assistant Editor, or click
    the Assistant Editor icon in the upper right corner of the Xcode
    window. Xcode shows the Main.storyboard side by side with the
    ViewController.swift file.

6. Move the mouse pointer over the text field, hold down the Control
    key, and Ctrl-drag under the class ViewController line in the
    ViewController.swift file.

7. Release the Control key and the left mouse button. A popup
    window appears.

8. Click in the Name text field, type **myTextField**, and click the Connect button. Xcode creates the following IBOutlet:

   @IBOutlet var myTextField: UITextField!

9. Move the mouse pointer over the WebKit View, hold down the Control key, and Ctrl-drag under the class ViewController line in the ViewController.swift file.

10. Release the Control key and the left mouse button. A popup window appears.

11. Click in the Name text field, type **webView**, and click the Connect button. Xcode creates the following IBOutlet:

    @IBOutlet var webView: WKWebView!

12. Choose View ➤ Standard Editor ➤ Show Standard Editor, or click the Standard Editor icon in the upper right corner of the Xcode window.

13. Click the ViewController.swift file in the Navigator pane.

14. Add the following underneath the import UIKit line:

    import WebKit

15. Edit the class ViewController line as follows:

    class ViewController: UIViewController, UITextFieldDelegate {

    This adds the UITextField Delegate to allow the text field to detect when editing has been completed by detecting when the user presses the Return or Enter key.

16. Add the following below the IBOutlets:

    var myView = WKWebView()

17. Edit the viewDidLoad method as follows:

```
override func viewDidLoad() {
    super.viewDidLoad()
    myTextField.delegate = self
    myTextField.clearButtonMode = .always
    lookupWebPage(address: "https://www.yahoo.com")
}
```

This defines the text field's delegate as the ViewController.swift file and displays a clear button at the far right of the text field so users can clear the text in the text field easily. Finally, it calls a function called lookupWebPage and sends it the web address of `https://www.yahoo.com`.

Note   WebKit View only allows secure connections defined by https:// and requires the complete spelling of the web site address such as `www.yahoo.com` instead of yahoo.com.

18. Add the following function below the viewDidLoad method:

```
func lookupWebPage(address: String) {
    let url = URL(string: address)
    let request = URLRequest(url: url!)
    webView.load(request)
}
```

This function accepts a string (a web site address) and stores it as a URL data type. Then it sends this URL address as a URLRequest, which is then passed to the load method. Assuming the web site address is valid, the web page will then appear inside the webView (WebKit View).

19. Add the following two functions to remove the virtual keyboard (if it's visible) when the user presses Return or Enter and sends the text stored in the text field as a web site address to retrieve:

```swift
func textFieldDidEndEditing(_ textField: UITextField) {
    if let webAddress = myTextField.text {
        lookupWebPage(address: webAddress)
    }
}

func textFieldShouldReturn(_ textField: UITextField) -> Bool {
    textField.resignFirstResponder()
    return true
}
```

The textFieldDidEndEditing function will take whatever the user typed into the text field and use that as a valid web site address. Of course, this will only work if the text is a valid web site address formatted like https://www.website.com.

The textFieldShouldReturn function runs the resignFirstResponder, which hides the virtual keyboard if it's visible. Then it returns true, which means that the text field will end editing when the user presses the Enter or Return key.

The entire ViewController.swift file should look like this:

```swift
import UIKit
import WebKit

class ViewController: UIViewController, UITextFieldDelegate {

    @IBOutlet var webView: WKWebView!
    @IBOutlet var myTextField: UITextField!
    var myView = WKWebView()

    override func viewDidLoad() {
        super.viewDidLoad()
        myTextField.delegate = self
```

```
        myTextField.clearButtonMode = .always
        lookupWebPage(address: "https://www.yahoo.com")
    }

    func lookupWebPage(address: String) {
        let url = URL(string: address)
        let request = URLRequest(url: url!)
        webView.load(request)
    }

    func textFieldDidEndEditing(_ textField: UITextField) {
        if let webAddress = myTextField.text {
            lookupWebPage(address: webAddress)
        }
    }

    func textFieldShouldReturn(_ textField: UITextField) -> Bool {
        textField.resignFirstResponder()
        return true
    }

}
```

20. Click the Run button or choose Product ➤ Run. The Simulator
     screen appears. As long as your Macintosh has an Internet
     connection, the WebKitApp displays the Yahoo web site as shown
     in Figure 14-2.

Figure 14-2. *The Yahoo web site displayed in the Simulator*

21. Click in the text field at the top of the screen and type a web site
     address (including https://) such as **https://www.apple.com** and
     press Enter. The Simulator screen now shows Apple's web site.

22. Choose Simulator ➤ Quit Simulator to return back to Xcode.

Displaying HTML Files

While the WebKit View can display web pages off the Internet, it can also display HTML
files stored in the app itself. Since WebKit View is essentially a complete browser, it can
display fairly sophisticated HTML files to create interested visual effects within an app.

You can create an HTML file using a separate editor (such as Adobe Dreamweaver) or you can create an HTML directly in Xcode. Dedicated HTML editors often let you create web pages visually, while creating HTML files in Xcode requires typing HTML commands.

To see how to create an HTML file in Xcode, follow these steps:

1. Create a new iOS Single View App project and name it HTMLApp.

2. Choose File ➤ New ➤ File. A template dialog appears.

3. Scroll down to the Other category and click the Empty icon as shown in Figure 14-3.

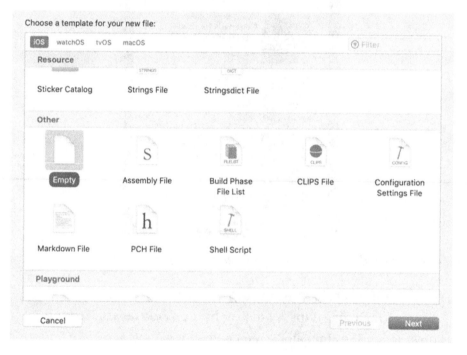

Figure 14-3. *Choosing an Empty file to add in an Xcode project*

4. Click the Next button. Another dialog appears, asking for a file name.

5. Type **readme.html** and then click the Create button. Xcode adds the readme.html file in the Navigator pane.

6. Click the readme.html file in the Navigator pane. The middle pane of Xcode displays the Empty file along with line numbers.

7. Type the following:

```
<!DOCTYPE html>
<html>
    <body>

        <p><b>This text is bold</b></p>
        <p><i>This text is italic</i></p>
        <p>This is what<sub> subscript</sub> and
        <sup>superscript</sup> look like</p>

    </body>
</html>
```

8. Click the Main.storyboard file in the Navigator pane.

9. Add the following underneath the import UIKit line:

```
import WebKit
```

10. Click the Library icon and drag and drop a WebKit View onto the user interface. You may want to resize the WebKit View so it takes up more space.

11. Choose Editor ➤ Resolve Auto Layout Issues ➤ Reset to Suggested Constraints. Xcode adds constraints to the WebKit View.

12. Choose View ➤ Assistant Editor ➤ Show Assistant Editor, or click the Assistant Editor icon in the upper right corner of the Xcode window. Xcode shows the Main.storyboard side by side with the ViewController.swift file.

13. Move the mouse pointer over the WebKit View, hold down the Control key, and Ctrl-drag under the class ViewController line in the ViewController.swift file.

14. Release the Control key and the left mouse button. A popup window appears.

15. Click in the Name text field, type **webView**, and click the Connect button. Xcode creates the following IBOutlet:

```
@IBOutlet var webView: WKWebView!
```

16. Add the following underneath the IBOutlet:

```
var myView = WKWebView()
```

17. Edit the viewDidLoad method as follows:

```
override func viewDidLoad() {
    super.viewDidLoad()

    if let url = Bundle.main.url(forResource: "readme",
    withExtension: "html") {
        webView.loadFileURL(url, allowingReadAccessTo: url)
    }
}
```

This code first tries to load the readme.html file. Only if it can find a readme.html file does it load it in the WebKit View.

18. Click the Run button or choose Product ➤ Run. The Simulator screen appears and displays the contents of your readme.html page on the screen.

19. Choose Simulator ➤ Quit Simulator to return back to Xcode.

20. Click the readme.html file in the Navigator pane.

21. Edit the readme.html file as follows to make the text larger and add a button that allows the user to click it:

```
<!DOCTYPE html>
<html>
    <body>

        <font size = "7">

        <p><b>This text is bold</b></p>
        <p><i>This text is italic</i></p>
```

```
<p>This is what<sub> subscript</sub> and
<sup>superscript</sup> look like</p>

<h1>JavaScript example</h1>

<button type="button"
    onclick="document.getElementById('data').innerHTML =
    Date()"
    style="font-size : 36px; width: 100%; height: 100px;">
    Click to display the current date and time.</button>

<p id="data"></p>

</font>

    </body>
</html>
```

22. Click the Run button or choose Product ➤ Run. The Simulator screen appears. Notice that the text now appears much larger.

23. Click the button to display the current date and time. The current date and time appears as shown in Figure 14-4.

Figure 14-4. *Displaying JavaScript in a WebKit View*

    24.   Choose Simulator ➤ Quit Simulator to return back to Xcode.

If you're comfortable with HTML code, edit the readme.html file with more sophisticated HTML code such as displaying tables and images.

Summary

Adding a WebKit View to an app allows displaying HTML files whether stored locally in an app or retrieved off the Internet. By displaying HTML files, a WebKit View can create interesting visual effects and user interfaces that may not be easily created using standard user interface objects. Best of all, experienced HTML developers can use their HTML skills to create a sophisticated app with little extra coding.

When loading HTML files, always check to make sure the file exists and can load inside a WebKit View. Displaying web pages or HTML files inside an app just gives you one more way to create interesting user interfaces for your apps.

CHAPTER 15

Displaying Animation

Most user interfaces are static, which is fine as long as the user can easily find commands and control the app. However to make a user interface visually interesting, consider adding animation to your apps. Animation can be as simple as moving an item on the screen or as sophisticated as displaying several seconds of multiple objects moving, spinning, and changing color on the screen.

Animation can involve one or more of the following:

- Moving an item from one location to another

- Resizing an item

- Changing transparency

- Rotating an item

To create basic animation, we need to use this code:

```
UIView.animate(withDuration: 2.0) {
    // animation code here
}
```

User interface objects such as buttons and labels are based on the UIControl class, which is based on UIView. So ultimately any user interface object can be animated as a UIView. The numeric value defines how long to make the animation run measured in seconds such as 2.0 seconds. The code inside the curly brackets then provides the actual animation.

© Wallace Wang 2019
W. Wang, *Pro iPhone Development with Swift 5*, https://doi.org/10.1007/978-1-4842-4944-4_15

Moving Items with Animation

To move an item, you need to define its starting and ending location. You can define the ending location of an item by visually placing it on the user interface. Then you can define the starting location through Swift code. Once you know where an item starts and ends up, you can define how long you want the movement animation to last.

For this example, we want to animate items as soon as the user interface loads. That means we need to define the initial location before the user interface loads. To do this, we'll need to specify the initial location in the viewWillAppear method, which runs right before the user interface appears on the screen.

To see how to move items with animation, follow these steps:

1. Create a new iOS Single View App project and name it AnimationMoveApp.

2. Click the Main.storyboard file in the Navigator pane.

3. Click the Library icon and drag and drop a label, a text field, and an image view onto the user interface. Resize the text field and label.

4. Double-click the label, type **This is a label**, and press Enter. The user interface should look similar to Figure 15-1.

Figure 15-1. *The user interface of the AnimationMoveApp project*

5. Choose Editor ➤ Resolve Auto Layout Issues ➤ Reset to Suggested Constraints. Xcode adds constraints to the label, text field, and image view.

6. Click the image view and choose View ➤ Inspectors ➤ Show Attributes Inspector, or click the Attributes Inspector icon in the upper right corner of the Xcode window.

7. Click the Background popup menu and choose a color such as orange. This will make the image view easy to see when it moves.

8. Click View in the Document Outline, choose View ➤ Inspectors ➤ Show Attributes Inspector, or click the Attributes Inspector icon in the upper right corner of the Xcode window.

9. Click the Background popup menu and choose a color such as yellow. This will make it easier to see the label and text field against a colored background.

10. Choose View ➤ Assistant Editor ➤ Show Assistant Editor, or click the Assistant Editor icon in the upper right corner of the Xcode window. Xcode shows the Main.storyboard side by side with the ViewController.swift file.

11. Move the mouse pointer over the label, hold down the Control key, and Ctrl-drag under the class ViewController line in the ViewController.swift file.

12. Release the Control key and the left mouse button. A popup window appears.

13. Click in the Name text field, type **myLabel**, and click the Connect button. Xcode creates the following IBOutlet:

    @IBOutlet var myLabel: UILabel!

14. Move the mouse pointer over the text field, hold down the Control key, and Ctrl-drag under the class ViewController line in the ViewController.swift file.

15. Release the Control key and the left mouse button. A popup window appears.

16. Click in the Name text field, type **myTextField**, and click the
     Connect button. Xcode creates the following IBOutlet:

     `@IBOutlet var myTextField: UITextField!`

17. Move the mouse pointer over the image view, hold down the
     Control key, and Ctrl-drag under the class ViewController line in
     the ViewController.swift file.

18. Release the Control key and the left mouse button. A popup
     window appears.

19. Click in the Name text field, type **myImageView**, and click the
     Connect button. Xcode creates the following IBOutlet:

     `@IBOutlet var myImageView: UIImageView!`

20. Choose View ➤ Standard Editor ➤ Show Standard Editor, or click
     the Standard Editor icon in the upper right corner of the Xcode
     window.

21. Click the ViewController.swift file in the Navigator pane.

22. Add the following viewWillAppear method:

```
override func viewWillAppear(_ animated: Bool) {
    myLabel.center.x -= view.bounds.width
    myTextField.center.x -= view.bounds.width
    myImageView.center.x -= view.bounds.width
}
```

Right before the view appears on the screen, this code moves the
label, text field, and image view to the left the exact width of the
entire view. This essentially hides the label, text field, and image
view from sight.

If you wanted to move the label, text field, and image view to the right side of the screen, you would simply add the view width to the center of each item such as

```
override func viewWillAppear(_ animated: Bool) {
    myLabel.center.x += view.bounds.width
    myTextField.center.x += view.bounds.width
    myImageView.center.x += view.bounds.width
}
```

If you wanted to move the label, text field, and image view to the top of the screen, you would simply subtract the view height to the center of each item such as

```
override func viewWillAppear(_ animated: Bool) {
    myLabel.center.x -= view.bounds.height
    myTextField.center.x -= view.bounds.height
    myImageView.center.x -= view.bounds.height
}
```

23. Edit the viewDidLoad method as follows:

```
override func viewDidLoad() {
    super.viewDidLoad()

    UIView.animate(withDuration: 2.0) {
        self.myLabel.center.x += self.view.bounds.width
        self.myTextField.center.x += self.view.bounds.width
        self.myImageView.center.x += self.view.bounds.width
    }
```

The viewWillAppear method moved the label, text field, and image view off to the left by the width of the view (which will change depending on the iOS device the app runs on). The viewDidLoad method now uses the UIView.animate method to move the label, text field, and image view to the right by the width of the view. This animation takes 2.0 seconds.

The entire ViewController.swift file should look like this:

```swift
import UIKit

class ViewController: UIViewController {

    @IBOutlet var myLabel: UILabel!
    @IBOutlet var myTextField: UITextField!
    @IBOutlet var myImageView: UIImageView!

    override func viewWillAppear(_ animated: Bool) {
        myLabel.center.x -= view.bounds.width
        myTextField.center.x -= view.bounds.width
        myImageView.center.x -= view.bounds.width
    }

    override func viewDidLoad() {
        super.viewDidLoad()

        UIView.animate(withDuration: 2.0) {
            self.myLabel.center.x += self.view.bounds.width
            self.myTextField.center.x += self.view.bounds.width
            self.myImageView.center.x += self.view.bounds.width
        }

    }

}
```

24. Click the Run button or choose Product ➤ Run. The Simulator
screen appears, and the label, text field, and image view slide out
from the left and onto the user interface as shown in Figure 15-2.

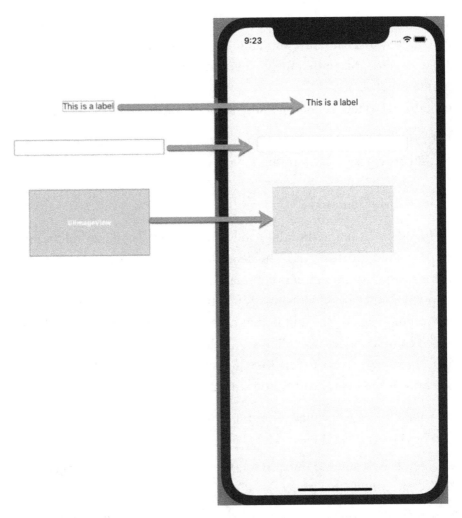

Figure 15-2. *The label, text field, and image view slide onto the user interface from the left*

25.   Choose Simulator ➤ Quit Simulator to return back to Xcode.

Customizing Animation with Delays and Options

Rather than have multiple items move at the same time, you may want them to move individually. To do this, you need to introduce a delay for one or more animations, so rather than starting immediately, an animation may wait a fixed amount of time (such as 0.25 or 2.8 seconds) before running. By delaying animation, you can let one item animate before another starts, or stagger animation among multiple items so they start and finish animating at different times.

Normally animation runs just once and then stops. However, you can define two additional options that cause the animation to repeat indefinitely or to run forward and backward while repeating indefinitely. This can be useful to display animation to attract the user's attention.

The modified UIView.animate command to include delays and options looks like this:

```
UIView.animate(withDuration: 3.4, delay: 2.3, options: [.repeat,
.autoreverse], animations: {
    // animate code here
}, completion: nil)
```

The withDuration defines how long the animation takes. Higher values take longer while shorter values take less time. The delay defines how long to wait before running the code inside the UIView.animate command.

The options can be listed individually (such as .repeat) or grouped in an array (such as [.repeat, .autoreverse]). The animations area is where you type Swift code to animate an item. The completion handler allows for a closure to run after the animation finishes. If you don't want any closure to run, then just set completion to nil.

To see how to add delays and options to animation, follow these steps:

1. Create a new iOS Single View App project and name it AnimationDelayApp.

2. Create the same user interface as the AnimationMoveApp project (or just modify that project).

3. Create three IBOutlets for the label, text field, and image view as follows:

```
@IBOutlet var myLabel: UILabel!
@IBOutlet var myTextField: UITextField!
@IBOutlet var myImageView: UIImageView!
```

4. Change the background color for both the view and the image view to make them easier to see.

5. Add the following viewWillAppear method:

```
override func viewWillAppear(_ animated: Bool) {
    myLabel.center.x -= view.bounds.width
    myTextField.center.x -= view.bounds.width
    myImageView.center.x -= view.bounds.width
}
```

6. Add the following in the viewDidLoad method:

```
UIView.animate(withDuration: 2.0) {
    self.myLabel.center.x += self.view.bounds.width
}
```

This animates the label exactly like the AnimateMoveApp project to make it easier to see how the next two animations differ.

7. Add the following in the viewDidLoad method to delay animation and repeat and autoreverse animation continually:

```
UIView.animate(withDuration: 3.4, delay: 2.3, options: [.repeat,
.autoreverse], animations: {
    self.myTextField.center.x += self.view.bounds.width
}, completion: nil)
```

8. Add the following in the viewDidLoad method to delay animation and only repeat the animation:

```
UIView.animate(withDuration: 1.4, delay: 3.5, options: .repeat,
animations: {
    self.myImageView.center.x += self.view.bounds.width
}, completion: nil)
```

The entire ViewController.swift file should look like this:

```
import UIKit

class ViewController: UIViewController {

    @IBOutlet var myLabel: UILabel!
    @IBOutlet var myTextField: UITextField!
```

```
@IBOutlet var myImageView: UIImageView!

override func viewWillAppear(_ animated: Bool) {
    myLabel.center.x -= view.bounds.width
    myTextField.center.x -= view.bounds.width
    myImageView.center.x -= view.bounds.width
}

override func viewDidLoad() {
    super.viewDidLoad()

    UIView.animate(withDuration: 2.0) {
        self.myLabel.center.x += self.view.bounds.width
    }

    UIView.animate(withDuration: 3.4, delay: 2.3, options:
    [.repeat, .autoreverse], animations: {
        self.myTextField.center.x += self.view.bounds.width
    }, completion: nil)

    UIView.animate(withDuration: 1.4, delay: 3.5, options:
    .repeat, animations: {
        self.myImageView.center.x += self.view.bounds.width
    }, completion: nil)

    }

}
```

9. Click the Run button or choose Product ➤ Run. The Simulator screen appears. Notice how the three different items appear animated. The label slides into place and stops. The text field slides right and then left. The image view slides right, disappears from view, and repeats over and over again.

10. Choose Simulator ➤ Quit Simulator to return back to Xcode.

Customizing Animation with Damping and Velocity

Another way to modify the movement of animated objects is to define a velocity and a damping ratio. The velocity defines how fast an object moves, measured in seconds. Higher values create faster movement, while lower values create slower movement.

The damping ratio creates a "spring" effect that makes a moving object appear to oscillate. A value of 1.0 creates no oscillation, while values closer to 0 create much greater oscillation.

The modified UIView.animate command to include velocity and damping looks like this:

```
UIView.animate(withDuration: 2.0, delay: 0.5,
usingSpringWithDamping: 0.1, initialSpringVelocity: 0.5, options:
[.repeat, .autoreverse], animations: {
    // animate code here
}, completion: nil)
```

To see how to add delays and options to animation, follow these steps:

1. Create a new iOS Single View App project and name it AnimationDampingApp.

2. Create the same user interface as the AnimationMoveApp project (or just modify that project).

3. Create three IBOutlets for the label, text field, and image view as follows:

```
@IBOutlet var myLabel: UILabel!
@IBOutlet var myTextField: UITextField!
@IBOutlet var myImageView: UIImageView!
```

4. Change the background color for both the view and the image view to make them easier to see.

5. Add the following in the viewDidLoad method to create ordinary animation without velocity or damping to make it easy to see the difference:

```
UIView.animate(withDuration: 4.5) {
    self.myLabel.center.x += self.view.bounds.width
}
```

6. Add the following in the viewDidLoad method to add damping and velocity:

```
UIView.animate(withDuration: 2.0, delay: 0.5,
usingSpringWithDamping: 0.75, initialSpringVelocity: 0.2, options:
[.repeat, .autoreverse], animations: {
    self.myTextField.center.x += self.view.bounds.width
}, completion: nil)
```

7. Add the following in the viewDidLoad method to see how different damping and velocity values affect the animation:

```
UIView.animate(withDuration: 2.0, delay: 0.5,
usingSpringWithDamping: 0.1, initialSpringVelocity: 0.5, options:
[.repeat, .autoreverse], animations: {
    self.myImageView.center.x += self.view.bounds.width
}, completion: nil)
```

The entire ViewController.swift file should look like this:

```
import UIKit

class ViewController: UIViewController {

    @IBOutlet var myLabel: UILabel!
    @IBOutlet var myTextField: UITextField!
    @IBOutlet var myImageView: UIImageView!

    override func viewDidLoad() {
        super.viewDidLoad()

        UIView.animate(withDuration: 4.5) {
            self.myLabel.center.x += self.view.bounds.width
        }

        UIView.animate(withDuration: 2.0, delay: 0.5,
        usingSpringWithDamping: 0.75, initialSpringVelocity: 0.2,
        options: [.repeat, .autoreverse], animations: {
            self.myTextField.center.x += self.view.bounds.width
        }, completion: nil)
```

```
UIView.animate(withDuration: 2.0, delay: 0.5,
usingSpringWithDamping: 0.1, initialSpringVelocity: 0.5,
options: [.repeat, .autoreverse], animations: {
    self.myImageView.center.x += self.view.bounds.width
}, completion: nil)

    }

}
```

8. Click the Run button or choose Product ➤ Run. The Simulator screen appears. Notice how the three different items appear animated. The label slides into place and stops. The text field slides right and then left. The image view slides right and then left with greater oscillation than the text field.

9. Choose Simulator ➤ Quit Simulator to return back to Xcode.

Resizing Items with Animation

Besides moving an item from one location to another, you can also resize an item by changing its width, height, or both its width and height. To change a user interface object's width or height, you need to specify the IBOutlet name of the object you want to resize and then specify a width or height value change such as

```
IBOutletName.frame.size.width += value
IBOutletName.frame.size.height += value
```

To see how to resize user interface objects, follow these steps:

1. Create a new iOS Single View App project and name it AnimationResizeApp.

2. Create the same user interface as the AnimationMoveApp project (or just modify that project).

3. Hold down the Command key and click the label, text field, and image view to select them all.

4. Click the Align icon to display a popup window.

5. Select the Horizontally in Container check box and click the Add 3 Constraints button as shown in Figure 15-3.

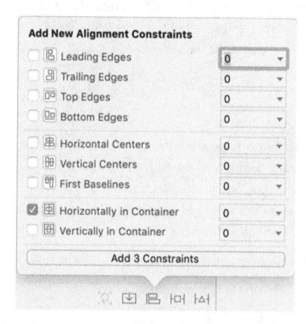

Figure 15-3. *Adding horizontal constraints on the label, text field, and image view*

6. Choose Editor ➤ Resolve Auto Layout Issues ➤ Add Missing Constraints in the bottom half of the submenu. Xcode adds additional constraints to the label, text field, and image view.

7. Create three IBOutlets for the label, text field, and image view as follows:

```
@IBOutlet var myLabel: UILabel!
@IBOutlet var myTextField: UITextField!
@IBOutlet var myImageView: UIImageView!
```

8. Change the background color for both the view and the image view to make them easier to see.

9.   Edit the viewDidLoad method as follows:

```
override func viewDidLoad() {
    super.viewDidLoad()

    myLabel.text = "This is a label displaying text on a user interface."

    UIView.animate(withDuration: 2.0, delay: 0.0, options:
    [.repeat, .autoreverse], animations: {
        self.myLabel.frame.size.width += 25
        self.myLabel.frame.size.height += 25
    }, completion: nil)

    UIView.animate(withDuration: 3.5, delay: 0.45, options:
    [.repeat, .autoreverse], animations: {
        self.myTextField.frame.size.width += 50
    }, completion: nil)

    UIView.animate(withDuration: 2.5, delay: 1.5, options:
    [.repeat, .autoreverse], animations: {
        self.myImageView.frame.size.height += 20
        self.myImageView.frame.size.width += 20
    }, completion: nil)

}
```

The entire ViewController.swift file should look like this:

```
import UIKit

class ViewController: UIViewController {

    @IBOutlet var myLabel: UILabel!
    @IBOutlet var myTextField: UITextField!
    @IBOutlet var myImageView: UIImageView!

    override func viewDidLoad() {
        super.viewDidLoad()

        myLabel.text = "This is a label displaying text on a user
        interface."
```

```
UIView.animate(withDuration: 2.0, delay: 0.0, options:
[.repeat, .autoreverse], animations: {
    self.myLabel.frame.size.width += 25
    self.myLabel.frame.size.height += 25
}, completion: nil)

UIView.animate(withDuration: 3.5, delay: 0.45, options:
[.repeat, .autoreverse], animations: {
    self.myTextField.frame.size.width += 50
}, completion: nil)

UIView.animate(withDuration: 2.5, delay: 1.5, options:
[.repeat, .autoreverse], animations: {
    self.myImageView.frame.size.height += 20
    self.myImageView.frame.size.width += 20
}, completion: nil)

    }

}
```

10. Click the Run button or choose Product ➤ Run. The Simulator screen appears. Notice the label, text field, and image view appear to grow and shrink over and over again.

11. Choose Simulator ➤ Quit Simulator to return back to Xcode.

Rotating Items with Animation

Rotating an item involves defining a rotation angle using the transform property and the CGAffineTransform command as follows:

```
IBOutletName.transform = CGAffineTransform(rotationAngle: value)
```

The CGAffineTransform command rotates items by radians, so if you're more comfortable specifying angles in degrees, we need to convert degrees into radians using a command from the GLKit framework like this:

```
import GLKit
```

Once the GLKit framework is imported into a project, we can access the GLKMathRadiansToDegrees function that accepts degrees and converts them to radians like this:

```
GLKMathDegreesToRadians(45)
```

To see how to rotate user interface objects, follow these steps:

1. Create a new iOS Single View App project and name it AnimationResizeApp.

2. Create the same user interface as the AnimationMoveApp project (or just modify that project).

3. Choose Editor ➤ Resolve Auto Layout Issues ➤ Reset to Suggested Constraints in the bottom half of the submenu. Xcode adds additional constraints to the label, text field, and image view.

4. Create three IBOutlets for the label, text field, and image view as follows:

```
@IBOutlet var myLabel: UILabel!
@IBOutlet var myTextField: UITextField!
@IBOutlet var myImageView: UIImageView!
```

5. Change the background color for both the view and the image view to make them easier to see.

6. Add the following under the import UIKit line:

```
import GLKit
```

7. Edit the viewDidLoad method as follows:

```
override func viewDidLoad() {
    super.viewDidLoad()

    let rotateMe = GLKMathDegreesToRadians(45)

    UIView.animate(withDuration: 2.0, delay: 0.0, options:
    [.repeat, .autoreverse], animations: {
        self.myLabel.transform = CGAffineTransform(rotationAngle:
        CGFloat(rotateMe))
```

```
    }, completion: nil)

    UIView.animate(withDuration: 3.5, delay: 0.45, options:
    [.repeat, .autoreverse], animations: {
        self.myTextField.transform = CGAffineTransform(rotation
        Angle: CGFloat(-rotateMe))
    }, completion: nil)

    UIView.animate(withDuration: 2.5, delay: 1.5, options:
    [.repeat, .autoreverse], animations: {
        self.myImageView.transform = CGAffineTransform(rotation
        Angle: CGFloat(rotateMe))
    }, completion: nil)
}
```

The entire ViewController.swift file should look like this:

```
import UIKit
import GLKit

class ViewController: UIViewController {

    @IBOutlet var myLabel: UILabel!
    @IBOutlet var myTextField: UITextField!
    @IBOutlet var myImageView: UIImageView!

    override func viewDidLoad() {
        super.viewDidLoad()

        let rotateMe = GLKMathDegreesToRadians(45)

        UIView.animate(withDuration: 2.0, delay: 0.0, options:
        [.repeat, .autoreverse], animations: {
            self.myLabel.transform = CGAffineTransform(rotation
            Angle: CGFloat(rotateMe))
        }, completion: nil)

        UIView.animate(withDuration: 3.5, delay: 0.45, options:
        [.repeat, .autoreverse], animations: {
```

```
        self.myTextField.transform = CGAffineTransform(rotation
        Angle: CGFloat(-rotateMe))
    }, completion: nil)

    UIView.animate(withDuration: 2.5, delay: 1.5, options:
    [.repeat, .autoreverse], animations: {
        self.myImageView.transform = CGAffineTransform(rotation
        Angle: CGFloat(rotateMe))
    }, completion: nil)
  }

}
```

8. Click the Run button or choose Product ➤ Run. The Simulator
    screen appears, and the animation begins on all three user
    interface objects as shown in Figure 15-4.

Figure 15-4. *Rotating a label, text field, and image view*

    9.   Choose Simulator ➤ Quit Simulator to return back to Xcode.

Changing Transparency with Animation

Rather than move or rotate an item, you might want to change its appearance instead. One way to do this is to change the transparency of an object. This can make an object gradually disappear and reappear again.

    To see how to change the transparency of a user interface objects, follow these steps:

    1.   Create a new iOS Single View App project and name it AnimationColorApp.

2. Create the same user interface as the AnimationMoveApp project (or just modify that project).

3. Create three IBOutlets for the label, text field, and image view as follows:

```
@IBOutlet var myLabel: UILabel!
@IBOutlet var myTextField: UITextField!
@IBOutlet var myImageView: UIImageView!
```

4. Change the background color for both the view and the image view to make them easier to see.

5. Edit the viewDidLoad method as follows:

```
override func viewDidLoad() {
    super.viewDidLoad()

    UIView.animate(withDuration: 2.0, delay: 0.0, options:
    [.repeat, .autoreverse], animations: {
        self.myLabel.alpha = 0.0
        self.myLabel.backgroundColor = UIColor.lightGray
    }, completion: nil)

    UIView.animate(withDuration: 3.5, delay: 0.45, options:
    [.repeat, .autoreverse], animations: {
        self.myTextField.alpha = 0.0
        self.myTextField.backgroundColor = UIColor.green
    }, completion: nil)

    UIView.animate(withDuration: 2.5, delay: 1.5, options:
    [.repeat, .autoreverse], animations: {
        self.myImageView.alpha = 0.0
    }, completion: nil)

}
```

The entire ViewController.swift file should look like this:

```
import UIKit

class ViewController: UIViewController {

    @IBOutlet var myLabel: UILabel!
    @IBOutlet var myTextField: UITextField!
    @IBOutlet var myImageView: UIImageView!

    override func viewDidLoad() {
        super.viewDidLoad()

        UIView.animate(withDuration: 2.0, delay: 0.0, options:
        [.repeat, .autoreverse], animations: {
            self.myLabel.alpha = 0.0
            self.myLabel.backgroundColor = UIColor.lightGray
        }, completion: nil)

        UIView.animate(withDuration: 3.5, delay: 0.45, options:
        [.repeat, .autoreverse], animations: {
            self.myTextField.alpha = 0.0
            self.myTextField.backgroundColor = UIColor.green
        }, completion: nil)

        UIView.animate(withDuration: 2.5, delay: 1.5, options:
        [.repeat, .autoreverse], animations: {
            self.myImageView.alpha = 0.0
        }, completion: nil)

    }

}
```

6. Click the Run button or choose Product ➤ Run. The Simulator screen appears, and the animation begins on all three user interface objects as they appear and disappear.

7. Choose Simulator ➤ Quit Simulator.

Animating Transitions Between View Controllers

When an app has multiple views, it needs a way to switch from one view controller to another. By using a navigation or tab bar controller, you can get a simple animation that slides one view controller over the other, but you can also create your own animation for transitions between view controllers.

To see how to create custom animation transitions between view controllers, follow these steps:

1. Create a new iOS Single View App project and name it AnimationTransitionApp.

2. Click the Main.storyboard file in the Navigator pane.

3. Click the Library icon and drag and drop a button anywhere on the user interface.

4. Double-click this button, type **Show**, and press Enter.

5. Choose Editor ➤ Resolve Auto Layout Issues ➤ Reset to Suggested Constraints. Xcode adds constraints to the button.

6. Choose View ➤ Assistant Editor ➤ Show Assistant Editor, or click the Assistant Editor icon in the upper right corner of the Xcode window. Xcode shows the Main.storyboard side by side with the ViewController.swift file.

7. Move the mouse pointer over the button, hold down the Control key, and Ctrl-drag above the last curly bracket at the bottom of the ViewController.swift file.

8. Release the Control key and the left mouse button. A popup window appears.

9. Click in the Name text field, type **openView**, click the Type popup menu and choose UIButton, and click the Connect button. Xcode creates an openView IBAction method.

10. Click the Library icon and drag and drop a View Controller in the storyboard.

11. Move the mouse pointer over the yellow circle at the top of the first view controller, hold down the Control key, and Ctrl-drag anywhere over the second view controller as shown in Figure 15-5.

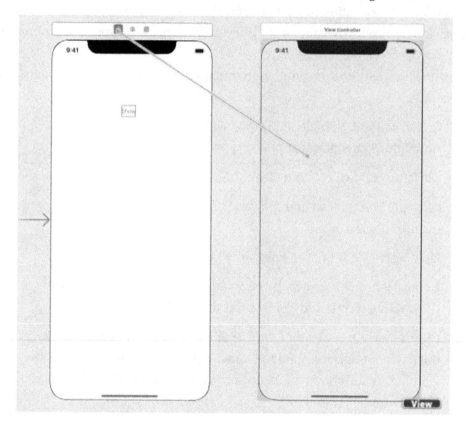

Figure 15-5. *Ctrl-dragging from the first view controller to the second view controller*

12. Release the Control key and the left mouse button. A popup window appears as shown in Figure 15-6.

Figure 15-6. *Choosing a Custom segue*

380

13. Choose Custom. Xcode draws a segue connecting the two view controllers.

14. Click View under the second view controller in the Document Outline.

15. Choose View ➤ Inspectors ➤ Show Attributes Inspector, or click the Attributes Inspector icon in the upper right corner of the Xcode window.

16. Click the Background popup menu and choose a color such as orange. This will make the second view controller easy to see when it appears.

17. Click the Library icon and drag and drop a button on the second view controller.

18. Double-click this button, type **Hide**, and press Enter.

19. Choose Editor ➤ Resolve Auto Layout Issues ➤ Reset to Suggested Constraints. Xcode adds constraints to the button.

20. Choose File ➤ New ➤ File. A template dialog appears.

21. Choose Cocoa Touch Class under the iOS category and click the Next button.

22. Click in the Class text field and type **SecondViewController**.

23. Click the Subclass of popup menu and choose UIViewController. Then click the Next and Create button. Xcode adds the SecondViewController.swift file to the Navigator pane.

24. Click the Main.storyboard file in the Navigator pane.

25. Click the yellow circle at the top of the second view controller to select it.

26. Choose View ➤ Inspectors ➤ Show Identity Inspector, or click the Identity Inspector icon in the upper right corner of the Xcode window.

27. Click the Class popup menu and choose SecondViewController.

28. Choose View ➤ Assistant Editor ➤ Show Assistant Editor, or click the Assistant Editor icon in the upper right corner of the Xcode window. Xcode shows the Main.storyboard side by side with the SecondViewController.swift file.

29. Move the mouse pointer over the button, hold down the Control key, and Ctrl-drag above the last curly bracket at the bottom of the SecondViewController.swift file.

30. Release the Control key and the left mouse button. A popup window appears.

31. Click in the Name text field, type **dismissButton**, click the Type popup menu and choose UIButton, and click the Connect button. Xcode creates an dismissButton IBAction method.

32. Edit the dismissButton IBAction method as follows:

```
@IBAction func dismissButton(_ sender: UIButton) {
    dismiss(animated: true, completion: nil)
}
```

33. Choose View ➤ Standard Editor ➤ Show Standard Editor, or click the Standard Editor icon in the upper right corner of the Xcode window.

34. Click File ➤ New ➤ File. A template dialog appears.

35. Choose Cocoa Touch Class under the iOS category and click the Next button.

36. Click in the Class text field and type **CustomSegue** as shown in Figure 15-7.

37. Click the Subclass of popup menu and choose UIStoryboardSegue as shown in Figure 15-7.

Choose options for your new file:

Class: CustomSegue

Subclass of: UIStoryboardSegue

☐ Also create XIB file

Language: Swift

Cancel   Previous   Next

Figure 15-7. *Creating a UIStoryboardSegue .swift class file*

38. Click the Next and Create button. Xcode adds the SecondViewController.swift file to the Navigator pane.

39. Click the Main.storyboard file in the Navigator pane.

40. Click Custom segue to "View Controller" in the Document Outline.

41. Choose View ➤ Inspectors ➤ Show Attributes Inspector, or click the Attributes Inspector icon in the upper right corner of the Xcode window.

42. Click in the Identifier text field and type **custom**. (This can be any arbitrary text.)

43. Click the Class popup menu and choose CustomSegue as shown in Figure 15-8.

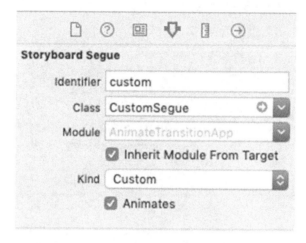

Figure 15-8. *Adding an Identifier and Class to the segue*

44. Click the ViewController.swift file in the Navigator pane.

45. Edit the openView IBAction method as follows:

```
@IBAction func openView(_ sender: UIButton) {
    self.performSegue(withIdentifier: "custom", sender: self)
}
```

The entire ViewController.swift file should look like this:

```
import UIKit

class ViewController: UIViewController {

    override func viewDidLoad() {
        super.viewDidLoad()
        // Do any additional setup after loading the view.
    }

    @IBAction func openView(_ sender: UIButton) {
        self.performSegue(withIdentifier: "custom", sender: self)
    }
}
```

The entire SecondViewController.swift file should look like this:

```swift
import UIKit

class SecondViewController: UIViewController {

    override func viewDidLoad() {
        super.viewDidLoad()
        // Do any additional setup after loading the view.
    }

    @IBAction func dismissButton(_ sender: UIButton) {
        dismiss(animated: true, completion: nil)
    }
}
```

At this point, we've created the basic structure for defining an animated transition between the two view controllers. The final step involves defining this animation in the CustomSegue.swift file.

Creating a custom transition involves creating a segue between two view controllers and giving it a name. Then that segue needs its own .swift file that defines the actual animation between the two view controllers. This segue .swift file defines the starting and ending point of the animation. Some different ways to transition between view controllers include

- Sliding the second view controller over the first from different angles

- Scaling the second view controller so it appears to grow and cover the first view controller

- Rotating the second view controller into place over the first view controller

When sliding the second view controller over the first, you need to define an x and y starting and ending point for the upper left corner of the second view controller. The origin (0,0) is defined by the upper left corner of the screen as shown in Figure 15-9.

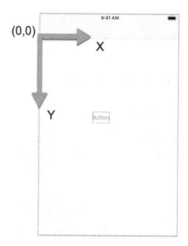

Figure 15-9. *The origin (0,0) appears in the upper left corner of the screen*

The starting point of the second view controller defines the upper left corner, which should place it off the screen. If you wanted the second view controller to slide into place from the bottom right corner, you would need to define its starting point at the bottom right corner like this:

```
secondVC.view.transform = CGAffineTransform(translationX: firstVC.view.
bounds.width, y: firstVC.view.bounds.height)
```

Then the ending point of the second view controller needs to be the origin (0,0) like this:

```
secondVC.view.transform = CGAffineTransform(translationX: 0.0, y: 0.0)
```

No matter what starting point you define for the second view controller, its ending point will always be the origin (0,0). By defining different values for the x and y starting point, you can make the second view controller slide into place from different angles as shown in Figure 15-10.

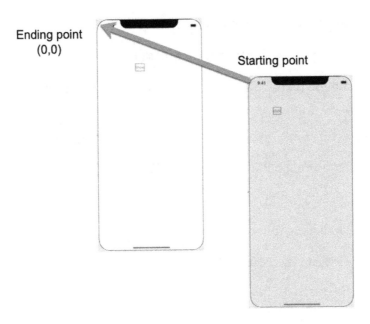

Figure 15-10. *The ending point is always (0,0), but the starting point defines the upper left corner position*

Scaling involves changing the width (x) and height (y) of the second view controller. A scaling value of 0 means the size of the second view controller is also zero, making the second view controller invisible. A scaling value of 1 means the size of the second view controller is its normal size. So animation involves defining a scaling value of 0 and an ending value of 1 like this:

```
secondVC.view.transform = CGAffineTransform(scaleX: 0.0, y: 0.0)
secondVC.view.transform = CGAffineTransform(scaleX: 1.0, y: 1.0)
```

Rotating means defining the starting rotation angle. The ending rotation angle is always 0. Since the rotation angle is measured in radians, we can use degrees and then convert those degrees into radians. That involves importing the GLKit framework and using the GLKMathDegreesToRadians function like this:

```
GLKMathDegreesToRadians(45)
```

The starting rotation angle can be any value you wish such as

```
let angle = GLKMathDegreesToRadians(125)
secondVC.view.transform = CGAffineTransform(rotationAngle:
CGFloat(angle))
```

387

Then the ending rotation angle is always 0 like this:

```
secondVC.view.transform = CGAffineTransform(rotationAngle: 0.0)
```

To define animation for the transition between two view controllers, follow these steps:

1. Click the CustomSegue.swift file in the Navigator pane.

2. Add the following under the import UIKit line:

   ```
   import GLKit
   ```

3. Add the following function:

   ```
   override func perform() {

   }
   ```

4. Add these three lines inside the perform() function:

   ```
   override func perform() {
       let firstVC = self.source
       let secondVC = self.destination

       firstVC.view.addSubview(secondVC.view)
   ```

   The source is the first view controller, while the destination is the second view controller that will transition onto the first view controller. The third line adds the second view controller onto the first view controller, making it visible.

5. Add the next lines in the perform() function:

   ```
   //secondVC.view.transform = CGAffineTransform(translationX: firstVC.view.bounds.width, y: firstVC.view.bounds.height)
   ```

   ```
   //secondVC.view.transform = CGAffineTransform(scaleX: 0.0, y: 0.0)
   ```

   ```
   let angle = GLKMathDegreesToRadians(125)
   secondVC.view.transform = CGAffineTransform(rotationAngle: CGFloat(angle))
   ```

   ```
   //secondVC.view.alpha = 0
   ```

These lines define the starting point for the second view controller. The first commented line is used to slide the second view controller into position and places the second view controller's upper left corner at the bottom right corner of the first view controller.

The second commented line is used to scale the second view controller and defines its scale as 0, which makes the second view controller so small that it's invisible.

The two uncommented lines first convert 125 degrees into radians and then define the starting rotation of the second view controller at 125 degrees.

The last uncommented line defines a transparency of 0, which makes the second view controller invisible.

6. Add the following animation code in the perform() function:

```
UIView.animate(withDuration: 0.8, animations: {
    //secondVC.view.transform = CGAffineTransform(translationX:
    0.0, y: 0.0)
    //secondVC.view.transform = CGAffineTransform(scaleX: 1.0, y: 1.0)
    secondVC.view.transform = CGAffineTransform(rotationAngle: 0.0)
    //secondVC.view.alpha = 1
}) { (finished) in
    firstVC.present(secondVC, animated: false, completion: nil)
}
```

This UIView.animate command defines how long the animation lasts (0.8 seconds) and includes code to define the ending point for all transitions.

The first commented line moves the upper left corner of the second view controller at (0,0), which is the upper left corner of the screen.

The second commented line scales the second view controller with a value of 1, which makes the second view controller appear full size on the screen.

The uncommented line defines the ending rotation angle as 0, which makes the second view controller appear correctly on the screen.

The last commented line defines the second view controller's transparency as 1, which makes it fully visible.

After the animation is complete, a closure presents the second view controller but without animation so it will use our defined animation.

The entire CustomSegue.swift file should look like this:

```swift
import UIKit
import GLKit // Only needed if you want to convert degrees into
           //    radians for rotation

class CustomSegue: UIStoryboardSegue {

    override func perform() {
        let firstVC = self.source
        let secondVC = self.destination

        firstVC.view.addSubview(secondVC.view)

        //secondVC.view.transform = CGAffineTransform(translationX:
        //    firstVC.view.bounds.width, y: firstVC.view.bounds.height)

        //secondVC.view.transform = CGAffineTransform(scaleX: 0.0,
        //    y: 0.0)

        let angle = GLKMathDegreesToRadians(125)
        secondVC.view.transform = CGAffineTransform(rotationAngle:
            CGFloat(angle))

        //secondVC.view.alpha = 0

        UIView.animate(withDuration: 0.8, animations: {
            //secondVC.view.transform =
            //    CGAffineTransform(translationX: 0.0, y: 0.0)
            //secondVC.view.transform = CGAffineTransform(scaleX:
            //    1.0, y: 1.0)
            secondVC.view.transform = CGAffineTransform(rotation
                Angle: 0.0)
```

```
            //secondVC.view.alpha = 1
        }) { (finished) in
            firstVC.present(secondVC, animated: false,
            completion: nil)
        }

    }

}
```

7. Click the Run button or choose Product ➤ Run. The Simulator screen appears and displays the Show button.

8. Click the Show button. The second view controller rotates into position.

9. Click the Hide button to return back to the first view controller.

10. Choose Simulator ➤ Quit Simulator to return back to Xcode.

Experiment by commenting out the rotation angle code and uncommenting the translation code like this:

```
secondVC.view.transform = CGAffineTransform(translationX: firstVC.
view.bounds.width, y: firstVC.view.bounds.height)


//secondVC.view.transform = CGAffineTransform(scaleX: 0.0, y: 0.0)

//let angle = GLKMathDegreesToRadians(125)
//secondVC.view.transform = CGAffineTransform(rotationAngle:
CGFloat(angle))

UIView.animate(withDuration: 0.8, animations: {
    secondVC.view.transform = CGAffineTransform(translationX: 0.0,
    y: 0.0)
    //secondVC.view.transform = CGAffineTransform(scaleX: 1.0, y: 1.0)
    //secondVC.view.transform = CGAffineTransform(rotationAngle: 0.0)
}) { (finished) in
    firstVC.present(secondVC, animated: false, completion: nil)
}
```

Then repeat except uncommenting out the scaling code and commenting out the other animation code like this:

```
//secondVC.view.transform = CGAffineTransform(translationX:
firstVC.view.bounds.width, y: firstVC.view.bounds.height)

secondVC.view.transform = CGAffineTransform(scaleX: 0.0, y: 0.0)

//let angle = GLKMathDegreesToRadians(125)
//secondVC.view.transform = CGAffineTransform(rotationAngle:
CGFloat(angle))

UIView.animate(withDuration: 0.8, animations: {
    //secondVC.view.transform = CGAffineTransform(translationX:
    0.0, y: 0.0)
    secondVC.view.transform = CGAffineTransform(scaleX: 1.0, y: 1.0)
    //secondVC.view.transform = CGAffineTransform(rotationAngle: 0.0)
}) { (finished) in
    firstVC.present(secondVC, animated: false, completion: nil)
}
```

Finally, uncomment out the transparency code and comment out the other animation code like this:

```
//secondVC.view.transform = CGAffineTransform(translationX:
firstVC.view.bounds.width, y: firstVC.view.bounds.height)

//secondVC.view.transform = CGAffineTransform(scaleX: 0.0, y: 0.0)

//let angle = GLKMathDegreesToRadians(125)
//secondVC.view.transform = CGAffineTransform(rotationAngle:
CGFloat(angle))

secondVC.view.alpha = 0

UIView.animate(withDuration: 0.8, animations: {
    //secondVC.view.transform = CGAffineTransform(translationX:
    0.0, y: 0.0)
    //secondVC.view.transform = CGAffineTransform(scaleX: 1.0, y: 1.0)
    //secondVC.view.transform = CGAffineTransform(rotationAngle: 0.0)
```

```
        secondVC.view.alpha = 1
    }) { (finished) in
        firstVC.present(secondVC, animated: false, completion: nil)
    }
```

Simple Animation Transition Between View Controllers

Rather than define your own animation transitions between view controllers, Xcode offers a Transition Style option that lets you choose how a view controller appears on the screen. The four different Transition Styles include

- Cover Vertical – The view controller slides up from the bottom of the screen (default).

- Flip Horizontal – The current view controller flips from right to left in 3D as if the new view controller were on back of the previous view controller.

- Cross Dissolve – The current view controller fades out, while the new view controller fades in.

- Partial Curl – The current view controller curls up from the bottom right corner like turning the page of a book, revealing the new view controller underneath.

To see how to choose these different animation transitions between view controllers, follow these steps:

1. Create a new iOS Single View App project and name it OpenViewApp.

2. Click the Main.storyboard file in the Navigator pane.

3. Click the Library icon and drag and drop a button on the view controller.

4. Choose Editor ➤ Resolve Auto Layout Issues ➤ Reset to Suggested Constraints. Xcode adds constraints to the button.

5. Choose View ➤ Assistant Editor ➤ Show Assistant Editor, or click the Assistant Editor icon in the upper right corner of the Xcode window. Xcode shows the Main.storyboard side by side with the ViewController.swift file.

6. Move the mouse pointer over the button, hold down the Control key, and Ctrl-drag above the last curly bracket at the bottom of the ViewController.swift file.

7. Release the Control key and the left mouse button. A popup window appears.

8. Click in the Name text field, type **openView**, click the Type popup menu and choose UIButton, and click the Connect button. Xcode creates an IBAction method.

9. Modify this openView IBAction method as follows:

```
@IBAction func openView(_ sender: UIButton) {
    let vc = self.storyboard?.instantiateViewController
    (withIdentifier: "second")
    present(vc!, animated: true, completion: nil)
}
```

The first line creates a "vc" constant that represents a view controller in the storyboard that has a StoryID called "second" (this can be any arbitrary text you wish). Then the second line displays this view controller. That means we need to add a second view controller to the storyboard and give it a Storyboard ID of "second".

10. Click the Library icon and drag and drop a View Controller in the storyboard.

11. Click the Library icon and drag and drop a button on this second view controller in the storyboard.

12. Move the mouse pointer over this button on the second view controller, hold down the Control key, and Ctrl-drag over the first view controller.

13. Release the Control key and the left mouse button. A popup menu appears.

14. Choose Show.

15. Click View (under the second View Controller) in the Document Outline.

16. Choose View ➤ Inspectors ➤ Show Attributes Inspector, or click the Attributes Inspector icon in the upper right corner of the Xcode window.

17. Click the Background popup menu and choose a distinctive color for this second view controller.

18. Click the Transition Style popup menu and choose Flip Horizontal as shown in Figure 15-11.

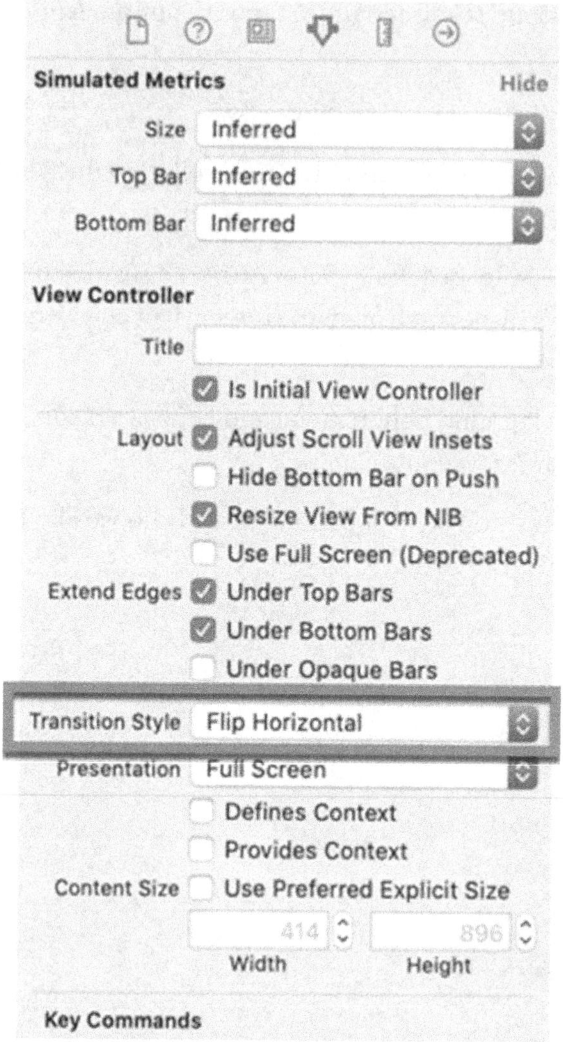

Figure 15-11. *The Transition Style popup menu*

19. Click the second View Controller Scene in the Document Outline
     or click the yellow circle icon at the top of this second view
     controller to select this newly added view controller.

20. Choose View ➤ Inspectors ➤ Show Identity Inspector, or click
     the Identity Inspector icon in the upper right corner of the Xcode
     window.

21. Click in the Storyboard ID text field, type **second**, and press Enter
     as shown in Figure 15-12.

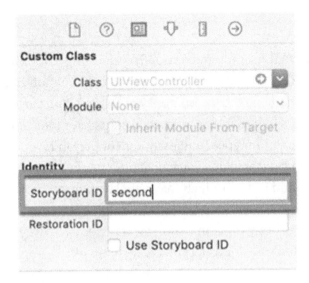

Figure 15-12. *The Storyboard ID text field*

22. Click the first View Controller Scene in the Document Outline or click the yellow circle icon at the top of the first view controller to select the initial view controller (with the white background).

23. Choose View ➤ Inspectors ➤ Show Attributes Inspector, or click the Attributes Inspector icon in the upper right corner of the Xcode window.

24. Click the Transition Style popup menu and choose Flip Horizontal.

25. Click the Run button or choose Product ➤ Run. The Simulator screen displays the user interface.

26. Click the button. Notice that the second view controller appears to flip around because of the Flip Horizontal transition style.

27. Click the button on this second view controller. Notice that the first view controller appears to flip around because it also has a Flip Horizontal transition style.

28. Choose Simulator ➤ Quit Simulator.

By experimenting with different transition styles such as Partial Curl or Cross Dissolve, you can create different ways to display view controllers on the screen.

Summary

Animation can make your user interface visually interesting to look at while also emphasizing any important parts of the user interface. Animation can involve moving, resizing, rotating, or changing the transparency of an item. You can define how long animation lasts and add delays so one animation starts later than another animation. You can also make animation repeat endlessly and/or play in reverse.

By adding damping and velocity, you can define how fast the animation starts and how it oscillates back and forth. Oscillation can make animated items appear to bounce on the screen.

Finally, you can create custom animation for transitions between two view controllers. Such custom transitions let you create more interesting and unique transitions from one view controller to another. If you'd rather not create a custom transition, you can choose different transition styles for your view controllers instead.

CHAPTER 16

Using Machine Learning

Artificial intelligence (AI) has been around since the 1960s. In those early days, computer scientists dreamed of intelligent computers that could think, but the reality proved far less breathtaking. The biggest obstacle to AI was that computer scientists had to mimic intelligence by anticipating all situations. In limited domains like chess, this worked, but when dealing with large amounts of data, this primitive solution failed because it's impossible to anticipate all possible situations that might occur in most cases. That's why the latest developments in AI focus less on hand coding all possibilities and focus more on machine learning.

Machine learning has proven valuable for creating "smarter" programs, especially when they must deal with previously unknown data. For example, credit card companies use machine learning to track your spending patterns. With so many customers, it's impossible for people to track each customer's spending patterns so that's why they rely on machine learning instead.

Machine learning can analyze your spending patterns, and the moment it detects something unusual, such as a purchase in another country or a large, out of the ordinary purchase, the machine learning program flags that as suspicious. Since your spending patterns may change subtly over time, the machine learning program can adjust and recognize valid purchases while spotting suspicious ones. In this way, machine learning adapts to new situations and appears "smarter."

Machine learning is best used for dealing with data that can't be anticipated ahead of time although many programs can adapt machine learning to make the program easier to use. For example, when you type text to write an e-mail or a note, the virtual keyboard displays words and phrases it thinks you're likely to write. By tapping on a word or phrase, you can type faster without writing out the entire word or phrase.

Machine learning can make apps more responsive and versatile. In this chapter, you'll learn how to incorporate machine learning in iOS apps.

© Wallace Wang 2019
W. Wang, *Pro iPhone Development with Swift 5*, https://doi.org/10.1007/978-1-4842-4944-4_16

Understanding Machine Learning

The main idea behind machine learning is that computer scientists create generic algorithms that they train using large amounts of data. When the algorithm gets the problem right, it modifies its own code so it can identify similar types of problems in the future. When the algorithm gets the problem wrong, it also modifies its own code to reduce the chance of making the same mistake again. Such training and feedback creates a program that literally learns, hence the term machine learning. Best of all, the algorithm trains itself based on data it receives so there's no need for a human programmer to modify the algorithm by hand, which would be tedious and inefficient.

Machine learning lets programs deal with situations it has never encountered before. One common machine learning problem involves image recognition. You can train an algorithm to recognize a dog or a boat in a picture, but that algorithm must eventually learn to recognize dogs or boats in pictures it has never seen before.

Most people may be familiar with an early form of machine learning that appeared in spam filters for e-mail. It's impossible to identify all possible spam because spammers can simply modify their spam. As a result, spam filters use machine learning to identify possible spam. When you confirm that a message is spam, you're training the spam filter to recognize similar types of spam in the future. That's why over time, spam filters tend to get better simply because they keep getting trained by new data.

Machine learning involves three steps:

- Developing and writing algorithms

- Training the algorithm with large amounts of data

- Using the trained algorithm (called a machine learning model)

Creating algorithms can be difficult and training algorithms can be time-consuming. In 2018, Apple introduced Create ML, which allows you to create your own machine learning models using Swift. This involves exposing the Create ML machine learning model to lots of data to gradually train it to recognize the data you want. Fortunately, if you don't have the time to design your own machine learning models, you can take trained machine learning models and simply use them without writing your own algorithms or training it with large amounts of data.

Note   Apple's Create ML framework is based on Turi Create, a machine learning company that Apple acquired in 2016. Turi Create was designed to let you create machine learning models using the Python programming language. Create ML is basically Turi Create redesigned for Apple's Swift programming language. You can learn more about Create ML from Apple's documentation (`https://developer.apple.com/documentation/createml`).

The advantages of simply using a trained machine learning model is that you can add artificial intelligence to your iOS apps quickly and easily. The drawback is that you need to find trained machine learning models that do what you need. In addition, you cannot increase the trained machine learning model's intelligence. You're essentially taking a fixed machine learning model that won't improve over time.

Since most people aren't able to write machine learning algorithms and train it with large amounts of data, they must rely on machine learning models that others have created. There are two sources or machine learning models:

- Core ML models

- Non-Core ML models

When you add a machine learning model to an iOS project, it must be stored in a file format known as Core ML (which stands for Core Machine Learning). Since Core ML is a new file format, most machine learning models are stored in different file formats. Fortunately, Apple has converted some popular machine learning models into the Core ML format. That means you can use these machine learning models in your iOS apps right away.

The main purpose for adding machine learning to your iOS apps is so your app can anticipate the user's needs. When you type text in many iOS apps, you'll see a list of words or phrases the app thinks you want to type. Rather than type the entire word or phrase yourself, you can just tap on the suggested word or phrase displayed. Over time, the app will tend to suggest common words and phrases you use most often, so the app customizes itself to your behavior, making typing text faster and easier for you.

Essentially machine learning lets your app become smarter. The smarter your app is able to respond to the user, the happier the user will be. Machine learning gives your app new capabilities without requiring you to exhaustively write instructions yourself.

What this chapter will focus on is finding Core ML models, adding them to iOS projects, and using them in your iOS app.

Finding a Core ML Model

The simplest way to find a Core ML model to use is to visit Apple's Developer web site on machine learning at https://developer.apple.com/machine-learning. Apple provides a growing library of tested Core ML models that you can add to an iOS project. While this list may be relatively small, it will grow over time.

Besides Apple's site, you may also be able to find Core ML models on third-party sites where people have created or converted other machine learning model formats into Core ML. For the truly adventurous, you can find Core ML conversion tools on Apple's Developer web site. By using these Core ML conversion tools, you can search for other machine learning models stored in different file formats and convert them into the Core ML format. This process of converting machine learning models into the Core ML format involves using the Python programming language and is beyond the scope of this chapter.

When evaluating different Core ML models to use, you need to look at what the machine learning model does and how large its file may be as shown in Figure 16-1.

SqueezeNet

Detects the dominant objects present in an image from a set of 1000 categories such as trees, animals, food, vehicles, people, and more. With an overall footprint of only 5 MB, SqueezeNet has a similar level of accuracy as AlexNet but with 50 times fewer parameters.

View original model details ›

Download Core ML Model ⊕

Figure 16-1. *Core ML models briefly describe what the model does and how large its file is*

The Core ML model described in Figure 16-1 tells you that it's an image recognition model that's 5 MB in size. The size of Core ML models can vary dramatically so you need to weigh the benefits of each model with its size. Adding 5 MB to the size of your iOS app may be reasonable, but adding 553.5 MB may not. There's often a trade-off between large file size and greater accuracy, but sometimes smaller models can outperform larger ones so you may need to experiment with different models until you find the right one for your app that balances accuracy and file size.

Image Recognition

At the time of this writing, most of the Core ML models available on Apple's machine learning site focuses on image recognition. This can work in two ways:

- Your app can load an image stored in the Photos app.

- Your app can view an item through the camera.

First, we'll start simple and add an image to an Xcode project. This will only allow us to recognize that single image hard-coded into the app, but it will let us focus on getting the Core ML model working within an app. Once we know the Core ML model works, we can focus on the non-machine learning functions to retrieve an image from the Photos app or from the iPhone/iPad camera.

The first step is to download a Core ML model to your computer. Visit `https://developer.apple.com/machine-learning` and download the MobileNet and SqueezeNet models. Both models focus on image recognition and both are fairly small in size. By experimenting with two different Core ML models, you can see how accurate both of them might be and how using any Core ML model works in similar ways.

The second step is to visit any search engine and look for images of any object such as a car, dog, computer, or bird. The exact image doesn't matter but choose an image that has a blank background such as all white. By choosing an image that's isolated and not cluttered with other items, you'll improve the Core ML model's chance of recognizing it correctly.

Obviously in real apps, you can't always choose pictures that are easiest for the Core ML model to identify, but for our purposes, we just want to get the Core ML model working to identify items in a picture. Once you have downloaded the Core ML models (SqueezeNet and MobileNet) and a single image of any object, you're ready to create the Xcode project to use machine learning.

To see how to use a Core ML file, follow these steps:

1. Create a new iOS Single View App project and name it CoreMLImageApp.

2. Click the ViewController.swift file in the Navigator pane.

3. Under the import UIKit line, add the following:

   ```
   import CoreML
   import Vision
   ```

   The "import CoreML" line simply lets your project recognize and use the Core ML model added to your project. The "import Vision" line lets your project use the Vision framework for recognizing items in an image.

4. Drag and drop the MobileNet Core ML model from a Finder window to the Navigator pane of your Xcode project as shown in Figure 16-2. When a dialog appears, click the Finish button.

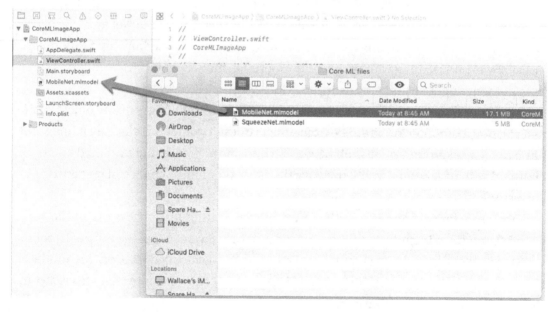

Figure 16-2. *Drag and drop the Core ML model into Xcode*

5. Drag and drop an image into the Navigator pane, and when a dialog appears, click the Finish button. Make sure this image file has a descriptive name such as "cat.jpg" or something similar.

6. Click the image file you added to the Navigator pane. Xcode displays that image.

7. Choose View ➤ Inspectors ➤ Show the File Inspector, or click the File Inspector icon in the upper right corner of the Xcode window.

8. Look under the Target Membership category and make sure the check box is selected. If you named your Xcode project CoreMLImageApp, then make sure the CoreMLImageApp check box is selected under the Target Membership category.

9. Click the MobileNet.mlmodel file in the Project navigator. The middle Xcode pane displays information about the machine learning model such as its authors and how it works. More importantly, the Model Evaluation Parameters describe the input the model expects and the data it outputs.

   In the case of the MobileNet.mlmodel file, it expects an input of an image. Once it receives an image, it outputs a dictionary (a string and a double) that displays the probability that it accurately identified the image. It also outputs a string that identifies the image.

10. Choose View ➤ Inspectors ➤ Show the File Inspector, or click the File Inspector icon in the upper right corner of the Xcode window.

11. Look under the Target Membership category and make sure the check box is selected. If you named your Xcode project CoreMLImageApp, then make sure the CoreMLImageApp check box is selected under the Target Membership category as shown in Figure 16-3.

Figure 16-3. *Viewing the details of the MobileNet model*

12.   Click the Main.storyboard file in the Navigator pane.

13.   Click the Library icon and drag and drop a label and image view.
      Resize the label and image view so it looks similar to Figure 16-4.

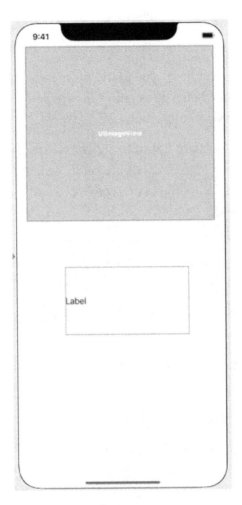

Figure 16-4. *Designing the user interface*

14. Click the image view and then choose View ➤ Utilities ➤ Show
     Attributes Inspector, or click the Attributes Inspector icon in the
     upper right corner of the Xcode window.

15. Click the Image text field and choose the file name of your image
     such as "cat.jpg". This will make the image view display the image
     you stored in your Xcode project.

16. Click the Content Mode popup menu and choose Aspect Fit. This
     will make the image appear correctly proportioned in the image
     view. At this point, you should see your chosen image appear in
     the image view.

17. Click the label and make sure the Attributes Inspector is still visible. (If not, click View ➤ Utilities ➤ Show Attributes Inspector.)

18. Click in the Lines text field, type 0, and press Enter. Defining 0 lines makes the label display as many lines as needed depending on the text you store in that label.

19. Choose View ➤ Assistant Editor ➤ Show Assistant Editor, or click the Assistant Editor icon in the upper right corner of the Xcode window. Xcode displays the Main.storyboard and ViewController. swift files side by side.

20. Move the mouse pointer over the image view, hold down the Control key, and Ctrl-drag from the image view to under the class ViewController line in the ViewController.swift file.

21. Release the Control key and the left mouse button. A popup window appears.

22. Click in the Name text field, type **imageView**, and click the Connect button. Xcode creates the following IBOutlet:

```
@IBOutlet var imageView: UIImageView!
```

23. Move the mouse pointer over the label, hold down the Control key, and Ctrl-drag from the label to under the class ViewController line in the ViewController.swift file.

24. Release the Control key and the left mouse button. A popup window appears.

25. Click in the Name text field, type **labelDescription**, and click the Connect button. Xcode creates the following IBOutlet:

```
@IBOutlet var labelDescription: UILabel!
```

26. Choose View ➤ Standard Editor ➤ Show Standard Editor, or click the Standard Editor icon in the upper right corner of the Xcode window.

At this point, we've created the user interface. Now it's time to write Swift code. The machine learning model needs an image as input, so we need to identify the image file you added to your Xcode project. This involves two steps. First, you need to identify the file name, file extension of the image, and path of that image. Second, you need to store this information as a URL to give to the Core ML model.

To make the ModelNet machine learning work, follow these steps:

1. Click the ViewController.swift file in the Navigator pane.

2. Add the following line in the viewDidLoad method:

```swift
let imagePath = Bundle.main.path(forResource: "Cat", ofType: "jpg")
```

   In the preceding code, the constant name is "imagePath" but you can choose any name you wish. The file name is "Cat" but you need to replace this with the name of your image file. The file extension is "jpg" and you'll need to replace it with the file extension of your image file as well. The preceding code creates an optional variable because it's possible that the file can't be found.

3. Add the following line under the previously added line in the viewDidLoad method:

```swift
let imageURL = NSURL.fileURL(withPath: imagePath!)
```

   In the preceding code, the constant name is "imageURL" but you can choose any name you wish. The image path is identified as "imagePath", which must be identical to the constant you created using the Bundle.main.path command. Notice that you must explicitly unwrap the "imagePath" optional variable using the exclamation point.

   Now that we've stored the image file, extension, and path in a constant ("imageURL"), it's time to work with the Core ML model. First, create a constant to represent the Core ML model added to your Xcode project, such as MobileNet.mlmodel.

4. Add the following line under the previously added line in the viewDidLoad method:

```
let modelFile = MobileNet()
```

The "modelFile" constant can actually be any name you wish. MobileNet() identifies the MobileNet.mlmodel file added in your Xcode project. If you use a different Core ML model such as SqueezeNet.mlmodel, then you would replace "MobileNet" with "SqueezeNet".

Next, we need to tell your app to use the chosen Core ML model (identified by the "modelFile" constant) with the Vision framework. This means creating another constant with an arbitrary name (such as "model").

5. Add the following line under the previously added line in the viewDidLoad method:

```
let model = try! VNCoreMLModel(for: modelFile.model)
```

Now the next step is to let the Core ML model examine the image. We already defined the image name, extension, and path in the "imageURL" constant, so we can use this to define an image request.

6. Add the following line under the previously added line in the viewDidLoad method:

```
let handler = VNImageRequestHandler(url: imageURL)
```

After requesting an image to examine, the next step is to request that your app actually use the Core ML model stored in the "model" constant. The Core ML model needs to examine the image and compare it to its trained data multiple times to maximize the chances of identifying it correctly. That means you need to request that the Core ML model run and provide it with a completion handler that defines what the Core ML model does when it identifies the image.

7. Add the following two lines under the previously added line in the viewDidLoad method:

```
let request = VNCoreMLRequest(model: model, completionHandler:
findResults)
try! handler.perform([request])
```

The last step is to write the function for the completion handler, which is called "findResults".

8. Create a separate function in the ViewController.swift file as follows:

```
func findResults(request: VNRequest, error: Error?) {

}
```

This findResults function runs when the Core ML model examines an image. The first step for this findResults function is to make sure it can examine the image. If not, it needs to prevent the rest of its code from running. To check if the Core ML model can successfully examine an image, we can use a guard statement.

9. Add the following in the findResults function:

```
guard let results = request.results as?
[VNClassificationObservation] else {
    fatalError("Unable to get results")
}
```

Assuming that the Core ML model can examine the image, we need to keep track of its guesses with two variables that can be any arbitrary name.

10. Add the following in the findResults function:

```
var bestGuess = ""
var bestConfidence: VNConfidence = 0
```

The "bestGuess" variable will hold the Core ML model's current prediction of what it thinks the item in an image might be. The "bestConfidence" variable will hold the confidence level. Note that the "bestConfidence" variable must be defined as a VNConfidence data type, which holds a Float value.

Finally, we need a loop to exhaustively examine the image to determine the Core ML model's best guess of what that object might be. This loop assigns a confidence level and an identifier to the "bestConfidence" and "bestGuess" variables, respectively. Each time it comes across a prediction with a higher confidence level, it stores it in the "bestGuess" variable.

11. Add the following in the findResults function:

```swift
for classification in results {
    if (classification.confidence > bestConfidence) {
        bestConfidence = classification.confidence
        bestGuess = classification.identifier
    }
}
```

Finally after the loop has exhaustively searched through all possible predictions for what the item in the image might be, the loop stops and the "bestGuess" variable contains the guess and the "bestConfidence" variable contains that confidence level. Now we need one last line of code to display this information in the label on the user interface.

12. Add the following in the findResults function:

```swift
labelDescription.text = "Image is: \(bestGuess) with
confidence \(bestConfidence)) out of 1"
```

The entire ViewController.swift file should look like this:

```swift
import UIKit
import CoreML
import Vision

class ViewController: UIViewController {

    @IBOutlet var imageView: UIImageView!
    @IBOutlet var labelDescription: UILabel!

    override func viewDidLoad() {
        super.viewDidLoad()
```

```swift
    let imagePath = Bundle.main.path(forResource: "Cat",
    ofType: "jpg")
    let imageURL = NSURL.fileURL(withPath: imagePath!)

    let modelFile = MobileNet()

    let model = try! VNCoreMLModel(for: modelFile.model)

    let handler = VNImageRequestHandler(url: imageURL)

    let request = VNCoreMLRequest(model: model,
    completionHandler: findResults)
    try! handler.perform([request])
}

func findResults(request: VNRequest, error: Error?) {
    guard let results = request.results as?
    [VNClassificationObservation] else {
        fatalError("Unable to get results")
    }

    var bestGuess = ""
    var bestConfidence: VNConfidence = 0

    for classification in results {
        if (classification.confidence > bestConfidence) {
            bestConfidence = classification.confidence
            bestGuess = classification.identifier
        }
    }

    labelDescription.text = "Image is: \(bestGuess) with
    confidence \(bestConfidence)) out of 1"
}

}
```

13. Click the Run button or choose Product ➤ Run. The Simulator
screen appears, displaying the image you added to the image view
along with the Core ML model's guess and confidence level of the
image as shown in Figure 16-5.

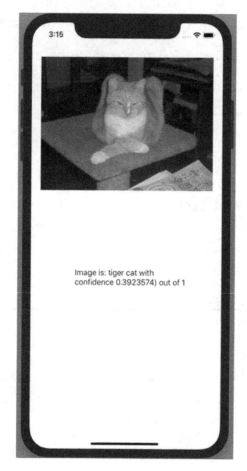

Figure 16-5. Recognizing an image using a Core ML model

14. Choose Simulator ➤ Quit Simulator to return to Xcode.

If you modify your project by adding a different Core ML model, you'll notice that
each Core ML model identifies the same object in slightly different ways with different
confidence levels. You can also try modifying your project by adding different image
files containing cars, trees, horses, or airplanes to see how accurately it identifies the

displayed item. Machine learning models aren't perfect, but you can see that we've created an app that can identify items with very little coding. Instead, we've let a trained machine learning model do all the hard work of identifying items in an image.

Identifying Objects from the Camera

The first app we built in this chapter simply examined a single image file. If we wanted to examine a different image, we'd have to add that new image to the Xcode project, modify the code slightly to reflect the different image file name, and then run the app all over again.

A far more versatile solution is to simply use the built-in camera on an iPhone or iPad to aim and point at an object. Then have the Core ML model try to identify what that object might be. To do this, you'll need to physically connect an iPhone or iPad to your Macintosh while running Xcode since you cannot test the camera on the Simulator.

To see how to use a Core ML file, follow these steps:

1. Create a new iOS Single View App project and name it CoreMLCameraApp.

2. Click the Main.storyboard file in the Navigator pane.

3. Click the Library icon and drag and drop a view and a label. Resize the view and label so it looks similar to Figure 16-6.

Figure 16-6. *Designing the user interface for the CoreMLCameraApp project*

4. Choose Editor ➤ Resolve Auto Layout Issues ➤ Reset to Suggested Constraints in the bottom half of the submenu. Xcode adds constraints to the view and label.

5. Click the label to select it.

6. Choose View ➤ Inspectors ➤ Show Attributes Inspector, or click the Attributes Inspector icon in the upper right corner of the Xcode window.

7. Click the Center icon to center text inside the label.

8. Click the Background popup menu and choose light color such as white or light yellow. This will make the label easier to see on an actual iOS screen.

9. Choose View ➤ Assistant Editor ➤ Show Assistant Editor, or click the Assistant Editor icon in the upper right corner of the Xcode window. Xcode displays the Main.storyboard and ViewController. swift files side by side.

10. Move the mouse pointer over the view, hold down the Control key, and Ctrl-drag from the view to under the class ViewController line in the ViewController.swift file.

11. Release the Control key and the left mouse button. A popup window appears.

12. Click in the Name text field, type **videoFeed**, and click the Connect button. Xcode creates the following IBOutlet:

    @IBOutlet var videoFeed: UIView!

13. Move the mouse pointer over the label, hold down the Control key, and Ctrl-drag from the label to under the class ViewController line in the ViewController.swift file.

14. Release the Control key and the left mouse button. A popup window appears.

15. Click in the Name text field, type **resultLabel**, and click the Connect button. Xcode creates the following IBOutlet:

    @IBOutlet var resultLabel: UILabel!

16. Choose View ➤ Standard Editor ➤ Show Standard Editor, or click the Standard Editor icon in the upper right corner of the Xcode window.

17. Click the ViewController.swift file in the Navigator pane.

18. Under the import UIKit line, add the following:

```
import AVFoundation
import CoreML
import Vision
```

The AVFoundation framework lets us access the camera, while the CoreML framework lets us access a machine learning model and the Vision framework lets us recognize images.

19. Underneath the IBOutlets, add the following three variables to represent the camera output, the capture session, and the video preview layer. The camera output is what the iPhone/iPad camera receives. The capture session coordinates the flow of data from the camera. The video preview layer displays the video the iPhone/iPad camera captures:

```
var cameraOutput : AVCapturePhotoOutput!
var previewLayer : AVCaptureVideoPreviewLayer!
var captureSession : AVCaptureSession!
```

Once we've created these IBOutlets and variables, we need to write a function that store and display data captured through the camera. Inside this function we need to create an AVCaptureSession, which can capture different types of data such as audio or video. Then we need to capture photographic images through the camera.

20. Add the following function in the ViewController.swift file:

```
func useCamera() {
    captureSession = AVCaptureSession()
    captureSession.sessionPreset = AVCaptureSession.Preset.photo
}
```

Now we need to store the captured video from the camera in the cameraOutput variable.

21. Add the following in the useCamera function:

```
cameraOutput = AVCapturePhotoOutput()
```

Finally, we need to retrieve video and determine if it's successful or not. That involves creating a constant called "device" to capture video. Then we need to use an if statement to determine if the camera is successfully capturing video. This involves defining a "device" constant and then using an if statement.

22. Add the following to the useCamera function:

```
let device = AVCaptureDevice.default(for: AVMediaType.video)
if let input = try? AVCaptureDeviceInput(device: device!) {

} else {
    print ("No video feed available")
}
```

If there is no video feed, then the else portion runs and prints "No video feed available". If there is video, then we need to check if the video can be successfully displayed in the UIView through its IBOutlet named videoFeed.

Once we know we can retrieve video, two more if statements check if it's possible to get input and output from the camera.

23. Modify the if let statement as follows:

```
if let input = try? AVCaptureDeviceInput(device: device!) {
    if (captureSession.canAddInput(input)) {
        captureSession.addInput(input)

        if (captureSession.canAddOutput(cameraOutput)) {
            captureSession.addOutput(cameraOutput)
        }
    }
} else {
    print ("No video feed available")
}
```

Finally, we need to display the captured video onto the UIView on the user interface. To do this, we need to define the previewLayer to the captureSession (the video feed from the camera) and define how that video appears inside the UIView such as Aspect Fill.

24.   Modify the if let statement as follows:

```
if let input = try? AVCaptureDeviceInput(device: device!) {
    if (captureSession.canAddInput(input)) {
        captureSession.addInput(input)

        if (captureSession.canAddOutput(cameraOutput)) {
            captureSession.addOutput(cameraOutput)
        }

        previewLayer = AVCaptureVideoPreviewLayer(session:
        captureSession)
        previewLayer.videoGravity = AVLayerVideoGravity.
        resizeAspectFill

    } else {
        print ("No video feed available")
    }
}
```

The last step is to actually display the video inside the UIView, which is defined by the IBOutlet called videoFeed. First, we need to define the frame of the preview layer to match the size of the UIView on the user interface. Next, we need to add that previewLayer to the UIView layer. Finally, we need to start capturing the video.

25.   Modify the useCamera function so the entire function looks like this:

```
func useCamera() {
    captureSession = AVCaptureSession()
    captureSession.sessionPreset = AVCaptureSession.Preset.photo
    cameraOutput = AVCapturePhotoOutput()
```

```
    let device = AVCaptureDevice.default(for: AVMediaType.video)
    if let input = try? AVCaptureDeviceInput(device: device!) {
        if (captureSession.canAddInput(input)) {
            captureSession.addInput(input)

            if (captureSession.canAddOutput(cameraOutput)) {
                captureSession.addOutput(cameraOutput)
            }

            previewLayer = AVCaptureVideoPreviewLayer(session:
            captureSession)
            previewLayer.videoGravity = AVLayerVideoGravity.
            resizeAspectFill
            previewLayer.frame = videoFeed.bounds
            videoFeed.layer.addSublayer(previewLayer)
            captureSession.startRunning()
        } else {
            print ("Could not get any input")
        }
    } else {
        print ("No video feed available")
    }

}
```

26. Modify the viewDidLoad method to call the "useCamera" function
     like this:

```
override func viewDidLoad() {
    super.viewDidLoad()
    useCamera()
}
```

The entire ViewController.swift file should look like this:

```
import UIKit
import AVFoundation
import CoreML
import Vision
```

```swift
class ViewController: UIViewController {
    @IBOutlet var videoFeed: UIView!
    @IBOutlet var resultLabel: UILabel!

    var cameraOutput : AVCapturePhotoOutput!
    var previewLayer : AVCaptureVideoPreviewLayer!
    var captureSession : AVCaptureSession!

    override func viewDidLoad() {
        super.viewDidLoad()
        useCamera()
    }

    func useCamera() {
        captureSession = AVCaptureSession()
        captureSession.sessionPreset = AVCaptureSession.Preset.photo
        cameraOutput = AVCapturePhotoOutput()

        let device = AVCaptureDevice.default(for: AVMediaType.video)
        if let input = try? AVCaptureDeviceInput(device: device!) {
            if (captureSession.canAddInput(input)) {
                captureSession.addInput(input)

                if (captureSession.canAddOutput(cameraOutput)) {
                    captureSession.addOutput(cameraOutput)
                }

                previewLayer = AVCaptureVideoPreviewLayer(session:
                captureSession)
                previewLayer.videoGravity = AVLayerVideoGravity.
                resizeAspectFill
                previewLayer.frame = videoFeed.bounds
                videoFeed.layer.addSublayer(previewLayer)
                captureSession.startRunning()
            } else {
                print ("Could not get any input")
            }
        } else {
```

```
        print ("No video feed available")
    }

  }


}
```

27. Connect your iOS device to your Macintosh through a USB cable.

28. Click the Active Scheme icon at the top of the Xcode window to display a menu. At the top of this menu, choose your iOS device under the Device category as shown in Figure 16-7.

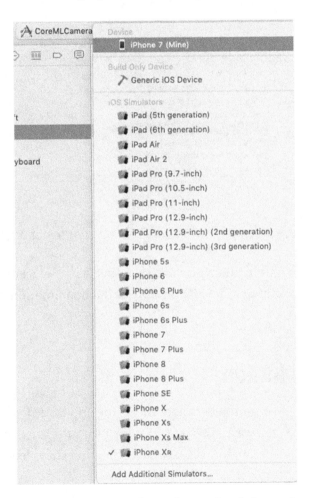

Figure 16-7. *Choosing an iOS device from the Active Scheme icon*

423

Once you've defined an actual iOS device to run your Xcode CoreMLCameraApp project, the last step is to give your app permission to access the camera.

29.   Click the Info.plist file in the Navigator pane.

30.   Move the mouse pointer over the bottom row until a + and – icon appears.

31.   Click the + icon. Xcode adds a new row.

32.   Click in the Key column in the newly added row so a popup menu appears and choose Privacy – Camera Usage Description as shown in Figure 16-8.

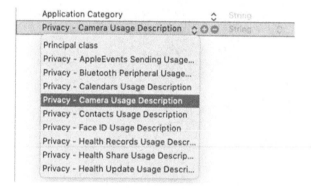

Figure 16-8.   *Defining privacy settings to allow use of the camera*

Click in the Value column and type a message such as "App needs to access camera". The exact text does not matter as it will only appear the first time your app runs on an iOS device.

Analyzing an Image

At this point the code in your project simply allows the app to retrieve video from a connected iOS device's camera and display it on the user interface. The next step is to actually capture and analyze an individual image from that video feed so the Core ML model can recognize the object viewed by the camera.

We'll need to create a function that retrieves an image from the video feed and another function to analyze that image using a Core ML model. First, we need to capture an image from the video feed with a function called recognizeImage() and call that function at the end of the useCamera method.

1. Click the ViewController.swift file in the Navigator pane.

2. Edit the class ViewController line like this:

```
class ViewController: UIViewController, AVCapturePhotoCaptureDelegate {
```

The AVCapturePhotoCaptureDelegate allows capturing of images through the camera.

3. Edit the last few lines of the useCamera function like this:

```
} else {
    print ("No video feed available")
}
recognizeImage()

}
```

4. Add a recognizeImage function underneath the useCamera function like this:

```
@objc func recognizeImage() {
}
```

Note   The @obj keyword allows Swift and Objective-C code to work together. In this case, this allows Swift code to work with Objective-C code that's part of Apple's framework for creating apps.

The first step is to create an object that allows the capture of an image, which is an AVCapturePhotoSettings object. Then we need to capture the actual image and define its format. Finally, we need to capture an image.

5. Add the following to the recognizeImage function:

```
let settings = AVCapturePhotoSettings()
settings.previewPhotoFormat = settings.embeddedThumbnailPhotoFormat
cameraOutput.capturePhoto(with: settings, delegate: self)
```

After the recognizeImage() function retrieves an image from the video feed, we need another function to convert this image into a UIImage.

6. Add the following function to the ViewController.swift file:

```
func photoOutput(_ output: AVCapturePhotoOutput,
didFinishProcessingPhoto photo: AVCapturePhoto, error: Error?) {
    if let error = error {
        print ("Error code: \(error.localizedDescription)")
    }

    if let imageData = photo.fileDataRepresentation(), let image =
    UIImage(data: imageData) {
        predictItem(image: image)
    }
}
```

The photoOutput function stores the captured image as a UIImage and also calls a function called predictItem, which we'll need to write later. This predictItem function will need to use a Core ML model to analyze the image captured from the video feed.

Since the Core ML model needs to know where to find that image, we'll first need to write a function that returns a URL.

7. Add the following function in the ViewController.swift file:

```
func getDocumentsDirectory() -> URL {
    let paths = FileManager.default.urls(for: .documentDirectory,
    in: .userDomainMask)
    let documentsDirectory = paths[0]
    return documentsDirectory
}
```

8. Drag and drop the SqueezeNet Core ML file into the Navigator pane, and when a dialog appears, click the Finish button.

9. Add the following predictItem function:

```
func predictItem(image: UIImage) {
    if let data = image.pngData(){
        let fileName = getDocumentsDirectory().
        appendingPathComponent("image.png")
        try? data.write(to: fileName)

        let modelFile = SqueezeNet()
        let model = try! VNCoreMLModel(for: modelFile.model)

        let request = VNCoreMLRequest(model: model,
        completionHandler: finalGuess)
        let handler = VNImageRequestHandler(url: fileName)
        try! handler.perform([request])
    }
}
```

This code uses the SqueezeNet Core ML model, but you can substitute the name of a different Core ML model if you wish. By experimenting with different Core ML models, you can see how accurate (or poorly) different Core ML models are at recognizing and identifying items in a picture.

The predictItem function calls another function called finalGuess, which runs after the Core ML model analyzes the image. The finalGuess function runs each time the Core ML model guesses what an item is in an image. Each time the Core ML model makes a guess, it gives a confidence level between 0 and 1 where 1 is highly confident.

10. Add the finalGuess function in the ViewController.swift file as follows:

```swift
func finalGuess(request: VNRequest, error: Error?) {
    guard let results = request.results as?
    [VNClassificationObservation] else {
        fatalError("Unable to get a prediction")
    }

    var bestGuess = ""
    var confidence: VNConfidence = 0
    for classification in results {
        if classification.confidence > confidence {
            confidence = classification.confidence
            bestGuess = classification.identifier
        }
    }
    resultLabel.text = bestGuess + "\n"
    Timer.scheduledTimer(timeInterval: 5.0, target: self,
    selector: #selector(self.recognizeImage), userInfo: nil,
    repeats: false)
}
```

The finalGuess function simply analyzes each prediction by the Core ML model and checks its confidence level. If the Core ML model is more confident that it's found a better match, it uses that prediction instead. Eventually after the Core ML analyzes all possible items it can recognize, the one item with the highest confidence level will be left and that will be the answer displayed on the label on the user interface.

The entire ViewController.swift file should look like this:

```swift
import UIKit
import AVFoundation
import CoreML
import Vision
```

```swift
class ViewController: UIViewController, AVCapturePhotoCaptureDelegate {

    @IBOutlet var videoFeed: UIView!
    @IBOutlet var resultLabel: UILabel!

    var cameraOutput : AVCapturePhotoOutput!
    var previewLayer : AVCaptureVideoPreviewLayer!
    var captureSession : AVCaptureSession!

    override func viewDidLoad() {
        super.viewDidLoad()
        useCamera()
    }

    func useCamera() {
        captureSession = AVCaptureSession()
        captureSession.sessionPreset = AVCaptureSession.Preset.photo
        cameraOutput = AVCapturePhotoOutput()

        let device = AVCaptureDevice.default(for: AVMediaType.video)
        if let input = try? AVCaptureDeviceInput(device: device!) {
            if (captureSession.canAddInput(input)) {
                captureSession.addInput(input)

                if (captureSession.canAddOutput(cameraOutput)) {
                    captureSession.addOutput(cameraOutput)
                }

                previewLayer = AVCaptureVideoPreviewLayer(session:
                captureSession)
                previewLayer.videoGravity = AVLayerVideoGravity.
                resizeAspectFill
                previewLayer.frame = videoFeed.bounds
                videoFeed.layer.addSublayer(previewLayer)
                captureSession.startRunning()
            } else {
                print ("Could not get any input")
            }
```

```swift
        } else {
            print ("No video feed available")
        }
        recognizeImage()

    }

    @objc func recognizeImage() {
        let settings = AVCapturePhotoSettings()
        settings.previewPhotoFormat = settings.
        embeddedThumbnailPhotoFormat
        cameraOutput.capturePhoto(with: settings, delegate: self)
    }

    func photoOutput(_ output: AVCapturePhotoOutput,
    didFinishProcessingPhoto photo: AVCapturePhoto, error: Error?) {
        if let error = error {
            print ("Error code: \(error.localizedDescription)")
        }

        if let imageData = photo.fileDataRepresentation(), let
        image = UIImage(data: imageData) {
            predictItem(image: image)
        }
    }

    func getDocumentsDirectory() -> URL {
        let paths = FileManager.default.urls(for:
        .documentDirectory, in: .userDomainMask)
        let documentsDirectory = paths[0]
        return documentsDirectory
    }

    func predictItem(image: UIImage) {
        if let data = image.pngData() {
            let fileName = getDocumentsDirectory().
            appendingPathComponent("image.png")
            try? data.write(to: fileName)
```

```swift
            let modelFile = SqueezeNet()
            let model = try! VNCoreMLModel(for: modelFile.model)

            let request = VNCoreMLRequest(model: model,
            completionHandler: finalGuess)
            let handler = VNImageRequestHandler(url: fileName)
            try! handler.perform([request])
        }
    }

    func finalGuess(request: VNRequest, error: Error?) {
        guard let results = request.results as?
        [VNClassificationObservation] else {
            fatalError("Unable to get a prediction")
        }

        var bestGuess = ""
        var confidence: VNConfidence = 0
        for classification in results {
            if classification.confidence > confidence {
                confidence = classification.confidence
                bestGuess = classification.identifier
            }
        }
        resultLabel.text = bestGuess + "\n"
        Timer.scheduledTimer(timeInterval: 5.0, target: self,
        selector: #selector(self.recognizeImage), userInfo: nil,
        repeats: false)
    }
}
```

11. Make sure you have an iOS device connected to your Macintosh
    and click the Run button, or choose Product ➤ Run.

12. Point your camera at an item to see what the Core ML model
    thinks that item might be as shown in Figure 16-9. (Don't be
    shocked if the accuracy of most Core ML models is surprisingly
    low.)

Figure 16-9. Identifying an item through the camera of an iPhone

13.   Click the Stop button in Xcode to stop the app from running.

Summary

As you can see, Core ML models can be impressive in giving your app the ability to recognize items in images, but they still have limitations in failing to recognize everything with perfect accuracy. Not all Core ML models are equal in accuracy or size so you may need to experiment with different Core ML models until you find the one that works best with your app.

The main idea behind Core ML is that you can add the ability to deal with unknown data by simply using a trained machine learning model. Apple will continue adding new Core ML models that will likely offer different features beyond just image recognition. Over time, you'll be able to add these trained machine learning models to your apps and give your app artificial intelligence with little effort.

CHAPTER 17

Using Facial and Text Recognition

In the previous chapter, you learned about Core ML, which lets you use machine learning models in your apps. However, iOS also offers another form of artificial intelligence that doesn't require finding and adding a trained machine learning model to your app. Instead, you can simply use the Vision framework that can recognize objects in pictures such as faces or text.

At the simplest level, facial recognition can identify the number of faces in a picture and also draw rectangles in an image to show exactly all the faces the app recognized. On a more advanced level, facial recognition can also identify eyes, noses, and mouths and other parts of a face.

Beyond recognizing faces in a picture, the Vision framework can also recognize and identify text in a picture by displaying a rectangle around text. Just remember that text recognition works best with text that's easy to see such as black text against a white background (or white text against a dark background). Text that appears too similar to the background may get overlooked.

Although facial recognition and text recognition may not be perfect, it can be accurate enough to give your app extra features that require you to write little additional code on your own.

Recognizing Faces in Pictures

To use facial recognition, you must import the Vision framework. In this app we'll be analyzing pictures stored in the Photos app so you also need to import the Photos framework.

© Wallace Wang 2019
W. Wang, *Pro iPhone Development with Swift 5*, https://doi.org/10.1007/978-1-4842-4944-4_17

To see how to use facial recognition, follow these steps:

1. Create a new iOS Single View App project and name it FacialRecognitionApp.

2. Click the ViewController.swift file in the Navigator pane.

3. Under the import UIKit line, add the following:

```
import Vision
import Photos
```

Since this app will need to pick pictures stored in the Photos app, we'll need to import the Photos framework and make the ViewController.swift file adopt the UIImagePickerControllerDelegate along with the UINavigationControllerDelegate.

4. Modify the class ViewController line like this:

```
class ViewController: UIViewController, UIImagePickerController
Delegate, UINavigationControllerDelegate {
```

5. Click the Main.storyboard file in the Navigator pane.

6. Click the Library icon and drag and drop a button, image view, and label.

7. Double-click the button, type **Get Image**, and press Enter.

8. Click the label and choose View ➤ Inspectors ➤ Show Attributes Inspector, or click the Attributes Inspector icon in the upper right corner of the Xcode window.

9. Click the Center icon in the Alignment group to center text in the label.

10. Resize the label and image view so the user interface looks similar to Figure 17-1.

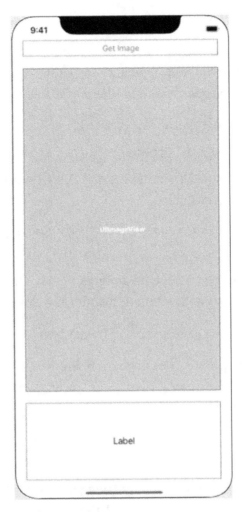

Figure 17-1. *A button, label, and image view define the user interface*

11. Choose Editor ➤ Resolve Auto Layout Issues ➤ Reset to Suggested
    Constraints in the bottom half of the submenu. Xcode adds
    constraints to the user interface items.

12. Choose View ➤ Assistant Editor ➤ Show Assistant Editor, or click
    the Assistant Editor icon in the upper right corner of the Xcode
    window. Xcode shows the Main.storyboard and ViewController.
    swift file side by side.

13. Move the mouse pointer over the label, hold down the Control
    key, and Ctrl-drag under the class ViewController line in the
    ViewController.swift file.

14. Release the Control key and the left mouse button. A popup window appears.

15. Click in the Name text field, type **messageLabel**, and click the Connect button. Xcode creates an IBOutlet as follows:

    @IBOutlet var messageLabel: UILabel!

16. Move the mouse pointer over the image view, hold down the Control key, and Ctrl-drag under the class ViewController line in the ViewController.swift file.

17. Release the Control key and the left mouse button. A popup window appears.

18. Click in the Name text field, type **pictureChosen**, and click the Connect button. Xcode creates an IBOutlet as follows:

    @IBOutlet var pictureChosen: UIImageView!

19. Move the mouse pointer over the button, hold down the Control key, and Ctrl-drag above the last curly bracket in the ViewController.swift file.

20. Release the Control key and the left mouse button. A popup window appears.

21. Click in the Name text field, type **getImage**, click the Type popup menu and choose UIButton, and click the Connect button. Xcode creates a getImage IBAction method.

22. Edit this getImage IBAction method as follows:

    ```
    @IBAction func getImage(_ sender: UIButton) {
        getPhoto()
    }
    ```

    The getImage IBAction method needs to call a function called getPhoto, which will let the user view and retrieve an image stored in the Photos app.

23. Add the following function in the ViewController.swift file:

```swift
func getPhoto() {
    let picker = UIImagePickerController()
    picker.delegate = self
    picker.sourceType = .savedPhotosAlbum
    present(picker, animated: true, completion: nil)
}
```

Note   For the picker.sourceType, you can choose either .savedPhotosAlbum or .photoLibrary.

Once the user selects an image, the next step is to display that image in the UIView on the user interface and analyze that image to look for faces. To do this, we need to create another function called imagePickerController that runs after the user picks an image from the Photos album.

24. Add the following function in the ViewController.swift file:

```swift
func imagePickerController(_ picker: UIImagePickerController,
didFinishPickingMediaWithInfo info: [UIImagePickerController.
InfoKey : Any]) {
    if let gotImage = info[UIImagePickerController.InfoKey.
    originalImage] as? UIImage {
        picker.dismiss(animated: true, completion: nil)
        pictureChosen.image = gotImage
        analyzeImage(image: gotImage)
    }
}
```

This function first dismisses the image picker. Then it verifies that a picture has been chosen. Once it has verified that the user chose a picture, it displays that image in the UIView connected to the IBOutlet named pictureChosen. Finally it calls another function to analyze the image, called analyzeImage.

25.   Add the following function in the ViewController.swift file:

```swift
func analyzeImage(image: UIImage) {
    let handler = VNImageRequestHandler(cgImage: image.cgImage!,
    options: [ : ])

    messageLabel.text = "Analyzing picture..."

    let request = VNDetectFaceRectanglesRequest(completionHandler:
    handleFaceRecognition)
    try! handler.perform([request])
}
```

This function uses VNDetectFaceRectanglesRequest in the Vision framework to detect faces in a picture. After it analyzes a picture, it runs another function called handleFaceRecognition.

This handleFaceRecognition function simply displays the number of faces in the UILabel on the user interface. Keep in mind that the facial recognition feature may not always be accurate for images where faces may be too small or may appear to blend in with the background.

26.   Add the following to the ViewController.swift file:

```swift
func handleFaceRecognition(request: VNRequest, error: Error?) {
    guard let foundFaces = request.results as? [VNFaceObservation]
    else {
        fatalError ("Can't find a face in the picture")
    }
    messageLabel.text = "Found \(foundFaces.count) faces in the picture"
}
```

The complete ViewController.swift file should look like this:

```swift
import UIKit
import Vision
import Photos
```

```swift
class ViewController: UIViewController,
UIImagePickerControllerDelegate, UINavigationControllerDelegate {

    @IBOutlet var messageLabel: UILabel!
    @IBOutlet var pictureChosen: UIImageView!

    override func viewDidLoad() {
        super.viewDidLoad()
        // Do any additional setup after loading the view.
    }

    func handleFaceRecognition(request: VNRequest, error: Error?) {
        guard let foundFaces = request.results as? [VNFaceObservation]
        else {
            fatalError ("Can't find a face in the picture")
        }
        messageLabel.text = "Found \(foundFaces.count) faces in the
        picture"
    }

    func analyzeImage(image: UIImage) {
        let handler = VNImageRequestHandler(cgImage: image.
        cgImage!, options: [ : ])

        messageLabel.text = "Analyzing picture..."

        let request = VNDetectFaceRectanglesRequest(completionHand
        ler: handleFaceRecognition)
        try! handler.perform([request])
    }

    func imagePickerController(_ picker: UIImagePickerController,
    didFinishPickingMediaWithInfo info: [UIImagePickerController.
    InfoKey : Any]) {
        if let gotImage = info[UIImagePickerController.InfoKey.
        originalImage] as? UIImage {
            picker.dismiss(animated: true, completion: nil)
            pictureChosen.image = gotImage
            analyzeImage(image: gotImage)
        }
```

```
    }

    func getPhoto() {
        let picker = UIImagePickerController()
        picker.delegate = self
        picker.sourceType = .savedPhotosAlbum
        present(picker, animated: true, completion: nil)
    }

    @IBAction func getImage(_ sender: UIButton) {
        getPhoto()
    }
}
```

You can test this project on either the Simulator or on an actual iOS device connected to your Macintosh through a USB cable. If you want to test this project on the Simulator, you'll need to add pictures of people in the Simulator's Photos app. To do this, run this project on the Simulator, then choose Hardware ➤ Home to display the Home screen.

Now click the Safari icon (and make sure your Macintosh has an Internet connection). This will load Safari and from there, visit any site that contains pictures of people. When you see an image that you want to store in the Photos app in the Simulator, move the mouse pointer over that image, hold down the mouse/trackpad button, and slide up until a menu appears at the bottom of the screen as shown in Figure 17-2.

Figure 17-2. *Saving an image in Safari running on the Simulator*

Tap the Save Image button to save the image in the Photos app on the Simulator. Once you've got at least one picture stored in the Simulator's Photos app, follow these steps to test the FacialRecognitionApp project:

1. Make sure the FacialRecognitionApp project is loaded in Xcode.

2. Click the Run button or choose Product ➤ Run. The FacialRecognitionApp screen appears.

3. Click the Get Image button. The Simulator's Photos app appears.

4. Click a picture that displays faces. The app displays the number of faces it found in the image as shown in Figure 17-3.

Figure 17-3. *Running the FacialRecognition app in the Simulator*

Highlighting Faces in an Image

Just identifying the number of faces in an image is fine, but you can also highlight each face with a rectangle to show you exactly which parts of a picture the Vision framework recognized as a face. There are two parts to identify faces in a picture with a rectangle. First, you need to use the VNFaceLandmarkRegion2D class to identify the face in the image. In the Vision framework, landmarks are identifying parts of an image where the most obvious landmark to identify is a face.

Once you identify a landmark (face) in an image, the second step is to draw a rectangle around that landmark (face). The final step is to take this image, with rectangles around one or more faces, and display it on the UIView on the user interface.

To see how to identify faces in a picture by drawing a rectangle around them, follow these steps:

1. Create a new iOS Single View App project and name it AdvancedFacialRecognitionApp.

2. Click the Main.storyboard file and design the user interface exactly like the FacialRecognitionApp with a button, an image view, and a label (see Figure 17-1).

3. Under the import UIKit line, add the following:

```
import Vision
import Photos
```

4. Modify the class ViewController line like this:

```
class ViewController: UIViewController,
UIImagePickerControllerDelegate, UINavigationControllerDelegate {
```

5. Click the Main.storyboard file in the Navigator pane and design the same user interface as the FacialRecognitionApp that includes a button, image view, and label (see Figure 17-1).

6. Ctrl-drag the label and image view into the ViewController.swift file to create two IBOutlets as follows:

```
@IBOutlet var messageLabel: UILabel!
@IBOutlet var pictureChosen: UIImageView!
```

7. Ctrl-drag the button into the bottom of the ViewController.swift file to create an IBAction method named getImage.

8. Modify the getImage IBAction method as follows and add the getPhoto function:

```
func getPhoto() {
    let picker = UIImagePickerController()
    picker.delegate = self
    picker.sourceType = .savedPhotosAlbum
    present(picker, animated: true, completion: nil)
}
```

```
@IBAction func getImage(_ sender: UIButton) {
    getPhoto()
}
```

9. Add the following functions to detect faces in a picture:

```
func imagePickerController(_ picker: UIImagePickerController,
didFinishPickingMediaWithInfo info: [UIImagePickerController.
InfoKey : Any]) {
    if let gotImage = info[UIImagePickerController.InfoKey.
    originalImage] as? UIImage {
        picker.dismiss(animated: true, completion: nil)
        pictureChosen.image = gotImage
        identifyFacesWithLandmarks(image: gotImage)
    }
}

func identifyFacesWithLandmarks(image: UIImage) {
    let handler = VNImageRequestHandler(cgImage: image.cgImage!,
    options: [ : ])

    messageLabel.text = "Analyzing picture..."

    let request = VNDetectFaceLandmarksRequest(completionHandler:
    handleFaceLandmarksRecognition)
    try! handler.perform([request])
}

func handleFaceLandmarksRecognition(request: VNRequest, error:
Error?) {
    guard let foundFaces = request.results as? [VNFaceObservation]
    else {
        fatalError ("Problem loading picture to examine faces")
    }
    messageLabel.text = "Found \(foundFaces.count) faces in the picture"
```

```
for faceRectangle in foundFaces {

    let landmarkRegions: [VNFaceLandmarkRegion2D] = []

    drawImage(source: pictureChosen.image!, boundary:
    faceRectangle.boundingBox, faceLandmarkRegions:
    landmarkRegions)
}
}
```

The first function retrieves an image and then calls the identifyFacesWithLandmarks function, which detects the faces. This identifyFacesWithLandmarks function then calls the handleFaceLandmarksRecognition function to detect faces and call a drawImage function to draw rectangles around those faces.

10. Add the following function to draw rectangles around faces in a picture:

```
func drawImage(source: UIImage, boundary: CGRect,
faceLandmarkRegions: [VNFaceLandmarkRegion2D]) {
    UIGraphicsBeginImageContextWithOptions(source.size, false, 1)
    let context = UIGraphicsGetCurrentContext()!
    context.translateBy(x: 0, y: source.size.height)
    context.scaleBy(x: 1.0, y: -1.0)
    context.setLineJoin(.round)
    context.setLineCap(.round)
    context.setShouldAntialias(true)
    context.setAllowsAntialiasing(true)

    let rect = CGRect(x: 0, y:0, width: source.size.width, height:
    source.size.height)
    context.draw(source.cgImage!, in: rect)

    //draw rectangles around faces
    let fillColor = UIColor.white
    fillColor.setStroke()
```

```
let rectangleWidth = source.size.width * boundary.size.width
let rectangleHeight = source.size.height * boundary.size.height

context.addRect(CGRect(x: boundary.origin.x * source.size.
width, y:boundary.origin.y * source.size.height, width:
rectangleWidth, height: rectangleHeight))
context.drawPath(using: CGPathDrawingMode.stroke)

let modifiedImage : UIImage =
UIGraphicsGetImageFromCurrentImageContext()!
UIGraphicsEndImageContext()
pictureChosen.image = modifiedImage
}
```

The entire ViewController.swift file should look like this:

```
import UIKit
import Vision
import Photos

class ViewController: UIViewController,
UIImagePickerControllerDelegate, UINavigationControllerDelegate {

    @IBOutlet var messageLabel: UILabel!
    @IBOutlet var pictureChosen: UIImageView!

    override func viewDidLoad() {
        super.viewDidLoad()
        // Do any additional setup after loading the view.
    }

    func imagePickerController(_ picker: UIImagePickerController,
    didFinishPickingMediaWithInfo info: [UIImagePickerController.
    InfoKey : Any]) {
        if let gotImage = info[UIImagePickerController.InfoKey.
        originalImage] as? UIImage {
            picker.dismiss(animated: true, completion: nil)
            pictureChosen.image = gotImage
```

```
        identifyFacesWithLandmarks(image: gotImage)
    }
}

func identifyFacesWithLandmarks(image: UIImage) {
    let handler = VNImageRequestHandler(cgImage: image.
    cgImage!, options: [ : ])
    messageLabel.text = "Analyzing picture..."

    let request = VNDetectFaceLandmarksRequest(completionHandl
    er: handleFaceLandmarksRecognition)
    try! handler.perform([request])
}

func handleFaceLandmarksRecognition(request: VNRequest, error:
Error?) {
    guard let foundFaces = request.results as?
    [VNFaceObservation] else {
        fatalError ("Problem loading picture to examine faces")
    }
    messageLabel.text = "Found \(foundFaces.count) faces in the
    picture"

    for faceRectangle in foundFaces {

        let landmarkRegions: [VNFaceLandmarkRegion2D] = []

        drawImage(source: pictureChosen.image!, boundary:
        faceRectangle.boundingBox, faceLandmarkRegions:
        landmarkRegions)
    }
}

func drawImage(source: UIImage, boundary: CGRect,
faceLandmarkRegions: [VNFaceLandmarkRegion2D]) {
    UIGraphicsBeginImageContextWithOptions(source.size, false, 1)
    let context = UIGraphicsGetCurrentContext()!
    context.translateBy(x: 0, y: source.size.height)
    context.scaleBy(x: 1.0, y: -1.0)
```

447

```
        context.setLineJoin(.round)
        context.setLineCap(.round)
        context.setShouldAntialias(true)
        context.setAllowsAntialiasing(true)

        let rect = CGRect(x: 0, y:0, width: source.size.width,
        height: source.size.height)
        context.draw(source.cgImage!, in: rect)

        //draw rectangles around faces
        let fillColor = UIColor.white
        fillColor.setStroke()

        let rectangleWidth = source.size.width * boundary.size.width
        let rectangleHeight = source.size.height * boundary.size.height

        context.addRect(CGRect(x: boundary.origin.x * source.size.
        width, y:boundary.origin.y * source.size.height, width:
        rectangleWidth, height: rectangleHeight))
        context.drawPath(using: CGPathDrawingMode.stroke)

        let modifiedImage : UIImage =
        UIGraphicsGetImageFromCurrentImageContext()!
        UIGraphicsEndImageContext()
        pictureChosen.image = modifiedImage
    }

    func getPhoto() {
        let picker = UIImagePickerController()
        picker.delegate = self
        picker.sourceType = .savedPhotosAlbum
        present(picker, animated: true, completion: nil)
    }

    @IBAction func getImage(_ sender: UIButton) {
        getPhoto()
    }
}
```

11. Click the Run button or choose Product ➤ Run. The Simulator screen appears.

12. Click the Get Image button to display a list of pictures stored in the Photos app.

13. Click the picture that displays faces. The app displays white rectangles around all detected faces as shown in Figure 17-4.

Figure 17-4. *Displaying rectangles around faces in a picture*

14. Choose Simulator ➤ Quit Simulator.

Highlighting Parts of a Face in an Image

Besides identifying faces in an image with a rectangle, the Vision framework can also identify and highlight the following parts of a face:

- Contour of the face

- Nose and nosecrest

- Inner and outer lips

- Eye, eyebrow, and pupil for both the left and right eyes

- Median line

Note   To get a complete listing of all the parts of a face the Vision framework can identify, visit Apple's developer's web site at `https://developer.apple.com/documentation/vision/vnfacelandmarks2d`.

To identify facial features, we need to modify the code in the AdvancedFacialRecognitionApp project. Within the handleFacelandmarksRecognition function, we'll need to look for landmarks within a face in an image by using this code:

```
guard let landmarks = faceRectangle.landmarks else {
        continue
}
```

Next we'll need to look for specific landmarks such as a left eye or nose. Once we find a specific facial feature, we need to store this in the landmarkRegions array using code such as the following:

```
if let faceContour = landmarks.faceContour {
    landmarkRegions.append(faceContour)
}
if let leftEye = landmarks.leftEye {
    landmarkRegions.append(leftEye)
}
```

```
    if let rightEye = landmarks.rightEye {
        landmarkRegions.append(rightEye)
    }
    if let nose = landmarks.nose {

        landmarkRegions.append(nose)
    }
```

The complete handleFaceLandmarksRecognition function should look like this:

```
func handleFaceLandmarksRecognition(request: VNRequest, error: Error?) {
    guard let foundFaces = request.results as? [VNFaceObservation] else {
        fatalError ("Problem loading picture to examine faces")
    }
    messageLabel.text = "Found \(foundFaces.count) faces in the picture"

    for faceRectangle in foundFaces {

        guard let landmarks = faceRectangle.landmarks else {
            continue
        }

        var landmarkRegions: [VNFaceLandmarkRegion2D] = []

        if let faceContour = landmarks.faceContour {
            landmarkRegions.append(faceContour)
        }
        if let leftEye = landmarks.leftEye {
            landmarkRegions.append(leftEye)
        }
        if let rightEye = landmarks.rightEye {
            landmarkRegions.append(rightEye)
        }
        if let nose = landmarks.nose {
            landmarkRegions.append(nose)
        }
```

```
        drawImage(source: pictureChosen.image!, boundary:
        faceRectangle.boundingBox, faceLandmarkRegions:
        landmarkRegions)
    }
}
```

The drawImage function needs to be modified to highlight any chosen facial features. First, change the fillColor constant to a variable like this:

```
var fillColor = UIColor.white
```

Then define a color, such as red, to highlight facial features and draw those lines as follows:

```
fillColor = UIColor.red
fillColor.setStroke()
context.setLineWidth(2.0)
for faceLandmarkRegion in faceLandmarkRegions {
    var points: [CGPoint] = []
    for i in 0..<faceLandmarkRegion.pointCount {
        let point = faceLandmarkRegion.normalizedPoints[i]
        let p = CGPoint(x: CGFloat(point.x), y: CGFloat(point.y))
        points.append(p)
    }
    let facialPoints = points.map { CGPoint(x: boundary.origin.x *
    source.size.width + $0.x * rectangleWidth, y: boundary.origin.y *
    source.size.height + $0.y * rectangleHeight) }
    context.addLines(between: facialPoints)
    context.drawPath(using: CGPathDrawingMode.stroke)
}
```

The complete drawImage function should look like this:

```
func drawImage(source: UIImage, boundary: CGRect, faceLandmarkRegions:
[VNFaceLandmarkRegion2D])  {
    UIGraphicsBeginImageContextWithOptions(source.size, false, 1)
    let context = UIGraphicsGetCurrentContext()!
    context.translateBy(x: 0, y: source.size.height)
```

```
context.scaleBy(x: 1.0, y: -1.0)
context.setLineJoin(.round)
context.setLineCap(.round)
context.setShouldAntialias(true)
context.setAllowsAntialiasing(true)

let rect = CGRect(x: 0, y:0, width: source.size.width, height:
source.size.height)
context.draw(source.cgImage!, in: rect)


//draw rectangles around faces
var fillColor = UIColor.white
fillColor.setStroke()

let rectangleWidth = source.size.width * boundary.size.width
let rectangleHeight = source.size.height * boundary.size.height

context.addRect(CGRect(x: boundary.origin.x * source.size.width,
y:boundary.origin.y * source.size.height, width: rectangleWidth,
height: rectangleHeight))
context.drawPath(using: CGPathDrawingMode.stroke)

//draw facial features
fillColor = UIColor.red
fillColor.setStroke()
context.setLineWidth(2.0)
for faceLandmarkRegion in faceLandmarkRegions {
    var points: [CGPoint] = []
    for i in 0..<faceLandmarkRegion.pointCount {
        let point = faceLandmarkRegion.normalizedPoints[i]
        let p = CGPoint(x: CGFloat(point.x), y: CGFloat(point.y))
        points.append(p)
    }
    let facialPoints = points.map { CGPoint(x: boundary.origin.x *
    source.size.width + $0.x * rectangleWidth, y: boundary.origin.y *
    source.size.height + $0.y * rectangleHeight) }
```

```
        context.addLines(between: facialPoints)
        context.drawPath(using: CGPathDrawingMode.stroke)
    }


    let modifiedImage : UIImage =
    UIGraphicsGetImageFromCurrentImageContext()!
    UIGraphicsEndImageContext()
    pictureChosen.image = modifiedImage
}
```

The complete ViewController.swift file should look like this:

```
import UIKit
import Vision
import Photos

class ViewController: UIViewController,
UIImagePickerControllerDelegate, UINavigationControllerDelegate {

    @IBOutlet var messageLabel: UILabel!
    @IBOutlet var pictureChosen: UIImageView!

    override func viewDidLoad() {
        super.viewDidLoad()
        // Do any additional setup after loading the view.
    }

    func imagePickerController(_ picker: UIImagePickerController,
    didFinishPickingMediaWithInfo info: [UIImagePickerController.
    InfoKey : Any]) {
        if let gotImage = info[UIImagePickerController.InfoKey.
        originalImage] as? UIImage {
            picker.dismiss(animated: true, completion: nil)
            pictureChosen.image = gotImage
            identifyFacesWithLandmarks(image: gotImage)
        }
    }
```

```
func identifyFacesWithLandmarks(image: UIImage) {
    let handler = VNImageRequestHandler(cgImage: image.cgImage!,
    options: [ : ])

    messageLabel.text = "Analyzing picture..."

    let request = VNDetectFaceLandmarksRequest(completionHandler:
    handleFaceLandmarksRecognition)
    try! handler.perform([request])
}

func handleFaceLandmarksRecognition(request: VNRequest, error:
Error?) {
    guard let foundFaces = request.results as? [VNFaceObservation]
    else {
        fatalError ("Problem loading picture to examine faces")
    }
    messageLabel.text = "Found \(foundFaces.count) faces in the
    picture"

    for faceRectangle in foundFaces {

        guard let landmarks = faceRectangle.landmarks else {
            continue
        }

        var landmarkRegions: [VNFaceLandmarkRegion2D] = []

        if let faceContour = landmarks.faceContour {
            landmarkRegions.append(faceContour)
        }
        if let leftEye = landmarks.leftEye {
            landmarkRegions.append(leftEye)
        }
        if let rightEye = landmarks.rightEye {
            landmarkRegions.append(rightEye)
        }
```

```
        if let nose = landmarks.nose {
            landmarkRegions.append(nose)
        }

        drawImage(source: pictureChosen.image!, boundary:
        faceRectangle.boundingBox, faceLandmarkRegions:
        landmarkRegions)
    }
}

func drawImage(source: UIImage, boundary: CGRect,
faceLandmarkRegions: [VNFaceLandmarkRegion2D]) {
    UIGraphicsBeginImageContextWithOptions(source.size, false, 1)
    let context = UIGraphicsGetCurrentContext()!
    context.translateBy(x: 0, y: source.size.height)
    context.scaleBy(x: 1.0, y: -1.0)
    context.setLineJoin(.round)
    context.setLineCap(.round)
    context.setShouldAntialias(true)
    context.setAllowsAntialiasing(true)

    let rect = CGRect(x: 0, y:0, width: source.size.width, height:
    source.size.height)
    context.draw(source.cgImage!, in: rect)

    //draw rectangles around faces
    var fillColor = UIColor.white
    fillColor.setStroke()

    let rectangleWidth = source.size.width * boundary.size.width
    let rectangleHeight = source.size.height * boundary.size.height

    context.addRect(CGRect(x: boundary.origin.x * source.size.
    width, y:boundary.origin.y * source.size.height, width:
    rectangleWidth, height: rectangleHeight))
    context.drawPath(using: CGPathDrawingMode.stroke)
```

```swift
    //draw facial features
    fillColor = UIColor.red
    fillColor.setStroke()
    context.setLineWidth(2.0)
    for faceLandmarkRegion in faceLandmarkRegions {
        var points: [CGPoint] = []
        for i in 0..<faceLandmarkRegion.pointCount {
            let point = faceLandmarkRegion.normalizedPoints[i]
            let p = CGPoint(x: CGFloat(point.x), y: CGFloat(point.y))
            points.append(p)
        }
        let facialPoints = points.map { CGPoint(x: boundary.origin.x
        * source.size.width + $0.x * rectangleWidth, y: boundary.
        origin.y * source.size.height + $0.y * rectangleHeight) }
        context.addLines(between: facialPoints)
        context.drawPath(using: CGPathDrawingMode.stroke)
    }

    let modifiedImage : UIImage =
    UIGraphicsGetImageFromCurrentImageContext()!
    UIGraphicsEndImageContext()
    pictureChosen.image = modifiedImage
}

func getPhoto() {
    let picker = UIImagePickerController()
    picker.delegate = self
    picker.sourceType = .savedPhotosAlbum
    present(picker, animated: true, completion: nil)
}

@IBAction func getImage(_ sender: UIButton) {
    getPhoto()
}
}
```

Running this project will then highlight the face contour, nose, and left and right eyes as shown in Figure 17-5.

Figure 17-5. *Highlighting facial features in a picture*

Recognizing Text in an Image

Besides recognizing text, the Vision framework can also recognize text in an image or through a camera. Just like recognizing faces, text recognition can recognize text, even if that text appears in different languages. To see how the Vision framework can detect text, follow these steps:

1.   Create a new iOS Single View App project and name it TextRecognitionApp.

2.   Click the ViewController.swift file in the Navigator pane.

3. Under the import UIKit line, add the following to allow access to the camera and vision recognition frameworks:

```
import Vision
import AVFoundation
```

4. Edit the class ViewController line to adopt the delegate for capturing video output as follows:

```
class ViewController: UIViewController,
AVCaptureVideoDataOutputSampleBufferDelegate {
```

5. Click the Main.storyboard file in the Navigator pane.

6. Click the Library icon and drag and drop an image view. The exact placement doesn't matter, but you'll want the UIImageView to be as large as possible because this is where you'll see the video output that identifies text.

7. Choose Editor ➤ Resolve Auto Layout Issues ➤ Reset to Suggested Constraints.

8. Choose View ➤ Assistant Editor ➤ Show Assistant Editor, or click the Assistant Editor icon in the upper right corner of the Xcode window. Xcode shows the Main.storyboard and ViewController.swift file side by side.

9. Move the mouse pointer over the image view, hold down the Control key, and Ctrl-drag under the class ViewController line in the ViewController.swift file.

10. Release the Control key and the left mouse button. A popup window appears.

11. Click in the Name text field, type **textImage**, and click the Connect button. Xcode creates an IBOutlet as follows:

```
@IBOutlet var textImage: UIImageView!
```

Now we need to create one variable to capture video from the camera and a second variable to analyze the image.

12. Add the following underneath the IBOutlet:

```
var session = AVCaptureSession()
var requests = [VNRequest]()
```

There are two steps to identify text in an image through the camera. First, we need to get an image from the camera. Second, we need to identify text in that image.

13. Modify the viewDidLoad method as follows:

```
override func viewDidLoad() {
    super.viewDidLoad()
    getVideo()
    detectText()
}
```

To getVideo function needs to define the camera to record video and then capture that video. Finally, it must display that video in the UIImageView using the textImage IBOutlet.

14. Add the following getVideo function:

```
func getVideo() {
    session.sessionPreset = AVCaptureSession.Preset.photo
    let camera = AVCaptureDevice.default(for: AVMediaType.video)

    let cameraInput = try! AVCaptureDeviceInput(device: camera!)
    let cameraOutput = AVCaptureVideoDataOutput()
    cameraOutput.videoSettings = [kCVPixelBufferPixelFormatTypeKey
    as String: Int(kCVPixelFormatType_32BGRA)]
    cameraOutput.setSampleBufferDelegate(self, queue:
    DispatchQueue.global(qos: DispatchQoS.QoSClass.default))
    session.addInput(cameraInput)
    session.addOutput(cameraOutput)

    let videoLayer = AVCaptureVideoPreviewLayer(session: session)
    videoLayer.frame = textImage.bounds
    textImage.layer.addSublayer(videoLayer)
    session.startRunning()
}
```

15. Add the following function to capture an image from the camera:

```
func captureOutput(_ output: AVCaptureOutput, didOutput
sampleBuffer: CMSampleBuffer, from connection:
AVCaptureConnection) {
    guard let pixelBuffer = CMSampleBufferGetImageBuffer
    (sampleBuffer) else {
        return
    }

    var requestOptions:[VNImageOption : Any] = [:]

    if let cameraData = CMGetAttachment(sampleBuffer, key:
    kCMSampleBufferAttachmentKey_CameraIntrinsicMatrix,
    attachmentModeOut: nil) {
        requestOptions = [.cameraIntrinsics:cameraData]
    }

    let imageRequestHandler = VNImageRequestHandler(cvPixelBuffer:
    pixelBuffer, orientation: CGImagePropertyOrientation
    (rawValue: 6)!, options: requestOptions)

    do {
        try imageRequestHandler.perform(self.requests)
    } catch {
        print(error)
    }
}
```

All this code so far simply gets the camera to work on an iOS device, but the app won't be able to access the camera until the user gives permission to do so. The final step is to click the Info.plist file in the Navigator pane and add the Privacy – Camera Usage Description key. Under the Value column, type descriptive text such as "Need to use camera to view text" as shown in Figure 17-6.

16. Click the Info.plist file in the Navigator pane.

17. Move the mouse pointer over the bottom row until a + and – icon appears.

18. Click the + icon. Xcode adds a new row.

19. Click in the Key column in the newly added row so a popup menu appears and choose Privacy – Camera Usage Description as shown in Figure 17-6.

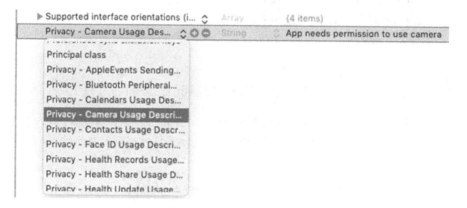

Figure 17-6. *Editing the Info.plist file lets an app ask for permission to use the camera*

20. Click in the Value column and type a message such as "App needs permission to use camera".

21. Click the ViewController.swift file in the Navigator pane.

22. Add the following function to detect text in an image:

```
func detectText() {
    let textRequest = VNDetectTextRectanglesRequest
    (completionHandler: handleText)
    textRequest.reportCharacterBoxes = true
    requests = [textRequest]
}
```

Once this function identifies text in an image, it calls a second function called handleText to define where to display a rectangle on the image. Another function called identifyWords does the actual work of drawing a rectangle where text appears.

23.   Add the following functions in the ViewController.swift file:

```swift
func handleText(request: VNRequest, error: Error?) {
    guard let observations = request.results else {
        print ("No text found")
        return
    }

    let result = observations.map({$0 as? VNTextObservation})

    DispatchQueue.main.async() {
        self.textImage.layer.sublayers?.removeSubrange(1...)
        for region in result {
            guard let foundRegion = region else {
                continue
            }

            self.identifyWords(box: foundRegion)
        }
    }
}

func identifyWords(box: VNTextObservation) {
    guard let rectangle = box.characterBoxes else {
        return
    }
    var maxX: CGFloat = 9999.0
    var minX: CGFloat = 0.0
    var maxY: CGFloat = 9999.0
    var minY: CGFloat = 0.0

    for char in rectangle {
        if char.bottomLeft.x < maxX {
            maxX = char.bottomLeft.x
        }
        if char.bottomRight.x > minX {
            minX = char.bottomRight.x
        }
```

```
        if char.bottomRight.y < maxY {
            maxY = char.bottomRight.y
        }
        if char.topRight.y > minY {
            minY = char.topRight.y
        }
    }

    let xCord = maxX * textImage.frame.size.width
    let yCord = (1 - minY) * textImage.frame.size.height
    let width = (minX - maxX) * textImage.frame.size.width
    let height = (minY - maxY) * textImage.frame.size.height

    let outline = CALayer()
    outline.frame = CGRect(x: xCord, y: yCord, width: width,
    height: height)
    outline.borderWidth = 2.0
    outline.borderColor = UIColor.red.cgColor

    textImage.layer.addSublayer(outline)
}
```

The entire ViewController.swift file should look like this:

```
import UIKit
import Vision
import AVFoundation

class ViewController: UIViewController,
AVCaptureVideoDataOutputSampleBufferDelegate {

    @IBOutlet var textImage: UIImageView!
    var session = AVCaptureSession()
    var requests = [VNRequest]()

    override func viewDidLoad() {
        super.viewDidLoad()
        getVideo()
        detectText()
    }
```

```
func getVideo() {
    session.sessionPreset = AVCaptureSession.Preset.photo
    let camera = AVCaptureDevice.default(for: AVMediaType.video)

    let cameraInput = try! AVCaptureDeviceInput(device: camera!)
    let cameraOutput = AVCaptureVideoDataOutput()
    cameraOutput.videoSettings =
    [kCVPixelBufferPixelFormatTypeKey as String: Int(kCVPixelF
    ormatType_32BGRA)]
    cameraOutput.setSampleBufferDelegate(self, queue:
    DispatchQueue.global(qos: DispatchQoS.QoSClass.default))
    session.addInput(cameraInput)
    session.addOutput(cameraOutput)

    let videoLayer = AVCaptureVideoPreviewLayer(session: session)
    videoLayer.frame = textImage.bounds
    textImage.layer.addSublayer(videoLayer)
    session.startRunning()
}

func captureOutput(_ output: AVCaptureOutput, didOutput
sampleBuffer: CMSampleBuffer, from connection:
AVCaptureConnection) {
    guard let pixelBuffer = CMSampleBufferGetImageBuffer(sampl
    eBuffer) else {
        return
    }

    var requestOptions:[VNImageOption : Any] = [:]

    if let cameraData = CMGetAttachment(sampleBuffer, key:
    kCMSampleBufferAttachmentKey_CameraIntrinsicMatrix,
    attachmentModeOut: nil) {
        requestOptions = [.cameraIntrinsics:cameraData]
    }

    let imageRequestHandler = VNImageRequestHandler(cvPixelBuf
    fer: pixelBuffer, orientation: CGImagePropertyOrientation(
    rawValue: 6)!, options: requestOptions)
```

```swift
    do {
        try imageRequestHandler.perform(self.requests)
    } catch {
        print(error)
    }
}

func detectText() {
    let textRequest = VNDetectTextRectanglesRequest(completion
    Handler: handleText)
    textRequest.reportCharacterBoxes = true
    requests = [textRequest]
}

func handleText(request: VNRequest, error: Error?) {
    guard let observations = request.results else {
        print ("No text found")
        return
    }

    let result = observations.map({$0 as? VNTextObservation})

    DispatchQueue.main.async() {
        self.textImage.layer.sublayers?.removeSubrange(1...)
        for region in result {
            guard let foundRegion = region else {
                continue
            }

            self.identifyWords(box: foundRegion)
        }
    }
}

func identifyWords(box: VNTextObservation) {
    guard let rectangle = box.characterBoxes else {
        return
    }
```

```
var maxX: CGFloat = 9999.0
var minX: CGFloat = 0.0
var maxY: CGFloat = 9999.0
var minY: CGFloat = 0.0

for char in rectangle {
    if char.bottomLeft.x < maxX {
        maxX = char.bottomLeft.x
    }
    if char.bottomRight.x > minX {
        minX = char.bottomRight.x
    }
    if char.bottomRight.y < maxY {
        maxY = char.bottomRight.y
    }
    if char.topRight.y > minY {
        minY = char.topRight.y
    }
}

let xCord = maxX * textImage.frame.size.width
let yCord = (1 - minY) * textImage.frame.size.height
let width = (minX - maxX) * textImage.frame.size.width
let height = (minY - maxY) * textImage.frame.size.height

let outline = CALayer()
outline.frame = CGRect(x: xCord, y: yCord, width: width,
height: height)
outline.borderWidth = 2.0
outline.borderColor = UIColor.red.cgColor

textImage.layer.addSublayer(outline)
    }

}
```

Note   To test this app, you'll need to connect an iPhone or iPad with a camera to your Macintosh using a USB cable.

24. Connect an iOS device to your Macintosh through its USB cable.

25. Click the Scheme menu and choose your iOS device.

26. Click the Run button or choose Product ➤ Run. The app appears.

27. Point the camera at text. Whatever the camera sees appears inside the UIImageView on the user interface and displays rectangles around text. While the Vision framework may not always be accurate in identifying text in an image, it can recognize text in different languages as shown in Figure 17-7.

Figure 17-7. *Identifying text on a sign through the iPhone camera*

28. Click the Stop button in Xcode, or choose Product ➤ Stop.

Summary

As you can see, the Vision framework contains enough artificial intelligence to identify and recognize faces in a picture. Not only can you identify the number of faces, but you can also identify the faces by drawing a rectangle around them in a picture.

Besides recognizing faces, the Vision framework can also identify specific facial features such as eyes, nose, and lips. If your app works with images containing people or text, you can use the Vision framework to identify faces, facial features, and text (even in different languages) to give your app extra features without writing much code yourself.

CHAPTER 18

Using Speech

The Speech framework lets apps recognize audio commands as a supplement to taps and gestures. In addition, the Speech framework can also transcribe speech into text. By adding speech recognition features, your app can offer more ways for the user to interact in a natural manner that's easy for everyone to do.

Before an app can use speech recognition, the user must give permission for the app to access the microphone and use speech recognition. You may also want to make your users aware that speech recognition may send audio data to Apple's servers over the Internet to improve accuracy. That's why it's important to get the user's permission to use the microphone and use speech recognition due to privacy concerns.

By adding speech recognition to your app, your user interface is no longer limited to the touch screen. Speech recognition may never replace the touch screen, but it can give users another way to interact with your app by just speaking to it out loud.

Note You can only test speech recognition on an actual iOS device. You cannot test speech recognition with the Simulator program.

Converting Speech to Text

The Speech framework that Apple provides can convert spoken words into printed text, even in different languages based on your current location. To see how this speech to text recognition feature works, follow these steps:

1. Create a new iOS Single View App project and name it Speech2TextApp.

2. Click the Info.plist file in the Navigator pane.

© Wallace Wang 2019

W. Wang, *Pro iPhone Development with Swift 5*, https://doi.org/10.1007/978-1-4842-4944-4_18

3. Move the mouse pointer over the bottom row until a + and – icon appears.

4. Click the + icon. Xcode adds a new row.

5. Click in the Key column in the newly added row so a popup menu appears and choose Privacy – Speech Recognition Usage Description. Then click in the Value column and type descriptive text such as "Need to send data to Apple's servers".

6. Repeat steps 3–5 except choose Privacy – Microphone Usage Description, click in the Value column, and type descriptive text such as "Must use the microphone to hear speech" as shown in Figure 18-1.

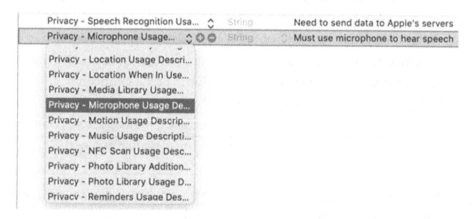

Figure 18-1. *Adding two privacy settings in the Info.plist file*

7. Click the Main.storyboard file in the Navigator pane.

8. Click the Library icon and drag and drop a label and two buttons.

9. Double-click one button, type **Start Recognizing Speech**, and press Enter.

10. Double-click the second button, type **Stop Recording**, and press Enter.

11. Click the label and choose View ➤ Inspectors ➤ Show Attributes Inspector, or click the Attributes Inspector icon in the upper right corner of the Xcode window.

12. Click in the Lines text field, type 0, and press Enter.

13. Resize the label so it's tall and wide enough to display text. The entire user interface should look something like Figure 18-2.

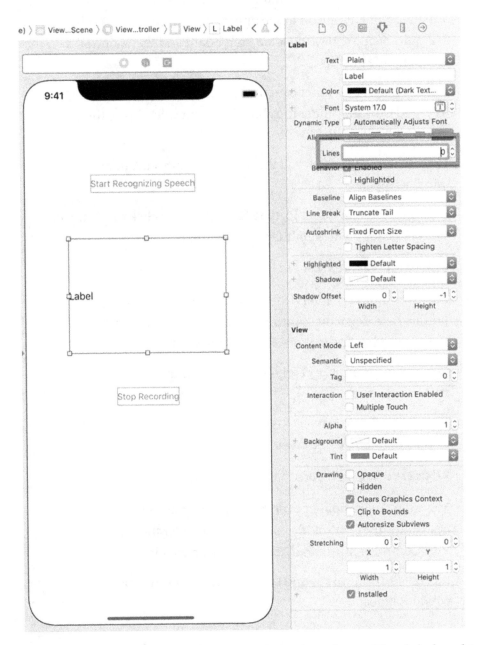

Figure 18-2. *Designing the Speech2TextApp user interface with a label and two buttons*

14. Choose Editor ➤ Resolve Auto Layout Issues ➤ Reset to Suggested Constraints at the bottom of the menu to define constraints for all items.

15. Choose View ➤ Assistant Editor ➤ Show Assistant Editor, or click the Assistant Editor icon in the upper right corner of the Xcode window. Xcode shows the Main.storyboard and ViewController. swift file side by side.

16. Move the mouse pointer over the label, hold down the Control key, and Ctrl-drag under the class ViewController line in the ViewController.swift file.

17. Release the Control key and the left mouse button. A popup window appears.

18. Click in the Name text field, type **textLabel**, and click the Connect button. Xcode creates an IBOutlet as follows:

```
@IBOutlet var textLabel: UILabel!
```

19. Move the mouse pointer over the Start Recognizing Speech button, hold down the Control key, and Ctrl-drag under the class ViewController line in the ViewController.swift file.

20. Release the Control key and the left mouse button. A popup window appears.

21. Click in the Name text field, type **recordButton**, and click the Connect button. Xcode creates an IBOutlet as follows:

```
@IBOutlet var recordButton: UIButton!
```

22. Move the mouse pointer over the Stop Recording button, hold down the Control key, and Ctrl-drag under the class ViewController line in the ViewController.swift file.

23. Release the Control key and the left mouse button. A popup window appears.

24. Click in the Name text field, type **stopButton**, and click the
    Connect button. Xcode creates an IBOutlet as follows:

    @IBOutlet var stopButton: UIButton!

25. Move the mouse pointer over the Start Recognizing Speech
    button, hold down the Control key, and Ctrl-drag above the last
    curly bracket in the ViewController.swift file.

26. Release the Control key and the left mouse button. A popup
    window appears.

27. Click in the Name text field, type **startRecording**, click the Type
    popup menu and choose UIButton, and click the Connect button.
    Xcode creates an IBAction method.

28. Move the mouse pointer over the Stop Recording button, hold
    down the Control key, and Ctrl-drag above the last curly bracket in
    the ViewController.swift file in the ViewController.swift file.

29. Release the Control key and the left mouse button. A popup
    window appears.

30. Click in the Name text field, type **stopRecording**, click the Type
    popup menu and choose UIButton, and click the Connect button.
    Xcode creates an IBAction method.

31. Choose View ➤ Standard Editor ➤ Show Standard Editor, or click
    the Standard Editor icon in the upper right corner of the Xcode
    window.

32. Click the ViewController.swift file in the Navigator pane.

33. Under the import UIKit line, add the following to import the
    Speech framework:

    import Speech

34. Edit the class ViewController line to adopt the
    SFSpeechRecognizerDelegate like this:

    class ViewController: UIViewController, SFSpeechRecognizerDelegate {

35. Under the IBOutlet, add the following to create an instance of the AVAudioEngine class:

```
let audioEngine = AVAudioEngine()
```

36. Add a speech recognizer and define a location to detect a specific type of language like this:

```
let speechRecognizer = SFSpeechRecognizer(locale: Locale(identifier: "en-US"))
```

37. Add a request to detect spoken audio:

```
var request = SFSpeechAudioBufferRecognitionRequest()
```

38. Add an optional variable to store the recognition task. Since the task may or may not succeed, it needs to be an optional variable:

```
var recognitionTask : SFSpeechRecognitionTask?
```

39. Modify the two IBAction methods for the two buttons as follows:

```
@IBAction func startRecording(_ sender: UIButton) {
    recordButton.isEnabled = false
    stopButton.isEnabled = true
    recognizeSpeech()
}

@IBAction func stopRecording(_ sender: UIButton) {
    recordButton.isEnabled = true
    stopButton.isEnabled = false
    stopSpeech()
}
```

At this point we need to write two functions: recognizeSpeech() and stopSpeech().

40. Add the stopSpeech() function as follows:

```
func stopSpeech() {
    audioEngine.stop()
    request.endAudio()
```

```
    recognitionTask?.cancel()
    audioEngine.inputNode.removeTap(onBus: 0)
}
```

41. Add a recognizeSpeech() function as follows:

```
func recognizeSpeech() {
    let node = audioEngine.inputNode

    request = SFSpeechAudioBufferRecognitionRequest()
    request.shouldReportPartialResults = true

    let recordingFormat = node.outputFormat(forBus: 0)
    node.installTap(onBus: 0, bufferSize: 1024, format:
    recordingFormat) { (buffer, _) in
        self.request.append(buffer)
    }

    audioEngine.prepare()
    do {
        try audioEngine.start()
    } catch {
        return print (error)
    }

    guard let recognizeMe = SFSpeechRecognizer() else {
        return
    }

    if !recognizeMe.isAvailable {
        return
    }

    recognitionTask = speechRecognizer?.recognitionTask(with:
    request, resultHandler: {result, error in
        if let result = result {
            let transcribedString = result.bestTranscription.
            formattedString
            self.textLabel.text = transcribedString
```

477

```
    } else if let error = error {
        print(error)
    }
})
```

```
}
```

The first few lines of the recognizeSpeech() function require an audio engine to process data in nodes, so we need to get that data and create a request to recognize speech. The first few lines of code in the recognizeSpeech function do this:

```
let node = audioEngine.inputNode
```

```
request = SFSpeechAudioBufferRecognitionRequest()
request.shouldReportPartialResults = true
```

```
let recordingFormat = node.outputFormat(forBus: 0)
node.installTap(onBus: 0, bufferSize: 1024, format:
recordingFormat) { (buffer, _) in
    self.request.append(buffer)
}
```

Next we need to catch potential errors in case the audio engine can't start or if the speech recognizer cannot be accessed:

```
audioEngine.prepare()
do {
    try audioEngine.start()
} catch {
    return print (error)
}
```

```
guard let recognizeMe = SFSpeechRecognizer() else {
    return
}
```

```
if !recognizeMe.isAvailable {
    return
}
```

Finally, we need to recognize the spoken speech and transcribe it to text, which will appear in the textLabel IBOutlet:

```
recognitionTask = speechRecognizer?.recognitionTask(with: request,
resultHandler: {result, error in
    if let result = result {
        let transcribedString = result.bestTranscription.
        formattedString
        self.textLabel.text = transcribedString
    } else if let error = error {
        print(error)
    }
})
```

The entire ViewController.swift file should look like this:

```
import UIKit
import Speech

class ViewController: UIViewController, SFSpeechRecognizerDelegate {

    @IBOutlet var recordButton: UIButton!
    @IBOutlet var stopButton: UIButton!
    @IBOutlet var textLabel: UILabel!

    let audioEngine = AVAudioEngine()
    let speechRecognizer = SFSpeechRecognizer(locale:
    Locale(identifier: "en-US"))
    var request = SFSpeechAudioBufferRecognitionRequest()
    var recognitionTask : SFSpeechRecognitionTask?

    override func viewDidLoad() {
        super.viewDidLoad()
        // Do any additional setup after loading the view.
    }

    func stopSpeech() {
        audioEngine.stop()
        request.endAudio()
```

```
        recognitionTask?.cancel()
        audioEngine.inputNode.removeTap(onBus: 0)
    }

    func recognizeSpeech() {
        let node = audioEngine.inputNode

        request = SFSpeechAudioBufferRecognitionRequest()
        request.shouldReportPartialResults = true

        let recordingFormat = node.outputFormat(forBus: 0)
        node.installTap(onBus: 0, bufferSize: 1024, format:
        recordingFormat) { (buffer, _) in
            self.request.append(buffer)
        }

        audioEngine.prepare()
        do {
            try audioEngine.start()
        } catch {
            return print (error)
        }

        guard let recognizeMe = SFSpeechRecognizer() else {
            return
        }

        if !recognizeMe.isAvailable {
            return
        }

        recognitionTask = speechRecognizer?.recognitionTask(with:
        request, resultHandler: {result, error in
            if let result = result {
                let transcribedString = result.bestTranscription.
                formattedString
                self.textLabel.text = transcribedString
            } else if let error = error {
```

```
                print(error)
            }
        })
    }

    @IBAction func startRecording(_ sender: UIButton) {
        recordButton.isEnabled = false
        stopButton.isEnabled = true
        recognizeSpeech()
    }

    @IBAction func stopRecording(_ sender: UIButton) {
        recordButton.isEnabled = true
        stopButton.isEnabled = false
        stopSpeech()
    }
}
```

42. Connect an iOS device to your Macintosh through its USB cable.

43. Click the Scheme popup menu in the upper left corner of the Xcode window and choose your iOS device.

44. Click the Run button or choose Product ➤ Run. The first time you run the app, it will ask permission to access the microphone and send your data to Apple's servers.

45. Tap the Start Recognizing Speech button.

46. Speak a sentence and the transcribed text should appear in the label. Then tap the Stop Recording button when you're done. The transcribed text may make mistakes, but in general, you'll find it's fairly accurate in transcribing common words into text as shown in Figure 18-3.

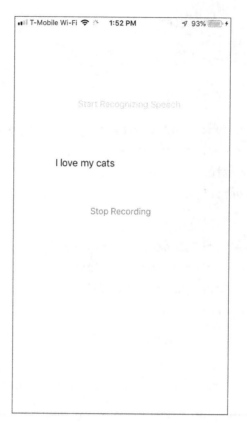

Figure 18-3. *Running the Speech2Text project on an iPhone*

47. Click the Stop button in Xcode, or choose Product ➤ Stop.

Recognizing Spoken Commands

Besides transcribing spoken speech into text, the Speech framework can also recognize specific spoken words that you must define ahead of time. This gives your app the ability to respond to spoken commands as a way to interact with the user.

Just be aware that in most languages, words may sound alike but be spelled differently. For example, in English, "red" and "read" sound the same and "too," "to," and "two" also sound alike. When identifying spoken commands, be aware of words that sound alike but may have completely different meanings.

To recognize spoken commands, we simply need to use a switch statement to detect a specific word or phrase. To see how to recognize spoken commands, follow these steps:

1. Make sure the Speech2TextApp project is loaded into Xcode.

2. Click the ViewController.swift file in the Navigator pane.

3. Add the following function to define specific words to recognize as spoken commands:

```
func checkSpokenCommand (commandString: String) {
    switch commandString {
    case "Purple":
        textLabel.backgroundColor = UIColor.purple
    case "Green":
        textLabel.backgroundColor = UIColor.green
    case "Yellow":
        textLabel.backgroundColor = UIColor.yellow
    default:
        textLabel.backgroundColor = UIColor.white
    }
}
```

If the user says "purple," "green," or "yellow," the app will change the UILabel background to a different color. If the user says anything else, the UILabel background will turn to white. Now we need to call this checkSpokenCommand function inside the recognizeSpeech function like this:

```
// Chezzzzzzzzzzzck for spoken command
self.checkSpokenCommand(commandString: transcribedString)
```

4. Modify the recognizeSpeech() function as follows:

```
func recognizeSpeech() {
    let node = audioEngine.inputNode

    request = SFSpeechAudioBufferRecognitionRequest()
    request.shouldReportPartialResults = true
```

```swift
let recordingFormat = node.outputFormat(forBus: 0)
node.installTap(onBus: 0, bufferSize: 1024, format:
recordingFormat) { (buffer, _) in
    self.request.append(buffer)
}

audioEngine.prepare()
do {
    try audioEngine.start()
} catch {
    return print (error)
}

guard let recognizeMe = SFSpeechRecognizer() else {
    return
}

if !recognizeMe.isAvailable {
    return
}

recognitionTask = speechRecognizer?.recognitionTask(with:
request, resultHandler: {result, error in
    if let result = result {
        let transcribedString = result.bestTranscription.
        formattedString
        self.textLabel.text = transcribedString

        // Check for spoken command
        self.checkSpokenCommand(commandString:
        transcribedString)

    } else if let error = error {
        print(error)
    }
})

}
```

5. Connect an iOS device to your Macintosh through its USB cable.

6. Click the Scheme popup menu in the upper left corner of the Xcode window and choose your iOS device.

7. Click the Run button or choose Product ➤ Run.

8. Tap the Start Recognizing Speech button.

9. Say one of the three words ("purple," "green," or "yellow") that will change the background color of the label. When the app recognizes one of these three command words, it changes the label background color as shown in Figure 18-4.

Figure 18-4. Running the Speech2Text project on an iPhone to change the background color of the label

10. Click the Stop button in Xcode, or choose Product ➤ Stop.

Turning Text to Speech

Just as Swift can recognize spoken commands and convert spoken words into text, so can Swift do it the other way around by reading text out loud. To read text out loud, you need to use the AVFoundation framework, which gives your app access to a speech synthesizer.

This speech synthesizer is based on your current location and default language such as American English, Australian English, or United Kingdom English. Then the speech synthesizer can read text stored in a string that can be read at a fast or slow rate.

To see how to use the speech synthesizer, follow these steps:

1. Create a new iOS Single View App project and name it Text2SpeechApp.

2. Click the Main.storyboard file in the Navigator pane.

3. Click the Library icon and drag and drop a slider, button, and text view.

4. Double-click the button, type **Read Text Out Loud**, and press Enter.

5. Resize the text view, double-click the text view, and type some text such as **This is a test of the emergency broadcasting system. This is only a test.** The user interface should look similar to Figure 18-5.

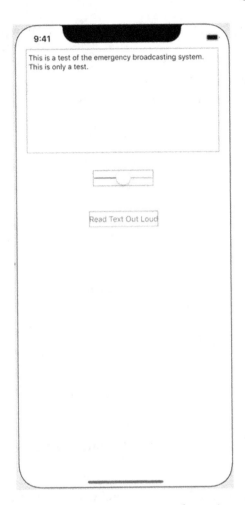

Figure 18-5. *The user interface for the Text2Speech project*

6. Choose Editor ➤ Resolve Auto Layout Issues ➤ Reset to Suggested Constraints at the bottom of the menu to define constraints for all items.

7. Choose View ➤ Assistant Editor ➤ Show Assistant Editor, or click the Assistant Editor icon in the upper right corner of the Xcode window. Xcode shows the Main.storyboard and ViewController. swift file side by side.

8. Move the mouse pointer over the text view, hold down the Control key, and Ctrl-drag under the class ViewController line in the ViewController.swift file.

9. Release the Control key and the left mouse button. A popup window appears.

10. Click in the Name text field, type **textView**, and click the Connect button. Xcode creates an IBOutlet as follows:

@IBOutlet var textView: UITextView!

11. Move the mouse pointer over the slider, hold down the Control key, and Ctrl-drag under the class ViewController line in the ViewController.swift file.

12. Release the Control key and the left mouse button. A popup window appears.

13. Click in the Name text field, type **rateSlider**, and click the Connect button. Xcode creates an IBOutlet as follows:

@IBOutlet var rateSlider: UISlider!

14. Move the mouse pointer over the button, hold down the Control key, and Ctrl-drag above the last curly bracket at the bottom of the ViewController.swift file.

15. Release the Control key and the left mouse button. A popup window appears.

16. Click in the Name text field, type **readText**, click the Type popup menu and choose UIButton, and click the Connect button. Xcode creates a readText IBAction method.

17. Choose View ➤ Standard Editor ➤ Show Standard Editor, or click the Standard Editor icon in the upper right corner of the Xcode window.

18. Click the ViewController.swift file in the Navigator pane.

19. Under the import UIKit line, add the following to access the speech synthesizer:

import AVFoundation

20. Add the following under the IBOutlets to add an AVSpeechSynthesizer class:

```
let audio = AVSpeechSynthesizer()
```

21. Add the following to use the AVSpeechUtterance class to read text out loud:

```
var convertText = AVSpeechUtterance(string: "")
```

22. Edit the readText IBAction method as follows:

```
@IBAction func readText(_ sender: UIButton) {
    convertText = AVSpeechUtterance(string: textView.text)
    convertText.rate = rateSlider.value
    audio.speak(convertText)
}
```

This function first retrieves any text stored in the textView IBOutlet. Then it retrieves the value defined by the slider, which varies from 0 to 1.0 to define the rate that the speech synthesizer will speak. A low number makes the speech synthesizer speak slowly, while a higher number makes the speech synthesizer speak faster. Finally the speech synthesizer uses the rate and text to read the text out loud.

The entire ViewController.swift file should look like this:

```
import UIKit
import AVFoundation

class ViewController: UIViewController {

    @IBOutlet var textView: UITextView!
    @IBOutlet var rateSlider: UISlider!

    let audio = AVSpeechSynthesizer()
    var convertText = AVSpeechUtterance(string: "")

    override func viewDidLoad() {
        super.viewDidLoad()
        // Do any additional setup after loading the view.
    }
```

```
@IBAction func readText(_ sender: UIButton) {
    convertText = AVSpeechUtterance(string: textView.text)
    convertText.rate = rateSlider.value
    audio.speak(convertText)
}

}
```

Note   You can run this app on either the Simulator program or on an actual iOS device.

---

23. Click the Run button or choose Product ➤ Run. The Simulator screen appears displaying your app's user interface.

24. Click the Read Text Out Loud button. The app starts reading the text stored in the text view.

25. Experiment with dragging the slider left or right to adjust the rate of the speech synthesizer, and experiment with typing different text in the text view.

26. Choose Simulator ➤ Quit Simulator to return back to Xcode.

Summary

Adding speech recognition requires the Speech framework, while adding a speech synthesizer to read text out loud requires the AVFoundation framework. Speech recognition gives users another way to interact with your app, while the speech synthesizer lets your app read short strings or even long amounts of text out loud. This can be handy for people with visibility problems or to provide information to users if they can't look at the iPhone screen, such as when they're driving.

By adding speech recognition and a speech synthesizer, your app can use audio as another part of its user interface to allow users to give and receive data from your app.

CHAPTER 19

Understanding SiriKit

In the previous chapter, you learned how to do simple speech recognition. However since there are multiple ways to say the same thing, recognizing voice commands can be difficult when commands get more complex than simple one-word options. To help your app recognize more complicated voice commands, you can add the features of Siri to your app through the SiriKit framework.

Siri essentially takes care of the difficult task of recognizing words and turning them into commands. Then your app has the task of responding to voice commands identified through Siri. Once your app identifies a user's intent through recognized voice commands, your app may need to ask additional questions to clarify the user's intent. Finally, your app can respond intelligently using Siri as its user interface. By using SiriKit, your app can gain the power of Siri with little additional work on your part.

The main limitation is that SiriKit restricts your app to one of several domains that define the user's intent such as sending a message, making a call, browsing through photos, sending money, or making an appointment with a ride-sharing service.

Note   To view a list of all possible Intent domains SiriKit can recognize, visit `https://developer.apple.com/documentation/sirikit`.

Intent domains make it easier for Siri to understand what the user says. For example, if you said, "Send 25 dollars to Fred" within a money payment app, Siri could correctly identify the recipient (Fred) and the amount of money to send (25 dollars). At this point, your app would need to do the actual work of sending money to Fred along with verifying that Fred was a valid person and that your account had enough money to send in the first place.

SiriKit works by recognizing speech, extracting possible actions within a limited domain, asking the user for additional information if necessary, then converting that spoken speech into text for your app to process.

491

© Wallace Wang 2019
W. Wang, *Pro iPhone Development with Swift 5*, https://doi.org/10.1007/978-1-4842-4944-4_19

How SiriKit Works

SiriKit works with an app through two types of files called extensions. An Intents App extension contains Swift code to respond to the user's voice commands after they're interpreted by Siri. An Intents UI App extension allows your app to customize the appearance of data displayed within Siri. At the very least, every app that connects to SiriKit needs an Intents App extension. An Intents UI App extension simply makes your app look more professional but isn't absolutely necessary.

To create a SiriKit app, follow these steps:

1. Create a new iOS Single View App project and name it SiriApp.

2. Choose File ➤ New ➤ Target. A template dialog appears.

3. Click the iOS category and click Intents Extension as shown in Figure 19-1.

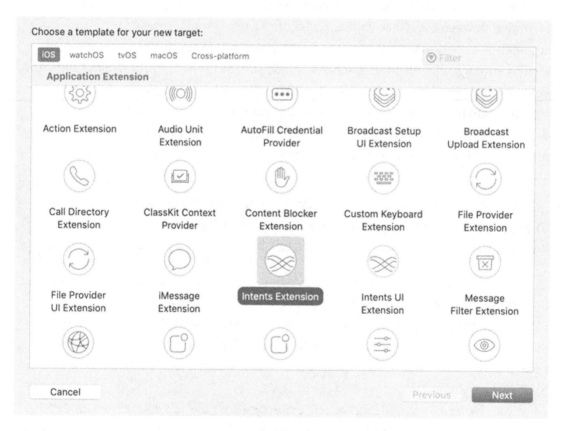

Figure 19-1.   *Adding an Intents Extension file to a project*

4.   Click the Next button. A window appears, asking for a product name for the extension.

5.   Click in the Product Name text field and type **MessageExtension**. Make sure the Include UI Extension check box is selected.

6.   Click the Finish button. When a dialog appears asking if you want to activate the scheme, click the Activate button. Xcode creates two new folders called MessageExtension and MessageExtensionUI as shown in Figure 19-2.

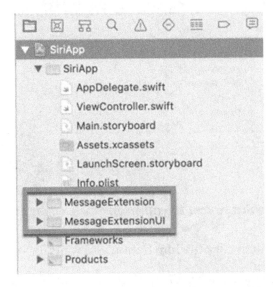

Figure 19-2.   *Xcode adds two new folders for your Intents Extension*

The MessageExtension folder contains an IntentHandler.swift file. This is where you write code to handle commands captured by Siri.

The MessageExtensionUI folder contains a MainInterface. storyboard file along with an accompanying IntentViewController. swift file. The Main.storyboard file appears within Siri to let users know they're interacting with your app through Siri. If you do not customize this Main.storyboard file, your app will display a generic dialog within Siri.

7.   Connect an iOS device to your Macintosh through its USB cable.

8. Click the Scheme popup menu in the upper left corner of the Xcode window and choose your iOS device.

9. Click the Run button or choose Product ➤ Run. A dialog appears, asking you to choose an app to run as shown in Figure 19-3.

Figure 19-3. *Choosing Siri to run in your app*

10. Click Siri and then click the Run button. Siri waits for you to speak.

11. Say "Send a message using SiriApp." The first time you run the SiriApp project, Siri will ask for permission to use SiriApp as shown in Figure 19-4.

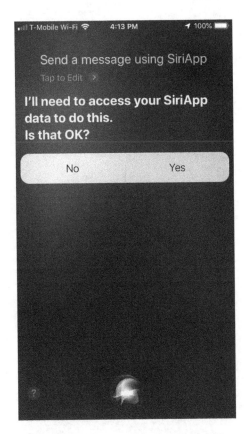

Figure 19-4. *Running the Speech2Text project on an iPhone*

12.   Tap the Yes button. Siri then asks where you want to send the
        message as shown in Figure 19-5.

Figure 19-5. *Running the Speech2Text project on an iPhone*

This generic SiriApp dialog is what's defined by the Main.storyboard file under the MessageExtensionUI folder.

13. State a name stored in your Contacts app. Siri will then ask for the message to send.

14. Recite any message you like. Notice that Siri may not always understand the words you speak accurately. Siri will then ask for confirmation to send it. Although Siri will say it sent the message, nothing will actually be sent.

15. Click the Stop button in Xcode, or choose Product ➤ Stop.

Just with this short demo, you can see how SiriKit works by integrating your app in Siri and allowing Siri to work as your app's user interface.

Now let's go back to Xcode and understand the details of your
SiriApp project and how it works.

Defining How Siri Interacts with the User

In both the MessageExtension and MessageExtensionUI folder of your SiriApp
project, you'll see an Info.plist file. Each of these files defines what Siri recognizes
and responds to. In each Info.plist file, click under the NSExtension heading, then the
NSExtensionAttributes, and finally under IntentsSupported. The Info.plist file under the
MessageExtension folder supports three intents as shown in Figure 19-6.

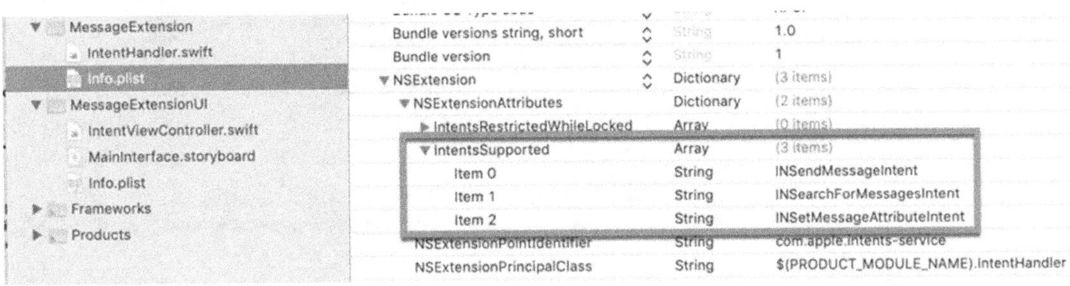

Figure 19-6.   *The Info.plist contents under the MessageExtension folder*

This means that Siri will let you send, search for, and modify the attributes of a
message such as whether it's been marked as read or not.

If you were creating an app in a different domain such as making payments or
creating notes, you would need to change the IntentsSupported items to something
else such as INSendPaymentIntent or INCreateNoteIntent. The exact intent you'd add
depends on the Intent domain your app will handle and which intents your app will
support. By looking up a particular SiriKit domain, such as creating notes, you can see all
possible intents available as shown in Figure 19-7.

Create Note

```
protocol INCreateNoteIntentHandling
```
The handler interface for creating notes.

```
class INCreateNoteIntent
```
A request to create a new note.

```
class INCreateNoteIntentResponse
```
Your app's response to a request to create a note.

Append to Note

```
protocol INAppendToNoteIntentHandling
```
The handler interface for appending content to a note.

```
class INAppendToNoteIntent
```
A request to append content to a note.

```
class INAppendToNoteIntentResponse
```
Your app's response to a request to append content to a note.

Search for Notebook Items

```
protocol INSearchForNotebookItemsIntentHandling
```
The handler interface for searching for notes, tasks, and reminders.

```
class INSearchForNotebookItemsIntent
```
A request to search for notes, tasks, and reminders.

```
class INSearchForNotebookItemsIntentResponse
```
Your app's response to a request to search for notes, tasks, or reminders.

Figure 19-7. *Apple's documentation lists all possible intents for a particular domain such as note creation*

Click the Info.plist file in the MessageExtensionUI folder. If you expand NSExtension, NSExtensionAttributes, and IntentsSupported, you can see that the user interface of Siri supports the INSendMessageIntent as shown in Figure 19-8.

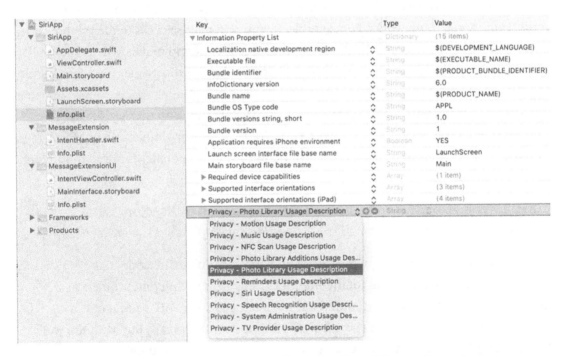

Figure 19-8. *The Info.plist file in the MessageExtensionUI folder*

In any app that works with SiriKit, make sure you modify the Info.plist files to define the intents your app will support for a particular domain such as ride booking, messaging, or photos.

One final Info.plist file you may need to modify is the one stored in your main project's folder. For example, if your app will work with SiriKit to allow searching of photos stored in the Photos album, you'll need to modify the Info.plist file to allow photo library usage as shown in Figure 19-9.

Figure 19-9. *Adding privacy settings in the Info.plist of the main project*

Some common privacy settings you may need to modify include

- Calendar usage

- Contacts access

- Music library access

- Photo library access

- Reminders usage

Understanding the IntentHandler.swift File

Once you have modified the Info.plist files for any privacy settings and to define the intents your app will handle through Siri, the next step is to modify the IntentHandler. swift file located in the Extension folder (not the ExtensionUI folder).

The IntentHandler.swift file imports the Intents framework, but you may need to import additional frameworks. For example, if your app needs access to the Photos library, you'll need to import the Photos framework. If your app makes VoIP calls, you'll need to import the CallKit framework. Make sure you import the proper framework your app needs.

After importing any additional frameworks, the next step is to make sure your IntentHandler class adopts handling protocols for your chosen domain. In our SiriApp project, our IntentHandler class adopts protocols for sending, searching, and modifying messages as follows:

```
class IntentHandler: INExtension, INSendMessageIntentHandling,
INSearchForMessagesIntentHandling, INSetMessageAttributeIntentHandling {
```

If your app is not working in the messaging domain, delete the code in the IntentHandler.swift file and adopt the IntentHandler class to different protocols such as the INStartAudioCallIntentHandling protocol to work with VoIP calling or the INStartWorkoutIntentHandling protocol. (SiriKit protocols typically end with the word "Handling".) The following code adopts protocols for the workout domain:

```
class IntentHandler: INStartWorkoutIntentHandling,
INPauseWorkoutIntentHandling, INResumeWorkoutIntentHandling,
INCancelWorkoutIntentHandling, INEndWorkoutIntentHandling {
```

Regardless of the specific SiriKit protocols your IntentHandler class adopts, you'll need to create functions to conform to those protocols. In our SiriApp project, the IntentHandler.swift file contains code for working with messaging. When working with SiriKit with messaging or any other domain such as workouts or payments, users can give commands in several ways. Ideally, users will give complete commands that identify at least three items:

- The name of your app

- The recipient of your action

- The content of your action

If your app used Siri to work in the payment domain, users could give a command like "Pay Fred ten dollars using SiriApp." In this example, Fred is the recipient of the action, ten dollars is the content of your action, and SiriApp is the name of the app the user wants to use.

However, most times users will not give complete commands. Instead, they may give a partial command like "Use SiriApp to pay Fred." When Siri hears the name of the app, it knows which app to use. Then it uses the person's name (Fred) as the recipient, assuming Fred is stored in your Contacts app and you have given the app permission to access the Contacts app database.

However, Siri won't know the amount, so at this point, it will need to ask an additional question for the amount. When the user states the amount, then Siri can complete the action. When Siri doesn't have complete information, it needs to ask for the missing information, which is called disambiguation.

Note   Although the IntentHandler.swift file uses a switch statement to verify names, it doesn't contain any code to actually access or verify if a name is stored in the Contacts app database or not.

In our SiriApp project, Siri needs to resolve two possible pieces of missing information:

- Who the recipient is

- What the message may be

In the IntentHandler.swift file of our SiriApp project, there are two functions to handle these issues. The first function is called resolveRecipients. Notice there's a switch statement that deals with three cases. First, if the user gives a name that matches multiple people. For example, if you want to send a message to Fred but you have a Fred Johnson, Fred Murray, and Fred Billingsly in your contacts database, Siri will need to ask the user which person in particular:

```
case 2 ... Int.max:
    // We need Siri's help to ask user to pick one from the matches.
    resolutionResults += [INSendMessageRecipientResolutionResult.
    disambiguation(with: matchingContacts)]
```

If the user gives one name and that name matches exactly one person in the Contacts app, then the app can perform the complete action:

```
case 1:
        // We have exactly one matching contact
        resolutionResults += [INSendMessageRecipientResolutionResult.
        success(with: recipient)]
```

Of course, the user may give a name that isn't in the contacts database. In that case, the code will need to let Siri know that the task cannot be completed. This means Siri will need to inform the user of this and ask for a new name:

```
case 0:
        // We have no contacts matching the description provided
        resolutionResults += [INSendMessageRecipientResolutionResult.
        unsupported()]
```

The IntentHandler.swift file contains another function called resolveContent. This function checks if the user specifies a message to send. For example, the user could say, "Send a message with SiriApp to Fred." This identifies the app to use (our SiriApp project) and the recipient (Fred). But since the user didn't specify a message, Siri will need to resolve this by asking for a message. That's the purpose of the resolveContent function:

```
func resolveContent(for intent: INSendMessageIntent, with completion:
@escaping (INStringResolutionResult) -> Void) {
    if let text = intent.content, !text.isEmpty {
```

```
        completion(INStringResolutionResult.success(with: text))
    } else {
        completion(INStringResolutionResult.needsValue())
    }
}
```

Once Siri has a valid recipient and message to send, it uses a confirm function to ask the user to verify everything is ready.

Note   The template code in the IntentHandler.swift file does not actually send out messages even though Siri will claim that it has sent the message. To actually send a message, you'll need to write additional code.

```
func confirm(intent: INSendMessageIntent, completion: @escaping
(INSendMessageIntentResponse) -> Void) {
    // Verify user is authenticated and your app is ready to send a
    message.

    let userActivity = NSUserActivity(activityType: NSStringFromClass
    (INSendMessageIntent.self))
    let response = INSendMessageIntentResponse(code: .ready,
    userActivity: userActivity)
    completion(response)
}
```

Finally, the handle function actually takes action after Siri has gotten the recipient's name and message from the user. The handle function in the IntentHandler.swift file looks like this:

```
func handle(intent: INSendMessageIntent, completion: @escaping
(INSendMessageIntentResponse) -> Void) {
    // Implement your application logic to send a message here.

    let userActivity = NSUserActivity(activityType: NSStringFromClass
    (INSendMessageIntent.self))
```

```
    let response = INSendMessageIntentResponse(code: .success,
    userActivity: userActivity)
    completion(response)
}
```

Note that all of these functions include the keyword INSendMessageIntent or INSendMessageIntentResponse. If you look at the bottom of the IntentHandler.swift file, there are two handle functions, but one is designed to deal with searching for messages (INSearchForMessageIntent) and the second is designed to deal with changing attributes of a message (INSetMessageAttributeIntent).

Understanding the ExtensionUI Folder

The IntentHandler.swift file in the Extension folder contains code to link your app to Siri. To customize the appearance of your app within Siri, you have the option of customizing a storyboard file that appears within Siri. The purpose of this storyboard file is to display information to the user within Siri. By default, your app will display a generic user interface inside Siri, but you can display a custom user interface by modifying the two files inside the ExtensionUI folder.

The IntentViewController.swift file contains Swift code for customizing your app's user interface within Siri. The MainInterface.storyboard file defines the actual user interface as shown in Figure 19-10.

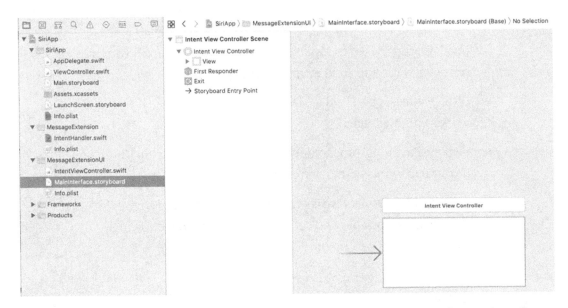

Figure 19-10. *The MainInterface.storyboard file defines your app's user interface in Siri*

If you want to define a custom user interface that appears inside Siri, you'll need to write Swift code in the IntentViewController.swift file and add user interface items onto the MainInterface.storyboard file such as a UILabel or UITextView. Then you'll need to create IBOutlets between the .storyboard file and the IntentViewController.swift file.

To see how to customize the Siri user interface for your app, follow these steps:

1. Make sure the SiriApp project is loaded in Xcode.

2. Click the IntentViewController.swift file in the MessageExtensionUI folder.

3. Make the IntentViewController class adopt the INUIHostedViewsSiriProviding protocol by modifying it as follows:

```
class IntentViewController: UIViewController,
INUIHostedViewControlling, INUIHostedViewSiriProviding {
```

Next, we'll need to set one of three variables to true:

- displaysMap – Used to replace a default Map interface if your app relies on Maps app such as ride booking

- displaysMessage – Used to display a custom interface if your app works with messages

- displaysPaymentTransaction – Used to display a custom interface if your app works with payments

4. Since our SiriApp project works with messages, we need to use the displaysMessage variable and set it to true, so add the following above the viewDidLoad method:

```
var displaysMessage: Bool {
    return true
}
```

The final step is to modify the configure function to display your .storyboard file within Siri. Remember, each time Siri asks a question to the user, it will display your .storyboard file so you need to define what type of information to display in the user interface each time Siri asks a question.

5. To see how to display a custom user interface within Siri, click the MainInterface.storyboard file in the MessageExtensionUI folder and click the Library icon.

6. Drag and drop a label onto the view. Center it and expand its width so it looks like Figure 19-11.

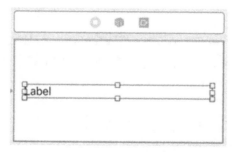

Figure 19-11. *Placing a label on the MainInterface.storyboard file*

7. Choose View ➤ Assistant Editor ➤ Show Assistant Editor, or click the Assistant Editor icon in the upper right corner of the Xcode window. Xcode displays the MainInterface.storyboard and IntentViewController.swift file side by side.

8. Move the mouse pointer over the label, hold down the Control key, and Ctrl-drag above the var displaysMessage line.

9. Release the Control key and the left mouse button. A popup window appears.

10. Click in the Name text field, type **messageLabel**, and click the Connect button. Xcode creates an IBOutlet as follows:

```
@IBOutlet var messageLabel: UILabel!
```

11. Modify the configureView function as follows:

```
func configureView(for parameters: Set<INParameter>,
of interaction: INInteraction, interactiveBehavior:
INUIInteractiveBehavior, context: INUIHostedViewContext,
completion: @escaping (Bool, Set<INParameter>, CGSize) -> Void) {

    if let messageIntent = interaction.intent as?
    INSendMessageIntent {

        guard messageIntent.content != nil else {
            return completion(true, parameters, CGSize.zero)
        }

        messageLabel.text = "Your message = \(messageIntent.
        content ?? "")"
    }

    completion(true, parameters, self.desiredSize)
}
```

Essentially this function checks if the user has added content to a message. If not, then display the MainInterface.storyboard file as size zero, which effectively hides it from view.

12. Connect an iOS device to your Macintosh through its USB cable.

13. Click the Scheme popup menu in the upper left corner of the Xcode window and choose your iOS device.

14. Click the Run button or choose Product ➤ Run. A dialog appears, asking you to choose an app to run (see Figure 19-3).

15. Click Siri and then click the Run button. Siri waits for you to speak.

16. Say "Send a message using SiriApp."

17. State a name stored in your Contacts app. Siri will then ask for the message to send.

18. Recite any message you like such as **Hello there**. The MainInterface.storyboard file appears as shown in Figure 19-12.

Figure 19-12. *The MainInterface.storyboard appears within Siri*

19. Click the Stop button in Xcode, or choose Product ➤ Stop.

The entire contents of the IntentViewController.swift file should look like this:

```swift
import IntentsUI

class IntentViewController: UIViewController,
INUIHostedViewControlling, INUIHostedViewSiriProviding {
    @IBOutlet var messageLabel: UILabel!

    var displaysMessage: Bool {
        return true
    }

    override func viewDidLoad() {
        super.viewDidLoad()
        // Do any additional setup after loading the view.

    }

    // MARK: - INUIHostedViewControlling

    // Prepare your view controller for the interaction to handle.
    func configureView(for parameters: Set<INParameter>,
    of interaction: INInteraction, interactiveBehavior:
    INUIInteractiveBehavior, context: INUIHostedViewContext,
    completion: @escaping (Bool, Set<INParameter>, CGSize) -> Void) {

        if let messageIntent = interaction.intent as?
        INSendMessageIntent {

            guard messageIntent.content != nil else {
                return completion(true, parameters, CGSize.zero)
            }

            messageLabel.text = "Your message = \(messageIntent.
            content ?? "")"
        }

        completion(true, parameters, self.desiredSize)
    }
```

```
        var desiredSize: CGSize {
            return self.extensionContext!.hostedViewMaximumAllowedSize
        }

    }
```

Creating a Payment App with Siri

In our SiriApp project, we simply used code created by Xcode to send a message. In this project, we're going to create a simple payment app that works with Siri so you can see the differences between this project and the previous SiriApp project along with seeing what you need to modify when working with an app outside of the messaging domain.

1. Create a new iOS Single View App project and name it CatPay.

2. Choose file ➤New ➤ Target. A template dialog appears.

3. Click the iOS category and click Intents Extension (see Figure 19-1).

4. Click the Next button. A window appears, asking for a product name for the extension.

5. Click in the Product Name text field and type **PayExtension**. Make sure the Include UI Extension check box is selected.

6. Click the Finish button. When a dialog appears asking if you want to activate the scheme, click the Activate button. Xcode creates two new folders called PayExtension (containing the IntentHandler.swift file) and PayExtensionUI (containing the IntentViewController.swift file and the MainInterface.storyboard file).

   For our simple payment app, we're only going to allow sending a payment, so we need to modify the Info.plist file in both the PayExtension and PayExtensionUI folders. You'll need to expand NSExtension, NSExtensionAttributes, and IntentsSupported. By default, the items in the Info.plist file will contain message sending intents such as INSendMessageIntent, but our app will be sending payments instead.

7. Click the Info.plist file in the PayExtension folder and expand IntentsSupported.

8. Move the mouse pointer over Item 0 so a + and – icon appears.

9. Click the – icon to delete Item 0.

10. Repeat steps 8 and 9 to delete the next Item 0. Xcode displays a single Item 0.

11. Click in the Value column of Item 0 and type INSendPaymentIntent as shown in Figure 19-13.

Figure 19-13. *Modifying the Info.plist file to support INSendPaymentIntent*

12. Click the Info.plist in the PayExtensionUI folder.

13. Expand IntentsSupported and change the value to INSendPaymentIntent.

14. Click the IntentHandler.swift file in the PayExtension folder.

15. Modify the class declaration at the top of the file to focus on INSendPaymentIntentHandling instead of messages like this:

```
class IntentHandler: INExtension, INSendPaymentIntentHandling {
```

16. Edit the handle function to deal with the INSendPaymentIntent like this:

```
func handle(intent: INSendPaymentIntent, completion: @escaping
(INSendPaymentIntentResponse) -> Void) {
    let userActivity = NSUserActivity(activityType:
    NSStringFromClass(INSendMessageIntent.self))
    completion(INSendPaymentIntentResponse(code: .success,
    userActivity: userActivity))
}
```

17. Just as you need to modify the handle function to work with
    INSendPaymentIntent (instead of INSendMessageIntent), so
    you need to also modify the confirm function to deal with the
    INSendPaymentIntent like this:

```
func confirm(intent: INSendPaymentIntent, completion:
@escaping (INSendPaymentIntentResponse) -> Void) {
    let userActivity = NSUserActivity(activityType:
    NSStringFromClass(INSendPaymentIntent.self))
    let response = INSendPaymentIntentResponse(code: .ready,
    userActivity: userActivity)
    completion(response)
}
```

The entire IntentHandler.swift file should look like this:

```
import Intents

class IntentHandler: INExtension, INSendPaymentIntentHandling  {

    override func handler(for intent: INIntent) -> Any {
        // This is the default implementation.  If you want
        different objects to handle different intents,
        // you can override this and return the handler you want
        for that particular intent.

        return self
    }

    func handle(intent: INSendPaymentIntent, completion: @escaping
    (INSendPaymentIntentResponse) -> Void) {
        let userActivity = NSUserActivity(activityType:
        NSStringFromClass(INSendMessageIntent.self))
        completion(INSendPaymentIntentResponse(code: .success,
        userActivity: userActivity))
    }
```

```
func confirm(intent: INSendPaymentIntent, completion:
@escaping (INSendPaymentIntentResponse) -> Void) {
    let userActivity = NSUserActivity(activityType:
    NSStringFromClass(INSendPaymentIntent.self))
    let response = INSendPaymentIntentResponse(code: .ready,
    userActivity: userActivity)
    completion(response)
}

}
```

Now it's time to create a custom user interface for appearing within Siri.

18. Click the MainInterface.storyboard in the PayExtensionUI folder.

19. Choose View ➤ Assistant Editor ➤ Show Assistant Editor, or click the Assistant Editor icon in the upper right corner of the Xcode window. Xcode displays the MainInterface.storyboard and IntentViewController.swift file side by side.

20. Click the Library icon and drag and drop a label. You may want to resize the label to make it wider.

21. Move the mouse pointer over the label, hold down the Control key, and Ctrl-drag above the var displaysMessage line.

22. Release the Control key and the left mouse button. A popup window appears.

23. Click in the Name text field, type **contentLabel**, and click the Connect button. Xcode creates an IBOutlet as follows:

```
@IBOutlet var contentLabel: UILabel!
```

24. Choose View ➤ Standard Editor ➤ Show Standard Editor, or click the Standard Editor icon in the upper right corner of the Xcode window.

25. Click the IntentViewController.swift file in the PayExtensionUI folder.

26. Modify the IntentViewController.swift file to make it adopt the INUIHostedViewSiriProviding protocol like this:

```
class IntentViewController: UIViewController,
INUIHostedViewControlling, INUIHostedViewSiriProviding  {
```

27. Add the following displaysPaymentTransaction variable below the IBOutlet like this:

```
var displaysPaymentTransaction: Bool {
    return true
}
```

28. Modify the configureView function so it displays the MainInterface.storyboard within Siri like this:

```
func configureView(for parameters: Set<INParameter>,
of interaction: INInteraction, interactiveBehavior:
INUIInteractiveBehavior, context: INUIHostedViewContext,
completion: @escaping (Bool, Set<INParameter>, CGSize) -> Void) {
    if let paymentIntent = interaction.intent as?
    INSendPaymentIntent {

        guard let amount = paymentIntent.currencyAmount?.amount
        else {
            return completion(true, parameters, CGSize.zero)
        }

        let paymentDescription = "Sending \(amount)
        \(paymentIntent.currencyAmount?.currencyCode ?? "dollars")
        worth of cats"
        contentLabel.text = paymentDescription
    }
    completion(true, parameters, self.desiredSize)
}
```

The guard statement checks if the user specified an amount for payment. If not, then the user interface size is set to zero, which makes the default user interface appear instead.

If the user has specified an amount, then it displays a string in the UILabel defined by the IBOutlet called contentLabel. Notice that currencyCode represents the currency used in your region, but you need to specify a default value (in this case "dollars") in case your app can't define the region's currency code.

The complete IntentViewController.swift file should look like this:

```swift
import IntentsUI

class IntentViewController: UIViewController,
INUIHostedViewControlling, INUIHostedViewSiriProviding  {

    @IBOutlet var contentLabel: UILabel!

    var displaysPaymentTransaction: Bool {
        return true
    }

    override func viewDidLoad() {
        super.viewDidLoad()
        // Do any additional setup after loading the view.
    }

    func configureView(for parameters: Set<INParameter>,
    of interaction: INInteraction, interactiveBehavior:
    INUIInteractiveBehavior, context: INUIHostedViewContext,
    completion: @escaping (Bool, Set<INParameter>, CGSize) ->
    Void) {
        if let paymentIntent = interaction.intent as?
        INSendPaymentIntent {

            guard let amount = paymentIntent.currencyAmount?.
            amount else {
                return completion(true, parameters, CGSize.zero)
            }

            let paymentDescription = "Sending \(amount)
            \(paymentIntent.currencyAmount?.currencyCode ??
            "dollars") worth of cats"
```

```
                    contentLabel.text = paymentDescription
                }
            completion(true, parameters, self.desiredSize)
        }

        var desiredSize: CGSize {
            return self.extensionContext!.hostedViewMaximumAllowedSize
        }

    }
```

29. Connect an iOS device to your Macintosh through its USB cable.

30. Click the Scheme popup menu in the upper left corner of the Xcode window and choose your iOS device.

31. Click the Run button or choose Product ➤ Run. A dialog appears, asking you to choose an app to run (see Figure 19-3).

32. Click Siri and then click the Run button. Siri waits for you to speak.

33. Say "Send twenty-five dollars using CatPay." The first time you run the CatPay project, Siri will ask for permission to use CatPay. After you give Siri permission, Siri displays the MainInterface. storyboard user interface as shown in Figure 19-14.

Figure 19-14. *The MainInterface.storyboard appears within Siri*

34. When Siri asks if you want to send the payment, say "Send" and
     Siri will say it sent payment (although it really doesn't because you
     haven't written any code to define who to send the money to or
     how to withdraw funds from an account).

35. Click the Stop button in Xcode or choose Product ➤ Stop.

     Although you customized the MainInterface.storyboard with a
     label, you could easily add pictures or text that represents your
     app's logo. That way users can recognize your app within Siri.

Summary

SiriKit gives your apps the ability to connect to Siri so users can interact with your app using voice commands. Just remember that SiriKit can only handle a limited range of domains such as messaging, ride booking, VoIP calling, or payments.

When you create a target file for your project, Xcode creates template code for working with the messaging domain to send messages. You'll need to delete most of this code in the IntentHandler.swift file to customize it for a different domain such as photos or workouts.

Make sure you edit the Info.plist files in the Extension and ExtensionUI folders to define the specific domain intents your app will handle such as INSendPaymentIntent or INSendMessageIntent.

To customize your user interface within Siri, you'll need to modify the MainInterface. storyboard file and the IntentViewController.swift file.

By adding SiriKit to your app, you can make your app easier to use through the natural language processing capabilities of Siri.

CHAPTER 20

Understanding ARKit

One of the most popular mobile games in recent years was Pokemon Go, which displayed Pokemon characters overlaid over actual places when viewed through the iPhone camera. By aiming your iPhone camera at a park bench or a bush, you could see a Pokemon cartoon character as if it were really there.

This technology of displaying virtual objects over actual physical objects is known as augmented reality (AR). The idea behind augmented reality is to let you combine real-world objects with virtual objects that appear on your iPhone screen.

One use for augmented reality is to point your iPhone at a street so you can see street names and names of businesses in the surrounding area. Another use is to show you walking directions complete with arrows to show you how to navigate around large public places such as airport terminals or museums.

In the past, creating augmented reality apps required writing mathematic equations to track real-world objects and position virtual objects in the real world. Fortunately, Apple has made augmented reality much easier to create through a new software framework called ARKit. By using ARKit along with other frameworks such as SceneKit, you can create augmented reality apps quickly and easily.

Note   You can only test and run ARKit apps on an iPhone 6s or higher, an iPad Pro, or the latest iPad models.

How ARKit Works

At the simplest level, ARKit works by identifying surrounding areas called feature points. Once ARKit understands the physical objects viewed by an iOS device camera, it can then overlay a virtual object on top of the real image displayed by the camera.

519

© Wallace Wang 2019
W. Wang, *Pro iPhone Development with Swift 5*, https://doi.org/10.1007/978-1-4842-4944-4_20

To see an example of ARKit in action, follow these steps:

1. Choose File ➤ New ➤ Project. Xcode displays a template dialog as shown in Figure 20-1.

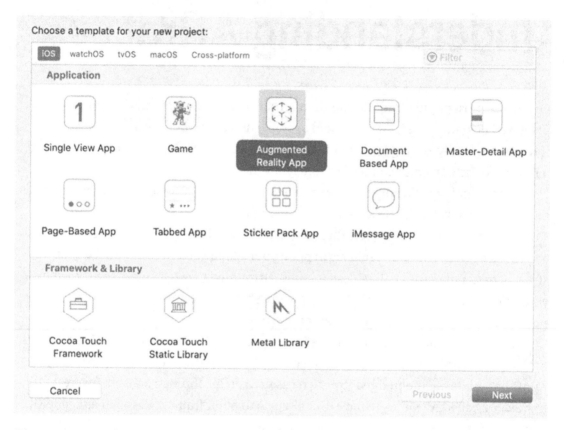

Figure 20-1. *The Augmented Reality App template*

2. Click the iOS category and click the Augmented Reality App icon. Then click the Next button and Create button. Another dialog appears.

3. Click in the Product Name text field and type ARTestApp. Make sure the Content Technology popup menu displays SceneKit. (The other two options in the Content Technology popup menu are Metal and SpriteKit. SpriteKit is designed for 2D images, while Metal is designed for advanced users who prefer to create their own code to create graphics. In most cases, you'll want to use SceneKit to display 3D images.)

4. Click the ViewController.swift file and you'll see code already written for you to create an augmented reality app. Notice that the ViewController.swift file contains three import statements:

```
import UIKit
import SceneKit
import ARKit
```

   UIKit creates an iOS app. SceneKit lets you display three-dimensional objects. ARKit lets you add augmented reality to your app.

5. Next, notice that the ViewController class adopts the ARSCNViewDelegate:

```
class ViewController: UIViewController, ARSCNViewDelegate {
```

   This protocol lets you display SceneKit images as augmented reality objects overlaid over real-world objects.

6. Next, notice that the ViewController.swift file already contains a single IBOutlet named sceneView:

```
@IBOutlet var sceneView: ARSCNView!
```

7. Click the Main.storyboard file in the Navigator pane. Notice that an ARKit SceneKit View already appears on the user interface as shown in Figure 20-2. This ARSCNView displays 3D SceneKit images on a camera background.

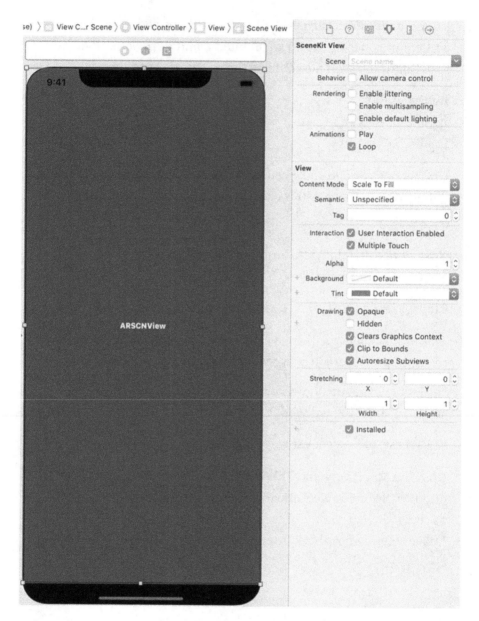

Figure 20-2. *An ARKit SceneKit View already appears on the user interface*

8.   Click the ViewController.swift file in the Navigator pane. Look in the
     viewWillAppear function and you'll see two lines of code that help create
     augmented reality in the app. The first line creates a constant called
     configuration, which represents an ARWorldTrackingConfiguration
     object. This object tracks an iOS device's orientation and position as well
     as detecting real-world surfaces.

```
let configuration = ARWorldTrackingConfiguration()
```

The second line actually displays the augmented reality image overlaid on the view displayed by the camera:

```
sceneView.session.run(configuration)
```

9. Look in the viewDidLoad function of the ViewController.swift file. First, there's a line that defines the ViewController.swift file as its delegate. Second, there's a line that displays frames per second (fps) and timing data at the bottom of the screen:

```
sceneView.showsStatistics = true
```

10. Look in the Navigator pane for an art.scnassets folder. If you expand this folder, you'll see that it contains two files: ship.scn and texture.png.

11. Click the ship.scn file, which contains a three-dimensional object as shown in Figure 20-3.

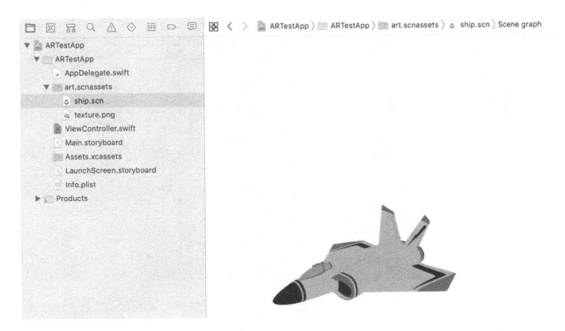

Figure 20-3. *Viewing the ship.scn file in Xcode*

Note   A .scn file stands for a SceneKit file format. Most 3D digital imaging programs can save files in a .dae (Digital Asset Exchange) file format. If you add a .dae file to Xcode, you can convert it to a .scn file format by adding the .dae file to the Navigator pane and then choosing File ➤ Export and save the file as a .scn file. If you want to create .dae files, you can use the free, open source Blender program (www.blender.org). You can also find free, public domain .dae files on the Internet.

Virtual objects consist of a shape (in this case, the ship.scn file) and a texture (texture.png) that gets applied on the shape. If you click the texture.png file, you'll see the color and graphics that appears on the ship.scn file.

12.   Click the texture.png in the Navigator pane. The texture appears as shown in Figure 20-4.

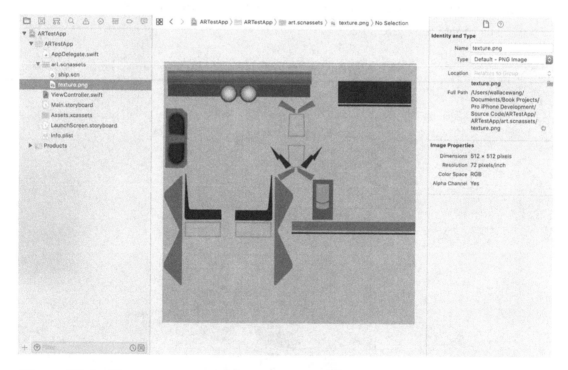

Figure 20-4. *The appearance of the texture.png file*

13.   Connect an iOS device to your Macintosh through a USB cable.

14. Make sure the Scheme menu in the upper left corner of the Xcode window displays your iOS device.

15. Click the Run button or choose Product ➤ Run. Point your iOS device camera anywhere. The virtual image of the ship.scn file should now appear over the real-world objects viewed by the camera as shown in Figure 20-5.

Figure 20-5. *Running the ARTestApp project in an iPhone*

16. Move your iOS device around to see different angles of the ship. scn image as if it were a real object in front of you. Also note that the bottom of the screen displays statistics about the augmented reality image such as its frames per second (fps).

17.   Choose Product ➤ Stop or click the Stop icon. At this point, you've seen a simple demonstration of how augmented reality works. By adding different texture files or replacing the ship.scn file with a different image, you can display custom images as seen through the iOS device camera.

18.   Edit the ViewController.swift file by commenting out the two lines that define the ship.scn file and then load that scene:

```
//let scene = SCNScene(named: "art.scnassets/ship.scn")!
//sceneView.scene = scene
```

19.   Add the following line after the commented out code. This line displays feature points and the world origin overlaid over the camera image:

```
sceneView.debugOptions = [ARSCNDebugOptions.showWorldOrigin,
ARSCNDebugOptions.showFeaturePoints]
```

Feature points appear as yellow dots that highlight surface areas that ARKit recognizes. The world origin appears where your iOS device appears when the app first run. The world origin displays x, y, and z axes where the x axis goes right, the y axis goes up, and the z axis points out of the screen toward the user.

Note   ARKit works best in clear lighting conditions with multiple objects visible so it can detect surface areas of tables, floors, and walls. Poor lighting conditions will hinder ARKit's ability to identify surface areas along with pointing the camera at a blank wall or floor.

The entire viewDidLoad function should look like this:

```
override func viewDidLoad() {
    super.viewDidLoad()

    // Set the view's delegate
    sceneView.delegate = self

    // Show statistics such as fps and timing information
    sceneView.showsStatistics = true
```

```
    // Create a new scene
    //let scene = SCNScene(named: "art.scnassets/ship.scn")!

    // Set the scene to the view
    //sceneView.scene = scene
    sceneView.debugOptions = [ARSCNDebugOptions.showWorldOrigin,
    ARSCNDebugOptions.showFeaturePoints]
}
```

20. Make sure an iOS device is connected to your Macintosh through a USB cable. Then click the Run button or choose Product ➤ Run. The world origin appears along with yellow dots on nearby areas that represent feature points as shown in Figure 20-6.

Figure 20-6. *The debugOptions line displays the origin and feature points*

21. Click the Stop button in Xcode or choose Product ➤ Stop.

Drawing Augmented Reality Objects

By replacing the ship.scn file with your own images, you can display anything you want as an augmented reality object. However, you can also display simple geometric shapes. Some of the available shapes you can draw include

- SCNBox – Draws a box

- SCNCapsule – Draws a cylinder whose ends are capped with hemispheres

- SCNCone – Draws a cone

- SCNCylinder – Draws a cylinder

- SCNFloor – Draws an infinite plane that can optionally reflect a scene

- SCNPlane – Draws a rectangular plane of a specific width and height

- SCNPyramid – Draws a pyramid

- SCNSphere – Draws a sphere

- SCNTorus – Draws a torus, ring-shaped object

- SCNTube – Draws a cylinder with a hole along its central axis

When displaying geometric shapes, you need to define three features:

- The object's physical dimensions such as its height and width

- The object's appearance such as its color

- The object's position relative to the world origin

Once you define an object's size, appearance, and position, you need to place it on the view displayed by the camera. To do this, you need to define a node. To see how to define a node, follow these steps:

1. Make sure the ARTestApp project is loaded in Xcode.

2. Click the ViewController.swift file in the Navigator pane.

3. Underneath the sceneView.debugOptions line, in the
    viewDidLoad method, add the following:

```
let node = SCNNode()
node.geometry = SCNPyramid(width: 0.1, height: 0.2, length: 0.1)
node.geometry?.firstMaterial?.diffuse.contents = UIColor.cyan
node.position = SCNVector3(0, -0.2, 0)
sceneView.scene.rootNode.addChildNode(node)
```

This first line creates a node, which defines where a geometric
shape will appear.

The second line defines a SCNPyramid with a width, height, and
length.

The third line defines the color of the shape, which is cyan.

The fourth line defines the pyramid's position relative to the world
origin. In this case, the base of the pyramid appears below the
origin at –0.2.

The fifth line adds the node to the scene so a cyan pyramid
appears directly under the world origin.

The entire viewDidLoad method should look like this:

```
override func viewDidLoad() {
    super.viewDidLoad()

    // Set the view's delegate
    sceneView.delegate = self

    // Show statistics such as fps and timing information
    sceneView.showsStatistics = true

    // Create a new scene
    //let scene = SCNScene(named: "art.scnassets/ship.scn")!

    // Set the scene to the view
    //sceneView.scene = scene
    sceneView.debugOptions = [ARSCNDebugOptions.showWorldOrigin,
    ARSCNDebugOptions.showFeaturePoints]
```

```
let node = SCNNode()
node.geometry = SCNPyramid(width: 0.1, height: 0.2,
length: 0.1)
node.geometry?.firstMaterial?.diffuse.contents = UIColor.cyan
node.position = SCNVector3(0, -0.2, 0)
sceneView.scene.rootNode.addChildNode(node)
```

    }

4. Make sure an iOS device is connected to your Macintosh through a USB cable and make sure the Scheme popup menu at the upper left corner of the Xcode window displays your connected iOS device.

5. Click the Run button or choose Product ➤ Run. A pyramid appears under the world origin as shown in Figure 20-7.

Figure 20-7. *Displaying a pyramid as an augmented reality object*

6.   Click the Stop button in Xcode or choose Product ➤ Stop.

Experiment by changing the values for the node.position along with the pyramid's width, height, and length. Also change the color of the pyramid from cyan to red or yellow. Rather than display a pyramid, choose a different shape such as a SCNBox, SCNTub, or SCNCone.

Resetting the World Origin

We created the ARTestApp project using the Augmented Reality App template, but we can easily give augmented reality capabilities to any project just by adding the ARKit and SceneKit frameworks. When you first run the ARTestApp project, it will define the world origin at the current location of your iPhone or iPad. If you take a few steps back, you'll see the origin displayed on the screen (see Figure 20-6). Unfortunately, the world origin will remain fixed until you run the app again.

To fix this problem, the next project you'll create will show a Reset button that will let you move your iPhone/iPad to a new location and redefine the origin at your new location. In this way, you can redefine the world origin position without having to restart the app.

To see how to create an augmented reality app from the Single View App template, follow these steps:

1.   Create a new iOS Single View App project and name it ARResetApp.

2.   Click the ViewController.swift file in the Navigator pane.

3.   Under the import UIKit line, add the following lines to add the SceneKit and ARKit frameworks like this:

```
import SceneKit
import ARKit
```

4. Modify the class ViewController line to adopt the ARSCNViewDelegate like this:

    ```
    class ViewController: UIViewController, ARSCNViewDelegate  {
    ```

5. Click the Info.plist file and add a Privacy – Camera Usage Description key. If you fail to do this, your app won't have access to the camera and won't be able to run.

6. Click the Main.storyboard file in the Navigator pane.

7. Click the Library icon and drag and drop a button onto the bottom of the user interface.

8. Resize the button so it spans the width of the screen.

9. Double-click the button, type **Reset**, and press Enter.

10. Click the Library icon and drag and drop an ARKit SceneKit View on the user interface.

11. Resize the ARKit SceneKit View so the user interface looks like Figure 20-8.

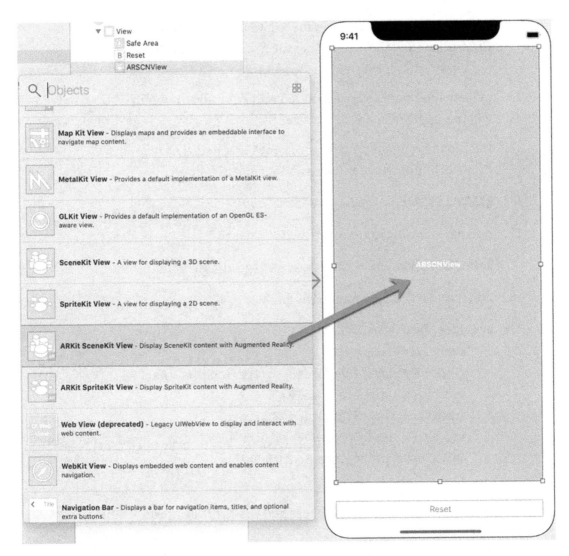

Figure 20-8. *The ARKit SceneKit View displays augmented reality objects*

12. Choose Editor ➤ Resolve Auto Layout Issues ➤ Reset to Suggested
     Constraints on the bottom half of the submenu. Xcode adds
     constraints to the button and ARKit SceneKit View.

13. Choose View ➤ Assistant Editor ➤ Show Assistant Editor, or click
     the Assistant Editor icon in the upper right corner of the Xcode
     window. Xcode shows the Main.storyboard and ViewController.
     swift file side by side.

14. Move the mouse pointer over the ARSCNView, hold down the Control key, and Ctrl-drag under the class ViewController line in the ViewController.swift file.

15. Release the Control key and the left mouse button. A popup window appears.

16. Click in the Name text field, type **sceneView**, and click the Connect button. Xcode creates an IBOutlet as follows:

```
@IBOutlet var sceneView: ARSCNView!
```

17. Add the following underneath the IBOutlet:

```
let configuration = ARWorldTrackingConfiguration()
```

18. Edit the viewDidLoad method as follows:

```
override func viewDidLoad() {
    super.viewDidLoad()
    // Do any additional setup after loading the view.
    sceneView.delegate = self
    sceneView.showsStatistics = true
    sceneView.debugOptions = [ARSCNDebugOptions.showWorldOrigin,
    ARSCNDebugOptions.showFeaturePoints]
}
```

19. Add the following viewWillAppear and viewWillDisappear functions:

```
override func viewWillAppear(_ animated: Bool) {
    super.viewWillAppear(animated)

    // Run the view's session
    sceneView.session.run(configuration)
}
```

```
override func viewWillDisappear(_ animated: Bool) {
    super.viewWillDisappear(animated)

    // Pause the view's session
    sceneView.session.pause()
}
```

20. Move the mouse pointer over the button, hold down the Control key, and Ctrl-drag above the last curly bracket in the ViewController.swift file.

21. Release the Control key and the left mouse button. A popup window appears.

22. Click in the Name text field, type **resetAR**, click the Type popup menu and choose UIButton, and click the Connect button. Xcode creates a resetAR IBAction method.

23. Edit this IBAction method as follows:

```
@IBAction func resetAR(_ sender: UIButton) {
    sceneView.session.pause()
    sceneView.session.run(configuration, options: [.resetTracking,
    .removeExistingAnchors])
}
```

The entire ViewController.swift should look like this:

```
import UIKit
import SceneKit
import ARKit

class ViewController: UIViewController, ARSCNViewDelegate  {

    @IBOutlet var sceneView: ARSCNView!

    let configuration = ARWorldTrackingConfiguration()

    override func viewDidLoad() {
        super.viewDidLoad()
        // Do any additional setup after loading the view.
        sceneView.delegate = self
```

```
            sceneView.showsStatistics = true
            sceneView.debugOptions = [ARSCNDebugOptions.
            showWorldOrigin, ARSCNDebugOptions.showFeaturePoints]
        }

        override func viewWillAppear(_ animated: Bool) {
            super.viewWillAppear(animated)

            // Run the view's session
            sceneView.session.run(configuration)
        }

        override func viewWillDisappear(_ animated: Bool) {
            super.viewWillDisappear(animated)

            // Pause the view's session
            sceneView.session.pause()
        }

        @IBAction func resetAR(_ sender: UIButton) {
            sceneView.session.pause()
            sceneView.session.run(configuration, options:
            [.resetTracking, .removeExistingAnchors])
        }
    }
```

24. Make sure an iOS device is connected to your Macintosh through a USB cable and make sure the Scheme popup menu at the upper left corner of the Xcode window displays your connected iOS device.

25. Click the Run button or choose Product ➤ Run. Step back to see the world origin (see Figure 20-6).

26. Aim the iOS device's camera in a different direction and tap the Reset button and step backward. You should now see the world origin defined in your new location and direction.

27. Click the Stop button in Xcode or choose Product ➤ Stop.

Drawing Custom Shapes

ARKit offers common geometric shapes you can create such as cylinders, cones, pyramids, boxes, and spheres. If none of those geometric shapes meet your needs, you can draw your own by defining a starting point and then adding lines to create a shape. Drawing lines to define a shape creates what's called a Bezier path.

The four main steps to creating a Bezier path include

- Defining a Bezier path

- Defining a starting point for drawing

- Drawing one or more lines

- Defining a SCNShape based on the Bezier path lines you've defined

To create a Bezier path, you need to define a BezierPath object like this:

```
let path = UIBezierPath()
```

Once you've created a Bezier path, you need to define its starting point like this:

```
path.move(to: CGPoint(x: 0, y: 0))
```

Now we need to draw one or more lines using the addLine method that defines the ending point of that line like this:

```
path.addLine(to: CGPoint(x: 0.2, y: 0.2))
```

Finally, we need to turn that Bezier path into a shape:

```
let shape = SCNShape(path: path, extrusionDepth: 0.1)
```

Once we have a shape, we can display it as an augmented reality object by defining it as a node with a color and position. Then we can finally add that node to the augmented reality view:

```
let node = SCNNode()
node.geometry = shape
node.geometry?.firstMaterial?.diffuse.contents = UIColor.yellow
node.position = SCNVector3(0,0, -0.4)
sceneView.scene.rootNode.addChildNode(node)
```

To see how to create an augmented reality app from the Single View App template, follow these steps:

1. Make sure the ARResetApp project is loaded in Xcode.

2. Click the ViewController.swift file in the Navigator pane.

3. Edit the viewDidLoad method as follows:

```
override func viewDidLoad() {
    super.viewDidLoad()
    // Do any additional setup after loading the view.
    sceneView.delegate = self
    sceneView.showsStatistics = true
    sceneView.debugOptions = [ARSCNDebugOptions.showWorldOrigin,
    ARSCNDebugOptions.showFeaturePoints]

    let path = UIBezierPath()
    path.move(to: CGPoint(x: 0, y: 0))
    path.addLine(to: CGPoint(x: 0.2, y: 0.2))
    path.addLine(to: CGPoint(x: 0.4, y: -0.2))
    let shape = SCNShape(path: path, extrusionDepth: 0.1)
    let node = SCNNode()
    node.geometry = shape
    node.geometry?.firstMaterial?.diffuse.contents = UIColor.
    yellow
    node.position = SCNVector3(0,0, -0.4)
    sceneView.scene.rootNode.addChildNode(node)
}
```

4. Make sure an iOS device is connected to your Macintosh through a USB cable and make sure the Scheme popup menu at the upper left corner of the Xcode window displays your connected iOS device.

5. Click the Run button or choose Product ➤ Run. A yellow triangular shape appears past the world origin as shown in Figure 20-9.

Figure 20-9. *Drawing a custom shape using a Bezier path*

6. Click the Stop button in Xcode or choose Product ➤ Stop.

Experiment with different colors and values for drawing a custom shape.

Modifying the Appearance of Shapes

Up until now, we've just created a shape and applied a color to it, but there are other ways to modify the appearance of a shape. Some ways to modify the appearance of a shape include changing the lighting, transparency, or texture. Lighting makes a shape look differently depending on the type of lighting and location of the light source. Transparency defines whether a shape appears solid or see-through. Texture applies a graphic image on the sides of a shape such as making a shape appear to be made out of bricks or sand. By modifying the appearance of a shape, you can make that shape more visually interesting.

To experiment with modifying the appearance of shapes, follow these steps:

1. Create a new Augmented Reality App project and name it
    ARAppearanceApp. Make sure the Content Technology uses
    SceneKit. The first way we're going to modify the appearance of an
    object is to use a graphic image that appears over that shape.

2. Search the Internet for "public domain texture images" and you'll
    find plenty of images that you can freely download and use. Texture
    images typically display a regular pattern such as bricks, water,
    fields, or materials such as wood or stone as shown in Figure 20-10.

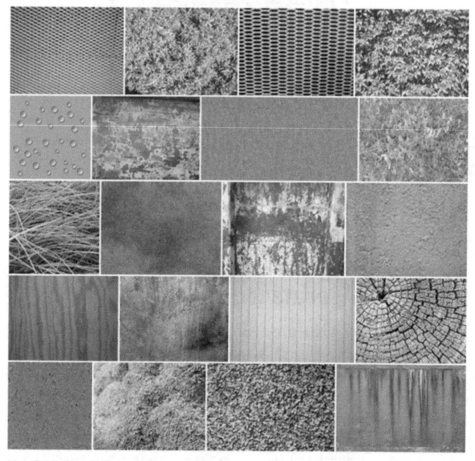

Figure 20-10. Searching for public domain texture images

3. Download a texture image and make sure it's stored in either the
    .png or .jpg file format. Then drag and drop it into the Navigator
    pane, and when a dialog appears, click the Finish button. Your
    chosen texture image appears in the middle Xcode pane as shown
    in Figure 20-11.

Figure 20-11. *Placing a texture image file in the Navigator pane*

4. Click the ViewController.swift file in the Navigator pane.

5. Modify the viewDidLoad method as follows:

```
override func viewDidLoad() {
    super.viewDidLoad()

    // Set the view's delegate
    sceneView.delegate = self

    // Show statistics such as fps and timing information
    sceneView.showsStatistics = true
```

```
sceneView.debugOptions = [ARSCNDebugOptions.showWorldOrigin,
ARSCNDebugOptions.showFeaturePoints]

let box = SCNBox(width: 0.1, height: 0.1, length: 0.2,
chamferRadius: 0.01)
let node = SCNNode()
let material = SCNMaterial()
material.diffuse.contents = UIImage(named: "rocks.jpg")
box.materials = [material]

node.geometry = box
node.position = SCNVector3(0, 0, -0.3)

sceneView.scene.rootNode.addChildNode(node)
}
```

This code defines a SCNBox geometric shape and also defines
a SCNMaterial array. That's because a shape can have multiple
materials. Then the code defines a graphic file called "rocks.jpg" as
its first material. Make sure you change this name to the name of
the texture image you dropped into the Navigator pane in step 3.

The entire ViewController.swift file should look like this:

```
import UIKit
import SceneKit
import ARKit

class ViewController: UIViewController, ARSCNViewDelegate {

    @IBOutlet var sceneView: ARSCNView!

    override func viewDidLoad() {
        super.viewDidLoad()

        // Set the view's delegate
        sceneView.delegate = self

        // Show statistics such as fps and timing information
        sceneView.showsStatistics = true
```

```
sceneView.debugOptions = [ARSCNDebugOptions.
showWorldOrigin, ARSCNDebugOptions.showFeaturePoints]

let box = SCNBox(width: 0.1, height: 0.1, length: 0.2,
chamferRadius: 0.01)
let node = SCNNode()
let material = SCNMaterial()
material.diffuse.contents = UIImage(named: "rocks.jpg")
box.materials = [material]

node.geometry = box
node.position = SCNVector3(0, 0, -0.3)

sceneView.scene.rootNode.addChildNode(node)
}

override func viewWillAppear(_ animated: Bool) {
    super.viewWillAppear(animated)

    // Create a session configuration
    let configuration = ARWorldTrackingConfiguration()

    // Run the view's session
    sceneView.session.run(configuration)
}

override func viewWillDisappear(_ animated: Bool) {
    super.viewWillDisappear(animated)

    // Pause the view's session
    sceneView.session.pause()
}

func session(_ session: ARSession, didFailWithError error:
Error) {
    // Present an error message to the user

}
```

```
func sessionWasInterrupted(_ session: ARSession) {
    // Inform the user that the session has been interrupted,
    for example, by presenting an overlay

}

func sessionInterruptionEnded(_ session: ARSession) {
    // Reset tracking and/or remove existing anchors if
    consistent tracking is required

    }
}
```

6. Make sure an iOS device is connected to your Macintosh through
    a USB cable and make sure the Scheme popup menu at the upper
    left corner of the Xcode window displays your connected iOS
    device.

7. Click the Run button or choose Product ➤ Run. A box appears
    with the texture image displayed on its surface as shown in
    Figure 20-12.

Figure 20-12. A stone image appears as material around a box shape

8. Click the Stop button in Xcode or choose Product ➤ Stop.

   Another way to modify the appearance of a shape is to change its transparency using a value between 0 (invisible) and 1 (solid).

9. Click the ViewController.swift file in the Navigator pane.

10. Add this transparency line right above the box.materials = [material] line like this:

```
material.transparency = 0.7
box.materials = [material]
```

The preceding code defines a transparency of 0.7 so the box appears semitransparent. The entire ViewController.swift file should look like this:

```swift
import UIKit
import SceneKit
import ARKit

class ViewController: UIViewController, ARSCNViewDelegate {

    @IBOutlet var sceneView: ARSCNView!

    override func viewDidLoad() {
        super.viewDidLoad()

        // Set the view's delegate
        sceneView.delegate = self

        // Show statistics such as fps and timing information
        sceneView.showsStatistics = true

        sceneView.debugOptions = [ARSCNDebugOptions.
        showWorldOrigin, ARSCNDebugOptions.showFeaturePoints]

        let box = SCNBox(width: 0.1, height: 0.1, length: 0.2,
        chamferRadius: 0.01)
        let node = SCNNode()
        let material = SCNMaterial()
        material.diffuse.contents = UIImage(named: "rocks.jpg")
        material.transparency = 0.7
        box.materials = [material]

        node.geometry = box
        node.position = SCNVector3(0, 0, -0.3)

        sceneView.scene.rootNode.addChildNode(node)
    }
```

```swift
override func viewWillAppear(_ animated: Bool) {
    super.viewWillAppear(animated)

    // Create a session configuration
    let configuration = ARWorldTrackingConfiguration()

    // Run the view's session
    sceneView.session.run(configuration)
}

override func viewWillDisappear(_ animated: Bool) {
    super.viewWillDisappear(animated)

    // Pause the view's session
    sceneView.session.pause()
}

func session(_ session: ARSession, didFailWithError error:
Error) {
    // Present an error message to the user

}

func sessionWasInterrupted(_ session: ARSession) {
    // Inform the user that the session has been interrupted,
    for example, by presenting an overlay

}

func sessionInterruptionEnded(_ session: ARSession) {
    // Reset tracking and/or remove existing anchors if
    consistent tracking is required

    }
}
```

11. Make sure an iOS device is connected to your Macintosh through a USB cable and make sure the Scheme popup menu at the upper left corner of the Xcode window displays your connected iOS device.

12. Click the Run button or choose Product ➤ Run. Notice that the box now appears somewhat transparent as shown in Figure 20-13.

Figure 20-13. *Changing the transparency value makes a shape look less solid*

     13.   Click the Stop button in Xcode or choose Product ➤ Stop.

Playing with Lighting

Besides applying textures and defining a transparency level, another way to change the appearance of a shape is through lighting. Lighting lets you create a light source that illuminates nearby shapes. Depending on the lighting you choose and the position of that light, you can create different types of visual effects on a shape.

To create a light source, you need to do the following:

- Define an SCNLight object.

- Define the SCNLight type.

- Assign the SCNLight object to an SCNNode.

- Define the position of the SCNNode.

- Add the SCNNode to the scene.

To define an SCNLight object, you just need to create a constant like this:

```
let spotLight = SCNLight()
```

Now define one of the following lighting types:

- ambient

- directional

- IES

- probe

- spot

Each lighting type highlights a shape in different ways, so let's start by experimenting with the directional lighting type:

```
spotLight.type = .directional
```

Now that you've defined a lighting type, you need to create a SCNNode like this:

```
let spotNode = SCNNode()
spotNode.light = spotLight
```

The first line creates an SCNNode object and the second line defines its light source as the spotlight (SCNLight) object that we created earlier.

Finally, we can position the SCNNode object based on the world origin. That means you need to define an x, y, and z value such as

```
spotNode.position = SCNVector3(0, 0.2, 0)
```

The preceding code places the light source 0.2 meters above the origin so the light shines down on the box we're going to create.

The final step is to add this light source node to the augmented reality scene:

```
sceneView.scene.rootNode.addChildNode(spotNode)
```

To experiment with lighting in augmented reality, follow these steps:

1. Make sure the ARAppearanceApp is loaded in Xcode.

2. Click the ViewController.swift file.

3. Edit the viewDidLoad method as follows:

```swift
override func viewDidLoad() {
    super.viewDidLoad()

    // Set the view's delegate
    sceneView.delegate = self

    // Show statistics such as fps and timing information
    sceneView.showsStatistics = true

    sceneView.debugOptions = [ARSCNDebugOptions.showWorldOrigin,
    ARSCNDebugOptions.showFeaturePoints]

    let box = SCNBox(width: 0.1, height: 0.1, length: 0.2,
    chamferRadius: 0.01)
    let node = SCNNode()
    let material = SCNMaterial()
    //material.diffuse.contents = UIImage(named: "rocks.jpg")
    //material.transparency = 0.7

    let spotLight = SCNLight()
    spotLight.type = .directional
    let spotNode = SCNNode()
    spotNode.light = spotLight
    spotNode.position = SCNVector3(0, 0.2, 0)

    material.diffuse.contents = UIColor.orange

    box.materials = [material]

    node.geometry = box
    node.position = SCNVector3(0, 0, -0.3)

    sceneView.scene.rootNode.addChildNode(node)
    sceneView.scene.rootNode.addChildNode(spotNode)
}
```

4. Make sure an iOS device is connected to your Macintosh through a USB cable and make sure the Scheme popup menu at the upper left corner of the Xcode window displays your connected iOS device.

5. Click the Run button or choose Product ➤ Run. Notice that an orange box appears, placed 0.3 meters behind the origin. Then the light source will appear 0.2 meters above the origin shining down on the orange box. Because the light type is directional, it only highlights the face of the box as shown in Figure 20-14.

Figure 20-14. *Directional lighting focuses on the front of the orange box*

6.   Click the Stop button in Xcode or choose Product ➤ Stop.

To see how a different light type changes the appearance of a shape, change the light type from directional to omni like this:

```
//spotLight.type = .directional  // illuminates only the front of
the box
spotLight.type = .omni  // illuminates the front and top of
the box
```

Now if you run this project, the omni lighting type highlights the front and the top of the box as shown in Figure 20-15.

Figure 20-15. *An omni light type illuminates the front and top of the orange box*

Apple's documentation defines how the different light types should behave so experiment with changing the light type and the position of the light source. By changing the position of a light source, you can illuminate different areas of a shape. By simply changing the light type, you can illuminate an object in different ways as shown in Figure 20-16.

| Ambient | Directional | Omni | Spot |

Figure 20-16. *How different lighting types work in highlighting a shape*

Summary

In this chapter, you've learned the basics of creating augmented reality objects using ARKit. You've learned how to place an augmented reality object on a scene and how to alter the appearance of an object by changing its color, transparency, and texture. In addition, you also learned how to draw your own objects and illuminate an object using a light source.

Augmented reality gives your apps the ability to overlay virtual objects over an actual scene. In the next chapter, you'll learn how to interact with augmented reality objects so you can control and manipulate them.

CHAPTER 21

Interacting with Augmented Reality

Displaying virtual objects on a real-world scene can be interesting, but you'll likely want to do more than just overlay static images on a scene. Besides displaying virtual objects on a scene, ARKit can also make virtual objects move on the screen and give users the ability to interact with virtual objects through touch gestures such as taps or swipes.

For example, a user might want to tap on a virtual object to make it move or respond in some way such as changing its appearance or moving on the screen. By making augmented reality interactive, your app can be more visually interesting and responsive to the user.

Note You can only test and run ARKit apps on an iPhone 6s or higher, an iPad Pro, or the latest iPad models.

For this example, we'll create an augmented reality app that displays a geometric shape on the screen. Then users can swipe on that shape to make it rotate. To do this, we'll need to learn several skills.

First, most people are familiar with manipulating geometric shapes using degrees, but Apple's SceneKit framework uses radians instead. We could write our own formula to convert degrees to radians, but Apple provides a mathematical framework called GLKit, which contains a function that can perform this calculation. As a general rule, it's always best to rely on Apple's frameworks as much as possible rather than write your own functions because Apple's frameworks are tested so you won't have to spend time debugging and testing your own functions.

© Wallace Wang 2019
W. Wang, *Pro iPhone Development with Swift 5*, https://doi.org/10.1007/978-1-4842-4944-4_21

To see an example of ARKit in action, follow these steps:

1. Create a new Augmented Reality App project and name it ARGestureApp.

2. Click the ViewController.swift file in the Navigator pane.

3. Underneath the import ARKit line, add the following:

```
import GLKit
```

4. Add the following under the IBOutlet to create a node like this:

```
let node = SCNNode()
```

5. Edit the viewDidLoad method to add debug options that will display the world origin and feature points on the screen. You may not want to display the world origin or feature points in a final app, but it can be helpful to make sure virtual objects appear correctly on the screen. Add the following line into the viewDidLoad method:

```
sceneView.debugOptions = [ARSCNDebugOptions.showWorldOrigin,
ARSCNDebugOptions.showFeaturePoints]
```

Storing and Accessing Graphic Assets

Now we need to create a geometric shape. In this case, we want to create a pyramid so we'll need to define its width, height, and length. In addition, we also want to apply a texture over our pyramid.

The Augmented Reality App project comes with two graphic files: ship.scn and texture.png. We won't be displaying the ship.scn file so you can delete the code that displays this ship.scn on the screen. However, we do want to use the texture.png file.

In the previous chapter, you saw how to apply a texture graphic image by simply defining its name like this:

```
let material = SCNMaterial()
material.diffuse.contents = UIImage(named: "rocks.jpg")
```

Defining the graphic file name is fine, but if you misspell the name or move the file, then Xcode won't know where to find that file. A safer approach is to store the graphic image in the Assets.xcassets folder and give it a descriptive name. Then you can reference this graphic image any time by using its descriptive name instead.

To see how to use the assets folder, follow these steps:

1. Make sure the ARGestureApp project is loaded into Xcode.

2. Click the Assets.xcassets folder in the Navigator pane to open a pane. Near the bottom left corner of this pane, click the + icon to display a popup menu as shown in Figure 21-1.

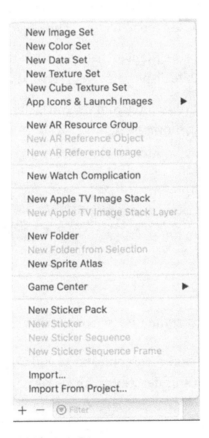

Figure 21-1. *Creating a New Image Set*

3. Click New Image Set. Xcode displays an Image name along with different magnification size images you can store as shown in Figure 21-2.

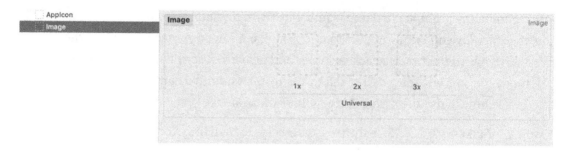

Figure 21-2. *Viewing an Image Set*

4. Click Image under the AppIcon set and press Return. Xcode highlights the Image name so you can type a more descriptive name. For our purposes, type "Texture" and press Enter.

5. Click the gray disclosure triangle that appears to the left of the art. scnassets folder. Xcode displays the ship.scn and texture.png files.

6. Drag and drop the texture.png from the Navigator pane onto the 1x dotted line box as shown in Figure 21-3.

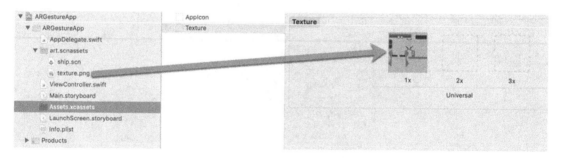

Figure 21-3. *Displaying a graphic image in an image set*

At this point, we've stored a graphic image and we can now refer to this image by using its descriptive image set name, which is Texture.

7. Click the ViewController.swift file in the Navigator pane.

8. Modify the viewDidLoad method by deleting this line:

```swift
let scene = SCNScene(named: "art.scnassets/ship.scn")!
```

9. Type the following in the viewDidLoad method where you deleted the previous line:

```
node.geometry = SCNPyramid(width: 0.15, height: 0.2, length: 0.1)
node.geometry?.firstMaterial?.diffuse.contents =
UIImage(imageLiteralResourceName: "Texture")
```

Notice that we can now refer to the texture by its image set name regardless of the actual file name such as texture.png. This reduces the chance of misspelling a file name.

10. Modify the viewDidLoad method by deleting this line:

```
sceneView.scene = scene
```

11. Type the following in the viewDidLoad method where you deleted the previous line:

```
node.position = SCNVector3(0, -0.2, 0)
sceneView.scene.rootNode.addChildNode(node)
```

Working with Touch Gestures

Once we've created a pyramid and applied a texture to it so it appears on the screen, the next step is to recognize when the user touches the pyramid. To do this, we need to create a gesture recognizer. There are several types of gestures you can recognize such as a swipe, tap, long press, pinch, or rotation motion. In our project, we're going to detect a right swipe gesture. When the user right swipes on the pyramid, we want the pyramid to rotate.

To detect a touch gesture, we need to create a constant that recognizes a specific type of gesture and defines a function to respond to that touch gesture.

1. Make sure the ARGestureApp project is loaded in Xcode.

2. Click the ViewController.swift file in the Navigator pane.

3. Add the following two lines inside the viewDidLoad method right under the two lines that define the pyramid and its texture as the "Texture" image set:

```
let swipeGesture = UISwipeGestureRecognizer(target: self, action:
#selector(handleSwipe))
sceneView.addGestureRecognizer(swipeGesture)
```

The first line creates a gesture recognizer constant that calls a handleSwipe function to deal with the swipe gesture.

The second line adds the gesture recognizer so the scene view can recognize the swipe gesture.

When we created a gesture recognizer, we also defined a function to handle the swipe when it's recognized. Now we need to create the handleSwipe function.

4. Add the following in the ViewController.swift file:

```
@objc func handleSwipe(sender: UISwipeGestureRecognizer) {
    let swipeArea = sender.view as! SCNView
    let touchCoordinates = sender.location(in: swipeArea)
    let touchedShape = swipeArea.hitTest(touchCoordinates,
    options: nil)

    if (sender.direction == .right) && (touchedShape.isEmpty !=
    true) {
        print ("Right swipe")

        let degrees: Float = 45
        let radians = GLKMathDegreesToRadians(degrees)

        let action = SCNAction.rotateBy(x: 0, y: CGFloat(radians),
        z: 0, duration: 5)
        node.runAction(action)
    }
}
```

This function retrieves the coordinates where the user swiped. Then it checks if the swipe gesture is to the right and within the pyramid boundaries. If so, then it prints "Right swipe" and defines degrees as a Float type with a value of 45.

Using the GLKMathDegreesToRadians function in the GLKit framework, it converts 45 degrees to radians and stores this value in the radians constant.

Then it defines an SCNAction to rotate by a fixed number of radians. In this case, rotation only occurs around the y axis so the pyramid appears to spin around. The time duration to spin completely around is defined as 5 seconds.

This rotation action is then applied to the node (pyramid) using the runAction method.

5. Make sure an iOS device is connected to your Macintosh through a USB cable and make sure the Scheme popup menu at the upper left corner of the Xcode window displays your connected iOS device.

6. Click the Run button or choose Product ➤ Run. A pyramid appears under the world origin, covered with the texture.png graphic image as shown in Figure 21-4.

Figure 21-4. *Running the ARGestureApp project in an iPhone*

7. Right swipe on the pyramid and it will rotate for 5 seconds before
   stopping.

8. Click the Stop button in Xcode or choose Product ➤ Stop.

   Right now, the pyramid rotates for 5 seconds and then stops.
   If you want the pyramid to rotate and never stop, modify the
   handleSwipe function like this:

```
        @objc func handleSwipe(sender: UISwipeGestureRecognizer) {
let swipeArea = sender.view as! SCNView
let touchCoordinates = sender.location(in: swipeArea)
let touchedShape = swipeArea.hitTest(touchCoordinates, options: nil)

if (sender.direction == .right) && (touchedShape.isEmpty != true) {
    print ("Right swipe")
```

```
        let degrees: Float = 45
        let radians = GLKMathDegreesToRadians(degrees)

        let action = SCNAction.rotateBy(x: 0, y: CGFloat(radians),
        z: 0, duration: 5)
        let forever = SCNAction.repeatForever(action)
        node.runAction(forever)
    }
}
```

The complete ViewController.swift file should look like this:

```
import UIKit
import SceneKit
import ARKit
import GLKit

class ViewController: UIViewController, ARSCNViewDelegate {

    @IBOutlet var sceneView: ARSCNView!

    let node = SCNNode()

    override func viewDidLoad() {
        super.viewDidLoad()

        // Set the view's delegate
        sceneView.delegate = self

        // Show statistics such as fps and timing information
        sceneView.showsStatistics = true

        sceneView.debugOptions = [ARSCNDebugOptions.showWorldOrigin,
        ARSCNDebugOptions.showFeaturePoints]

        // Create a new scene
        node.geometry = SCNPyramid(width: 0.15, height: 0.2, length: 0.1)
        node.geometry?.firstMaterial?.diffuse.contents =
        UIImage(imageLiteralResourceName: "Texture")
```

```swift
        let swipeGesture = UISwipeGestureRecognizer(target: self, action:
        #selector(handleSwipe))
        sceneView.addGestureRecognizer(swipeGesture)

        // Set the scene to the view
        node.position = SCNVector3(0, -0.2, 0)
        sceneView.scene.rootNode.addChildNode(node)
    }

    @objc func handleSwipe(sender: UISwipeGestureRecognizer) {
        let swipeArea = sender.view as! SCNView
        let touchCoordinates = sender.location(in: swipeArea)
        let touchedShape = swipeArea.hitTest(touchCoordinates, options: nil)

        if (sender.direction == .right) && (touchedShape.isEmpty != true) {
            print ("Right swipe")

            let degrees: Float = 45
            let radians = GLKMathDegreesToRadians(degrees)

            let action = SCNAction.rotateBy(x: 0, y: CGFloat(radians), z:
            0, duration: 5)
            //let forever = SCNAction.repeatForever(action)
            node.runAction(action) //node.runAction(forever)
        }
    }

    override func viewWillAppear(_ animated: Bool) {
        super.viewWillAppear(animated)
        // Create a session configuration
        let configuration = ARWorldTrackingConfiguration()

        // Run the view's session
        sceneView.session.run(configuration)
    }

    override func viewWillDisappear(_ animated: Bool) {
        super.viewWillDisappear(animated)
```

```
        // Pause the view's session
        sceneView.session.pause()
    }

    func session(_ session: ARSession, didFailWithError error: Error) {
        // Present an error message to the user

    }

    func sessionWasInterrupted(_ session: ARSession) {
        // Inform the user that the session has been interrupted, for
        example, by presenting an overlay
    }

    func sessionInterruptionEnded(_ session: ARSession) {
        // Reset tracking and/or remove existing anchors if consistent
        tracking is required

    }
}
```

Detecting a Horizontal Plane

Up until now, our augmented reality apps can appear at specific locations on the screen and can even respond to gestures such as a swipe. To make augmented reality more versatile, we're going to learn about plane detection.

Plane detection allows an iOS device to recognize a horizontal plane such as a table top or a floor. Once your app recognizes a horizontal surface, then it can place a virtual object on that surface such as a chair or a coffee mug. In this app, you'll learn how to detect horizontal planes and how to use tap gestures to place a virtual object on a horizontal plane.

1. Create a new Augmented Reality App project and name it ARPlaneApp. This will automatically create an art.scnassets folder with the ship.scn and texture.png art files. We'll be using the ship.scn file to place on a flat surface.

2. Click the ViewController.swift file in the Navigator pane.

3. Edit the viewWillAppear method as follows:

```
override func viewWillAppear(_ animated: Bool) {
    super.viewWillAppear(animated)

    // Create a session configuration
    let configuration = ARWorldTrackingConfiguration()

    configuration.planeDetection = .horizontal
    // Run the view's session
    sceneView.session.run(configuration)
}
```

4. Edit the viewDidLoad method as follows:

```
override func viewDidLoad() {
    super.viewDidLoad()

    // Set the view's delegate
    sceneView.delegate = self

    // Show statistics such as fps and timing information
    sceneView.showsStatistics = true

    sceneView.debugOptions = [ARSCNDebugOptions.showFeaturePoints,
    ARSCNDebugOptions.showWorldOrigin]

    let tapGesture = UITapGestureRecognizer(target: self, action:
    #selector(handleTap))
    sceneView.addGestureRecognizer(tapGesture)
}
```

When our app detects a horizontal plane, we want to tap on that area to add a virtual object. In this case, the virtual object will be the ship.scn image. To add a tap gesture, we need to create a tap gesture and then add it to the scene.

The first line defines a tap gesture that will be handled by a function called handleTap. The second line adds that tap gesture to the scene view. Now we need to create the handleTap function to respond to the tap gesture.

5. Add the following handleTap function inside the ViewController.
    swift file:

```swift
@objc func handleTap(sender: UITapGestureRecognizer) {
    let sceneView = sender.view as! ARSCNView
    let location = sender.location(in: sceneView)
    let hitTest = sceneView.hitTest(location, types:
    .estimatedHorizontalPlane)
    if !hitTest.isEmpty {
        addObject(hitTestResult: hitTest.first!)
    }
}
```

The first line defines the handleTap function as an Objective-C
function as defined by the @obj keyword. Then it retrieves the tap
gesture.

The second line creates a sceneView constant that receives the
data as an ARSCNView.

The third line identifies the location on the screen.

The fourth line checks if the tapped location appears within a
horizontal plane.

The fifth line checks if the user tapped within a horizontal plane.
If so, then it runs an addObject function that sends it the data
where the user tapped (hitTest.first!). Now we need to create this
addObject function.

6. Add the following function:

```swift
func addObject (hitTestResult: ARHitTestResult) {
    let scene = SCNScene(named: "art.scnassets/ship.scn")!
    let node = (scene.rootNode.childNode(withName: "ship",
    recursively: false))!

    let transform = hitTestResult.worldTransform.columns.3
    node.position = SCNVector3(transform.x, transform.y,
    transform.z)
    sceneView.scene.rootNode.addChildNode(node)
}
```

This function defines the ship.scn as the object to add to a scene.
The data received by this function contains the coordinates
of where the user tapped, which is stored in a 4x4 matrix
(worldTransform). The third column in this matrix contains the x,
y, and z coordinates where the user tapped.

The entire ViewController.swift file should look like this:

```swift
import UIKit
import SceneKit
import ARKit

class ViewController: UIViewController, ARSCNViewDelegate {

    @IBOutlet var sceneView: ARSCNView!

    override func viewDidLoad() {
        super.viewDidLoad()

        // Set the view's delegate
        sceneView.delegate = self

        // Show statistics such as fps and timing information
        sceneView.showsStatistics = true

        sceneView.debugOptions = [ARSCNDebugOptions.
        showFeaturePoints, ARSCNDebugOptions.showWorldOrigin]

        let tapGesture = UITapGestureRecognizer(target: self,
        action: #selector(handleTap))
        sceneView.addGestureRecognizer(tapGesture)
    }

    override func viewWillAppear(_ animated: Bool) {
        super.viewWillAppear(animated)

        // Create a session configuration
        let configuration = ARWorldTrackingConfiguration()
```

```swift
    configuration.planeDetection = .horizontal
    // Run the view's session
    sceneView.session.run(configuration)
}

override func viewWillDisappear(_ animated: Bool) {
    super.viewWillDisappear(animated)

    // Pause the view's session
    sceneView.session.pause()
}

@objc func handleTap(sender: UITapGestureRecognizer) {
    let sceneView = sender.view as! ARSCNView
    let location = sender.location(in: sceneView)
    let hitTest = sceneView.hitTest(location, types:
    .estimatedHorizontalPlane)
    if !hitTest.isEmpty {
        addObject(hitTestResult: hitTest.first!)
    }
}

func addObject (hitTestResult: ARHitTestResult) {
    let scene = SCNScene(named: "art.scnassets/ship.scn")!
    let node = (scene.rootNode.childNode(withName: "ship",
    recursively: false))!

    let transform = hitTestResult.worldTransform.columns.3
    node.position = SCNVector3(transform.x, transform.y,
    transform.z)
    sceneView.scene.rootNode.addChildNode(node)
}

func session(_ session: ARSession, didFailWithError error:
Error) {
    // Present an error message to the user

}
```

```
func sessionWasInterrupted(_ session: ARSession) {
    // Inform the user that the session has been interrupted,
    for example, by presenting an overlay

}

func sessionInterruptionEnded(_ session: ARSession) {
    // Reset tracking and/or remove existing anchors if
    consistent tracking is required

}
}
```

7. Make sure an iOS device is connected to your Macintosh through a USB cable and make sure the Scheme popup menu at the upper left corner of the Xcode window displays your connected iOS device.

8. Click the Run button or choose Product ➤ Run.

9. Point the iOS device's camera at a flat surface. When lots of yellow dots appear, tap the screen to display the airplane image as shown in Figure 21-5.

Figure 21-5. *Running the ARPlaneApp project in an iPhone*

10.   Click the Stop button in Xcode or choose Product ➤ Stop.

Modifying an Image

If you add some virtual objects to an augmented reality app, that image may be too large, too small, or positioned at an odd angle. Fortunately, you can always modify a virtual object to adjust its size and position.

To see how to do this, click the Navigator pane of the ARPlaneApp project, open the art.scnassets folder, and click the ship.scn file. Xcode displays the image so you can see its appearance. Click the Node Inspector icon or choose View ➤ Utilities ➤ Show Node Inspector. Then click the cartoon airplane. Now you can see the position, Euler angles, and scale of the ship.scn as shown in Figure 21-6.

Figure 21-6. *Editing an image with the Node Inspector*

The Position coordinates define the image's position based on the world origin.

The Euler coordinates define the rotation of the image around the x, y, and z axes (also known as the pitch, yaw, and roll, respectively).

The Scale coordinates define the size of the image.

Note When adding virtual image files to an Xcode project, you may need to modify that virtual image's position, rotation, and scale in the Node Inspector to suit your needs. Most virtual image files will not be perfectly sized and oriented for your augmented reality apps.

Creating Virtual Objects

In the last project, we used the ship.scn file that automatically comes with any project created using the Augmented Reality App project. In this next project, we're going to learn how to create simple virtual objects using common geometric shapes.

We've already seen how to create virtual objects out of common geometric shapes like cylinders, boxes, and pyramids using Swift code. Now we're going to see how to create common shapes and modify them to create simple virtual objects visually. You can create virtual objects and then modify them using Swift code later if you wish.

To see how to create virtual objects visually, follow these steps:

1. Create a new Augmented Reality App project and name it ARShapeApp.

2. Click the ViewController.swift file in the Navigator pane.

3. Type all the code from the ViewController.swift file in the ARPlaneApp project. (If you copy all the code from the ARPlaneApp project into this ARShapeApp project, make sure you reconnect the ARSCNView to the IBOutlet in the ViewController. swift file.

4. Click the art.scnassets folder and delete the ship.scn and texture. png files by clicking each file and pressing the Delete key (or choosing Edit ➤ Delete).

5. Click the ARShapeApp folder and choose File ➤ New ➤ File. A template window appears. Click the iOS category and scroll down until you see the Resource category as shown in Figure 21-7.

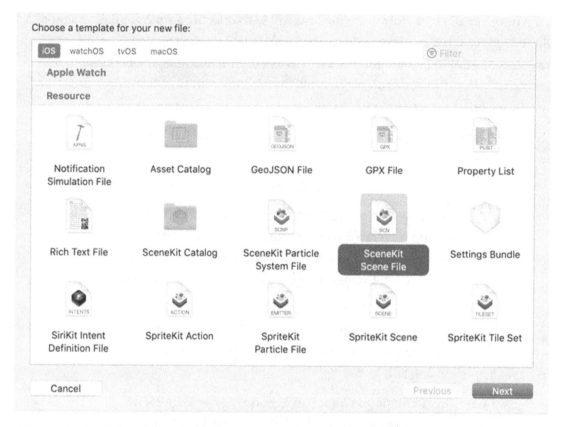

Figure 21-7. *Choosing a SceneKit Scene File in the template window*

6. Click the SceneKit Scene File icon and click the Next button.
    A Save As dialog appears.

7. Click in the Save As text field, type **MyShape**, and click Create.
    This creates an empty .scn file for us to modify.

8. Drag and drop your newly created .scn file into the art.scnassets
    folder.

9. Click the Library icon and you can see a variety of different objects
    and modifications you can add to your .scn file as shown in
    Figure 21-8.

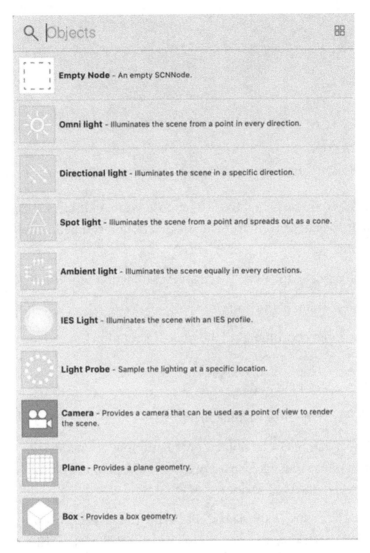

Figure 21-8. *The Object Library displays different items to add to a .scn file*

10. To create a virtual object, we need to start with an empty node,
     so click the Empty Node icon in the Object Library and drag and
     drop it on the scene. This displays x, y, and z axes on the scene as
     shown in Figure 21-9.

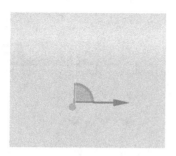

Figure 21-9. *Placing an Empty Node on a scene displays x, y, and z axes*

11. Click the Node Inspector icon (or choose View ➤ Utilities ➤ Show Node Inspector). From the Node Inspector, you can define the following:

   • The name of the node (used for identification purposes)

   • The position of the node

   • The Euler coordinates of the node (its rotation around the x, y, and z axes)

   • The scale of the node

   • The opacity (how visible the node is)

   We'll be creating virtual objects out of multiple shapes so let's create a house that will consist of a box and a pyramid on top with a plane to represent the door.

12. With the Node Inspector visible, click in the Name text field under the Identity category and type House. If you click the Show/Hide the Scene Graph View icon, you can see that the node you named appears with House appearing in the Scene Graph View and the Name text field in the Node Inspector pane as shown in Figure 21-10.

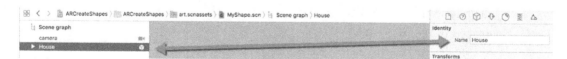

Figure 21-10. *Defining a name for a node*

In the Object Library pane, you'll need to add the following:

- Box

- Pyramid

- Plane

13. Click the Show/Hide the Scene Graph View icon to make sure the Scene Graph View pane is visible as shown in Figure 21-11.

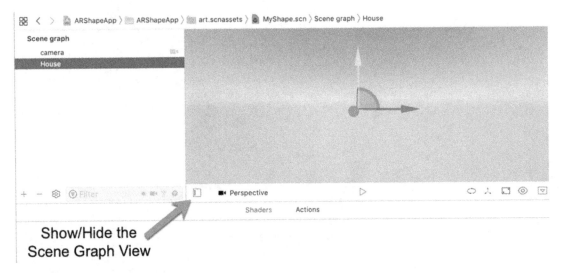

Figure 21-11. *The Show/Hide the Scene Graph View icon*

14. Drag and drop the Box from the Object Library window to the Scene Graph View pane indented under the House title as shown in Figure 21-12.

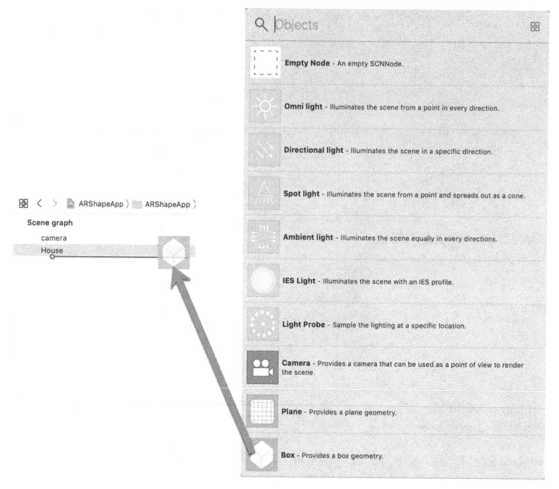

Figure 21-12. *Make sure a blue line appears indented under the House category when dragging and dropping items*

15.   After you add a box, you may need to scroll around to find a white box displayed on the screen. Since white can be hard to see, let's change the box's color. Click the box name in the Scene Graph View pane and click the Material Inspector icon (or choose View ➤ Utilities ➤ Show Material Inspector).

16.   Click the Diffuse popup menu to display a Colors window, and click a color such as blue.

17. Now we need to position the box in a specific location so click the Node Inspector icon (or choose View ➤ Utilities ➤ Show Node Inspector). Make sure the x, y, and z text boxes in the Position category are all set to 0. You should now have a box appearing in your chosen color at positions 0, 0, 0.

18. Add a pyramid by dragging and dropping it in the Scene Graph View pane so it appears indented under the House title. This creates a white pyramid. Let's move this pyramid so it has a color and appears on top of the box.

19. Click pyramid in the Scene Graphic View pane and click the Materials Inspector icon (or choose View ➤ Utilities ➤ Show Material Inspector). Click the Diffuse popup menu and choose a different color such as orange. Now we need to move the pyramid on top of the box.

20. Click the Node Inspector icon (or choose View ➤ Utilities ➤ Show Node Inspector). Change the x and z text boxes in the Position category to 0 but make the y value 0.5. This should place the pyramid on top of the box.

21. Finally, we need to add a plane to create a door to the side of the box. Drag and drop a plane indented under the House title.

22. Click the Node Inspector icon (or choose View ➤ Utilities ➤ Show Node Inspector). Change the x text boxes in the Position category to 0. Change the y text box value to –0.25. Change the z text box value to 0.52. This value of 0.52 places the plane slightly in front of the box so it's visible.

23. Click the Attributes Inspector icon (or choose View ➤ Utilities ➤ Show Attributes Inspector). In the Size text boxes, change the width to 0.25 and the height to 0.5.

24. Finally, click House in the Scene Graph View pane and then click
the Node Inspector icon (or choose View ➤ Utilities ➤ Show Node
Inspector). Change the x, y, and z values in the Scale category to
0.2. This shrinks the entire house image so it's much smaller. The
final result should show a house with a pyramid on top of a box
and a plane in one side as shown in Figure 21-13.

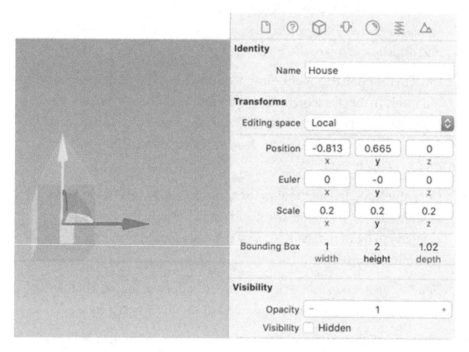

Figure 21-13. *Creating a house out of a pyramid, box, and a plane*

25. Copy all the functions from the previous ARPlaneApp project's
ViewController.swift file. Since we now want to display the house
image (instead of the ship.scn image), modify the first two lines of
the addObject function as follows:

```
let scene = SCNScene(named: "art.scnassets/MyShape.scn")!
let node = (scene.rootNode.childNode(withName: "House",
recursively: false))!
```

Notice that the first line defines the actual MyShape.scn file. Then
the second line defines the node, which we named "House". Your
entire ViewController.swift file should look like this:

```swift
import UIKit
import SceneKit
import ARKit

class ViewController: UIViewController, ARSCNViewDelegate {

    @IBOutlet var sceneView: ARSCNView!

    override func viewDidLoad() {
        super.viewDidLoad()

        // Set the view's delegate
        sceneView.delegate = self

        // Show statistics such as fps and timing information
        sceneView.showsStatistics = true

        sceneView.debugOptions = [ARSCNDebugOptions.
        showFeaturePoints, ARSCNDebugOptions.showWorldOrigin]

        let tapGesture = UITapGestureRecognizer(target: self,
        action: #selector(handleTap))
        sceneView.addGestureRecognizer(tapGesture)
    }

    override func viewWillAppear(_ animated: Bool) {
        super.viewWillAppear(animated)

        // Create a session configuration
        let configuration = ARWorldTrackingConfiguration()

        configuration.planeDetection = .horizontal
        // Run the view's session
        sceneView.session.run(configuration)
    }
```

```swift
override func viewWillDisappear(_ animated: Bool) {
    super.viewWillDisappear(animated)

    // Pause the view's session
    sceneView.session.pause()
}

@objc func handleTap(sender: UITapGestureRecognizer) {
    let sceneView = sender.view as! ARSCNView
    let location = sender.location(in: sceneView)
    let hitTest = sceneView.hitTest(location, types:
    .estimatedHorizontalPlane)
    if !hitTest.isEmpty {
        addObject(hitTestResult: hitTest.first!)
    }
}

func addObject (hitTestResult: ARHitTestResult) {
    let scene = SCNScene(named: "art.scnassets/MyShape.scn")!
    let node = (scene.rootNode.childNode(withName: "House",
    recursively: false))!

    let transform = hitTestResult.worldTransform.columns.3
    node.position = SCNVector3(transform.x, transform.y,
    transform.z)
    sceneView.scene.rootNode.addChildNode(node)
}

func session(_ session: ARSession, didFailWithError error:
Error) {
    // Present an error message to the user

}

func sessionWasInterrupted(_ session: ARSession) {
    // Inform the user that the session has been interrupted,
    for example, by presenting an overlay

}
```

```
func sessionInterruptionEnded(_ session: ARSession) {
    // Reset tracking and/or remove existing anchors if
    consistent tracking is required

    }
}
```

26. Make sure an iOS device is connected to your Macintosh through a USB cable and make sure the Scheme popup menu at the upper left corner of the Xcode window displays your connected iOS device.

27. Click the Run button or choose Product ➤Run.

28. Point the iOS device's camera at a flat surface. When lots of yellow dots appear, tap the screen to display the house image as shown in Figure 21-14.

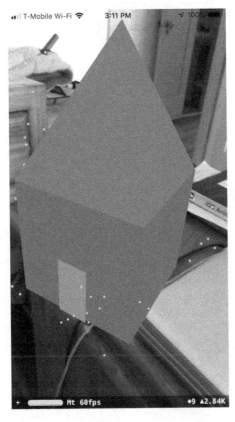

Figure 21-14. *Displaying a house image in augmented reality*

29.   Click the Stop button in Xcode or choose Product ➤ Stop.

There are two ways to design virtual objects. One way is to define everything using Swift code. The second way is to design virtual objects visually, which can make it easier to create objects out of multiple geometric shapes such as a pyramid on a box to create a house.

If you need to create realistic images, you'll likely need a 3D image editor, but for simple shapes, creating virtual objects can be simple and easy.

Summary

In this chapter, you learned more about working with augmented reality objects. First, you learned how to store images by name and access them without typing the entire file name and extension. Next, you learned how to use a gesture to swipe on a virtual object and make it move.

You also learned how to detect horizontal planes in the real world and how to edit and modify virtual images by changing its position, size, rotation, and scale. More importantly, you also learned how to create geometric shapes visually and combine them to create new objects. By knowing how to modify, store, and create virtual objects, you can now create anything you wish to display in augmented reality.

Index

A, B

© Wallace Wang 2019
W. Wang, *Pro iPhone Development with Swift 5*, https://doi.org/10.1007/978-1-4842-4944-4

CPSIA information can be obtained
at www.ICGtesting.com
Printed in the USA
LVHW100044250619
622192LV00005BA/12/P